The Body in Parts

The Body in Parts

Fantasies of Corporeality in Early Modern Europe

EDITED BY

David Hillman

AND

Carla Mazzio

Routledge *New York and London*

Published in 1997 by
Routledge
29 West 35th Street
New York, NY 10001

Published in Great Britain by
Routledge
11 New Fetter Lane
London EC4P 4EE

Library of Congress Cataloging-in-Publication Data

The body in parts : fantasies of corporeality in early modern Europe /
    edited by David Hillman and Carla Mazzio.
        p.   cm.
    Includes bibliographical references and index.
    ISBN 0-415-91693-3 (alk. paper). — ISBN 0-415-91694-1 (pbk. :
alk. paper)
    1. Body, Human, in literature.   2. European literature—History and
criticism.   3. Literature and science—Europe.   4. Literature and
culture—early modern.   I. Hillman, David   (David A.), 1963–   .
II. Mazzio, Carla
PN56.B62B65   1997
809'.9336—DC21   97-1481
                                                              CIP

Contents

IV. Parting Words

List of Figures

Acknowledgments

We would first of all like to thank our "organ donors," all of whom gave us not only wonderful essays but also warm and enthusiastic reactions to the idea of this book. We are especially grateful to Marge Garber for her encouragement, advice, and unstinting support from the very beginning of the project. Many thanks to those at Routledge who helped with the book, especially Bill Germano for his patience and wit, and Christine Cipriani for her careful editing. We are grateful to Rachen Tiven for indexing the volume with skill and surprisingly good cheer. The staff at Harvard's Countway Medical Library have been unfailingly friendly and helpful. Of the many who have supported our work on the book, we would particularly like to thank Stanley Cavell, Gwynne Evans, Daria Keynan, Jeffrey Masten, Ruth Nevo, Derek Pearsall, Anne Lake Prescott, Sharonda Rivera, John Tobin, and the members of the Harvard Renaissance Colloquium. Most of all, for their warmth, humor, and inspiration, we thank Linda Schlossberg and Alexis Susman.

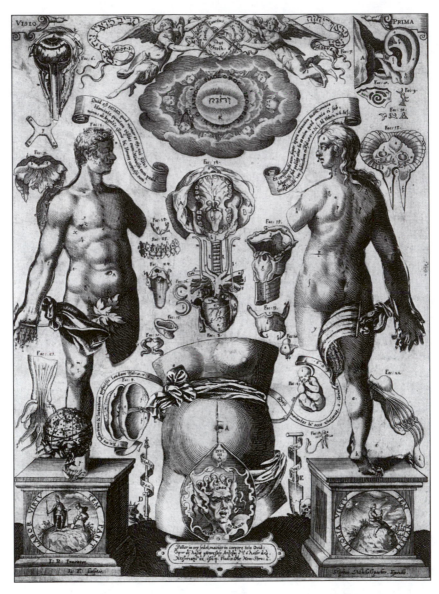

1. "Multi-layered flap anatomy with mobile shutters and detachable internal organs," from Johann Remmelin's *Catoptrum Microcosmicum* (Augsburg, 1619).

1

Introduction

Individual Parts

DAVID HILLMAN AND CARLA MAZZIO

> *Members. Begin There....* Imagine the body as a body full of thinking members.
> —Pascal, *Pensées*

Parts of the body are scattered throughout the literary and cultural texts of sixteenth- and seventeenth-century Europe. The proliferation of social and symbolic practices of "piecing out" the body in the early modern period (be it by punitive dismemberment, pictorial isolation, poetic emblazoning, mythic *spargamos,* satirical biting, scientific categorizing, or medical anatomizing) has generated a significant body of recent criticism about the logic of fragmentation.[1] Indeed, the very title of this book may seem to invoke the spectre of violence and disintegration: the Foucauldian episteme of ruptured social and symbolic fields, or the Lacanian *corps morcelé,* the psychic "body in bits and pieces." But the body in parts is not always the body in pieces. While the essays below examine the ways in which social and psychic conditions of fragmentation were encoded in practices of bodily partitioning, they also examine, collectively, the body that is "in" parts, that is constituted by a multiplicity of individuated organs. The extent to which aspects of culture were imagined to reside in, on, and about individual parts of the body is the subject of this volume.

"The subject of both kinds of Anatomy as well Historicall as Scientificall is a Part," writes Helkiah Crooke in his great compendium of anatomical knowledge, *Microcosmographia: A Description of the Body of Man* (London, 1616). Inverting Crooke's syntax, we would like to argue that it is equally accurate to say that the part, in the "Historicall" and "Scientificall" texts of the period, is a subject, both in the sense that it is increasingly marked and elaborated upon in a range of visual and textual spaces, and in the sense that it is frequently imagined to take on attributes of agency and subjectivity.[2] The ontological status of the part is revealed again and again in the essays here to be in endless flux between the positions of subject and object: as vehicles of culture and symbolization, as organs with eerily individuated agencies, as objects of libidinal cathexes, as instruments of sentient experience, as imagined *loci* of self-knowledge and self-alienation. What is imagined here is indeed, as Pascal vividly put it, "a body full of thinking members."[3]

The relations between bodily and cognitive systems of organization are in many ways most powerfully encoded by the symbolics of any given part, where the tensions between the metaphoric and the metonymic, between the floating and the firmly contextualized, or more generally between conditions of autonomy and dependence are powerfully articulated. As Elizabeth Grosz writes, "human bodies have the wonderful ability, while striving for integration and cohesion, organic and psychic wholeness, to also provide for and indeed produce fragmentations, fracturings, dislocations that orient bodies and body parts toward other bodies and body parts."[4] Because corporeal parts have individuated functions, locations, and differentiated relations to the body as a whole, they can become concentrated sites where meaning is invested and often apparently stabilized. But while the invocation of a specific body part may generate the illusion of a narrowed sphere of reference, it is in fact precisely this specificity that creates, in the corporeal fragment, a remarkable density of implication. As Jean Starobinski writes in his "Short History of Bodily Sensation": "I believe that the most fruitful generalizations are those arising from fairly precise studies of limited topics."[5]

The body has become an object of such extensive critical scrutiny in recent years that, in the words of Caroline Walker Bynum, it has become "no topic or, perhaps, almost all topics."[6] The elevation of the fragment to a position of central significance is, indeed, very much a topical matter in contemporary culture; the rejection of all forms of totality, including the corporeal, is one of the defining characteristics of postmodernism. But what the essays collected here reveal is that early moderns, no less than postmoderns, were deeply interested in the corporeal "topic"; for long before "topical" came to mean "of current interest, contemporary," the term (from the Greek *topos*, place) meant "of or applied to an isolated part of the body"; and it is suggestive that the first use of the word in this sense is recorded by the *Oxford English Dictionary* as dating to 1608. Moreover, the earliest English meaning of the term (the one closest to its Greek root)—"of or belonging to a particular location or place" (1588, according to the *OED*)—may remind us that the spatially imagined body was perhaps the most common vehicle for the making of social and cosmic metaphors in early modern Europe.[7]

It would be a mistake to underestimate the important role of corporeal partitioning in medieval life and thought: religious relics, venerated body parts of saints, zodiac figures (with each sign of the zodiac corresponding to parts of the body), the scandalously circulating organs of the fabliaux, and accounts of phantom limbs all marked the body as a charged site of fragmentation.[8] Indeed, Carolyn Bynum has theorized about the gradually increasing interest in body parts as objects of veneration in the religious life of medieval Europe.[9] But, as the very title of Bynum's recent book—*Fragmentation and Redemption*—might suggest, the medieval Christian understanding of the relation between corporeal fragmentation and wholeness tends to adhere to the Pauline view that "as the body is one, and hath many members, and all the members of that one body, being many, are one body: so also is Christ";[10] thus Erasmus could use almost exactly these words at the beginning of the sixteenth century in his discussion of the nature of bodily multiplicity.[11] By the end of the century, however, such a profession of confidence in the ultimate unity of religious and social systems modeled on bodily organization was no longer viable.

The transformations undergone by European culture and society during this period have been characterized variously as "the ultimate desertion of the universal for the particular,"[12] or the end of the "age of resemblance" and the beginning of modernity's "analytico-referential discourse."[13] It is not difficult to list elements that contributed to (and were given impetus by) this pervasive sense of fragmentation: the "more atomistic and individualistic" society associated with the advent of print technology and the end of feudalism;[14] the schisms in the church; the Copernican revolution, which shook notions of microcosmic-macrocosmic correspondence and symmetry; or the rise of anatomy and its corresponding "culture of dissection."[15] These "impulse[s] to ... distinction and individuation"[16] put increasing stress on the possibility of the recuperation of part into whole. The negotiation between parts and wholes thus became an especially vexed issue in the somatic structures of early modern Europe. The rhetorical trope in which these relations are configured (and disfigured) is synecdoche, a term that signifies the way in which a part is "taken for" a whole. Insofar as parts were imagined as dominant vehicles for the articulation of culture, the early modern period could be conceptualized as an age of synecdoche.[17] What we would like to emphasize here, however, is precisely the way in which the impossibility of fully integrating parts into wholes brought about a privileging of the body part as such.

Thus, for example, the anatomist's dismemberment of the body has been characterized by several critics recently as being in the service of the creation of "a new, more comprehensive order," a unified "body of knowledge";[18] but what often goes unnoticed is the elaborate attention given and significance attributed to the body part *in and of itself.* Similarly, the Renaissance artist's detailed anatomical study of the body, muscle by muscle and limb by limb, ostensibly enables the creation of the finished masterpiece; but Leonardo's, or Michelangelo's, or Dürer's gorgeous portraits of individual organs of the body stand as finished works of art in their own right, and attest to the lavish attention each gave to the isolated part; as Leonardo wrote of his anatomical drawings, "You will become acquainted with every part and every whole *by means of a demonstration of each part.*"[19] So too the Petrarchan poet's emblazoning of the beloved's body, while creating a new aesthetic whole—a sestina, an entire sonnet-sequence, the *Rime sparse*—foregrounds the individual body part so radically that it undermines, as Nancy Vickers will tell us here, "the descriptive mode itself." Or again, when John Donne describes the internal strife in his own body in the *Devotions Upon Emergent Occasions,* these countervailing impulses lie on the surface of his text: "Why dost thou melt me, scatter me?" he asks, lamenting the fact that "Man consists of more pieces, more parts, than the world."[20] And though his urgent desire to "recompact the scatter'd body"[21] always returns him to a vision of wholeness and unity—"Pray unto the Lord, and hee will make thee whole"[22]—his extraordinary meditations on particular body parts (heart, bowels, hand, eye)[23] speak to the energy generated by (and devoted to) individual organs.[24] All of these instances attest to the emergence in early modern culture of what may be called a new aesthetic of the part, which is to say an aesthetic that did not demand or rely upon the reintegration of the part into a predetermined whole.[25]

The Burckhardtian notion of the Renaissance as a period marked by the rise of the individual could, in this respect, be reformulated as a period marked by the rise of the individual part. Much like post-Burckhardtian notions of the individual, the isolated part can never be fully autonomous. If Burckhardt emphasized the self-constituting individual, the "individual" body part is an oxymoron. Its status as "part" implies by definition a relation. Indeed, in early modern England, "individual," as Peter Stallybrass has argued, "whatever its range of possible meanings, suggests a *relation* (of part to whole, of part to part, of member to body, of body to body) not a separate entity."[26] The dialectic implied by the configuration of any given body part is analogous to that implied by the competing uses of the word "individual" in the period. As Stallybrass makes clear, "the uses of 'individual' suggesting indivisibility and those suggesting divisibility emerge *together*"[27] in the seventeenth century. Similarly, the individual part, though singled out in a range of textual and iconographic spaces, always suggests a series of relations—to a normative, pathological, or utterly elusive whole, or to other (dominant or submissive, cooperative or uncooperative) parts, and to the range of symbolic structures that are based on those relations.

Perhaps not surprisingly, early modern anatomies—texts that depend upon the textual and pictorial isolation of parts of the body—are conspicuously fraught with anxiety regarding this dialectic of unity and partition. These texts are repeatedly characterized by a defensive insistence that the part is by definition a part only in relation to the whole: "A Part may be thus defined," writes Thomas Gibson at the opening of his *Anatomy of Humane Bodies Epitomized*:

> viz., *It is a bodily or solid Substance, cohering with, making up, and partaking of the life of, the whole* .... It must *cohere* with the whole. ... It (with others) must serve to *compleat* or *make up* the whole. ... It must partake of the *life* of the whole."[28]

Or, as Crooke would write, "*A part is a body cohearing or cleaving to the whole.*"[29] "Cleaving," a word suggesting at once conditions of attachment and detachment, encapsulates the contradictory impulses evident within medical anatomies about the dissection, representation, and elaboration of single body parts.

Such tensions inform the illustration that serves as the frontispiece to our introduction, the "Visio Prima" (first image) of Johann Remmelin's *Catoptrum Microcosmicum* (Microcosmic mirror; originally published in 1613), an anatomical atlas reprinted many times throughout northern Europe during the seventeenth (and well into the eighteenth) century. The body parts in this flap-anatomy with mobile shutters and multi-layered interiors are at once disconcertingly dismembered, scattered, and decontextualized, *and* set in relation to a series of possible sites within larger physiological, cultural, allegorical, and religious contexts. At first glance, the print seems a chaos of incomplete bodies, internal organs, and external body parts, all spilling over into representational space. (Indeed, so full of body parts is the illustration that both the fetus and the newborn infant in it are configured as no more than parts of the body; as if to say that we all start off as simply that—a body part waiting to be detached.) Upon closer inspection, though, the illustration is not only legible but carefully designed to ward off the very possibility of scattering and dismemberment, of representational collapse. The illustration is organized by a series of dominant oppositions: male and female, inner and outer, divine ethereality in the celestial sphere and monstrous embodiment in the nether regions.[30]

What begins to surface out of the spectre of bodily disorganization is a totalizing system of categorical order. A suggestive gloss here might be Lacan's description of the formation of subjectivity in the mirror stage, in which a sense of "primordial Discord" emerges alongside an image of corporeal totality, creating a fantasy of "the body in bits and pieces" as a retrospective representation of presymbolic chaos.[31] The fantasy, as Lacan articulates it, often resembles

> a jig-saw puzzle, with the separate parts of the body of a man or an animal in disorderly array ... incongruous images in which strange trophies, trunks, are cut up in slices and stuffed with the most unlikely fillings, strange appendages in eccentric positions, reduplications of the penis, images of the cloaca represented as a surgical excision.[32]

For Lacan, what eventually emerges from the mirror stage is not only an image of the self as inhabiting a complete, unified body but also (through the so-called Name of the Father) the entire symbolic structures of self and other, male and female, permitted and forbidden. For Remmelin, the Name of the Father, "Jehovah," is quite literally inscribed (in Hebrew) at the top of the illustration; positioned structurally as the counterpart and implicit threat to this name is the figure of Medusa.

The Medusa, as Marjorie Garber and Nancy Vickers have emphasized, is a famously apotropaic icon that embodies contradictory logics of "disease and cure, threat and protection, poison and remedy."[33] Here the image effects a displacement downward of the viewer's gaze,[34] uncannily anticipating the Freudian logic that explicitly links the Medusa to anxieties about castration: Freud's perception that "Medusa's head takes the place of a representation of the female genitals"[35] is stunningly prefigured by Remmelin's placement of the Medusa head over the female sexual organs.[36] But Remmelin's illustration seems to foreground another, broader interpretation of Medusa; for while, as Freud argues, castration may often be what is signified by decapitation, the latter is first of all a dismemberment, a corporeal partitioning. And Medusa's head is itself a horrific configuration of the body-in-parts, at once a decapitated head and a frightening assemblage of exaggerated parts—monstrous hair, grotesque ears, and a gaping mouth. From this perspective, what Remmelin's Medusa appears to be warning against is not so much a specific anatomical loss as the loss of bodily coherence—and ultimately of coherence as such.[37] For the body part, cut off from the totalized body, works to challenge the very structure upon which meaning is based. To return for a moment to Lacan, it is precisely this loss of coherence—this presymbolic chaos—that is figured by the body in bits and pieces. Such a reading brings out the possibility that the tension between body parts and corporeal wholes lies at the very heart of social and symbolic structuration. In an uncanny corporealization of illegibility—and a remarkably apt description of the icon in Remmelin's print—Lacan configures Medusa as an open mouth that empties the world of meaning. He calls Medusa's head, "[t]his something, which properly speaking is unnameable, the back of this throat, the complex, unlocatable form, which also makes it into the primitive object *par excellence*, the abyss of the feminine organ from which all life emerges, this gulf of the mouth, in which everything is swallowed up."[38] From this perspective, the "unnameable" body part always potentially threatens the symbolic order of the Name of the Father, the order of meaning itself.

But if the order of meaning is threatened by this severed head, it is also created and in many ways stabilized by it. Remmelin added the Medusa to the first authorized edition (three earlier editions had been circulated, much to his dismay) to protect against what he perceived to be the unauthorized scattering and dismembering of his own text.[39] Viewed from this perspective, Medusa appears to embody, to take upon herself, almost literally, anxieties about both textual and medical dismemberment; Perseus-like, Remmelin has "decapitated" the torso at the foot of his illustration and placed the head of Medusa, in the manner of a shield, as an apotropaic device to guard against the threat of symbolic and corporeal disfiguration.

It is worth pointing out that the attention to isolated parts of the body in early modern Europe was not always a source of anxiety.[40] Any reading of cultural pathologies implicit in the decontextualized or dramatically foregrounded organ would also have to consider the more normative models of bodily partition that would, for example, enable the queen of England to be officially represented (in the famous "Rainbow Portrait") wearing a gown covered with eyes, ears, and mouths,[41] or enable an early modern religious order, "the Cult of the Sacred Heart," to be organized around a single body part.

Similarly, any definition of the constitution of a body part would have to consider the fluidity of the rhetoric of bodily partitioning in the period. In anatomy texts, the rehearsal of the terminology of corporeal fragments (member, piece, part, particle, organ) was commonplace, establishing a veritable lexicon for the articulation of parts.[42] Influential natural philosophers like Paracelsus and Van Helmont went so far as to argue that parts were individuated not only lexically and physiologically but also ontologically: to the isolated organs belonged what were termed *ideae singularum partium*—so that, for instance, there existed an *idea ocularis* in the eye, or an *idea sanguinis* in the heart—imparting integrity and spiritual significance to each part of the body.[43]

If the discourse of "the part" was endlessly self-reflexive in medical texts (which were largely influenced by Galen's *De usu partium*), so too it was in the range of dramatic, textual, and iconographic allegories of the senses (based on Aristotle's *De sensu*), which carved out mythologies and personalities around body parts and bodily functions. We may say, in fact, that in early modern Europe more generally, the multiple traditions of medical and anatomical description, of Petrarchism, of religious and cultural iconography, converged to give individual parts of the body more semiotic complexity than they had ever had before. Nowhere in this period is the status of the part simply a given.[44]

The attention paid in this volume to the specific configuration of meanings clustered around particular corporeal parts ultimately suggests that in early modern representations, even or especially as a fantasy of the "whole body" emerges, the body is at the same time always, and perhaps inevitably, a body in parts.

> Being now to dissolve this goodly frame of Nature, and *to take in pieces this Maister-piece*, it shall not be amisse to take a light survey of all the parts as they lye in order.
>
> —Crooke, *Microcosmographia*[45]

The ordering of parts in this volume is necessarily problematic. We would not, perhaps, go so far as to echo Montaigne, who called his essays "grotesques and monstrous bodies, pieced together of diverse members, without definite shape, having no order, sequence, or proportion other than accidental."[46] But each of this volume's "essays in flesh and bone"[47] has very much its own area of interest and methodology; each is partial, in every sense of the word; and the volume as a whole makes no pretense at being either exhaustive or orderly. As bodies go, the one we have put together here is particularly grotesque.

Nonetheless, the pieces are arranged with some semblance of "order, sequence, or proportion." Those in the first section ("Subjecting the Part") examine the ways in which (to return to our earlier formulation) the part, in the early modern period, becomes a *subject*, both in the sense of being "subjected"—of being isolated and disempowered—and of being "subjected"— imagined to be endowed with qualities of intention and subjectivity. These essays investigate the period's emergent forms of subjectivity, which are at once structured and disrupted by forms of embodiment associated with particular parts of the body: knees, elbows, and the jointed body; the mouth and tongue; viscera; and nerves.

Nancy Vickers's "Members Only: Marot's Anatomical Blazons" focuses on the range of body parts (hair, breast, eyebrow, foot, etc.) praised and blamed in the anatomical blazon, and examines the radical fragmentedness of the body part as such. Building upon her own seminal work on Petrarchism and the anatomical blazon, Vickers theorizes what she calls "the power of the part" in early modern French lyric poetry.[48] Tracing the rise of the literary "anatomistes" in the court of Francis I, she shows how the "tropic disfiguration" so integral to the blazon "almost literalizes the logic whereby the self is collected, defined, and displayed *through* the process of splitting and exhibiting the other." In their extreme foregrounding of isolated body parts, she argues, anatomical blazons make little or no attempt to recover the body's unity: "their subjects," writes Vickers, "were body parts not bodies."

The function of body parts in articulating conditions of subjectivity in the social and political worlds of early modern England is the subject of Marjorie Garber's essay. "Out of Joint," the phrase that forms the title, suggests at once conditions of bodily, social, and syntactic dislocation. She argues not only that paradigms of articulation and disarticulation hinge on the logic of the joint but that in early modern literature and culture more generally, the syntax of the skeleton and the syntax of the sentence are inextricably linked. The first part of her essay historicizes early modern semiotics of knees, elbows, and shoulders, based on the gender and class positions of individuated joints; the second part compares modern and early modern rhetorics of articulation and conceptualizations of the jointed body.

With a similar emphasis on somatic articulations, Carla Mazzio's article, "Sins of the Tongue" examines the way in which the tongue, signifying at once the bodily organ and speech itself, emerges within early modern somatic symbolism as a fantasized embodiment of "insubjectible subjectivity." In the increasingly textualized culture of early modern England, fantasies of oral dominance, she argues, register shifting and uncertain relations between the spoken and the written, orality and corporeality, male and female. In sermons, anatomical treatises, literary and philosophical texts, the tongue becomes increasingly fetishized as a means of localizing and controlling the source of discursive and moral contagion, and collective fears of self-alienation are displaced into the mouth of the individual subject.

David Hillman's essay, "Visceral Knowledge: Shakespeare, Skepticism, and the Interior of the Early Modern Body," also concentrates on the embodiment of knowledge and subjectivity in a particular corporeal site—the entrails. Arguing that entrails were a crucial locus of subjectivity in the culture of the period, Hillman examines the ways in which knowledge of interiority, or selfhood, was often fantasized as being equated with objective knowledge of the interior of the body. The skeptical impulse to access the visceral interior of the other's body, exemplified by the practice of anatomy, is vividly portrayed in several of Shakespeare's plays. But what these plays reveal, argues Hillman, is that the impulse to gain access to the other's entrails derives less from the desire to know the other than from a refusal to recognize her or him as other.

The internal workings of the body are the subject of Gail Kern Paster's "Nervous Tension: Networks of Blood and Spirit in the Early Modern Body." Focusing on Crooke's *Microcosmographia*, Paster examines the relationship between the interior passageways of the body and what she calls "the early modern subject's imagined physiology of self." Tracing the ways in which early modern writers described corporeal motion as a series of little explosions, the essay emphasizes the ways in which the vessels worked as "internal distribution systems of early modern subjectivity," and calls attention to physiological descriptions that often recapitulated master tropes of social narratives.

What almost all of the essays in this volume share is what Paster calls an "interpretive literalism," a resistance to the often-assumed "dead metaphoricity" of early modern tropes based upon corporeal functions, locations, parts.[49] While inevitably overlapping with the thematics of self and subjectivity, the essays in Part II, "Sexing the Part," explore the way in which the social logics of sex, gender, and sexuality are located in quite specific bodily sites; the anus, the breast, the clitoris, and (perhaps surprisingly, to modern ears) the eye. (We should perhaps point out that the most notably absent sexual organ in this volume is the penis. An argument could be made, however, that the male member functions almost literally as a floating signifier, surfacing throughout this volume in perhaps the most unexpected of places.)

Jeffrey Masten's essay, "Is the Fundament a Grave?" analyzes the "foundational" or "fundamental" role of the male anus in the rhetoric of early modern Europe. Questioning the often-assumed association between the anus and the "end" or grave of the self, Masten establishes links between the anal or "foundational" and the generative. Through an analysis of a wide range of texts, from the medical and anatomical to the dramatic and political, he (tentatively) posits the fundament as a site for the production of knowledge and health, noting "the alterity of this culture's conception of the anus and of the body attached to and articulated around it."

Kathryn Schwarz's article, "Missing the Breast: Desire, Disease, and the Singular Effect of Amazons," contextualizes the absent Amazon breast in terms of early modern medical and literary representations of the breast. Schwarz suggests that the breast was, in this period, a metonymic icon and a site of inescapable gender difference. At the same time, she argues, in its connection to erotic excess and excessive maternal control, the breast is always a site of potential danger, signifying beyond the logic of social structures. It is precisely this threat that is encoded in the mythologized image of the absent Amazon breast—an absence that, says Schwarz, comes to embody multiple anxieties about loss: loss of the mother, of gender stability, of referential certainty.

The anatomy and physiology of sexual difference in early modern France, as Katherine Park writes in "The Rediscovery of the Clitoris: French Medicine and the *Tribade*, 1570–1620," was in every way called into question by the ambivalent status of the clitoris. Park's article examines anxieties about gender and sexual difference that informed the "rediscovery of the clitoris" in medical texts of the period. The (long-ignored) clitoris was imagined to have exact structural analogies to the phallus, thereby marking all women as in some sense hermaphroditic, bearing both male and female sexual organs. Park's work thus challenges the notion of gender determined by an implicitly hierarchized physiological inversion, and examines the implications of the phallic clitoris in terms of fantasies of "hermaphroditic" physiology and female sexuality in general.

The relation between masculinity and the physiology of the eye is a central concern of "Taming the Basilisk," in which Sergei Lobanov-Rostovsky examines the double role of the eye as both producer and object of the gaze. He traces traditional conceptions of the eye as alternatively a penetrative (and hence implicitly masculine) agent or a passive (and implicitly feminine) receptor, and goes on to show how the practice of ocular anatomy in the sixteenth century threatened the eye's power by conceiving of it as merely an enfleshed and vulnerable object. Through a reading of a range of medical and literary texts, Lobanov-Rostovsky reveals how fantasies of the eye's power are often compensatory, effacing the potential reduction of gazing subject to partiality and materiality (and of the eye itself to vulnerable passivity), and work in this period to associate the eye with the empowered and masculine gaze.

If Lobanov-Rostovsky's article aligns enfleshment, and thus the potential for wounding and dismemberment, with loss of power, the essays in our third section ("Divining the Part") reveal ways in which not only the condition of embodiment but even the very vulnerability of the body can empower the believer, linking him or her to the central image of corporeal suffering in Christianity, the body of Christ.

Stephen Greenblatt's article, "Mutilation and Meaning," contextualizes the wounding of the body in terms of a historical moment when the overarching framework of somatic sacredness, of the "universal language of holy wounds," begins to crumble. He traces out the logic of what he calls an "early modern heterology," in which writers focused at once on the particularizing, socially and culturally determined meanings of forms of bodily mutilation, and the general, potentially universal language of bodies. Faced with alien peoples to whose languages and cultures Europeans had little access, he argues, these "heterologists" focused almost inevitably on the "recalcitrant practical otherness" of the strangers' physical existence. His essay examines the way in which early modern attempts to establish and understand universal languages of the body register a shift from predominantly religious to predominantly anthropological paradigms.

Greenblatt thus shows one way in which modalities of conceptualizing corporeality shifted dramatically in the early modern period. The essays in this section by Michael Schoenfeldt, Scott Manning Stevens, and Katherine Rowe share a concern with the ways in which individual parts of the body, in their imagined relationship to the divine, were invested with varying degrees of significance in the literature and culture of the period. For Schoenfeldt, the stomach is imagined in early modern texts as the most literal site of human, and specifically devotional, inwardness: "The stomach," he writes, "is the chamber where God is welcomed into the self." While the activities of ingestion, transformation, and assimilation associated with the stomach were easily translated into social metaphors, dietary regimes worked as a very literal mode of self-fashioning and hence as a way to avoid the more deterministic aspects of Galenic humoral physiology. In contrast to recent theories about the implicitly transgressive status of the uncontained body, he stresses the salutary components of an orderly flow of substances in and out of the self. Examining the combined emphasis in medical and religious texts on the importance of understanding the interior spaces of the consuming subject, he traces discourses that link gastrointestinal activities with the personal, social, and spiritual status of the self.

Stevens's chapter, "Sacred Heart and Secular Brain," is similarly interested in the dominance of a body part in the shifting structures of (in par-

ticular) religious belief. It begins by noting that during the seventeenth century—just as medical science unequivocally endorsed the brain as the center
of mental and emotional activity—much liturgical practice focused specifically on the heart of Jesus as the location of Christ's humanity. With
anatomy's improved understanding of the heart's mechanical use as simply a
blood pump, writes Stevens, the organ became less and less available for a
purely physiological explanation of consciousness; the embodiment of the
self was relocated in the brain, the physiology of which remained (and indeed
remains) largely obscure. But, as Stevens argues, the heart's importance in
the period's religious iconography can be understood in terms of the organ's
ability to reoccupy a simultaneously material and metaphorical space, to
bridge the sacred-secular divide.

The sacred-secular divide is, in quite another sense, the subject of
Katherine Rowe's "'God's handy worke': Divine Complicity and the Anatomist's Touch." She argues that the divisibility of the hand in the largely secular
activity of dissection is consistently framed, in early modern medical texts,
within a logic of sacred significance. Tracing linguistic and iconographic
strategies that aim to recuperate the severed or dissected hand, Rowe argues
that associations between the hand of the anatomist and the hand of God
work to configure not only the activity but the spectacle of manual dissection
in terms of a framework of epistemological coherence and totality.

Peter Stallybrass's "Footnotes" provides a coda for the volume as a
whole. Starting from the "disappearance" of the foot in modern ballet, Stallybrass works backward to explore the relation between feet and one's position
within the social and symbolic order in early modern England. Here, he
argues, social logics of power and subordination are heavily invested in the
position of the foot: "power is marked not by the absence of feet but by their
presence." Hence, he suggests, the shoemaker had a particularly charged relationship to social hierarchy, to the literal as well as symbolic body politic: it is
on this "basis" that the cobbler can become, in the Renaissance, a veritable
"Mender of bad Soules."

"The Soule of Man *is wholly in the whole, and wholly in every particular
part,*" writes Crooke.[50] As the essays in this volume reveal, the body's individual parts loom large across the horizons of the early modern world, organiz-
ing its structures of subjectivity, society, and divinity. Yet while the part may
often succeed in displacing the whole, it never quite manages to replace it; if
there is always a tension between part and whole, it is because neither can do
without the other. Both, ultimately, are fantasmatic entities: the body part
can take on mythic forms of agency and autonomy, yet it always remains a

part, set apart only in relation to a whole. And the whole is no less mythic a construction, an imaginary defense against the fragmentary nature of corporeal existence. As the philosopher Jean-Luc Nancy has written,

> The parts of the corpus do not combine into a whole, are not means to it or ends of it. Each part can suddenly take over the whole, can spread out over it, can become it, the whole—that never takes place. There is no whole, no totality of the body—but its absolute separation and sharing [*partage*].[51]

Absolute *partage* perhaps, but no absolute part. The body in parts, which occupies such a privileged place in the public and private fantasies of early modern Europe, perhaps does so because it ultimately never takes place.

Notes

For their insights and encouragement, we would like to thank the members of the Harvard Renaissance Colloquium who listened to an early draft of this essay. For editing the editors, for careful and insightful comments on the final draft, we would like to thank Marjorie Garber, Jeffrey Masten, and Linda Schlossberg. And most particularly, we thank Peter Stallybrass for his remarkably generous and thoughtful response to this introduction.

1. See for example, Jonathan Sawday, *The Body Emblazoned: Dissection and the Human Body in Renaissance Culture* (London: Routledge, 1995); Devon L. Hodges, *Renaissance Fictions of Anatomy* (Amherst: University of Massachusetts Press, 1985); Nancy J. Vickers, "Diana Described: Scattered Woman and Scattered Rhyme," *Critical Inquiry* 8 (1981): 265–79; Susanne L. Wofford, "The Body Unseamed: Shakespeare's Late Tragedies," in *Shakespeare's Late Tragedies: A Collection of Critical Essays*, ed. Susanne L. Wofford (Upper Saddle River, N.J.: Prentice Hall, 1996), 1–21. Also, on the body as an integrated system, see Leonard Barkan's important *Nature's Work of Art: The Human Body as Image of the World* (New Haven: Yale University Press, 1975).

2. The complex relations between subjects and objects in the early modern period are the subject of the wonderful new anthology *Subject and Object in Renaissance Culture*, ed. Margreta de Grazia, Maureen Quilligan, and Peter Stallybrass (Cambridge: Cambridge University Press, 1996).

3. Blaise Pascal, *Pensées*, trans. A. J. Krailsheimer (New York: Penguin, 1966), 135.

4. Elizabeth Grosz, *Volatile Bodies: Toward a Corporeal Feminism* (Bloomington: Indiana University Press, 1994), 13.

5. Jean Starobinski, "The Natural and Literary History of Bodily Sensation," in *Fragments for a History of the Human Body, part two,* ed. Michel Feher, with Ramona Naddaff and Nadia Tazi (New York: Zone Books, 1989), 353.

6. Carolyn Walker Bynum, "Why All the Fuss about the Body? A Medievalist's Perspective," *Critical Inquiry* 22, no. 1 (autumn 1995): 2.

7. Perhaps the most famous early modern example of society as a collection of body parts is the debate about the belly in act I of Shakespeare's *Coriolanus*. On the contested status of the body politic in *Coriolanus,* see especially Zvi Jagendorf's "*Coriolanus*: Body Politic and Private Parts," in *Shakespeare Quarterly* 41, no. 4 (winter 1990): 455–69: "Each side in this argument makes metaphors out of limbs, and the result is a foregrounding of the fragment at the expense of the whole" (460).

8. See especially Caroline Walker Bynum *Fragmentation and Redemption: Essays on Gender and the Human Body in Medieval Religion* (New York: Zone Books, 1992), and Miri Rubin, "The Body, Whole and Vulnerable, in Fifteenth-Century England," in *Bodies and Disciplines: Intersections of Literature and History in Fifteenth-Century England,* ed. Barbara A. Hanawalt and David Wallace. *Medieval Cultures,* vol. 9 (Minneapolis: University of Minnesota Press, 1996). On phantom limbs, see Douglas B. Price and Neil J. Twombly, *The Phantom Limb Phenomenon: A Medical, Folkloric, and Historical Study: Texts and Translations of 10th to 20th Century Accounts of the Miraculous Restoration of Lost Body Parts* (Georgetown: Georgetown University Press, 1978), and on the circulation of body parts in medieval fabliaux, see Howard Bloch, *The Scandal of the Fabliaux* (Chicago: University of Chicago Press, 1986).

9. See especially the introduction ("In Praise of Fragments") and chapter 7 of Bynum, *Fragmentation and Redemption.*

10. I Cor. 12:12; cf. John A. T. Robinson, *The Body: A Study in Pauline Theology* (London: SCM Press, 1952), 58–67.

11. See Desiderius Erasmus, *Enchiridion Militis Christiani,* trans. William Tyndale (London, 1533), ed. Anne M. O'Donnell. *Early English Text Society* (Oxford: Oxford University Press, 1981), 155. The Corinthian subtext was, of course, cited often throughout the Renaissance, but, we contend, with increasing anxiousness.

12. Hiram Haydn, *The Counter-Renaissance* (New York: Harcourt, Brace & World, 1950), 143.

13. Michel Foucault, *The Order of Things: An Archaeology of the Human Sciences* (New York: Vintage Books, 1973), 55; Timothy Reiss, *The Discourse of Modernism* (Ithaca: Cornell University Press, 1982), 9.

14. Elizabeth L. Eisenstein, *The Printing Press as an Agent of Change: Communications and Transformations in Early-Modern Europe* (Cambridge: Cambridge University Press, 1979), 132.

15. Sawday, *The Body Emblazoned,* vii.

16. Ernst Cassirer, *The Individual and the Cosmos in Renaissance Philosophy*, trans. Mario Domandi (Philadelphia: University of Pennsylvania Press, 1963), 3.

17. Of course, insofar as synecdoche implies a full representation or recuperation of the whole, one could configure the early modern period in terms of a *crisis* of synecdoche. Importantly, synecdoche is not only the taking of part for whole; it

is also, and inseparably, the substitution of the whole for the part—the word derives, in fact, from the Greek for "the act of taking together." Kenneth Burke, arguing that synecdoche implies a relation of convertibility between its terms, writes that

> the "noblest synecdoche," the perfect paradigm of prototype for all lesser usages, is found in metaphysical doctrines proclaiming the identity of "microcosm" and "macrocosm." In such doctrines, where the individual is treated as a replica of the universe, and vice versa, we have the ideal synecdoche, since microcosm is related to macrocosm as part to whole, and either the whole can represent the part or the part can represent the whole.

It is just this "noble synecdoche" that comes into crisis in the early modern period, where the capacity of the body to *represent* or mirror a social, religious, or cosmic whole is threatened by the increasing and often disruptive dominance of its parts. See Kenneth Burke, *A Grammar of Motives* (New York: Prentice Hall, 1945), 503–7. On synecdoche and dismemberment in Shakespeare, see Wofford, "The Body Unseamed," 1–21.

18. Hodges, *Renaissance Fictions of Anatomy*, 6.

19. Cited in K. B. Roberts and J. D. W. Tomlinson, *The Fabric of the Body: European Traditions of Anatomical Illustration* (Oxford: Clarendon Press, 1992), 104; emphasis added.

20. John Donne, *Devotions Upon Emergent Occasions*, ed. Anthony Raspa (Oxford: Oxford University Press, 1987), 12 (Expostulation II); 19 (Meditation IV).

21. Donne, "A Valediction of my Name, in the Window," in *The Complete Poetry of John Donne*, ed. John T. Shawcross (New York: Anchor Books, 1967), 111.

22. Donne, *Devotions*, 22 (Expostulation IV), quoting Ecclesiastes, 38:9.

23. See, e.g., *Devotions*, 56–61, 86–87, 44–45, 49–50.

24. As Donne wrote in the "First Anniversary: An Anatomy of the World," "The body will not last out to have read / On every part, and therefore men direct / Their speech to parts, that are of most effect." *The Complete Poetry*, 284–85 (ll. 436–38). Elaine Scarry writes, in "Donne: 'But yet the body is his booke,'"

> We today generally assume that the body should be thought of "as a whole" rather than as "parts," since the latter seems to imply an aggressive, if only mentally executed, dismemberment. While this reflex is generously motivated, it may also be a luxury of our relative immunity to disease. In the Renaissance, "part" and "whole" seem to have very different values: the naming of body parts often seems to be performed as a stay against disease which works to "spoil" part after part and eventually to take over the whole body, subverting the capacity to differentiate among parts: "As long," Donne writes, "as a man is alive, if there appear any offence in his breath, the physician will assign it to

some *one* corrupt *place*, his *lungs*, or *teeth*, or *stomach*, and thereupon apply convenient remedy thereunto. But if he be dead, and putrefied, no man askes *from whence that ill aire and offence comes*, because it proceeds from the whole carcasse" (*Sermons* 3:364). Throughout Renaissance medical treatises there recurs what could be called the "trope of the entire body," which signals the moment when the physicians have lost, the disease has won, the attempt to "track" the disease is no longer possible, it being everywhere.

In *Literature and the Body: Essays on Populations and Persons*, ed. Elaine Scarry (Baltimore: Johns Hopkins University Press, 1987), 102 n. 22.

25. The relation between part and whole is at once vividly demonstrated and problematized by the zodiac figure. Although Leonard Barkan writes that in astrology, "man's body is viewed as a whole rather than in a list of anatomical parts, and is isomorphic with the heavens" (*Nature's Work of Art*, 25), this is not always the case: in Ottavio Scarlatini's late sixteenth-century *Homo et ejus figuratus et symbolicus* (Bologna, 1684), for example, twelve detached body parts float above the heads of three heavily classicized figures; Francesco Minniti's *Armonia Astro-Medico-Anatomica* (Venice, 1690) conflates physiological and astrological symbolics of individuated parts; the zodiac man here is notable less for his embodiment of a whole system than for his status as a conglomeration of multiply coded parts.

26. Peter Stallybrass, "Shakespeare, the Individual, and the Text," in *Cultural Studies*, ed. Lawrence Greenberg, Cary Nelson, and Paula Treichler (New York: Routledge, 1992), 593–612, 606.

27. Ibid., 595.

28. Thomas Gibson, *The Anatomy of Humane Bodies Epitomized* (London, 1697), 2.

29. Crooke, *Microcosmographia* (London, 1616), 3.

30. Moreover, the heart and tilted-back head at the center, and the eye, ear, hand, and foot at the four corners, combine to create a kind of order modeled on the human form. On the eye and ear as antithetical modalities of understanding subjectivity in the early modern period, see Joel Fineman, "Shakespeare's Ear," in *The Subjectivity Effect in the Western Literary Tradition: Essays Toward the Release of Shakespeare's Will* (Cambridge: MIT Press, 1991), 222–31; and Linda Woodbridge, *The Scythe of Saturn: Shakespeare and Magical Thinking* (Urbana: University of Illinois, 1994), 215–27.

31. Jacques Lacan, "The mirror stage as formative of the function of the I as revealed in psychoanalytic experience," in *Écrits: A Selection*, trans. Alan Sheridan (New York: Norton, 1977), 4. Lacan's theory of the infant's experience of the body is in many ways indebted to the work of Melanie Klein, for whom the baby's primitive, fragmented sense of self finds a correlative in the so-called part object—the fantasy of an agency-filled anatomical part of the body. See especially her "A Contribution to the Psychogenesis of Manic-Depressive States," in *The Works of Melanie Klein*, vol. 1, *Love, Guilt, and Reparation and Other Works, 1921–1945* (New York: Free Press, 1975), 262–89.

32. Jacques Lacan, "Some Reflections on the Ego," *International Journal of Psychoanalysis* 35 (1953): 13. Quoted in Grosz, *Volatile Bodies*, 43.

33. Marjorie Garber and Nancy Vickers's forthcoming *Don't Look Now: A Medusa Reader* (New York: Routledge, 1997), 1. Also, on the logics of the Medusa in anthropology, psychoanalysis, and literature, see Marjorie Garber, "*Macbeth*: The Male Medusa," in *Shakespeare's Ghost Writers: Literature as Uncanny Causality* (London: Methuen, 1987), 87–118; Nancy Vickers, "The Blazon of Sweet Beauty's Best: Shakespeare's *Lucrece*," in *Shakespeare and the Question of Theory*, ed. Patricia Parker and Geoffrey Hartman (New York: Routledge, 1985), 95–115.

34. The Medusa head is in fact literally displaced downward from its natural position on top of the torso—it is as if what we are seeing is the fallen head after it has been severed from Medusa's shoulders.

35. Sigmund Freud, "Medusa's Head," in *Sexuality and the Psychology of Love*, ed. Philip Rieff (New York: Macmillan, 1963), 213.

36. The presence of the image is all the more conspicuous in that it is entirely unnecessary because the genitals of the female torso it is supposedly hiding and protecting are already covered by a drape. Yet Remmelin found it necessary to add the Medusa image to the first authorized edition of his *Catoptrum*. See Kenneth F. Russel, *A Bibliography of Johann Remmelin the Anatomist* (Melbourne: Australia: J. F. Russel, 1991). In *The Body Emblazoned*, Sawday reads the anatomized interior of the body in early modern England as a kind of "Medusa head." What we hope to emphasize, however, is not so much Medusa's relation to the forbidden interior of the body as her relation to the logic of the body part as such.

37. As Marjorie Garber has suggested, in "*Macbeth*: The Male Medusa," "Medusa's head ends up being the displacement upward neither of the female nor of the male genitals but of gender undecidability as such. *That* is what is truly uncanny about it" (105).

38. Jacques Lacan, *The Second Seminar: The Ego in Freud's Theory and in the Technique of Psychoanalysis, 1954–1955*, ed. Jacques-Alain Miller, trans. Sylvana Tomaselli (New York: Norton, 1991), 164.

39. Despite the fact that Remmelin complained that the three earlier, unauthorized editions had been "teem[ing] with errors," the Medusa was one of the few changes he made to his own authorized edition. See Russel, *A Bibliography of Johann Remmelin*, 2–3.

40. Interestingly, the body part can embody both comic and tragic potential. (See, for example, Stallybrass's meditation on the clown's large feet and Garber's distinction between comically and tragically inflected joints in this collection.) There is a link to be made between Klein's theorization of the infant's ambivalent relation to the part object and these comic (or manic) and tragic (or depressive) potentials; see Vickers's discussion of Klein and the dialectic of praise and blame in her chapter here.

41. For a suggestive reading of the anxious subtext to the Rainbow Portrait, see Fineman, "Shakespeare's Ear." Fineman points out that the headdress worn by the queen is reminiscent of Medusa's head. Interestingly, there is no reference to

Medusa in the early version of Fineman's paper, published in *Representations* 28 (fall 1989), but, like Remmelin, he added the Medusa to a later version of his text, published in *The Subjectivity Effect in the Western Literary Tradition.*

42. According to the *OED*, the constellation of words with the root "part" in English emerged largely during the sixteenth century. Between 1523 and 1597, at least two dozen such words came into use, from "partnership," "departure," and "compartment" to "participant," "partake," "particularity," and "parturient."

43. See Walter Pagel, "Religious Motives in the Medical Biology of the Seventeenth Century, Part I," *Bulletin of the History of Medicine* 3, no. 2 (1935): 97–128, esp. 104–5 and 125–26: "Just as every being," he writes (describing Paracelsus's system), "is a peculiar entity the essence of which can never be the result of a simple mixture of matter, every organ within this being has its peculiar form, function and life" (104). Interestingly, even the experience of phantom body parts was given a name in the early modern period. Phantom limb syndrome, the sensation of having a body part that is not there, was considered to be a magical or miraculous event until the mid-sixteenth century, when it became a medical phenomenon, termed "dolor membri amputati" (the pain that remains after amputation). See Price and Twombly, *The Phantom Limb Phenomenon*, especially the introduction.

44. As Peter Stallybrass writes in a discussion of the publicly displayed heart, "[T]here is nothing given about the processes by which a particular body part is singled out for symbolic elaboration." "Dismemberments and Re-Memberments: Rewriting the *Decameron*, 4.1, in the English Renaissance," in *Studi Sul Bocaccio* 20 (1991): 299–323, at 318.

45. Crooke, *Microcosmographia*, 60.

46. Michel de Montaigne, *The Complete Essays of Montaigne*, trans. Donald M. Frame (Stanford: Stanford University Press, 1957), 135.

47. Montaigne, *Essays*, 640.

48. Nancy Vickers, "Diana Described: Scattered Woman and Scattered Rhyme."

49. For a brief discussion of "dead metaphoricity," see Jeffrey Masten's "Is the Fundament a Grave?" (this volume).

50. Crooke, *Microcosmographia*, 4.

51. Jean-Luc Nancy, "Corpus," in *Thinking Bodies*, ed. Juliet Flower MacCannell and Laura Zakarin (Stanford: Stanford University Press, 1994), 31.

Part I

❖

Subjecting the Part

Contre les

BLASONNEVRS
DES MEMBRES.

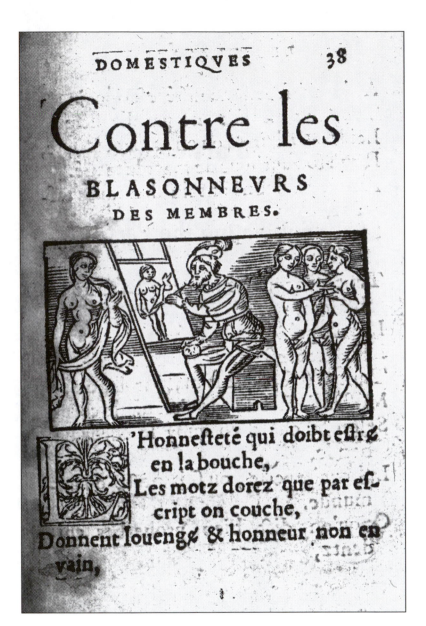

'Honnesteté qui doibt estre
en la bouche,
Les motz dorez que par es-
cript on couche,
Donnent louenge & honneur non en
vain,

2.1 From *Les Blasons domestiques* (Paris: Gilles Corrozet, 1539).

2

Members Only

Marot's Anatomical Blazons

❖

NANCY J. VICKERS

The image that introduces this essay is drawn from a 1539 volume, *Les Blasons domestiques*, published by Parisian poet-bookseller Gilles Corrozet (Figure 2.1). It stages a scene of composition: a courtly painter gestures toward a canvas and, in touching it with the instrument in his hand, perfects his representation of a female nude. A model poses before his easel; several models-in-waiting stand to the side. Though the woodcut's scene is in many senses elusive, we can approach its meaning by noting that it would probably be familiar to early modern readers of Parisian illustrated books. They might have recognized it, for example, as an imitation of a woodcut figuring prominently in Clément Marot's recent and best-selling edition of *Le Roman de la Rose* (*The Romance of the Rose*); they might even have noticed that the very same woodcut had then reappeared across a range of widely read, inexpensive little books about love.[1]

Marot, or his printer, had used the image to illustrate a story recounted in *Le Roman de la Rose* but borrowed from the ancients, that of the painter Zeuxis. Charged with the task of painting Helen, Zeuxis found no single model of sufficient beauty to pose for him. He thus worked from multiple models, adapting the best parts of each to assemble an idealized totality. His story is consistently invoked when the tension between body parts and whole bodies is at issue.[2] Indeed, Corrozet polemically remotivates it here to mount an argument "against the blazoners of body parts." He stages his "domestic blazons" (descriptive poems in praise of the parts of a respectable house) as correctives to "anatomical blazons" (descriptive poems in praise of the parts of the female body).

A literary fashion of their day,[3] the "anatomical blazons" circulated in the form of multiauthored anthologies in which each individual poet-painter praised one or more individual part(s). Only one poet, perhaps King Francis I, wrote in celebration of a full (though itemized) body. The *blasonneurs'* poems were thus the extension, the exaggeration to the point of violation, of the descriptive mode itself: they isolated each unit of conventional body-part enumeration; they attempted a microdescription that ultimately failed to be descriptive; and they diminished synecdoche (the part for the whole) as a properly operant trope by rhetorically stressing a fiction of lyric address in which the addressee was not a whole woman but, rather, a part of a woman—a nose, or a tooth, or a hand. For blazons not only describe the body parts they praise, they serenade them; they plead with them; they urge them to respond. What accounts for much of the perceived absurdity of body blazon is just this transposition, this shift in the traditional structure of seductive lyric address from "I" speaking to "you" (most excellent of ladies); to "I" speaking to "you" (most excellent of hands, feet, lips, eyes, or brows).[4] Each detail of the body is celebrated through a catalogue of qualities, a catalogue in which evocative units, like aphorisms, generally could stand alone, could assume another position without sacrificing meaning. The individual text expands a sequence of metaphors all triggered by the object named but ultimately rearrangeable. More important, both the poems' illustrations and their characteristic play with syntax (as in the insistent use of anaphora) focus the reader's eye, no matter what the text may say about a whole body, on but one detail. Thus, the traditional generic definition—descriptive verse in praise (blazon) or blame (counterblazon)—provides limited explanation; it neglects much of what is most striking about, or characteristic of, the genre.

The independent genre of the "anatomical blazon" had an identifiable and specific origin in the second quarter of the sixteenth century when a group of poets among the most respected men of vernacular letters in France—Antoine Héroet, Maurice Scève, and Claude Chappuys, among others—engaged in a literary contest. Seemingly inspired by a challenge posed in 1535 by the then exiled (and thus eager to please at court) Clément Marot, each composed at least one *blason anatomique*: the hair was Nature's masterpiece; the tooth, the pride of the anatomy; the fingernail, a mirror in which an ardent suitor could admire himself. These *blasons anatomiques*, collected and published first as supplements to other texts and later as independent volumes, are the products of a revealing moment in the history of one of the most conventional of conventions, examples of a descriptive boundary that would compel subsequent generations to seek alternate routes: "My mistress' eyes," wrote Shakespeare some sixty years later, "are nothing like the sun" (Sonnet 130, 1).

In their day the *blasons anatomiques* prompted bitter debate; in subsequent centuries they have been ignored, avoided, lost, and destroyed. In the 1950s, for example, Albert-Marie Schmidt still felt obliged in his anthology to use ellipsis in selected titles, to eliminate selected texts.[5] Indeed, modern editors have unfailingly truncated and imposed an order on the collection; they deny its unkempt plurality and correct its deformities. Misplaced limbs are set in proper sequence; misshapen ones, those of the *contreblasons*, are excluded. The very concept, moreover, of a collection of verse, composed by a loosely associated group of men, that figuratively dismembers the female body (be it in celebration or in vituperation) continues to seem if not aberrant at least unconventional.

From the beginning, blazon and counterblazon, fascination and repulsion, desire and disgust went hand in hand. Marot's original blazon of the breast ("Le Blason du tetin," 1535) was soon paired with his companion piece ("Le Contreblason du tetin," 1536), and these poems were consistently acknowledged as the models of the genre. Amused or dismissive responses to the *blasons anatomiques* may fashion themselves as straightforward, but most often read as mixed; they reenact an ambivalence inscribed in the texts, an ambivalence about bodies in general and women's bodies in particular.

Some blazoners transgressed the bounds of decorum, and others limited themselves to chaste appreciations; all, nonetheless, demonstrated an investment in the display of their own ingenuity. Less playful types were manifestly appalled. Corrozet, for example, considered the *blasonneurs'* manner (or style) to be "perfectly elegant" but judged their matter (or topic) to be the most disgusting ever developed: "But the subject is the most filthy and dirty [*ord et salle*] that was ever spoken about in a private or public room [*chambre ou salle*]." He termed their "deification" of female body parts "an idolatry" and insisted that right-thinking people found the *blasons anatomiques* offensive ("Les gens de bien en sont scandalisez").[6]

And yet despite, or perhaps because of, moral resistance, the popularity of anatomical blazon extended well into the century.[7] Editions were multiple; and, according to Marot's arch rival François Sagon, copies were "so available" as to be found "in every shop."[8] Momentum having been gained through the praise and blame of body parts, the genre's more corrective poets expanded and redefined appropriate blazon "matter" to include not only the domestic alternatives Corrozet proposed (household objects like pots and benches) but other topics such as garments, birds, and flowers— all the "banal objects," one critic notes, "given to man to serve him."[9]

Paradoxically, while these later blazons seemed to effect a defamiliarization of everyday "objects," they also reinforced and depended upon the very familiarity of their subject matter for poetic effect. But this banalization of the poems' "matter" was a move away from Marot's original *materia* for blazon—the description of the parts of the female body. The most extravagant celebrations to precede Marot of the anatomized woman had been penned by a *strambottista* associated with the court of Ferrara and known to French poets before 1536, Baldassare Olimpo da Sassoferrato. The *strambotto*, a highly repetitive eight-line lyric of popular origin, was practiced by poets such as Cariteo, Tebaldeo, and Serafino. Petrarch had praised individual parts of Laura's body, and Sanazzaro, imitating Petrarch, had written sonnets on a "beautiful hand."[10] The relationship of the *blasonneurs* to the Petrarchan tradition they embraced, however, was by no means a simple one. Some found in Petrarch a mirror revealing a complex psychology of love; for others, it was but a grotesquely distorted reflection. What could be serious in the context of Laura's expressive, inspiring eyes became absurd when applied to a random tooth or toe. It is, indeed, surprising that in 1581 an Italian scholar felt compelled to speculate in print as to why Petrarch had never celebrated Laura's nose:[11] a reading of the "Blason du Nez" ("O Noble Nose, odorative organ")[12] should have already provided ample explanation. The blazon, it is obvious, must often be read as parody; and yet, just as often it cannot. Maurice Scève, for example, in his "Blason du sourcil" ("Blazon of the eyebrow") strikes a lyric stance so similar to that of his 449-poem masterpiece, the *Délie* (1544), that to read the former as a spoof would imply a similar, patently unacceptable, reading of the latter. The "speaker" of the anatomical blazon, then, is as plural as the moods of the genre's many authors.

Some literary historians consider Olimpo's verses on the breast to be the source of Marot's original blazon; others trace its beginnings to medieval France. They derive blazon from the *dit*, or from a long tradition of Latin and vernacular salacious verse, or from medieval enumerative compendia on topics such as plants, animals, and stones. In any event, the *blasonneurs* stood in an ambivalent relation to the multiple traditions, sources, and contexts within which the poems were produced. We have already seen, for example, the dual impulses at work behind the *blasonneurs'* invocation of Petrarchan tropes. Similarly, the *blasons anatomiques* can be seen at once as figuring and disfiguring the conventional representations of body parts so integral to religious discourse. Indeed, the attention to isolated or scattered body parts in the religious polemics of the fifteenth and sixteenth centuries (relics, apocalyptic scattering, the worship of parts of Christ's body, etc.)[13] often served as an uncomfortable context for the *blasons*. Tropes of bodily fragmentation and individuation constitutive of the genre were seen, in many respects, as having potentially heretical overtones. For those of traditional religious conviction, the anatomical blazon, no matter how ostensibly playful, could well have seemed an offensive reversal—a desanctification of holy body parts corresponding in time to a sanctification of secular ones. Corrozet, for example, warned the reader of the blazon (whom he cast as both noble and male: "Et vous, Seigneurs, que ces Blasons lisez") that such worshipping of the creation (the body) instead of the creator (God) endangered his soul (276); Charles de la Hueterie parodically enacted this very substitution by announcing a shift in his address to the blazoned body from "*vous*" to "*tu*" (standard in speech to God) because the human anatomy now claimed such "great glory" that one owed it "the offering" ("Contre-blason du corps," ll. 21–24)

The association of the body part with divine "glory," while sarcastically inflected in the mouth of de la Hueterie, was a common trope of almost all anatomical treatises of the sixteenth century. These consistently associated the work of dissection and anatomical description with the revelation of the beauty of God's creation. Indeed, the descriptive elaboration of the singular body parts so central to both anatomical blazons and anatomical treatises can in many respects be seen as not only formally but also historically and contextually entwined. The authors of the blazon poems were called by themselves and by their contemporaries "*anatomistes*," and what they shared with their more concretely grounded practitioners was the circulation of printed texts that displayed the private, particularized body to the public gaze. It could be argued that what lay at the heart of both poetic and anatomical practices of dissection was the poet's or scientist's virtuoso display of a fundamentally scandalous art: it is in the masterful publishing of the secrets of the body by means of a masterful wielding of an instrument that the medical dissector's art meets that of the poet-rhetorician.

Jonathan Sawday has recently called attention to the relationship between medical and poetic strategies of dissecting the body, arguing that "the blazon formed a significant part of the culture of dissection which produced the partitioned body."[14] While it is a striking fact that the production of treatises on dissection and anatomical blazons coincided in time (the first independent collection, *Les Blasons anatomiques du corps fémenin,* appeared in the same year [1543] as Vesalius's *Fabrica*) and place (both were directly or indirectly associated with the Paris of Francis I),[15] there are also important distinctions to be drawn between the logic of bodily partitioning in medical and poetic practice.

The potential danger and transgressiveness of the partitioning of the body in the anatomical treatises was mitigated by a number of factors, not the least of which were the strategies of recuperation of corporeal wholeness commonly employed by these texts. The reliance of anatomical explication upon tropes and assumptions of contiguity and continuity, as well as the tendency of anatomical illustration to situate the body part consistently in relation to an image of a vital whole, worked to downplay the logic of fragmentation potentially associated with the actual practice of anatomy. The strategies of representing and elaborating upon individuated parts in the *blasons anatomiques*, in contrast, reveal a logic of more radical fragmentation: the body is individuated into single parts, and in the attention lavished upon particular members, few attempts are made to recover the body's unity.

The printed collections of anatomical blazons worked, in many ways, to emphasize the partiality of the despised or venerated bodily object. Throughout the sixteenth century, printed texts of *blasons anatomiques* combined a title, a picture, and a text on a single page. The poetry often affirmed the power of the part, its potential for action, its devastating effect on helpless admirers; reductive illustration not only isolated but also pinned the selected part to the page. The blazon's mode of illustration is key to its interpretation. While we do not know who introduced the pictures, and while we cannot tell whether poets had them in mind when they penned their texts or whether printers introduced them to enhance the market value of their products, they are a prominent feature of every extant sixteenth-century edition of *blasons anatomiques*. At most, they demonstrate that the genre was broadly conceived to be one of radical fragmentation; and at the very least, they leave us an invaluable document, a testimony to contemporary readings (those of the multiple printers) that interpret the poems as texts highlighting the part at the expense of the whole. The woodcuts were, in any case, deemed appropriate accompaniment to, and produced specifically for, these poems. Thus, unlike the more contextualized images in medical treatises, the blazons' woodcuts undermined any suggestion of bodily integrity the poems themselves might have made; they displayed a body disembodied, divided, and conquered.

2.2 "Blazon of the Hair," *Hecatomphile* (Paris: Pierre Sergent, 1539).

2.3 "Blazon of the Breast," *Hecatomphile* (Paris: Pierre Sergent, 1539).

This may be the place to dispel a common misapprehension about the anatomical blazon: namely, that the generic term *by definition* implies adherence to a comprehensive mode of describing. It certainly can be used to mean a descriptive catalogue of body parts (as it was by Roland Barthes, for example); indeed, early modern English usage conforms to this practice.[16] However, creating a "total picture" was never the overriding concern of the French anatomical *blasonneurs*; their subjects were body parts, not bodies, and their choice of topic was most graphically enacted in the radically fragmentary illustrations that preceded their poems: a foot without an attached leg resembles a broken piece of statuary; a single tear hangs in space; hair without a head is sketched on a blank field (figure 2.2); a breast is an isolated circle with a dot at the center (figure 2.3).

And every description of a part invited further description. The identification of new parts gave rise to new poems not through any desire to compile a coherent body but, rather, through a will to prolong poetic competition and proliferation. Marot's original "Blason du tetin," the poem that initiated the contest of poetic wits, received ten poems in response. Importantly, in contrast to the hierarchical and sequential models of bodily organization integral to medical, political, religious, and even earlier poetic discourse, the organization of blazoned parts into a collected volume resisted easy or cohesive systemization and integration. The first published group of *blasons anatomiques* (1536) included eleven unsigned blazons—essentially those listed in Marot's verse epistle ("Epistre XXX") to the early *blasonneurs* that twice catalogues parts blazoned: in sequence, breast, hair, heart, thigh, hand, eye, mind, mouth, tear, ear, and eyebrow; and later, hair, ears, eye, thigh, eyebrow, hand, heart, tear, mind, and mouth.[17] Marot's lists clearly defy or ignore conventions of bodily order: in his first, for example, he begins with the model poem (his own), concludes with that of the contest winner (Scève's on the eyebrow), and takes advantage of alliterative potential wherever he can.

A 1537 edition contains thirty-two blazons and again dramatically violates the rhetorical rules inherited from medieval "recipes" legislating head-to-toe sequence in body description.[18] In subsequent sixteenth-century volumes the pressure of convention tended to prevail, and the poems were reordered to reflect a general penchant for hierarchy—but not without admitting an occasional misplaced part or an inexplicable separation of identical parts. This evidence, given the persistent temptation to respect tradition (any status quo) and to build an integrated body, tends to demonstrate a relative disregard for coherence and system. When cataloguing blazons, Marot ignores convention; when writing blazons, he elects to write on only one body part in each. Olimpo da Sassoferrato, to cite an alternate example, had incorporated his *strambotto* on the breast into a single-authored sequence, a sequence that was both "inclusive" and sequential.[19] More important, certain early modern editors make no attempt at all at ordered cataloguing; others adopt it, but imperfectly. A number of prominent poets—Mellin de Saint-Gelais, Maclou de la Haye, and Bonaventure des Periers, to name only a few—wrote blazons that were never included in the collections but are found isolated in sixteenth-century editions of their works. Others, like Ronsard, wrote texts that might properly be classed as blazons but under different generic labels.

Marot's thirtieth verse epistle recounts an important early history of the anatomical blazon: he addresses himself to a group of followers, those new and noble French Apollos who will eventually surpass the classical poets; he lists the texts he received in response to his initiating blazon; and he invents both a contest and a winner, the "unknown" Maurice Scève who won the laurel crown with his "well sung Eyebrow" (ll. 21–26). Several poems listed by Marot allude to one another; they stage the competition between poets as a competition between parts. Four refer to other contestants: "Le Coeur" and "L'Oreille" by Albert le Grand (an undeciphered pseudonym); "La Cuisse" by Jacques le Lieur, a bourgeois *échevin* (alderman) from Rouen; and "La Main" by Claude Chappuys, an officer in the king's household. In each case a section of the *blason* enumerates body parts but mentions virtually no parts that are not among the subjects of other *blasonneurs*. The items detailed in these lists cannot be explained logically (in the sense that a tooth would be logical in the description of a mouth), unless one's logic is more poetic than corporeal. The selection of poetic "matter" seems driven by the existing "matter" already being celebrated by other poets. Consider, as example, these verses from the "Blason de la Cuisse":

> Cuisse la plus belle du monde.
> Cuisse qui fais *l'oeil* esmouvoir,
> Cuisse qui fais *Tetin* mouvoir.
> Cuisse qui fais parler *la bouche*,
> Un temps avant que l'on te touche.
> Cuisse qui fais *la main* servir,
> Cuisse qui te fais poursuyvir.

> (Most beautiful thigh in the world, / Thigh that moves the *eye,* / Thigh that moves the *breast,* / Thigh that makes the *mouth* speak / before one touches you, / Thigh that makes the *hand* serve, / Thigh you make yourself an object of pursuit.) (ll. 36–42; emphasis mine)

Although distinctions between the implied bodies of both speaker and addressee are extremely slippery in this text (whose "mouth," for example, speaks?), the association of the thigh to the eye, breast, mouth, and hand is strained. Through the use of the figure of anaphora (the repetition of a word or phrase at the beginning of successive syntactical units), this passage articulates a relationship of control: in the repeated "*Cuisse qui fais*" the thigh makes all other parts do things (move, speak, serve) until finally it makes itself an object of pursuit. Indeed, the passage's wit depends in part upon disrupting the order of governance conventional to the figure of the body politic; the received metaphor of a "head" of state (invoked in Scève's "Blason du Front" (Blazon of the Forehead) for example, which "by its movement governs the rest of the body," ll. 4–5) controls a descending hierarchy of members. Here bodily governance is comically displaced onto the lower stratum. An inappropriate part assumes control, and each subsequently enumerated member acts only through its sanction: the thigh prompts emotion in the eye; it makes the breast move; it makes the mouth speak; it makes the hand serve; it subjects other parts. Its superior status claims for it the rank of most excellent of parts and, by extension, for the poem that praises it, that of most excellent of blazons.

Paradoxically, the denigration of the body part in the paired genre of the *contreblason* stakes no less strong a claim for poetic preeminence. Marot himself sought to expand the original project precisely in this direction when, again in his verse epistle, he exhorted the *blasonneurs* to sing "the other side" (l. 57) and enclosed a counterblazon on the breast as a new model to imitate:

> Or chers Amys, par maniere de rire
> Il m'est venu voulenté de descrire
> A contre poil ung Tetin, que j'envoye
> Vers vous, affin que suiviez ceste voye.
> . . . .
> Mais voulentiers, qui l'Esprit exercite,
> Ores le Blanc, ores le Noir recite:
> Et est le Painctre indigne de louange,
> Qui ne sçait paindre aussi bien Diable qu'Ange.

> (Now for a laugh, dear friends, / I've decided to describe / a breast in reverse, that I send / to you so that you will follow my lead. . . . / And whosoever exercises his wit / must recite both black and white. / The painter is unworthy of praise / who can't paint a devil as well as an angel.) (ll. 37–40, 47–50)

Marot's self-appointment as leader of the *blasonneurs* and his not-so-modest proposal to his "dear friends" situate his poetic gesture, as well as his collective project, within the framework of epideictic, the branch of classical rhetoric in which oratorical skill is displayed through formal speeches of praise and/or blame.[20] His energetic call is for ingenious poetic display, for "exercise of wit" (l. 47), for the making of rhetorical "marvels" (l. 61). This significant casting of the function of epideixis not as rhetorical praise *or* blame (persuading an audience that the object described is intrinsically praiseworthy or blamable) but as poetic praise *and* blame (persuading the audience that the object described is both, or neither, or wholly irrelevant, but that the poet is a virtuoso) is at the heart of the blazon enterprise. For each *blason* in praise, Marot suggests matching verse in blame; the *blasonneur* might thus demonstrate his sophistic skill, his ability to argue imaginatively both sides of the matter within the context of an elegant rhetorical game. Clearly, the part described is postulated as secondary to the artful making of rhetorical moves, to what Shakespeare labeled "the quirks of blazoning pens" (*Othello* 2.1.63).

The nature of the game may be better understood when the *blasons* are read in terms of sixteenth-century poetic practice. In his *Art poëtique françoys* (1548), Thomas Sebillet, the "theorist" of the *école marotique*, defined blazon as follows:

> Blazon is perpetual praise or continuous blame of what one proposes to blazon. To this end, all of the figures of *demonstration* described by the Greek and Latin rhetoricians will well serve the poet who would write one. I say both on the side of praise and of blame. Because the ugly is as well blazoned as the beautiful, and the bad as the good: witness Marot and his Blazons of the beautiful and ugly breast: and they both emerge from one source, like praise and invective.[21]

It must be noted that none of the *blasonneurs* answered Marot's call to sing both the *pro* and the *contra* of their chosen body parts. The only significant blazons denigrating the body, the *contreblasons* of Charles de la Hueterie, are born of Marot's bitter exchange with Sagon and thus lack the playful mood of the proposal. Marot would engage the dynamic of a debate (between men) for and against women in order to enable a competition of wits. De la Hueterie refuses to enter into the spirit of the game; rather he sidesteps it; he rejects it as irreverent play; he condemns it as idolatrous celebration of the flesh in order to rebuke a Marot then exiled to Italy in the name of religion. Collectively his poems oppose, in favor of the soul, any celebration "in paints and colors" of mortal flesh ("Epistre," l. 24). They reduce the body to corruptible, disgusting matter and thus stand in serious contrast to the seductively human or stonily immortal forms sketched by the *blasonneurs*. De la Hueterie's "body" can be either male or female (though sex-specific parts are always female); his line of argument is not unlike that of other authors (Corrozet, for example) who take to task the very concept of anatomical blazon. But de la Hueterie's attack, in some sense, goes further, blaming the body itself for the fact that Marot and his followers worship it: "Not only do you [the body] have yourself praised, but you have your blazons sold, praised, and published" ("Continuation du corps humain," ll. 23–25).

Although Marot's proposal for the writing of counterblazon (a genre of staged virtuoso critique) and de la Hueterie's realization of it (a critique of a genre and, by extension, of its inventor) are clearly distinguished in kind, they are both informed by a similar logic of bifurcation, of placing or displacing blame onto the otherwise elevated body (or body part). They are also similarly linked by the masterful poetic reconfiguration of the body that they attempt to inscribe. In this sense, de la Hueterie's blame of the body (and the genre) might still be read as an extension of the competition between poets within the genre. The fact that the visual and rhetorical fragmentation and bifurcation of the female body was explicitly constitutive not only of the competition between the *blasonneurs* but, ultimately, of the collective product titled by 1543 the *Blasons anatomiques du corps fémenin* almost literalizes the logic whereby the self is collected, defined, and displayed *through* the process of splitting and exhibiting the other. The social and psychological dynamics implicit in the *blasons anatomiques* as a whole, as it were, were strikingly prefigured and exemplified by Marot's own blazon and counterblazon of the breast.

It is perhaps no coincidence in this respect that the original pair of good and bad parts, invoked primarily to enact and inspire poetic competition and authorial self-display, should be imagined in the form of the good breast and the bad breast. Through the lens of contemporary literary and psychoanalytic theory, the gender dynamics implicit in Marot's poetic gesture (the coextensive praising *and* blaming of the breast) take on an almost uncanny significance. Marot's choice of object, as well as his unique involvement in depicting both positive and negative versions of it, underline the broader ambivalence of the genre he made popular.[22] "The writer," reads the now familiar but still suggestive observation of Roland Barthes, "is someone who plays with his mother's body ... in order to glorify it, to embellish it, or in order to dismember it, to take it to the limit of what can be known about the body."[23] Here love/hate or use/abuse of the "mother tongue," the language literally learned at the maternal breast,[24] is grounded in opposition: to embellish/to dismember, to idealize/to disfigure. Development through symbiotic identification, then separation, and finally (for the male child) differentiation occurs in relation to a maternal body. It is initially a body in parts; and those parts, specifically the breast, both protect and threaten.

As the first source of erotic pleasure, the breast promises and nurtures: as the first menace, it denies and weans. Its duality, Melanie Klein postulates, is intolerable to the infant: it provokes, as a primary mode of "defense against anxiety," a split of the single part-object into two: a good breast and a bad breast.[25] The idealized good breast is the object of loving, erotic projection; the despised, persecuting breast, of hostile, destructive projection. Within the realm of infantile fantasy, Klein theorizes, these two attitudes coexist without dialectical resolution. They evolve into ambivalent feelings toward other part-objects and ultimately toward integrated objects (the good/bad mother, lover, friend, employer, etc.). Woman's body, then, if we follow Klein's argument, is the very ground of ambivalence; its representation, to whatever conscious end, stages the dual impulses of fascination and repulsion, of love and hate that it inspires. Marot's paired poems begin as follows (ll. 1-4; italics mine):

"Blason du tetin," 1535

Tetin refait plus blanc qu'un oeuf	Well formed *breast,* whiter than an egg,
Tetin de satin blanc tout neuf,	*Breast* of brand new white satin,
Tetin qui fais honte à la rose,	*Breast* which puts the rose to shame,
Tetin plus beau que nulle chose.	*Breast* more beautiful than any thing.

"Contreblason du tetin," 1536

Tetin qui n'as rien que la peau,	*Breast* which is nothing but skin,
Tetin flac, Tetin de drappeau	Flaccid breast, flagging *breast,*
Grande tetine, longue tetasse,	Big breast, long breast
Tetin, doy je dire bezasse?	*Breast,* or should I say old sack?

As these opening lines suggest, the poems are aligned by specific rhetorical homologies, by studied formal identifications. Each is in octosyllabic rhymed couplets; they are of similar length; in the definitive 1543 edition they share titles and illustrations. The *tetin* remains constant—only the genre varies ("Blason du tetin," and "Contreblason du tetin"); a single woodcut is duplicated to illustrate both texts.

In accordance with the guidelines established by the "ancients," the guidelines recommended to would-be *blasonneurs* in Sebillet's *Art poétique,* the blazon's rhetoric of *demonstration* is one of amplification through catalogue, comparison, metaphor, congeries, and figures of repetition. Anaphora is central among these and is perhaps the figure most characteristic of the genre. In the blazon it takes the form of the repetition of a name word—a signifier for the object-topic of the poem—that initiates parallel syntactical units.

In the texts constituting the first collection of *blasons anatomiques* (those poems sent to Marot and/or published in 1536), the frequent use of the "name word" is striking:[26] it appears in 40 percent of all lines at least once; it is the first word of a line 78 percent of the times it appears; and in 99 percent of the texts it is the first word of the poem. Marot's "breasts," as innovating models, determine these percentages in the blazons that imitate them. *Tetin* is the initial word of each of Marot's poems, the first word of a disproportionate number of lines, the object of constant repetition. This is, of course, a familiar *rhetoriqueur* strategy; but Marot adopts *rhetoriqueur* techniques selectively. A critical issue, then, resides not in the conventionality of the figure but, rather, in the circumstances of its use, in the interrogation of when, how, and to what end this convention is deployed. Here, in both the *blason du tetin* and the *contreblason du tetin*, a particularly insistent tropic disfiguration (the violence done to a full *descriptio* through the anaphoral privileging of a single signifier) parallels a fetishistic disfiguration (the violence done to the full body through the overdetermination of a single part).

Both texts are generated through the expansion of *tetin*: they develop along the parallel lines moving from a vocative ("*Tetin*," followed by adjectives) to repeated modifying phrases: ("*Tetin qui …*"; "*Tetin de …*"; "*Tetin au …*"; and so on). But Marot does more to establish a principle of identification between the two. He initiates each with essentially five *tetin*-initiated lines (line three of the counterblazon is an exception recuperated by "*Tetine*," "*Tetasse*"); he begins couplets eleven-twelve and fifteen-sixteen of both texts with the word "*Tetin*"; he returns the last movement of each blazon to another block of *tetin*-initiated lines; he repeats doubling structures within single lines (in the blazon—"*Tetin dur, non pas Tetin, voyre*," 1. 5; "*Tetin gauche, Tetin mignon*," 1. 15; "*Tetin meur, Tetin d'appetit*," 1. 26; in the counterblazon—"*Tetin flac, Tetin de drappeau*," 1. 2; "*Tetin grillé, Tetin pendant*," 1. 11; "*Tetin flaitry, tetin rendant*," 1. 12); and, most important, he incorporates verbatim at a parallel point in the counterblazon an entire block of verse from the blazon:

> *Quant on te voit il vient à maintz*
> *Une envie dedans les mains*
> *De te* taster, de te tenir,
> Mais il se fault bien contenir
> D'en approcher bon gré ma vie,
> Car il viendroit aultre envie.

(*On seeing you, many experience / a desire in their hands /* to touch *you*, to hold *you*; / but one must restrain oneself / from approaching, good grief! / For other desires might arise.) ("Blason du Tetin," ll. 19–24; emphasis mine)

> *Quand on te voit il vient à maintz*
> *Une envie dedans les mains*
> *De te* prendre avec gands doubles
> Pour en donner cinq ou six couples
> De souffletz sur le nez de celle
> Qui te cache soubz son esselle.

(*On seeing you, many experience / a desire in their hands /* to take *you* up in both gloves / and give five or six pairs / of punches to the nose of the woman / who hides you under her armpit.) ("Contreblason du tetin," ll. 25–30; emphasis mine)

The speaker's experience of both the beautiful and the monstrous, then, lit-erally and rhetorically centers on the transition from seeing to touching; the amplification of descriptive form, color, and mobility codes yields, first, to the evocation of tactile desire and, ultimately, to a suggestion of involuntary and as yet unrealized physical response. Marot thus sets before us two por-traits of a single body part; two variations on a single topic; two interpreta-tions of a single song ("one flat," as he advised in his epistle, and "one in key", l. 52). The very verses that in the blazon express the want of a tender, loving, erotic touch, in the counterblazon voice a desire to abuse, to equate contact with beating, to transform the breast into a weapon adapted to at-tack the body of which it is a part. Between the "moments" of these two texts there is a discontinuity, a gap, a time suggested but unspoken: in the blazon, we read ripeness (the untouched breast); in the counterblazon, we read depletion (the overtouched breast); but we never read fulfillment (the touch).

In these two texts Marot invokes specific conventions: a medieval de-scriptive canon (be it for the virgin or for the hag); *rhetoriqueur* technique; and a particularizing fashion inherited from Petrarch and his followers. And yet, Marot's "two breasts" reveal an imitative conflict—a self-conscious awareness of a debt to tradition and a persistent desire to do something new—in disfiguring the descriptive norm of the head-to-toe catalogue through hyperbolic (hypertrophic) variation on a single descriptive detail. In this sense these poems enact an ambivalent relation to their mother *cor-pus*: they disfigure the literary tradition that engenders them; they initiate a fad at once deeply Petrarchan and deeply anti-Petrarchan. Marot was, of course, the only poet within this strict context both to blazon and coun-terblazon woman's body, but when the *blasons anatomiques* finally appeared independently, their format mirrored his proposal; the anthology began with the assembled poems in praise (*laudatio*) and concluded with de la Hueterie's poems in blame (*vituperatio*). Marot's beautiful/ugly breast, therefore, served as an informing model; its deployment of the praise/blame opposition gave shape to the collective anthologies that followed.

For the ambivalence of the anatomical blazon is at issue even in texts unilaterally laudatory once we acknowledge that the object of veneration is not a beloved woman but a beloved part. Marot's fetishistic celebration of a lovely breast attempts and, I argue, fails at both midpoint and conclusion to recuperate the part into the whole. Though we are told that the "breast ... bears witness to the rest of the person" (1. 17–18), both illustration and text fix our gaze on the fragment and militate against our seeing the "entire and beautiful woman"(1. 34). Here "the woman" is absent; a fragment of her body, often reified and dehumanized, receives the devotion that had traditionally been her due. Mimetic representation, the "realistic" portrait, was admittedly not the conscious end of the *blasonneurs*. Virtuoso wordplay was Marot's chosen game. And the transgressive potential of that game was evident even to its inventor. His explanatory verse epistle, it must be noted, tellingly articulates concerns about insulting women (through verse in blame) and unleashing a *copia* of offensively salacious poetry (through verse in either praise or blame): "I must insist, in order to avoid trouble, that [the ugly breast] is not a French breast, and that I don't mean to unleash my words in such a way as to infuriate ladies" (ll. 42–46). He then goes on to caution would-be *blasonneurs* or *anatomistes* to avoid those "shameful parts" that should remain "covered," veiled, unseen (ll. 75–82). Marot's texts, then, signal that the affirming and negating anatomization of woman constituted a topic that was not just one among others, not just an arbitrary ground for rhetorical display. They acknowledge that this specific *amplificatio* entailed risk, that the extravagant display of female body parts repeated and enacted ambivalence within a space of play and poem.

Marot, the first anatomical blazoner, celebrated only one of woman's parts; his first wave of imitators celebrated only nine: the hair, the eyebrow, the eye, the tear, the ear, the mouth, the hand, the thigh, and the mind (as spirit or intellect, illustrated by an empty frame). What Marot assembled in 1535–1536, then, was by no means a "complete body." But the history of the early blazon is literally a generative one: one text became eleven; eleven became thirty-two; and thirty-two became thirty-seven (plus twenty-two counterblazons) by the time that, in 1543, a whole volume, a "corpus," was more or less fixed. And then that "definitive corpus" scattered its influence among the texts of subsequent poets. Marot had indeed sown the seed that brought forth a body of words. Had he composed in 1535 a traditional *effictio*, a head-to-toe portrait of a beautiful woman, he would have penned little more than a variation on a topos long practiced and long codified. His dismembering of that convention, his expansion of a single detail, exploited "infinite variety" to permit infinite poetic possibility. A described body has as many parts as it has names for parts: it can be re-divided (re-membered) in accordance with the lexicon applied to it by any inventive poet. If you can think of a new part, you can write a new poem. In 1967, for example, editor Jean-Clarence Lambert regretted the lack of the shoulder, the wrist, and the ankle.[27] A still more particularized scrutiny of the body would permit the making of still more rhetorical marvels, the generating of still more copious verse, the publishing of still more best-selling volumes.[28]

But the "speakers" of the blazon aspire not only to scrutinize. As we have seen in the case of Marot's two *tetins*, a trajectory from the visual to the tactile is central to the desire inscribed in these poems. When Marot called upon the *blasonneurs* to make new "marvels" in the form of *contre-blasons* ("*Là doncq, là doncq, poulsez, faictes merveilles*"), he not only urged them to describe the female anatomy, he equated description with striking, with laying a hand on the body: "*Pochez cest Oeil: fessez moy ceste Cuisse: / Descrivez. . . .*" ("Blacken the eye, spank the thigh, / describe. . . .") ("Epistre XXX," ll. 61, 64–65). The anatomical blazons return repeatedly to the temptation to touch conceived as a frustrated desire. Knowing himself "unworthy" of approaching (and even less of touching) an object as "holy" as the part he praises, the *blasonneur* contents himself with contemplating from afar and then putting his pen to page (Maurice Scève, "Blason de la Gorge," ll. 45–52). The blazon in praise would caress; the blazon in blame would beat; and both would utilize the site of the text to figuratively place the hand on ("*mettre la main à*") the matter ("*la matière*").[29] The rhetorical game is a game of gestures, but the object of the gestures is not arbitrary; the choice of the game is not unmotivated. The surface upon which this game is played, the matter to which the master painter-poet applies his caressing/abusing hand, is the model's nakedness as translated to his canvas. In the anatomical blazon, the body that is imagined in the most tactile and material of terms—that is partitioned, arranged, and rearranged under the scrutiny necessitated by the genre itself—ultimately vanishes beneath the "*anatomiste*'s" touch.

Notes

1. For the circulation of this image in relation to the early publishing history of the anatomical blazon, see my "The Unauthored 1539 Volume in which is Printed the *Hecatomphile, The Flowers of French Poetry*, and *Other Soothing Things*," in *Subject and Object in Renaissance Culture*, ed. Margreta de Grazia, Maureen Quilligan, and Peter Stallybrass (Cambridge: Cambridge University Press, 1996), 166–88.

2. For extended analysis of the early modern implications of the story of Zeuxis, see François Lecercle, *La Chimère de Zeuxis: Portrait poétique et portrait peint en France et en Italie à la Renaissance* (Tübingen: Gunter Narr Verlag, 1987).

3. On the French anatomical blazon, see Robert E. Pike, "The 'Blasons' in French Literature of the Sixteenth Century," *Romanic Review* 27 (1936); Kazimierz

Kupisz, "Des Recherches sur l'évolution du blason au XVI siècle," *Zagadnienia Rodzajów Literackich* 9, no. 2 (1967); Dudley B. Wilson, *Descriptive Poetry in France from Blason to Baroque* (New York: Barnes & Noble, 1967); Annette and Edward Tomarken "The Rise and Fall of the Sixteenth-Century French Blason," *Symposium* 29 (1975); Alison Saunders, "Sixteenth-Century Collected Editions of *Blasons Anatomiques*," *Library* 31 (1976), and *The Sixteenth-Century Blason Poétique* (Bern: Peter Lang, 1981); Lawrence D. Kritzman, *The Rhetoric of Sexuality and the Literature of the French Renaissance* (Cambridge: Cambridge University Press, 1991); and Jonathan Sawday, *The Body Emblazoned: Dissection and the Human Body in Renaissance Culture* (London: Routledge, 1995).

4. On the tension between the lyric and descriptive modes in blazon, see Kupisz, "Des Recherches sur l'évolucion du blason au XVI siècle," 67–81.

5. Albert-Marie Schmidt, *Poètes du XVIe siècle* (Paris: Gallimard, 1953), 293–364.

6. Corrozet, "Contre les blasonneurs des membres," in *Recueil de poésies françoises des XVe et XVIe siècles*, ed. A. de Montaiglon, vol. 6 (Paris: Jannet, 1857), 276. All further citations of Corrozet refer to this edition and appear in parentheses in my text. All translations from the French in this chapter are my own.

7. For a detailed history, see Saunders, "Sixteenth-Century Collected Editions."

8. François Sagon, "Epistre . . . ," in *Les Blasons anatomiques du corps fémenin* (Paris: Charles Langelier, 1543), ll. 100–1.

9. Kupisz, "Des Recherches sur l'évolucion du blason au XVI siècle," 77.

10. See James V. Mirollo, *Mannerism and Renaissance Poetry: Concept, Mode, Inner Design* (New Haven and London: Yale University Press, 1984), 125–59. On Petrarch's descriptive technique in relation to the blazon, see my "Diana Described: Scattered Woman and Scattered Rhyme," *Critical Inquiry* 8 (1981): 265–79.

11. L. Gandini, *Lettione . . . sopra un dubbio, come il Petrarca non lodasse Laura espressamente dal naso* (Venice, 1581), cited by Elizabeth Cropper in "On Beautiful Women, Parmigianino, *Petrarchismo*, and the Vernacular Style," *Art Bulletin* 58 (1976): 386 n. 68.

12. J. N. Darles, "Blason du Nez," *Les Blasons anatomiques du corps fémenin* (Paris: Charles Langelier, 1543), l. 1. All further references to the anatomical blazons and counterblazons will be to this edition and will appear in parentheses in my text.

13. See Caroline Walker Bynum, *Fragmentation and Redemption: Essays on Gender and the Human Body in Medieval Religion* (New York: Zone Books, 1991).

14. Sawday, *The Body Emblazoned*, 191.

15. Sawday, *The Body Emblazoned*, 195.

16. For Barthes, see *S/Z* (Paris: Seuil, 1970), 121; on early English usage, see Stephen Booth, ed. *Shakespeare's Sonnets* (New Haven: Yale University Press, 1977), 340–41, n. 5.

17. In *Oeuvres poétiques*, ed. Gérard Defaux, vol. 1 (Paris: Bordas, 1990), 337–40, ll.

9–16, 62–72. All further references to Marot's verse epistle will be to this edition and will appear in parentheses in my text.

18. Ernst Curtius describes medieval codes prescibing head-to-toe body description as "recipes," *European Literature in the Latin Middle Ages*, trans. W. R. Trask (1953; reprint, New York: Harper & Row, 1963), 181–82.

19. Baldassare Olimpo da Sassoferrato, *Gloria d'amore* (Venice: Antonio Remondin, n.d.).

20. For a useful discussion of the epideictic tradition in relation to poetry (or "second rhetoric"), see Joel Fineman, *Shakespeare's Perjured Eye: The Invention of Poetic Subjectivity in the Sonnets* (Berkeley, Los Angeles, London: University of California Press, 1986), 89–129.

21. Thomas Sebillet, in *Art poétique françoys*, ed. F. Gaiffe (Paris: E. Cornély, 1910), 169.

22. Mikhail Bakhtin suggestively adopts just this vocabulary in the few pages he devotes to the blazon: he speaks of "its dual fact, complete ambivalence, and contradictory fullness." In *Rabelais and His World*, trans. Hélène Iswolsky (Cambridge: M.I.T. Press, 1968), 429–30.

23. Roland Barthes, *The Pleasure of the Text*, trans. Richard Miller (New York: Farrar, Straus & Giroux, 1975), 37. On this passage in relation to anatomical blazon, also see Kritzman, *The Rhetoric of Sexuality and the Literature of the French Renaissance*, 8.

24. On the learning of the "mother tongue" at the nurse's breast, see Dante, *De Vulgari Eloquentia*, 1.1. 14–15.

25. The concepts outlined here are basic to Klein's work. A concise discussion appears in "Some Theoretical Conclusions Regarding the Emotional Life of the Infant," in *Envy and Gratitude and Other Works, 1946–1963* (New York: Delta, 1977), 61–67. For a psychoanalytic reading of Marot's texts as informed both by Klein and Julia Kristeva, see Kritzman, *The Rhetoric of Sexuality and the Literature of the French Renaissance*, 97–104.

26. On descriptive systems in poetry, see Michael Riffaterre, "Interpretation and Descriptive Poetry: A Reading of Wordsworth's 'Yew Trees,'" *New Literary History* 4 (1973), where he develops the concept of the "kernel word" (my "name word"), 234–37.

27. Preface to the *Blasons du corps fémenin* (Paris: André Balland, 1967), n.p.

28. Patricia Parker analyzes the copious potential of the blazon in relation to the logic of merchandising in *Literary Fat Ladies: Rhetoric, Gender, Property* (London and New York: Methuen, 1987), 126–54. See also my "Blazon of Sweet Beauty's Best": Shakespeare's *Lucrece*," in *Shakespeare and the Question of Theory*, ed. Patricia Parker and Geoffrey Hartman (New York and London: Methuen, 1985), 95–115.

29. For extended discussion of the notion of "placing the hand to the matter," see Claude-Gilbert Dubois, *Le Maniérisme* (Paris: Presses Universitaires de France, 1979).

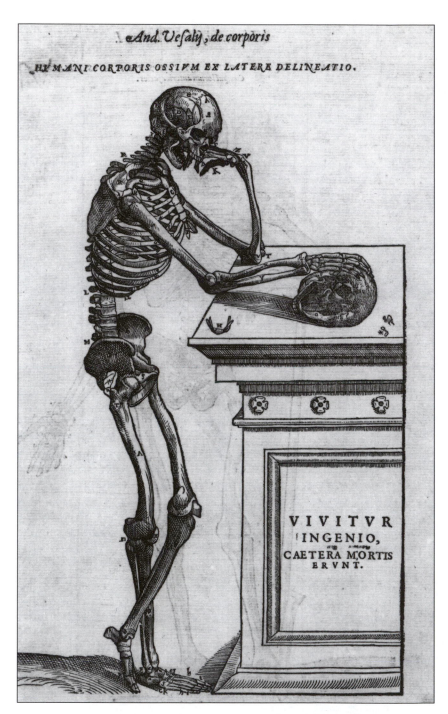

And. Vesalij, de corporis

HVMANI CORPORIS OSSIVM EX LATERE DELINEATIO.

VIVITVR
INGENIO,
CAETERA MORTIS
ERVNT.

3. Skeletal structure from Andreas Vesalius, *De humani corporis fabrica* (Venice, 1568).

3

Out of Joint

MARJORIE GARBER

Curst be he yt moves my bones.
—Epitaph on Shakespeare's grave,
Holy Trinity Church, Stratford

If anything, the linkage is just as natural the other way around.
—Peter Elbow, *What is English?*

The elephant, medieval scholars believed, had no joints. When Pope Leo X was presented with an elephant in 1514, the animal was made to kneel, partly as a sign of respect and partly to show that it could do so.

Fifteenth- and sixteenth-century observers began to refute the legend. "I must explain that these animals have knees, which they bend when walking,"[1] wrote one Italian commentator. The Frenchman André Thevet explained, likewise, that "they have joints in their knees, so that when their master commands them to kneel down, they kneel down promptly, which is contrary to the opinion of many who have described the Nature of the Elephant. . . . I myself saw them kneel down several times in the town of Cairo."[2] By the seventeenth century, Sir Thomas Browne could scoff at the "absurdity": "for first, they affirm it hath no joints, and yet concede it walks and moves about; whereby they conceive there may be a progression or advancement made in Motion without inflexion of parts."[3]

> The hint and ground of this opinion might be the gross and somewhat Cylindrical composure of the legs, the equality and less perceptible disposure of the joints, especially in the former legs of this Animal: they appearing when he standeth, like Pillars of flesh, without any evidence of articulation. (160)

"The elephant hath joints, but none for courtesy; his legs are legs for necessity, not for flexure," observes Ulysses tartly in Shakespeare's *Troilus and Cressida* (2.3.105). Like a proud man, said the proverb, the elephant will not kneel.

Knee-Jerk Responses

> All day long,
> My heart was in my knee.
> > —George Herbert, "Deniall"
>
> Genuflect! Genuflect! Genuflect!
> > —Tom Lehrer, "The Vatican Rag"

Of all early modern joints, the knee is arguably the most distinguished, at least in literary terms. The knee is an important articulation of the physical body politic, especially if the physical body politic is male.[4] As David Bevington points out in his account of the language of stage gesture, "Kneeling is a profound gesture of acknowledgment of the claims of hierarchy."[5] To bend the knee is to give homage, to assent to a political and social contract. Thus the knee in Shakespeare is often a figurative as well as a literal joint, appearing disproportionately in the history plays, both English and Roman. Indeed, it "can serve as the dominant expressive gesture at the point of dramatic reversal" (164)—functioning allegorically, we might say, as a joint of the dramatic action. A double joint. A hinge. Why this should be so and what it has to do with the knee as a physical joint of the body can be seen in the much-noticed and overdetermined function of kneeling in *Richard II*, Shakespeare's play of articulated and disarticulated homage.

Is patriotism a knee-jerk response? Should it be? Where does loyalty properly reside? The knee-plot of *Richard* stages these questions in vivid terms.

Bolingbroke affects homage and deference to the king in public ("let me kiss my sovereign's hand, / And bow my knee before his Majesty" [1.3.46–47]), but Richard scornfully describes his courtship of the common people: "Off goes his bonnet to an oyster-wench; / A brace of draymen ... had the tribute of his supple knee" (1.4.31–33). Acting as regent in Richard's absence from England, the loyal York clearly reads through this knee language when Bolingbroke drops to his knees before him: "Show me thy humble heart, and not thy knee. / Whose duty is deceivable and false" (2.3.83–84). By the time Richard returns from Ireland and greets his opponents from the walls of Flint Castle, the rebellion of the knee—the unjointed jointure of English hierarchy—is legible even to him. "We are amazed," he says to Northumberland, "and thus long have we stood,

> To watch [i.e., to wait for] the fearful bending of thy knee,
> Because we thought ourself the lawful king;
> And if we be, how dare thy joints forget
> To pay their awful duty to our presence?
>
> (3.3.72–76)

By the end of the scene Bolingbroke's gesture of kneeling to authority is frankly repudiated:

> Fair cousin, you debase your princely knee
> To make the base earth proud with kissing it. . . .
> Up cousin, up; your heart is up, I know,
> Thus high at least, although your knee be low.
>
> (3.3.191–95)

This encounter has been traditionally understood by critics and audiences as a symbolic turning point of high and low, anticipating Richard's image of the dipping well as a scale in the deposition scene (4.1). But the lying knee, the low knee, the knee whose duty, in York's phrase, is "deceivable and false," is also part of an articulated language of disarticulation, the breakdown, the dislocation, of a ceremonial culture of the body. The disturbingly comic scene of mass kneeling in act 5, scene 3, in which the entire York family, the elderly Duke and Duchess and their rebellious son Aumerle all kneel before Bolingbroke with a virtually audible creaking sound, extends this language to its inevitable and ludicrous conclusion, as the embarrassed and discomfited new king tries in vain to get these old people to rise up."[6]

"For ever will I walk upon my knees,"[7] declares the doughty Duchess, sinking to the ground. "Upon my mother's prayers I bend my knee," cries the son, hurling himself down. But York, professing loyalty to the king over loyalty to flesh and blood, claims that his own kneeling means something different—means obeisance rather than supplication, compliance rather than revolt: "Against them both my true joints bended be." York, who has begun his entreaty by describing his son as a "fest'red joint" that should be amputated for the health of the body politic ("This fest'red joint cut off, the rest rest sound"), announces that he possesses "true joints"—joints that join rather than put asunder or "out of joint." He thus raises the question of the joint moralisé—the signifying knee.

The Duchess suggests that her husband's real sentiments lie with the private body rather than the public one, while her and her son's posture should be read as both entreaty and homage: "His weary joints would gladly rise, I know; / Our knees still kneel till to the ground they grow." Desperate to get them *all* to rise—especially his aunt, whose age and sex both render her kneeling deeply unsuitable ("Good aunt, stand up," he says twice more, helplessly, as she continues to plead, volubly, from a kneeling position), Bolingbroke finally capitulates, pardoning Aumerle. "O happy vantage of a kneeling knee!" exults the Duchess (5.5. 89–130), perhaps now at last laboriously hauling herself to her feet. In these scenes, as indeed throughout Shakespeare's staging, public/private hierarchies are troubled by the knee-work.[8]

In later literature the knee, obedient or rebellious, bent or straight, would be used to reinforce the sense of hierarchy through a reanimation of the theory of the body politic. Spiritual size could be achieved not only in direct but also in inverse proportion to the physical. George Herbert's "Deniall" located the rebellious or resistant heart in the knee, the outward show of an obedient grace not yet achieved within. Herbert is here following a passage of church liturgy that itself derived from Clement and ultimately from the apocryphal *Oratio Manassae*: "*et nunc flecto genua cordis mei*," "and now bow I the knees of my heart."[9] The phrase "the knees of my heart"—disarticulated from its liturgical context—became a common citation, almost a cliché, in later years. Heinrich von Kleist, who—as we will see—plays a pivotal role in the story of the language of joints, used it both in his play *Penthesilea* and in a letter to Goethe in which he encloses a recent publication: "I present it to you 'on the knees of my heart.'"[10]

"It is so truly the mystery of the kneeling, of the deeply kneeling man; his being greater, by his spiritual responses, than he who stands!" wrote the poet Rilke in a letter to his mother. "He who kneels, who gives himself wholly to kneeling, loses indeed the measure of his surroundings, even looking up he would no longer be able to say what is great and what is small. But although in his bent posture he has scarcely the height of a child, yet he, this kneeling man, is not to be called small. With him the scale is shifted."[11] Rilke's observations could stand as a brilliant gloss on the fourth act of *King Lear*, when the formerly imperious king kneels to Cordelia, and she gently admonishes him: "No sir, you must not kneel" (*Lear* 4.7.58).

But the knee as body part does not always connote homage or prayer. Although it is *metaphorically* a sign of linkage and thus of obeisance, *metonymically* the knee rebels. "How long is't ago, Jack, since thou sawest thine own knee?" asks Prince Hal of Falstaff (*1 Henry IV* 2.4.328). Part of a continuing series of jokes about Falstaff's present girth (he responds by reminiscing about the tiny waist he had as a boy), this is also one of Hal's recurrent gibes about Falstaff's indifferent loyalty and questionable potency, since the knee was not only the bodily instrument of homage but also a location proximate to the genitals, often invoked as a kind of euphemism. Can you look down past your waistline at your lower body, Hal seems to be asking, and if so, what—if anything—do you see? The knee—the joint that bends, or not, obediently or rebelliously—becomes in Hal's little joke the unseen sign of Falstaff's unreliability.

Not for the first time, Falstaff becomes the "joint" or point of articulation between male and female. For—perhaps unsurprisingly, given the differential logics of power and hierarchy—joints like the knee often function *metaphorically* in men, who are part of the body politic, but *metonymically* in women, who derive their standing (or their kneeling) from adjacency. Women do use the supplicant knee in the ordinary way to petition grace or favor: Volumnia kneels to Coriolanus, and Isabella to Angelo. But the knee is a tricky joint, and a "trick knee" (from *trichier*, to deceive) is weak, deceptive, and liable to fail. Especially when it is the woman who is suspected of turning tricks.

More often than not, in early modern usage, the proximity of the knee to the genitals is noted in women rather than in men. An old man in *Iacke of Dover* (1604) keeps his wife in fancy stockings as a compensation: "Because I can not please her aboue the knee, I must needes please her below the knee." A seventeenth-century ballad describes a gardener who touched a carpenter's wife "a little above the knee" ("Five Merry Wives of Lambeth"), and another suggests that pregnancy may result from "tickl[ing] my knee" ("Young Mans Frolicks"). Defloration and impregnation are often figured in this period as a breaking of joints—most often knees, but occasionally elbows: "She has broken her leg above the knee (broken her elbow)" according to Tilley's proverbs, means "she has lost her virginity," or "she has become pregnant."[12] These "breaks" in jointed limbs both injure the connection and reinforce it.

When Freud describes the fetish as coming to life when "some process has been suddenly interrupted," he instances "the circumstance that the inquisitive boy used to peer up the woman's legs towards her genitals." For Freud, of course, the *absence* of the "longed-for penis" in women, the disappointed fantasy of the phallic woman, produces—by metonymy— the fetishization of the part nearby. In Freud's Vienna that "part" was often a foot or (its further metonymic emblem), the shoe; velvet or fur, he says, are acknowledged as signs of pubic hair. The woman's body is named by contiguity.

Contiguity, association, linkage—these elements of what is fundamentally metonymic logic are also (and not by accident) themselves joining or jointed functions, cognitive moves that depend upon a presumed coherence not only of parts but of connection. Early modern man kneels to demonstrate his entire connectedness to the body of the state. His knee is a hinge of rule. But the woman's knee is often a stand-in for her sexual parts, and women who kneel in homage like men are often, in literary terms, a cause of consternation.

Elbow Room

No man lives without jostling and being jostled; in all ways he has to elbow himself through the world, giving and receiving offense.
—Thomas Carlyle, "Sir Walter Scott"

Our horizon is never quite at our elbows.
—Henry David Thoreau, *Walden*, "Solitude"

The elbow, unlike its bodily equivalent, the knee, was and continues to be a relatively comical joint, linked to lower-class activities and to superstitions: To be out at elbow is to be threadbare; to shake one's elbow is to play at dice; to rub or scratch the elbow was, apparently, a sign of pleasure or satisfaction. In Shakespeare's *Love's Labour's Lost,* an offstage rehearsal of the disastrous Masque of the Muscovites meets with the approval of the commons: "One rubb'd his elbow thus, and fleer'd, and swore / A better speech was never spoke before" (5.2.109–10). An itchy elbow was a sign, though of what was not certain. When Conrade, summoned by the villain Borachio in *Much Ado* materializes "at thy elbow," Borachio observes with his customary elegance, "my elbow itch'd; I thought there would a scab follow" (3.3.98–100). Elbow grease, then as now, was a sign of industry, and may even (this is a guess) have meant "sweat," since it seemed to "smell."[13] (Modern pranksters, long after Shakespeare, would often tell a rube to go out and buy a container of "elbow grease" at the hardware store.)

Joaneath Spicer chronicles the "rise and apogee of the male elbow" as a sign of protectiveness and control in paintings—mostly portraits—in the period 1500 to 1650. Spicer argues that "the elbow in its most perfectly evolved form—the arms akimbo" will achieve in Holland "the status of a national attribute," marking the "alert, on guard, proud regent class."[14] In German and Italian painting, and in conduct books and manuals of gesture, the arm akimbo was often a sign of pride. Erasmus, among the first to comment on this attribute of male display, spoke slightingly of those who "stand or sit and set [the] one hand on[the] side which maner to some semeth comly like a warrior but it is not forthwith honest."[15] Bonifacio's *L'arte de' cenni* (1616) regards the elbow and arm akimbo as signs of strength, useful for pushing one's way through crowds but consequently "pushy" in a negative way, and John Bulwer's *Chironomia* of 1644 is similarly dismissive: "to set the arms agambo or aprank, and to rest the turned-in back upon the side is an action of pride and ostentation, unbeseeming the hand of an orator."[16] For soldiers and standard-bearers, however, the gesture was appropriate. Thus, presumably, the remark of Shakespeare's King John on his deathbed: "Now my soul hath elbow-room."(5.7.28).

Male portraits of the period, especially in Holland, displayed a hand on hip as a sign of cultural or military power. The same configurations can be found in Dutch group or corporate portraits, where artfully disposed limbs could produce a literalization of the "joint-stock company." Women, by contrast—unless they were monarchs or allegories—kept their elbows to themselves, and, in the language of the nursery rhyme (addressed to a hypothetical, ill-mannered "Mabel, Mabel") "off the table." These days the gesture—especially with *both* hands on hips, what Plautus called "handle men"—is most frequently used by women (and gay men) in musical comedy, where it appears to mark a certain kind of soubrette figure as waggish or scolding, and often appears as a prelude to breaking into song.

While the knee is often aligned with ascent and descent, with movements up and down, the elbows seem to work—literally and metaphorically—by a pushing in, out, and around. Thus the knee becomes connected to the tragic, the divine, and the narrowly hierarchical, while the elbow extends itself to the realm of the comic, the secular, and the broadly expansive. It is only when elbows are in a fixed position that they can work as emblems of power; it is the multidirectional mobility of the elbow that gives it its comic potential. [17] In terms of the social system, elbows can be in or out of joint. Oddly, though they are "above the knee" in anatomical terms, they are often below it in status: displacement, we see, does not always go upward, after all.

Taking Joint Stock

> The joint is jumpin'.
>
> —Fats Waller

> Remove the joint!
> —Lewis Carroll, *Through the Looking-Glass*

Twentieth-century readers tend to think of the phrase "out of joint" as a philosophical observation, a dead metaphor, a cliché.

"The time is out of joint. O cursed spite, / That ever I was born to set it right." The most familiar of quotations, this observation—made by Hamlet to his companions after the visitation of the Ghost—is glossed by Arden Shakespeare editor Harold Jenkins as "in utter disorder." [18] "Out of joint" in this sense is indeed something of a political cliché, embodying—and thus in a sense disembodying—the old image of the body politic.[19] The *Oxford English Dictionary* lists this example under "Out of joint," "*phrase, figurative*," and defines it as "disordered, perverted, out of order, disorganized. (Said of things, conditions, etc.; formerly also of persons in relation to conduct)." Reviewing French translations of the phrase, Jacques Derrida finds "Time is off its hinges" (*Le temps est hors de ses gonds*), "Time is broken down, unhinged, out of sorts" (*Le temps est détraqué*), "The world is upside down" (*Le monde est a l'envers*), "This age is dishonored" (*Cette époque est déshonorée*).[20] Derrida notes that the *OED*, unsurprisingly, "gives Hamlet's phrase as example of the ethico-political inflection."

For Slavoj Žižek, "out of joint" is an ontological and a philosophical condition, a matter of consciousness and of history. Reading F. W. J. Schelling and Fredric Jameson together, Žižek suggests that by their reasonings "every narrative eventually endeavours to provide an answer to the enigma of how things got out of joint, how the old 'authentic' ties disintegrated," how traditional societies became "modern, 'alienated,' unbalanced."[21] The logic of Schelling's thought, claims Žižek, "compels him to assert the inevitability of the 'out-of-jointness' and of man's Fall" (73). Elsewhere Žižek uses the same phrase to explain "the impossibility of locating the subject in the 'great chain of being,'" since "subject is in the most radical sense 'out of joint'; it constitutively lacks its own place."[22]

"In the most radical sense 'out of joint.'" But there is a different kind of "radical" sense that goes to the root of this oft-cited phrase. For directly above "out of joint," "*phrase, figurative*," the diligent *OED* browser will encounter, as he or she might expect, "out of joint," "*phrase, literal.* Said of a bone displaced from its articulation with another; dislocated; also of the part or member affected." A glance at the 1611 King James translation of the Bible reveals that it regularly describes body parts as "out of joint" in this literal anatomical way: (Genesis 32:25 "and the hollow of Jacob's thigh was out of joint"; Psalms 22:14 "I am poured out like water, and all my bones are out of joint"; Proverbs 25:19 "Confidence in an unfaithful man in time of trouble is like a broken tooth, and a foot out of joint"). Donne's "First Anniversary" blends the two frames of reference, political/philosophical and bodily: "So is the worlds whole frame / Quite out of joynt, almost created lame." Likewise in *Troilus and Cressida,* Ajax is described as a man who "hath the joints of every thing, but every thing so out of joint that he is a gouty Briareus, many hands and no use" (1.2.27–29).

"Ha! What news here?" demands the bastard Spurio in *The Revenger's Tragedy.* "Is the day out o' the socket, / That it is noon at midnight, the Court up? / How comes the guard so saucy with his elbows?" Here is the familiar and officious "handle-man" again, his elbows at the ready. "Out o' the socket" seems like a disturbingly literal and anatomical version of "out of joint."[23] The power of this image derives in part from its reliteralization. "Out o' the socket" sounds painful: we can almost supply the torturer and the rack. When Hamlet remarks that the time is out of joint and laments that he "was born to *set* it right," we may wonder, perhaps, whether that word "set" itself carries a strong or a weak meaning, a figurative or a literal one. A "bone-setter," after all, was a surgeon, responsible for "setting" dislocated or broken bones. "Can honor set to a leg?" asks Falstaff, rhetorically. Bones in Shakespeare may ache, rattle, be mocked, ground, gnawed, or hacked asunder, or, more peacefully, lie either in a tent or a grave. They are not usually "set," but they may indeed be "out of joint." It may be worth recalling that Heminge's and Condell's prefatory letter to the First Folio uses a similarly literal anatomical figure, describing Shakespeare's plays, restored to wholeness in their edition, as once "maimed, and deformed" but now "cur'd, and perfect of their limbes."[24] The texts of the plays, once out of joint, are now properly realigned, in effect, "set." Since in this period the word "set" itself carries a series of distinct connotations, from putting manuscript into type (1530) to placing in a certain sequence in a literary work (1535) to bone-setting (1572), the description of the plays as an anatomy or skeleton is itself troped on linkages between and among orthotic cultural practices.

Strikingly, however, the bodily member the *OED* singles out for special attention under the heading "out of joint" is "the nose," not a part that is normally thought of, these days, as being or having a joint at all. ("*To put one's nose out of joint*; see NOSE.") A modern slang dictionary notes that to "put someone's nose out of joint" = To make someone envious or jealous, but the use of the phrase goes back at least as far as Barnaby Rich in 1581. Dekker and Marston's *Satiromastix* uses the phrase ("Yonder bald Adams, is put my nose from his joint"), as does Robert Armin's *Fool upon Fool* ("The thought of the new come Foole so much mooued him . . . that he would put his nose out of ioynt"[25]).

"Nose" for penis in Western literature and culture goes at least as far back as Ovid (Publius Ovidius *Naso*) and as far forward as Pinocchio and Freud. Eric Partridge observes the frequency with which the nose in Shakespeare became a penis. "If you were but an inch of fortune better than I," asks Cleopatra's waiting-woman Charmian to her colleague Iras, "where would you choose it?" and Iras retorts, "Not in my husband's nose" (*A&C* 1.2.57–59). "Here," Partridge instructs firmly, "*nose* = proboscis = trunk = dangling projection."[26]

Metaphors of articulation are often generated by the physical functions, limitations, and possibilities of individual joints. Even joints that don't seem to have joints.

But could the "joint" be out of joint?

A "joint" in modern slang is a penis; a piece of meat. It is also a marijuana cigarette, a low dive, and a hangout.[27] To "unlimber the joint" is to urinate.[28] In the early modern period "joint" as "cut of meat" seems to have had a sexual flavor, too, both male and female. In *Pericles* a pimp and a bawd bicker about Marina's maidenhead: "Mistress, if I have bargain'd for the joint—" "Thou mayst cut a morsel off the spit" (4.2.130–31). But "joint" also regularly meant "penis," presumably because it bent, connected, and joined. In George Chapman's *Widow's Tears* the widow of the title laments to her companion, "One joint of him I lost was much more worth / Than the rack'd value of thy entire body"; the retort, not so sotto voce, is "I know what joint she means." In Sampson's *Vow-Breaker* (1625–1626) an old man rues his lack of potency: "I have daunc'd till every joynt about me growes stiffe but that which should be" (2.2.183)—obviously a familiar form of the joke—and there are dozens of similiar references, especially in the plays of the time.[29] Holofernes the pedant in *Love's Labour's Lost* announces that Costard the clown will play the part of a Roman hero: "this swain (because of his great limb or joint) shall pass Pompey the Great" (5.1.127–28). This is a laugh line if ever I heard one; "or joint" functions like an elbow in the ribs, and the jest is clearly dependent on the proverbial notion that fools and "naturals" were especially well-endowed.

In Shakespeare's plays, however, when the term "out of joint" is explicitly physical, it is often used in reference to the *shoulder.* "Thou hast drawn my shoulder out of joint," complains Hostess Quickly to the officers who arrest her and Doll Tearsheet at the end of *Henry IV, Part 2* (5.4.3). The rogue Autolycus, disguised as a robbed and beaten man and groveling in the dirt to cozen the clown in *The Winter's Tale*, complains (perhaps with equal falsehood), "I fear, sir, my shoulder-blade is out" (4.3.73). In Shakespeare, the shoulder is a site of honor ("which gently laid my knighthood on my shoulder" [*Richard II* 1.1.79]; fellowship ("they clap the lubber Ajax on the shoulder" [*Troilus* 3.3.279]; male beauty and heroism (Coriolanus is wounded "i' the shoulder and i' the' left arm," and will have scars to show the people [*Cor.* 2.1.147]; Pelops's ivory shoulder was a paradigm of perfection [*Two Noble Kinsmen* 4.2.21]). But dislocated shoulders—claimed, perhaps significantly in these examples by rebellious and socially marginal characters (the brothel hostess and the rogue)—are signs of something else: of, in fact, a social world "out of joint," signified by the *pretense* or excuse of forcible bodily dislocation.

As the case of Pelops suggests, the shoulder was a quintessentially "human" joint. John Donne pointed out in a sermon that "God is never said to have shoulders." Why? Because in essence he is "all shoulder," according to the Scriptures: "shoulders are the subjects of burdens, and therein the figures of patience, and so God is all shoulder, all patience."[30]

Like the elephant without knees, a God without shoulders (or a God who was all shoulder) demarcated the limits of a body at once allegorically and physiologically conceived.

What do joints do? They articulate and connect; they facilitate movement. "Animals use joints like a centre," declared Aristotle, "and the whole member, in which the joint is, becomes both one and two, both straight and bent, changing potentially and actually by reason of the joint."[31] Ulysses says with scornful lust that even Cressida's foot speaks; "her wanton spirits look out / At every joint and motive of her body" (*Troilus* 4.5.56–57). A joint literally "out of joint" is dislocated, disarticulated—and highly painful. "Let him die, / With every joint a wound" (*Troilus* 4.1.29–30). "To th' rack with him! We'll touze you / Joint by joint" (*Measure for Measure* 5.1.312). "By heaven, I will tear thee joint by joint, / And strew this hungry churchyard with thy limbs" (*Romeo and Juliet* 5.3.35–36).

Syntax

And as I prophesied, there was a noise, and behold a shaking, and the bones came together, bone to his bone.
—Ezekiel 37:7

The whole body fitly joined together and compacted by that which every joint supplieth, according to the effectual working of the measure of every part
—Paul to the Ephesians 4:16

The word "syntax" originally meant a systematic arrangement of parts and elements, like—and including—the constitution of the body. Thus Helkiah Crooke's *Microcosmographia, A Description of the Body of Man* (1615) asserted that "the universal compage of coagmentation of the bones is called a Syntax, and the backe of bones so fitted together is called a Sceleton."

The manner of this Syntax or composition is double, for it is made either by Articulation or by Coalition. Articulation we define to be a Naturall structure of the bones, where in the extremities or ends of two bones do touch one another. So that the whole Nature of Articulation consisteth of the Contraction of extremities or ends.[32]

A "compage" is a framework or system of conjoined parts, a complex structure, a means of joining. So *syntax*, in modern usage most frequently considered as an aspect of grammar, and *articulation*, frequently regarded as an aspect of speech, thus each inhabit, in their early modern forms, an intellectual and conceptual space modeled on the body, and, quite specifically, on its "connexions" or joints. "Their articulation doth not differ from the Syntax or coniunction of other parts," says Crooke (595), and John Edwards would declare in 1690 that "this single [argument] from the fabrick and syntax of man's body is sufficient to evince the truth of a Deity."[33] Physical motion becomes evidence of divine motion. As Aristotle had noted, "[T]his is our meaning when we speak of a point which is in potency one, but which becomes two in actual exercise. Now if the forearm were the living animal, somewhere in its elbow-joint would be the movement-imparting origin of the soul."[34] It is by a logic of connectedness that order is perceived, and, for a Christian like Edwards, "the Existence and Providence of God" deduced from the "naturalness" of order. "The hip bone's connected to the hip bone, the thigh bone's connected to the knee bone, the knee bone's connected to the leg bone, the leg bone's connected to the ankle bone . . ." In the case of the body and its joints, it was the joints that were articulate, that connected, that spoke.

But if they spoke, they also sometimes misspoke. In two key instances of inadvertent malapropism in Shakespeare's plays we can see how the expectation of organic form is disarticulated—how (as in the earlier example of Falstaff's invisible and rebellious knee) the very logic of bodily coherence and obedience can be challenged by the language of the joints. The dramatic episodes I have in mind, striking to modern as well as to early modern audiences, are the verbal miscues of Elbow the Constable and the language lesson of Princess Katherine of France.

A personification of the out-at-elbow "handle man," Shakespeare's "simple" Constable Elbow in *Measure for Measure*, is the butt of constant jokes about his name. "He's out at elbow" says Pompey the bawd, and the constable himself offers an early gloss on his comical "handle": "my name is Elbow. I do lean upon justice" (2.1.47–48). "Elbow," I should point out, is a not-uncommon English surname; Harvard's Widener Library houses works not only by Peter Elbow, cited above, but also by Gary, Linda, and Matthew Elbow, among others. Shakespeare is not merely being allegorical but also what a later age might call ethnographic, in giving his policeman this bare-bones name. Present-day authors by the name of Ankles, Shoulderblade, Knee and Kneebone likewise testify to the propensity of various cultures to tag their populations by anatomical features. But Elbow, the constable's name, performs itself not only in what may be characteristic postures of physical assertion but also in the way his character articulates—or, rather, disarticulates—language. He speaks of "my wife whom I detest [for *protest*] before heaven," (68) who "if she had been a woman cardinally [for *carnally*] given" (79); his malapropisms persist, with growing consequence, throughout the play. "Respected" for "suspected" (165). "Do you hear how he misplaces?" says the councillor Escalus to Angelo, the deputy. "Misplacing" here becomes a nonce rhetorical term for dislocation, and significantly, it is what might be called the "joints" of language, the prefixes and suffixes that alter meaning, that Elbow "misplaces," to produce meanings the contrary of what he (apparently) intends.

That such "misplacement" is in Shakespeare an articulate language of disarticulation can perhaps be seen even more clearly when language itself is the topic. In her comically pertinent (and impertinent) English-language lesson Katherine of France persistently mispronounces the word "elbow," first as "bilbow" and then as "ilbow." In the early modern period a "bilbo" was a both a sword and an iron bar with sliding fetters, used to shackle the feet of prisoners (probably from the town of Bilbao in Spain, famous for its ironworks). So the elbow as bilbow invokes another kind of joint, binding together prisoners who (to literalize Aristotle), though formally two "become one in actual exercise." The word "bilbo" appears elsewhere in Shakespeare in both senses.[35]

But what of "ilbow"? There is no such word in English; unlike "bilbo," it is not a verbal joke. Or is it? The princess, being French, gives the word its proper preposition: she says not "ilbow" but "de ilbow"; or dilbo; or—in this escalating feast of naughty half-rhyming words, dildo.

Malapropism is itself a kind of dislocation, as is clear from some of Katherine's other inadvertent *mots*: *nick* for neck, *sin* for chin, and, most notoriously, *coun* (cunt) for gown and the homonym *foot* (= French *foutre*, fuck) for English foot. What is dislocated here is not only a word from its socket of meaning but the sense of language itself as firmly jointed and joint. At once compound and complex, these are fractures of language ("fractured French" is indeed a modern term for fumbling attempts at Gallic speech). When the malapropism produces meaning, despite itself, it is said that the unconscious is speaking. The Princess of France, speculating about the swashbuckling "enemy" king who is destined to be her husband, misplaces foot, gown, chin, and elbow, and replaces them with foutre, coun, sin, and dildo. Her English has "english" on it; it spins out of control; it is out of joint.

We have been considering the dependence of certain implicit theories of language and structure upon the notion of organic form. The so-called body politic became the model for coherence and rule; mimesis, imitation, resemblance, and metaphor gave order and suggested "natural" hierarchies. The joint of the body could stand for the part-ness of the individual (again, normatively the male individual) in the unitary whole. But other theories of language that bear upon this same rhetoric of the joint and the body are, importantly, *not* based on organic form. Ferdinand de Saussure's theory of modern linguistics was based on a structuralist system of differences, not on resemblance or identity: a word is an element in a system. The "arbitrary nature of the sign" meant that the relationship between the signifier and the sign is never necessary or "motivated." The body—the natural body—was not the inevitable tenor for which particular words would be vehicles. Instead, it was the point of articulation itself, the relation, the joint, that gave meaning.

"Language might be called the domain of articulations," suggests Saussure in his *Course in General Linguistics.* "Each linguistic term is a member, an *articulus* in which an idea is fixed in a sound and a sound becomes the sign of an idea."[36] And again, "In Latin *articulus* means a member, part, or subdivision of a sequence; applied to speech, articulation designates either the subdivision of a spoken chain into syllables or the subdivision of the chain of meanings into significant units; *gegliederte Sprache* is used in the second sense in German" (10–11). *Geglierdert* means "jointed; articulate; constructed organically, organized." *Glied* is limb or member, and *gliederpuppe* is puppet, marionette, or jointed doll. What has the jointedness of puppets to do with the jointedness of language?

Pulling Strings

O, excellent motion! O exceeding puppet! Now will he interpret to her.
          —*Two Gentlemen of Verona* 2.1.94–95

Fie, fie, you counterfeit, you puppet, you!
          —*A Midsummer Night's Dream* 3.2.288

Come, children, let us shut up the box and the puppets, for our play is played out.
          —Thackeray, *Vanity Fair*

In Heinrich von Kleist's story "Über das Marionettentheater" (On the Puppet Theater, 1810), the narrator converses with a celebrated dancer, Mr. C., whom he has often encountered at "a puppet theater which had been hammered together in the marketplace, to entertain the crowds with little mock-heroic dramas." Dancers, says Mr. C., have much to learn from puppets about the graceful disposition of their own bodies.

The narrator is surprised "that he should signify with serious consideration this toy version of a high art."

> I inquired about the mechanism . . . and how it was possible, without myriad strings on the fingers, to control the separate members and their tie points as the rhythm of their movements or dances required.
>
> He answered that I must not imagine that each member, in the various motions of the dancer, had to be placed and pulled individually by the puppeteer.
>
> Each movement, he said, had its center of gravity; it would suffice to control that center, on the inside of the figure; the limbs, which are really nothing but pendulums, follow of themselves, in a mechanical way, without further aid.
>
> He added that this movement was a very simple one, that even when the center of gravity was directed in a *straight* line, the limbs began to describe *curves*; and that often, when shaken in a quite random way, the whole puppet assumed a kind of rhythmic motion that was very much like a dance. . . .
>
> The line that the center of gravity must describe is indeed very simple and, as he believed, in most cases straight. When it happens to be curved, the law of its curvature seemed only the first, and at most of the second order: and even in the latter case only elliptical, which form of movement happens to be the natural one for the extremities of the human body (because of the joints) and which would demand no great skill on the part of the puppeteer to describe.
>
> This line, however, considered from another point of view, is something very mysterious. For it is nothing less than *the path of the dancer's soul*.[37]

Mr. C. describes to the narrator with admiration the "mechanical legs that English craftsmen manufacture for hapless accident victims." Equipped with these prostheses, recipients not only "manage to dance," but dance with an extraordinary "lightness . . . serenity . . . and gracefulness that must amaze every thinking person." Such mechanically aided dancers, like the puppets that the same gifted English craftsman "could doubtless construct" to Mr. C.'s specifications, would have a key advantage over ordinary dancers, in that their members "are, as they should be, dead, pure, pendulums"—unlike, for example, the young dancer F., who, playing the part of Paris and extending an apple, finds that "his soul . . . actually settles in his elbow." The elbow here stands as emblem of all that is merely human: off-balance, intrusive, particular rather than general and ideal. These are "blunders," says Mr. C., unavoidable since the fall of man.

Kleist's dialogue is an early example of what would become "a virtual obsession with the puppet" in the theory and practice of European drama.[38] The modernist concern with the machine as an aesthetic object so intensely contemplated as to become a virtual subject enlisted the puppet, or the marionette, as part of a critique of naturalistic acting. William Butler Yeats, attending the premiere of Alfred Jarry's *Ubu Roi* in 1896, remarked that the actors were "hopping like wooden frogs" and looked like "dolls, toys, marionettes."[39] Maurice Maeterlinck in France and Gordon Craig in England were among others who saw the modernist puppet theater as a commentary on the impossibility of verisimilitude, the destabilization of authorship, and, ultimately, the vexed status of the subject.

We might recall Slavoj Žižek's observation that "subject is in the most radical sense 'out of joint': it constitutively lacks its own place." This quintessentially postmodern perception is, as Žižek shows, traceable back through Kant to Descartes, whose "I think" introduces "a crack in the ontologically consistent universe" by conjuring up the possibility of the "Evil Genius (*le malin genie*) who, behind my back, dominates me and pulls the strings of what I experience as 'reality.'"[40] To be "out of joint" is thus, for the human subject, to be subject to the machinations of an invisible puppeteer: "the prototype of the Scientist-Maker who creates an artificial man." Žižek's concern is with borderline "human" figures evoked by modern science, like the replicants in *Blade Runner* or the monster in *Frankenstein*. But his metaphor—"pulls the strings of what I experience as 'reality'"—returns "out of joint" to the time of its most familiar iteration: early modern England.

The early modern term for puppet show was "motion,"[41] which also became a shorthand word for puppet. Thus Ben Jonson's irritable Morose is reproved by the suddenly loquacious "silent woman" (actually a boy in disguise) he has taken for his wife: "[W]hy, did you thinke you had married a statue? or a motion, onely? one of the French puppets, with the eyes turn'd with a wire?"[42] As Scott Shershow notes, in the early modern period "the word *motion* constantly slips between the two sides of the physio-psychological opposition which it also predicates, linking biology and behavior, rhetoric and theater, within a transparent system of correspondences."[43] A curious reversal or inversion of meaning seems to have taken place in the process, however, where the puppet show was called a "motion" presumably because in it the inanimate moved, the puppet (or, as frequently, the human being compared to a puppet) was so-called because he or she did *not* move, or show animation.

Touring companies of Italian puppet-masters were popular in England and throughout Europe in the late sixteenth and seventeenth centuries, and the shows they presented were often related to the *commedia dell'arte*. Marionettes were not unknown in the period, especially in Italy, where an arrangement of rods and silk or cords were used to manipulate the arms and legs, "permitting all kinds of backward-bending joints,"[44] and some English references take note of them.[45] Beaumont and Fletcher's *The Woman Hater* compares a sexually unresponsive man to "dead motions moving upon wires,"[46] and a stage direction in a Cornish mystery play of 1611 calls for the appearance of "spirits on cords."[47] The famous *Hero and Leander* puppet show in Ben Jonson's *Bartholomew Fair* seems to have been of glove-puppets, made to move by the action of the fingers, wrist, and thumb because they are brought out in a basket. "Here is young Leander, is as proper an actor of his inches," says Leatherhead proudly, "and shakes his head like an ostler" (5.3.95–97). Even glove puppets had "joints," both human ones, inside the gloves, and represented ones. A character in Jonson's *Poetaster* asks derisively, "What's he with the half arms there, That salutes us out of his cloak, like a motion?."[48]

In *Bartholomew Fair* the puppet-master Leatherhead acts as "interpreter" for Littlewit's "motion" of *Hero and Leander*: "I am the mouth of 'em all," he declares (5.3.74). Deploring the fact that the time is "out of joint," Hamlet in effect proposes himself as the interpreter for the puppet government of the Claudius court. "I could interpret . . . if I could see the puppets dallying." Rejoining the old notion of the "body politic" with the perception that language itself was radically unstable and duplicitous, even the voice liable to be ventriloquized, the motion of the limbs (to borrow Kleist's terms) naturally elliptical ("which form of movement happens to be the natural one for the extremities of the human body [because of the joints]"), the early modern puppet marks the crisis point of articulation and disarticulation that is the theoretical space of the joint.

The unsettling movements of such "motions" can have their effect in the modern (and postmodern) theater as well. In the fall of 1995, for example, a series of Shakespeare plays performed by marionette companies played to sold-out houses in Berlin.[49] Presenting Shakespeare through puppet "actors" paradoxically brought the dramatic tensions closer to the surface, by defamiliarizing and estranging the realm of the psychological, and even the mimetic language of face and voice. In a comparable piece of spectacle, the George C. Wolfe production of *The Tempest* at New York's Public Theater, starring Patrick Stewart as Prospero, used puppets and stiltwalkers to produce a major part of the magical stage action. Naked "human" puppets like ventriloquists' dummies presided over the banquet scene, wielded by "unseen" Kuroko figures, actors dressed in black. The very limber jointedness of the puppets (designed by Barbara Pollitt), together with their human facial expressions and glistening nakedness (*not* a characteristic of most ventriloquists' dummies—imagine Charlie McCarthy with no clothes on), brilliantly and uncannily suggested both the living and the dead. We may recall that Freud's essay "The 'Uncanny'" took as one of its starting points Hoffmann's fantastic tale about the wooden doll Olympia, and the "impression made by waxwork figures, ingeniously constructed dolls, and other automata"; Freud singles out "dismembered limbs, a severed head, a hand cut off at the wrist, ... feet that dance by themselves"—all enabled by the movement of the joints—as "peculiarly uncanny ... especially when, as in the last instance, they prove capable of independent action."[50]

The Wolfe/Public Theater *Tempest* also included a number of "stiltwalkers," quite literally actors walking on stilts,[51] both to generate expressionistic stage action (in the opening storm the Neapolitans' ship was "tossed" on the waves of long cloth strips held at each end, and loosely fluttered, by an "invisible" figure on stilts) and, once again, to mark the uncanny. The wedding masque of Juno, Iris, and Ceres, often a ho-hum event in modern production, became a vivid and witty spectacle generating wonder because the three goddesses were all gigantic, walking on stilts. Moreover, the "feet" of the stilts wore dancers' toe–shoes (rather like the feet of the original Barbie doll). The effect was to render the audience, in Freud's terms, uncannily uncertain as to whether the legs they were looking at were "alive" (were these tall apparitions really two people, one on another's shoulders, the head and torso of the lower one hidden by the goddess's skirts?) or "dead" (the lower limbs not "human" but wooden, the "feet" not feet at all but painted poles?). If the effect was not precisely that of Freud's "feet that dance by themselves," it was, nonetheless, powerfully uncanny, precisely because of the unjointed "joints"—the "ankles" and "toes" that seemed to flex as they bore the goddesses' weight.

The word "stilt" was also used to mean "crutch," and may derive from a German word for "limp." Yet the novelist Thackeray would associate "stilts" with the larger-than-life appearance of figures on the stage when he described "the actors in the old tragedies, ... speaking from under a mask, and wearing stilts."[52] Limb or prosthesis? Human or puppet? Jacques Lacan described the "fragmented body-image" of the child (and the "aggressive disintegration" of the analysand) as manifesting itself "in the form of disjointed limbs."[53] The deliberate unjointing and rejointing of these superhuman figures, goddesses and "invisible" stagehands, produces the prosthetic joint as irreducible supplement to the human body, at once mimetic and fantasmatic.

Skeleton Keys

> The word of God is quick, and powerful, and sharper even than any two-edged sword, piercing even to the dividing asunder of soul and spirit, and of the joints and marrow.
> —The Epistle of Paul the Apostle to the Hebrews 4:12

> There is of course as much of metaphor as metonymy in prosthesis; in fact a powerful will-to-analogy functions through the narrative mode that attaches a wooden leg to a theoretical discussion.
> —David Wills, *Prosthesis*

"If hee had been made of one continuall bone," Helkiah Crooke wrote of mankind, at the beginning of the seventeenth century, "how could he have bent or extended or compassed his body? how could he have apprehended any thing or moved himselfe forward to attayne it? No; he must have stood like a trunke or a blocke." In this section of the *Microcosmographia*, called "of the structure and connexion of Bones," Crooke seems to suggest that the "connexion," the joint, was, in a sense, that which made human creatures human. Being not only conscious but jointed, man was enabled to "receive infinite images of Sensible things, and to flye and apply himselfe to the divers objects of his appetite." "Notwithstanding though this connexion be divers, yet it is so strangely fitted together that al seeme to be but one; one I say either by Continuity or by Contiguity at least." Continuity and contiguity are themselves tropes here, and indeed most familiar ones: we know them by names like metaphor and metonymy.[54] Metaphor is the seeming-to-be-one; metonymy is the linkage, the chain of associations, the joint. To be out of joint, to have the capacity to dislocate and be dislocated, is to recognize the fragility of the join, the point of vulnerability (call it an Achilles' heel) that is the corollary of the gift of movement, and in the register of language, the ambivalent task of the interpreter.

Paul de Man draws a connection between the uncanniness of the puppet figures in Kleist's allegorical tale and the political problematic of "the aesthetic," describing what he calls "the articulated puppets":[55]

> The puppets have no motion by themselves but only in relation to the motions of the puppeteer, to whom they are connected by a system of lines and threads. . . . The aesthetic power is located neither in the puppet nor in the puppeteer but in the text that spins itself between them. This text is the transformational system. . . . Tropes are quantified systems of motion. (285–86)

What de Man notes here is the illusion of freedom and universal order produced by an "ideology of the aesthetic" that encodes restriction and formalization under the sign of perfect art. His comparison text is a letter of Schiller's that extolls the traditional "English dance, composed of many complicated figures and turns" as "the perfect symbol of one's own individually asserted freedom" in a system in which "everything has [already] been arranged." "Caught in the power of gravity, the articulated puppets can rightly be said to be dead, hanging and suspended like dead bodies: gracefulness is directly associated with dead, albeit a dead cleansed of pathos. But it is also equated with a levity, an un-seriousness which is itself based on the impossibility of distinguishing between dead and play" (287). "The puppet's ground is not the ground of a stable cognition" (288).

Gravity and levity; "dead and play." "I could interpret between you and your love," says Hamlet to Ophelia, "if I could see the puppets dallying."[56]

The aesthetic is a principle of articulation, de Man suggests. "It is as a political force that the aesthetic still concerns us as one of the most powerful ideological drives to act upon the reality of history." "But what is then called . . . the *aesthetic*, is not a separate category but a principle of articulation between various known faculties, activities, and modes of cognition."[57] In the essay on Kleist's marionette theater, one of his few explicitly antifascist texts, de Man perceived that the idea of the "aesthetic state" in Schiller was the preference for the prosthetic grace of puppets or dead bodies in a harmony that can only be totalitarian. (Significantly, perhaps, Kleist's wonder-worker is an "English craftsman," who, like Schiller's "English dance," replaces the human member with a mechanical prosthesis.) The "aestheticization of politics" about which Walter Benjamin would speak so forcefully was precisely this kind of new, "improved" body politics in which prostheses, perfect, regular, and predictable, replaced the flawed and the human. And here too what was crucial was the logic, or pseudologic, of the joint.

Consider, as calculated theatrical examples, two signifying gestures from the political aesthetics of German fascism: the goose step and the Nazi salute. Both involve locking a joint—the knee, the elbow—rather than bending it (as for example in the parade march and bent-arm military salute favored by some other nations). In the goose step and Nazi salute, the body aspires to the condition of a machine, or a prosthesis, through the simulation of an unjointed limb that levitates, almost of its own accord, in response to the presence of the hero or the apparatus of state. (It is this automatism that Stanley Kubrick parodies, to such good effect, in *Dr. Strangelove*, and that Ian McKellen would later recall in his brilliant restaging of *Strangelove* as Shakespeare's Richard III.[58]) When thirty thousand hands were raised in the Nazi salute at the Nazi Party Congress in Nuremburg on September 4, 1934, Hitler had one of his officers proclaim: "The German form of life is definitely determined for the next thousand years. The Age of Nerves of the nineteenth century has found its close with us."[59] Nerves had been replaced by a "form of life" that aestheticized and mechanized the body: not a body without organs but a body without joints.

Characteristically, de Man's essay on Kleist cautions the reader against succumbing to pathos. "One should avoid the pathos of an imagery of bodily mutilation and not forget that we are dealing with textual models, not with the historical and political systems that are their correlate. The disarticulation produced by tropes is primarily a disarticulation of meaning; it attacks semantic units such as words and sentences."[60] Disarticulation— what later commentators have called "dislinkage"—is a product of figure itself: "the *dis*linkage precisely of cause and effect between the signifier and the world."[61] (Here we might perhaps usefully recall Peter Elbow's comment about writing: "If anything, the linkage is just as natural the other way around.")[62] This dislinkage is not a failure of reference but, rather, an estrangement, a "torsion" (3). Or, to put it in other words—in very familiar words—things are out of joint. Relations "between the signifier and the world" are strained—or sprained. Can they be set right? "Can honour set to a leg?" asked Falstaff, a performative deconstructor *avant la lettre*. "No. Or an arm? No.... Honour hath no skill in surgery then? What is honour? A word. What is in that word honour? What is that honour? Air" (*1 Henry IV* 5.1.131–36).

"One should avoid the pathos of an imagery of bodily mutilation." Yet, in early modern drama this is not so easily done, for to avoid the pathos of an imagery of bodily mutilation is, in effect, to avoid the theater and its peculiar power. We might recall Romeo's over-the-top threat to Paris, "By heaven, I will tear thee joint by joint, / And strew this hungry churchyard with thy limbs" (*Romeo and Juliet* 5.3.35–36). Achilles, encountering Hector for the first time, remarks that he has looked his fill: "I have with exact view perus'd thee, Hector / And quoted joint by joint" (*Troilus* 4.5.233). The "quote" comes from the register of language, but it parses a manifest threat in action: "I will. . . . As I would buy thee, view thee limb by limb" (237–38); "Tell me, you heavens, in which part of his body / Shall I destroy him— whether there, or there, or there?" (242–43). Pathos is not an incidental affect of theatrical representation; it is a key element of theatricality, ultimately inseparable from the words that produce it. What is torn is both body *and* words. The "joint" as body part and as the connective tissue of language is always *double-jointed*, figurative and literal at once. Which is the figure and which is the ground? Syntax or skeleton, homage or knee?

In Marlowe's *Doctor Faustus* the actor playing Faustus is furnished at one point with a prosthesis—a wooden leg.

> *Horse-courser.* Master doctor, awake and rise. . . . Master doctor! *He pulls off his leg.* Alas, I am undone; what shall I do? I have pulled off his leg. . . . [N]ow he has but one leg I'll outrun him, and cast this leg into some ditch or other. [*Exit*]
>
> *Faustus.* Stop him, stop him, stop him—ha, ha, ha! Faustus hath his leg again.
>
> 4.4.28–36[63]

Although the doctor exults at his deception, this comic scene prefigures his own later dismemberment: "See, here are Faustus' limbs, / All torn asunder by the hand of death. . . . We'll give his mangl'd limbs due burial" (5.3.6–7, 17).

The disarticulation of language from "historical and political systems," of the syntax of the sentence from the syntax of the skeleton, threatens to dislocate literature from culture, to put them "out of joint." But neither in early modern culture nor in dramatic literature more generally can one finally "avoid the pathos of an imagery of bodily mutilation." The materiality of the body and its vulnerable articulations not only exemplifies but constitutes the semantics of performance. Dismemberment is the hard connective tissue of drama, the skeleton beneath its scrim. Bodily pathos (and for that matter, bodily levity, too) manifested through the eloquent syntax of the jointed body has been the spectacular and articulate engine of theater since the *sparagmos* of Pentheus in Euripides' *Bacchae*, since the piecemeal excavations of a gravedigger in the *Hamlet* churchyard, since the cozened Horse-courser pulled the leg of Doctor Faustus—and the leg came off.

Notes

I thank David Hillman, Carla Mazzio, and Katherine Rowe (separately and jointly) for their encouragement and their wisdom in matters of the early modern body.

1. Ca'da Mosto, *The Voyages of Ca'da Mosto and other documents on West Africa in the second half of the Fifteenth Century* (London: Hakluyt Society, 1937), 46. Joan Barclay Lloyd, *African Animals in Renaissance Literature and Art* (Oxford: Clarendon Press, 1971), 117.

2. André Thevet, *Cosmographie de Levant* (1554), 69–73. Cited in Lloyd, *African Animals,* 116.

3. *The Works of Sir Thomas Browne,* vol. 2, *Pseudodoxia Epidemica,* Books I–VII, ed. Geoffrey Keynes (London: Faber & Faber, 1923), 157.

4. Women, of course, also kneel frequently in the dramatic literature of the period (as well as in court). Volumnia and Valeria kneel to Coriolanus, Isabella kneels in petition to Angelo ("Sweet Isabella, take my part! Lend me your knees," Mariana implores her [see *Measure for Measure* 5.1.435–47]).

5. David Bevington, *Action Is Eloquence: Shakespeare's Language of Gesture* (Cambridge and London: Harvard University Press, 1984), 164. Bevington's book offers a helpful discussion of "the visual significance" of kneeling "at moments of conflicting loyalty," with reference to plays from *Richard II* to *Measure for Measure, Coriolanus,* and *King Lear.*

6. Very fine readings of this scene are given by Sheldon P. Zitner, "Aumerle's Conspiracy," *Studies in English Literature* 14 (1974): 239–57, and Leonard Barkan, "The Theatrical Consistency of *Richard II*," *Shakespeare Quarterly* 29 (1978): 5–19.

7. Dover Wilson aptly compared this passage to More's lines to the rebellious commons in the Shakespearean additions to the play *Sir Thomas More:* "your unreverent knees / Make them your feet" (2.4.134–35).

8. The spectacle, at once comic and oddly moving, of a noblewoman past her youth kneeling in passionate suit to an obdurate monarch would be repeated in Shakespeare's *Coriolanus,* where Volumnia kneels to her son and pleads for Rome (5.3). Cleopatra kneels to Caesar and is told to "arise, you shall not kneel" (*Antony and Cleopatra* 5.2.114). Elsewhere an appalled Cordelia pleads with her father to rise. Brutus tells Portia not to kneel to him (*Julius Caesar* 2.1.278). Meantime, in *Hamlet,* Claudius invokes by his own (counter)example old York's notion of "true joints," discovering that his "stubborn knees" are reluctant to kneel in penitent prayer (3.3.70).

9. E. R. Curtius, *European Literature of the Latin Middle Ages,* trans. Willard Trask (New York: Harper & Row, 1963), 137–38; F. X. Funk, *Patres apostolici,* vol. I (1901), 172. The phrase "knees of the heart" is found in the *postcommunio* of the mass *pro reddendis gratiis.*

10. Heinrich von Kleist to Johann Wolfgang von Goethe, January 24, 1808. In *An Abyss Deep Enough: Letters of Heinrich von Kleist*, ed. and trans. Philip B. Miller (New York: Dutton, 1982), 178–79. *Penthesilea*, l. 2800.

11. Rainer Maria Rilke, letter to his mother (Phia Rilke), December 17, 1920. I am indebted to David Hillman for this reference.

12. In Fletcher's *Loyal Subject* (1618) a soldier's song anticipates the loss of virginity: "If her foot slip, an down fall she, And break her leg 'bove the knee" (3.5) and in the same playwright's *Wild Goose Chase* (1621) we hear that "She slip'd / And broke her leg about the knee" (4.1). In Heath's *Clarastella* (1650) it is the elbow, not the knee: "And so she broke her elbow 'gainst the bed"(2). By what is presumably a similar logic, Francis Grose's late-eighteenth-century *Glossary of Provincial and Local Words Used in England* (1785; reprint London: John Russell Smith, 1839), notes that "a girl who is got with child, is said to have sprained her ankle," and G. W. Matsell's nineteenth-century *Rogue's Lexicon* (New York: G. W. Matsell, 1859) defines both the possessor of a "broken leg" and a "sprained ankle" as "a woman that has had a child out of marriage."

13. Morris Palmer Tilley, *A Dictionary of the Proverbs in England in the Sixteenth and Seventeenth Centuries* (Ann Arbor: University of Michigan Press, 1950), 184.

14. Joaneath Spicer, "The Renaissance Elbow." *A Cultural History of Gesture*, ed. Jan Bremmer and Herman Roodenburg (Ithaca: Cornell University Press, 1992), 95.

15. Erasmus, *De civilitate morum puerilium* (1532), trans. as *A Lytell Booke of Good Maners for Chyldren* by Robert Whitinton. Also Spicer, "The Renaissance Elbow," 95.

16. John Bulwer, *Chirologia: or the Naturall Language of the Hand . . . Whereunto is added Chironomia: or the Arte of Manual Rhetoricke*, 2 vols. (London, 1644), chapter "Certain prevarications against the rule of rhetorical decorum, . . ." sect. 9. Also Spicer, "The Renaissance Elbow," 95.

17. The immobility of the elbow, of course, also has the potential to be parodied. In Shakespeare, the pretentious warrior with arms akimbo mocked by Erasmus makes his appearance in *Love's Labour's Lost* in the braggart soldier Don Armado, only to be taught that "folded arms" (3.1.181), "wreathed arms" (4.3.133) or "arms cross'd on [the] doublet like a rabbit on a spit" (3.1.18) with the elbows in marked the true posture of a lover. The same stereotypical postures appear in *The Two Gentlemen of Verona*, in *The Tempest*, and in *Hamlet*.

18. Jenkins cites a similar lament from Jerome Horsey's late-sixteenth-century *Travels in Russia*, "This turbulent time . . . all out of joint, not likely to be reduced a long time to any good form of peaceable government" (Jerome Horsey, "Travels in Russia," in Edward Bond, *Russia at the Close of the Sixteenth Century* [London: Hakluyt Society, 1927], 262) and compares Hamlet's remark to Claudius's suggestion, in the play's second scene, that Fortinbras dared to threaten Denmark because he regarded "our state" as "disjoint and out of frame" after the death of the former king.

19. Grafton's *Chronicle at large and meere history of the affayres of England* (1568) finds Thomas More concerned lest (in a phrase that might well have been on Claudius's—or Shakespeare's— mind) "they might peradventure bring the matter so farre out of joynt, that it should never be brought in frame againe." In Hoccleve's *To Sir John Oldcastle* (1415) the roistering knight is told, "Thow has been out of joynt al to longe."

20. Jacques Derrida, *Specters of Marx*, trans. Peggy Kamuf (New York: Routledge, 1994), 19. The *Hamlet* translations in question are Yves Bonnefoy (Paris: Gallimard, Folio, 1992); Jean Malaplate (Paris: Corti, 1991); Jules Derocquigny (Paris: Les Belles Lettres, 1989); and André Gide (Paris: Gallimard, Bibliothèque de la Pleiade, 1959). Derrida understands the phrase as describing "not a time whose joinings are negated, broken, mistreated, dysfunctional, disadjusted . . . but a time without *certain* joining or determinable conjunction" (18). In this discussion Derrida does not express an interest in the anatomical referent; "time," rather than "joint," is his principal concern: the "disjointure of the very presence of the present," the "non-contemporaneity of present time with itself" (25).

21. Slavoj Žižek, *The Indivisible Remainder: An Essay on Schelling and Related Matters* (London and New York: Verso, 1996), 42–43.

22. Slavoj Žižek, *Tarrying with the Negative: Kant, Hegel, and the Critique of Ideology* (Durham: Duke University Press, 1993), 12.

23. *The Revenger's Tragedy*, ed. Brian Gibbons (London: A. C. Black, 1990), 2.3. 44–46 and note. Gibbons, probably influenced by "noon" and "midnight," imagines the phrase to describe a torch out of a wall socket, or what he calls "a submerged link" with the play's images of skull and eye-socket."

24. John Heminge and Henrie Condell, "To the Great Variety of Readers" (prefatory letter to the First Folio of Shakespeare's Plays, 1623).

25. Tilley, *A Dictionary of the Proverbs in England*.

26. Eric Partridge, *Shakespeare's Bawdy*, 159. In general, Partridge is on the alert for these anatomical double meanings. Citing Lady Percy's mock threat to Hotspur to "break [his] little finger," he advises the reader that little finger for "penis" is "still current, among women, as a euphemism" (145; *Henry IV Part I*, 2.3.89–91). "Still current" presumably means in 1948, when the book was first published—or perhaps even in 1960, when the paperback edition appeared.

27. A famous Fats Waller recording of 1937, "The Joint Is Jumpin'" (with lyrics by Andy Rozaf and J. C. Johnson) described Harlem rent parties at their most raucous and lively: "The roof is rocking' / The neighbors are knockin' / We're all bums when the wagon comes / I'll say the joint is jumpin'." Across the Atlantic in the same years other joints were literally jumping, as the popular Cockney song "Knees-up, Mother Brown!"(1939) produced the slang term "knees-up" for a party or lively celebration.

    To be "in the joint" is to be in prison: "It's the black men who go to the joint, by and large" comments a *Boston Globe* column on prison reform. David Nyhan, "Bumper-Sticker Prison Reform," *Boston Globe*, December 6, 1995, 23.

28. *Brewer's Dictionary of Twentieth-Century Phrase and Fable.*

29. In Chapman's *All Fools* (1599–1604) a doctor assures his patient that he can cure venereal disease "without perishing of any joint," and is told, anxiously, "'Tis a joint I would be loath to lose for the best joint of mutton in Italy" (3.1.394). See Gordon Williams, *A Dictionary of Sexual Language and Imagery in Shakespearean and Stuart Literature* (London and Atlantic Highlands, N.J.: Athlone Press, 1994), 245.

30. John Donne, Sermon 5, in *Sermons*, vol. 9, ed. Evelyn Simpson and George Potter (Berkeley: University of California Press, 1958), 135.

31. Aristotle, *Movement of Animals*, trans. A.S.L. Farquarson, in *The Complete Works of Aristotle*, ed. Jonathan Barnes (Princeton: Bollingen, 1984), 1:1087.

32. Helkiah Crooke, *Microcosmographia, A Description of the Body of Man*, 2d ed. (London: M. Sparke, 1631), 930.

33. John Edwards, *A Demonstration of the Existence and Providence of God* (1690), 2:124.

34. Aristotle, *Movement of Animals*, 1:1087.

35. *Merry Wives of Windsor* 1.1.48; 3.5.92 (sword); *Hamlet* 5.2.96 (fetters).

36. Ferdinand de Saussure, *Course in General Linguistics*, ed. Charles Bally and Albert Sechehaye, trans. Wade Baskin (New York: McGraw-Hill, 1966), 112–13.

37. von Kleist, *An Abyss Deep Enough*, 211.

38. Scott Cutler Shershow, *Puppets and "Popular" Culture* (Ithaca and London: Cornell University Press, 1995), 184. Shershow's book is an illuminating account of the role of puppets and puppetry from Plato to the present.

39. William Butler Yeats, *The Autobiography of William Butler Yeats* (New York: Collier, 1965), 233. Cited by Shershow, *Puppets and "Popular" Culture*, 188.

40. Žižek, *Tarrying with the Negative*, 12.

41. For example, in Ben Jonson, *Bartholomew Fair* 5.3.

42. Ben Jonson, *Epicoene* 3.4.36–38. in *Ben Jonson*, ed. C. H. Hereford and Percy Simpson, 11 vols. (Oxford: Clarendon Press, 1925–1963).

43. Shershow, *Puppets and "Popular" Culture*, 75 (emphasis added). Shershow suggests that in *Religio Medici*, Sir Thomas Browne is "almost making a pun" when he says that he loves "to use the civility of my knee, my hat, and hand, with all those outward and sensible motions which may express or promote my invisible devotion." Thomas Browne, *Religio Medici*, pt. 1. sec. 3, in *The Works of Sir Thomas Browne*, ed. Geoffrey Keynes, 6 vols. (1928–1931; reprint Chicago: University of Chicago Press, 1964), 1:12–13.

44. George Speaight, *The History of the English Puppet Theatre* (London: Harrap, 1955), 36.

45. Ibid.

46. Beaumont and Fletcher, *The Woman Hater* (c. 1606) 3.1.

47. "A Note on the Chester Plays," by Robert Rogerrs, 1609 (Harl. MS 1944), quoted in *The Digby Plays*, Early English Text Society, Extra Series LXX (1896), cited by Speaight, *The History of the English Puppet Theater*, 279.

48. Theater historian George Speaight suggests that "a glove puppet, of which the arms are merely the fingers and thumb of the manipulator, does just exactly give the effect of having 'half arms' sticking—as if from the elbows—out of its costume." Speaight, *The History of the English Puppet Theater,* 65.

49. Stephen Kinzer, "Shakespeare, Icon in Germany," *New York Times,* December 30, 1995, 11. Shakespeare's plays had been performed by marionettes in London in the eighteenth century—in a theater run by the cross-dressing actress Charlotte Charke—and in the symbolist theater of Paris in the 1880s. See Shershow, *Puppets and "Popular" Culture* 156, 189, and Max von Boehn, *Dolls and Puppets*, trans. Josephine Nicoll (New York: Cooper Square, 1966), 346.

50. Sigmund Freud, "The 'Uncanny'" (1919), in *The Standard Edition of the Complete Psychological Works of Sigmund Freud*, ed. James Strachey (London: Hogarth Press and Institute of Psycho-analysis, 1955; reprint, 1986), 17:226, 244.

51. Stilts and stilt walkers date in Europe from the Middle Ages, when stilts were used not for theatrical purposes but for walking over marshes and streams. They could be strapped to the legs, or fastened beneath the feet, or held by the arms and hands. (The governor of the Belgian city of Namur in 1600 promised the archduke Albert a company of soldiers who would neither ride nor walk, and sent him stilt walkers; the city was rewarded by a pleased archduke with a perpetual exemption from the beer tax.)

52. William Makepeace Thackeray, *The History of Henry Esmond* (1852), introduction, 1.

53. Jacques Lacan, "The mirror stage as formative of the function of the I as revealed in psychoanalytic experience." (1949), in *Écrits: A Selection*, trans. Alan Sheridan (New York: Norton, 1977), 4.

54. Within the realm of the jointed body politic, "Continuity" needs "Contiguity" for success and succession, a little more than kin and less than kind. Claudius calls Gertrude "the imperial jointress" of his "warlike state," but the join there is fragile indeed: "our sometime sister, now our queen" (*Hamlet* 1.2.8-9). Lear, unwisely investing his sons-in-law Cornwall and Albany "jointly with my power" (*Lear* 1.1.130) loses both his power and his sanity, railing at a piece of household furniture as if it were his unkind daughter Goneril. "I cry you mercy, I took you for a join-stool" (3.6.52), quips the fool with mordant wit. A cliché of disparagement in the period, this proverbial phrase ("I cry you mercy, I took you for a joint-stool") is both literalized and banalized in the mad scene on the heath. (For other characteristic uses of the phrase, see, for example, John Withals, *A short dictionary for yonge begynners* [1553], and John Lyly, *Mother Bombie* [1594] 4.2.) Catachresis (e.g., the "leg" of a chair) becomes catastrophe: what was a jocular insult in the court becomes a hallucinatory delusion not altogether fool. That the "joiner" was a carpenter did not make it less likely that his work would be "anatomized." For an excellent treatment of carpentry, "artisinal 'joinery,'" and joinings in discourse and marriage, see Patricia Parker, "'Rude Mechanicals'" in *Subject and Object in Renaissance Culture*, ed. Margreta de Grazia, Maureen Quilligan, and Peter Stallybrass (Cambridge: Cambridge University Press, 1996), esp. 48–51.

55. Paul de Man, *The Rhetoric of Romanticism* (New York: Columbia University Press, 1984), 287.

56. *Hamlet* 3.2.246–47. Interpreters, somewhat like their twentieth century puppet-show counterparts (e.g., Fran Allison of "Kukla, Fran and Ollie," "Buffalo Bob" Smith of "Howdy Doody") spoke to and about the puppets, explaining the action, something especially necessary when the show itself was in a foreign tongue. The interaction of human and puppet also produced an odd, metatheatrical atmosphere, the puppets conventionally exhibiting "human" foibles that the interpreters had to both explain and, however futilely, try to control.

57. Paul de Man, "Aesthetic Formalization: Kleist's *Uber das Marionetten theater,*" in *The Rhetoric of Romanticism*, 264–65.

58. The reappropriation of this trope back into the realm of theatrical performance can be seen in a film like Stanley Kubrick's *Dr. Strangelove or: How I Learned to Stop Worrying and Love the Bomb* (1964) in which a fanatical German refugee scientist, the brains of the American nuclear bomb team, is unable to keep his gloved hand and crippled arm from suddenly extending in an apparently unwilled Nazi salute. (Here we might recall once more Žižek's evocation of the Evil Genius, the prototype of the Scientist-Maker, who "pulls the strings of what I experience as 'reality.'") Clearly indebted to *Dr. Strangelove*, is Ian McKellen's Richard III, played in a 1995 film version (with a screenplay adapted from Shakespeare by McKellen and director Richard Loncraine) as a self-enthralled fascist in the England of the 1930s. Richard's "deformity" in the film consists largely of stiffness, the inability to bend: his arm is thrust rigidly into his coat pocket, his stiff leg lags. The rhetoric of bodily organic form, as scholars of the play have often observed, leads to the phenomenon of Shakespeare's twisted Richard. But in this production it is not because his body fails to conform to "nature" but, rather, that it aspires to the condition of a machine.

   In the McKellen-Loncraine *Richard III*, the society band that plays at the film's outset (while a female singer jauntily warbles, to fox-trot rhythm, Marlowe's "Come Live With Me and Be My Love") offers another, debased version of Schiller's "English dance," itself once patterned on the heavenly music of the spheres. The dance-band's music stands display the entwined initials WS.

59. William L. Shirer, *The Rise and Fall of the Third Reich* (New York: Fawcett Crest, 1960), 318.

60. De Man, "Aesthetic Formalization," 289.

61. Andrew Parker and Eve Kosofsky Sedgwick, eds., *Performativity and Performance* (New York: Routledge, 1995), 2.

62. Peter Elbow, *What is English?* (New York: Modern Language Association, 1990), 136.

63. *The Plays of Christopher Marlowe*, ed. Roma Gill (London: Oxford University Press, 1971).

4.1 Emblem of the "Evill Tongue" from George Wither's *Collection of Emblemes* (London, 1635).

4

Sins of the Tongue

CARLA MAZZIO

With Gustus, Lingua dwells, his pratling wife,
Indu'd with strange and adverse qualities;
The nurse of hate and love, of peace and strife,
Mother of fairest truth, and foulest lies:
Of best or worst—no mean—made all of fire,
Which sometimes hell, and sometimes heav'ns inspire.
                    —Phineas Fletcher, *The Purple Island* (1633)

Lalangue est la condition du sens.
                    —Jacques Lacan, *Television*

Representations of the tongue in the early modern period often encode crises of logic, of language, and of sense. "O Ambivalent Organ," writes Erasmus in *Lingua* (1525), lamenting the fact that malevolent and benevolent discursive agencies emerge from one and the same bodily organ.[1] Erasmus, like many others, takes his cue from Proverbs (18:21) in noting the way in which the tongue is "ambi-valent," good and bad, always seeming to pull in two directions at once.[2] Indeed, the organ of speech, imagined in early modern religious, rhetorical, anatomical, and literary texts as the most powerful *and* the most vulnerable member of "man," is consistently coded as a member that seems to resist logical discriminations. Because "tongue" (like the Latin "*lingua*" and the Greek "*glossa*") also means "language," the very invocation of the word encodes a relation between word and flesh, tenor and vehicle, matter and meaning.[3] This relation, often configured as an intermingling of synecdoche and metonymy, is made explicit in Renaissance discourses about discourse such as Erasmus's *Lingua,* where the duplicities of language are imagined to emerge from the inherent slipperiness and duality of the organ of speech.[4]

What is particularly striking about early modern fantasies of the tongue is the way in which anxieties about the powers and vulnerabilities of language itself are consistently displaced onto what is otherwise, in Erasmus's words, just a "flabby little organ."[5] In George Wither's *Collection of Emblemes* (1635), for instance, the tongue, a synecdoche for the body and a metonymy for language, seems to have taken on a life of its own ("*No* Heart *can thinke*," the accompanying text reads, "*to what strange ends,* / The Tongues *unruely* Motion tends" [figure 4.1]).[6] Here, the tongue is estranged not only from its assumed interior counterpart, the heart, but from the whole body of which it is (or was) ostensibly a part. Like the famously disconcerting emblem of the winged lingua in Claude Paradin's *Devises Heroïques* (1551), or the emblem of a heart and tongue separated by hypocrisy in Georgette de Montenay's *Emblemes, ou Devises Chrestiennes* (1571), this image calls attention to both the materiality and the metaphoricity of signification.[7] The spectacle of the independent organ of speech, mobile even while dislodged from its bodily surround, in many ways perfectly embodies anxieties about reference itself, not only about the movement of speech *away* from the individual body but also about the movement of signs away from any singularly discernable, naturalized context.

Thomas Adams's *The Taming of the Tongue* (1619), a sermon on the abuses of speech, similarly imagines the tongue, the "wilde member," to be independent and isolated.[8] When he sets out to "examine the matter, and finde a stratagem to subdue it," he means to examine, quite literally, the tongue itself:

> We will observe 1. The Nature of the thing to be tamed. 2. The difficulty of accomplishing it. The insubjectible subject is the *Tongue:* which is 1. a member and 2. an Excellent, Necessary, Little, Singular Member, *It is a member.*[9]

An unruly "member," an "insubjectible subject," the tongue figures in a range of early modern discourses as a somatic manifestation of all that resists containment ("The eye, the eare, the foote, the hand, though wilde and *unruly* enough, have been *tamed*," writes Adams, "*but the tongue can no man tame*").[10] The linguistic, numerical, and conceptual repetitions here speak to the way in which that "insubjectible subject" seems to resist even representational constraints. Adams's insistence on the interlinked logics of autonomy and dependence, on both the "thing" to be tamed and the "membership" of that thing, reflects the slippery position of an organ that is both subject and object, that is and is not part of the self.[11] The "*Tongue* is the Subject (I meane in the discourse)," writes Adams, with a qualification that only seems to amplify the way in which this "topic," at once bodily and conceptual, encodes concerns about uncontrollable and contradictory forms of human subjectivity.[12]

"Oh necessary Tongue!" exclaims Adams, speaking to the organ of speech, "How many hearts would burst, if thou had not given them vent!"[13] The member that gives "vent" to voice and subjectivity, that bridges the individual and the collective, is also imagined to be a potentially autonomous and separate part of the self, a member that is always already dismembered. This essay will examine how representations of the disruptive and autonomous tongue functioned to locate and somatize multiple conditions of "insubjectible subjectivity" in the early modern period. It will then, by lingering on Thomas Tomkis's *Lingua: Or the Combat of the Tongue and the Five Senses for Superiority* (1607), move from questions about the somatization of speech to questions about the somatization of writing and textuality more generally, exploring the ways in which conditions of collective self-estrangement were located in the mouth of the individual subject, placed and displaced onto the very tip of the tongue.

Slips of the Tongue

> [The tongue] is one of the least members, most moveable, and least tyred: whereby man naturally runneth out in language the image of his life.
> —John Abernethy, *The Poysonous Tongue* (1622)

Early modern fantasies about the tongue often suggest a nervousness about its apparent agency. This is, in part, because of the deconstructive potential of the member. As the one organ that can move in and out of the body, its symbolic position in a range of discourses lies on the threshold between the framed and the unframed, between the space of the self and the space of the other.[14] "[The tongue] is both passive, and active: it is inflamed, and inflameth others. It is both *in it selfe* poysoned, and a poysoner of others," writes John Abernethy, Bishop of Cathnes, in *The Poysonous Tongue* (1622).[15] The notion of the organ as "*in it self*" boundless and paradoxical was of course not new to the early modern period, echoing as it did the *Epistle of James*, where the tongue is imagined as a horrifying mix of physiology and allegory:

> Even so the tongue is a little member, and boasteth great things. Behold, how great a matter a little fire kindleth! And the tongue *is* a fire, a world of iniquity: so is the tongue among our members, that it defileth the whole body, and setteth on fire the course of nature; and it is set on fire of hell (3:5–6).

But the referential fluidity of this fiery "little member" and its imagined capacity of "defil[ing] the whole body" had a range of analogues in the social logic of early modern somatic symbolism. Discussions about the uses and abuses of speech in the period increasingly drew on anatomical models, and the tongue was frequently singled out as a peculiarly unstable organ.[16] For many, the contradictory mechanical and functional properties of the tongue coded it as never quite set "among [the] members." William Gearing, for example, points out in *A Bridle for the Tongue* (1663) that unlike all other organs of sense, the tongue is both importer and "exporter," an instrument responsible for facilitating the movement of that which is out, in, and that which is in, out.[17] Early etymologies of "*lingua*" traced the word to its root in the activities of both eating and speaking; as Isidore of Seville writes, "Varro thinks that the tongue, *lingua*, was named from binding food, *ligare*; others because it binds words."[18] Contradictions are similarly encoded in the physical movement of the member that, in the words of Aristotle, is uniquely capable of "advancing and retiring in every direction,"[19] or as one seventeenth-century anatomist put it, "is the onely Muscle of the Body that is the opifex of two contrary motions."[20] Because the tongue can move in and out of the context of the body, and extend not only the linguistic but the material boundaries of the self, it constantly threatens distinctions between the classical and the grotesque body.[21]

Indeed, it is precisely the physical qualities of the tongue, its protean morphologies and contradictory capacities, that are imagined to disrupt dominant social codes emerging from the borders and symmetries of bodily form. The tongue defies the symmetrical logic of visible bodily organs; unlike the eyes, ears, nostrils, lips, and other visible parts that surround it, it has no double, twin, or as one early anatomist put it, it "hath no fellow."[22]

As John Bulwer writes emphatically, "*The tongue of man is not (indeed) double ... as in some Creatures, but simple and only one ...* "[23] In a body that is imagined to be perfectly paired, symmetrical, an image of cosmic and geometric order, the tongue seems, quite literally, a bit out of place.

The combined spatial and mechanical "ambivalence" of the organ easily translated into metaphoric configurations which seemed themselves capable "of advancing and retiring in every direction." Many noted, for example, the way in which the tongue, unlike the ears, hands, and feet, was able to move beyond the bounds of immediate material circumstances, to *literally* affect lives from a distance. As Adams puts it, "The hand spares to hurt the absent, the tongue hurts all.... The hand reacheth but a small compasse, the tongue goes through the world."[24] "It is *parvum,* but *pravum,*" he writes, "little in quantitie, but Great in iniquitie ... [It] hath not straiter limites, then the whole world to walke through."[25] The pedestrian metaphors often invoked to conjure the image of a mobile and independent tongue suggest at once the power and the violent synecdochal function of the unruly organ, emphasizing as much the replacement as the representation of the whole "man" by a singular corporeal part. Indeed, that "ungrateful medling of a busy-body," as Richard Allestree suggested in *The Government of the Tongue* (1674), seems to know no bounds; it travels at once to the furthest reaches of the cosmos and to the most "inward" spaces of the self:

> So unboundedly mischievous is that petulant member, that heaven and earth are not wide enough for its range, but it will find work at home too; and like the viper, that after it had devoured its companions prey'd upon itself, so it corrodes inward, and becomes often as fatal to its owner, as to all the world besides.[26]

Toxic, petulant, and all-consuming, the literal and figurative range of the tongue rendered it particularly suitable for the articulation of collapsing distinctions, be they linguistic, sociopolitical, geographic, or cosmic. Even *discussions* of sins of the tongue tended to generate anxieties about the inability of the very "topic" to fit within a systematic and ordered textual cosmos. While Erasmus's *Lingua* (following Plutarch's *De garrulitate*) is unusually disordered and seemingly endless, Allestree's *Government* begins with a disclaimer: "I shall not attempt a particular discussion of all the vices of the tongue: it doth indeed pass all Geography to draw an exact Map of that *world of iniquity,* as St. *James* calls it."[27]

Fantasies of the tongue's mobility were often explicitly linked to disturbances of social and political order. The capacities of the organ as a *vehicle*, as that which exists to carry and transport, led to its multiple personifications as porters, midwives, footmen, trumpeters, horses, and women, all roles that emphasized the tongue's ordained position to serve the higher-ups.[28] But the "orderly" was always potentially disorderly. The good tongue, according to Thomas Adams, is a "diligent messenger" and performs an "office, not unlike the Towne-clarkes, which if it performe not well, the Corporation is better without it."[29] In Phineas Fletcher's allegorical poem, *The Purple Island* (1633), the organ of taste is "a Groom with wonderous volubilitie," who "Delivers [food] unto neare officers, / Of nature like himself, and like agilitie."[30] Interestingly, the grammatically convenient misogyny that enables the officious organ of taste for Fletcher to be male ("tongue") and the "strange" organ of speech to be female ("lingua") emphasizes a logic of self-estrangement commonly encoded in textual, iconographic, and dramatic representations of male speech in the early modern period.[31]

In the words of Gerhard Richter, "strategic declarations of independence by individual body parts presuppose the prior dismemberment of the self-identical, whole body."[32] Accordingly, I want to suggest, the pervasive images of autonomous speech organs in the early modern period speak not only to conditions of linguistic and cultural fragmentation (what Terence Cave, for example, has called "the fragmentation of the logos")[33] but, more specifically, to conditions of psychic fragmentation, where introjected fantasies of corporeal alienation were that which in many ways secured the possibility of virtuous speech. In a range of early modern texts the tongue was imagined as a literal and symbolic internal *émigré:*[34] as Erasmus suggests, "So let each man say to his tongue whenever it is swept into speech or tickled into calumny, backbiting, and obscenity, 'O my tongue, where are you going? Are you preparing to do good or evil?'"[35] The fact that a conversation with one's tongue was even an imaginative possibility speaks to its status as an alternately scapegoated or sanctified body part. Despite the logistical problems of speaking to an organ of speech, in *The Arbor of Amitie* (1558), Thomas Howell goes so far as to write a poem about "He [who] accuseth his tongue": "Why fearefull tong: what menst thou thus / To fayle, thy maisters paines to paint, / In matters vaine: and frivolous, / Thou runst at rainge: & needes restraint."[36] As the many poems written to or about the disappointing organ suggest, the tongue was often upbraided for thwarting its owner's mastery.[37] Blaming the messenger could not have been more perfectly internalized.

Or indeed, externalized. For the involuntary motions attributed to this significant other might lead some to consider the isomorphic relations between the tongue and the penis, that other bodily member with an apparent will of its own. The relation between "the Egresse of the Tongue out of the mouth and of *Priapisme*," writes John Bulwer, "is a thing of very subtile Speculation":

> [T]he action in kissing, which some beastly Leachers use when their veines are inflate with lust would enduce one to think that there were some analogy between the extension of the two unruly members. The difference between the erection of both parts is that the viril member is not only encreased in length but in thicknesse and compasse: but the Tongue onely in length being not increased in all the dimensions of its body when it goes out of the mouth.[38]

While the two organs here are clearly differentiated, the homology emphasizes the way in which the tongue was imagined as even physiologically "other," as less subject to muscular control than other parts of the body. The increased attention to the muscular structure and the voluntary and involuntary motions of the human body in early modern anatomies led to numerous debates concerning the relationship between "the two unruly members." "[T]here are many that say," reads the first English translation of Berengario's *Microcosmographia* (1664),

> that the Tongue is not moved to the outward parts voluntarily, but meerly naturally from the imagination, as the Yard; and some say that it, and also the Yard are moved of muscles, and of the imagination together, and some of the imagination only, which by means of the spirit causeth a windiness, dilating, and erecting the Yard, and in like manner the Tongue, with bringing it out of the mouth.[39]

The physiology of genital and lingual "dilation" provides a striking analogue to the activity of narration itself ("to dilate" means both "to enlarge" and "to spread abroad or make large," to amplify, to tell).[40] As associations between the tongue and the penis became more explicit in the sixteenth and seventeenth centuries, so too did the imagined relationship between rhetorical and sexual performance.[41] This relationship was, for many midwifes and "gossips," a matter of fact. In Jacques Guillemeau's *Child-Birth* (1612), for example, it is said that

> the Navell must be tyed longer, or shorter, according to the difference of the sexe, allowing more measure to the males: because this length doth make their tongue, and privie members the longer: whereby they may

> both speake the plainer, and be more serviceable to Ladies ... [T]he Gossips commonly say merrily to the Midwife; if it be a boy, *Make him good measure*; but if it be a wench, *Tye it short*.[42]

Lingual and sexual performance, one's ability to speak effectively and "be more serviceable to the Ladies," are here intimately and physiologically entwined.

But such homologies might lead to uncomfortable morphologies: if, as Bulwer writes, the tongue is in some sense *virile* (meaning both manly and hard), it is also often imagined as its opposite, *mulier* (meaning both womanly and soft). The fact that one of the first early modern medical descriptions of the clitoris not only imagined it "as part of woman's 'shameful member' (*membre honteux*)" but as "'a little tongue' (*languette*),"[43] problematizes the gendering of the tongue (or speech itself) as "phallic." Frequently described in medical texts as one of the softest and most shapeless members of "man," and in religious and rhetorical texts as a surprisingly "little" member, the organ surfaces to give the lie to fantasies of phallogocentric self-expansion. Although the tongue is often well endowed with fantasies of insemination and phallic penetration, the "two unruly members" are, of course, very different. Indeed, the fact that the physiology of desire is less subject to the controlling forces of reason and volition than the activity of speech makes early modern configurations of the tongue as "*the* unruly member" all the more conspicuously phantasmatic. As Erasmus wrote, although "the tongue and the genitals [are] the two most rebellious organs ... the tongue ha[s] to be curbed with more care than the genitals."[44] The strategies of coding and "caring" for this most rebellious of members (including its symbolic displacement downward) encoded a logic of most uncomfortable consequences. It is significant in this respect that in early modern literary texts the tongue is an anatomical site frequently marked by loss.[45] If the sinful mouth was often configured as "a magazine of all offensive weapons ... [filled with] *spears and arrows and sharp swords*," the imagined vulnerability of the tongue made it an easy target (as the Malfonts and Pieros and Hieronimos of the period might suggest) for revenge.[46]

For the autonomous organ is also potentially the detached organ, a logic emphasized by a specular economy which, in much early modern literature and iconography, functioned to isolate and shame the extroverted member. The simultaneous strength and vulnerability of that "flabby little organ" is perhaps most spectacularly illustrated by Nicoletto da Modena's early sixteenth-century engraving *Le sort de la langue méchante* (*The fate of the evil tongue*; Figure 4.2). The popularity of the engraving seems to be

4.2 *Le sort de la langue méchante,* 1507 engraving by Nicoletto Rosex da Modena.

suggested both by its unusual number of impressions, as well as by the fact that despite its seemingly unappetizing subject matter, it was reproduced in full color on an Italian majolica plate.[47] The inscription, which reads *Lingua Pravorum Peribit* ("the evil tongue perishes"), is somewhat misleading. For the placement of the organ on an *anvil* under a cluster of blunt-edged instruments suggests that the tongue is as much an object of painstaking reform as it is the subject of brutal attack. While the detached lingua initially seems quite helpless, the two exhausted *putti*, with hammers in hand, speak to the implicit strength of even the dismembered organ. A perfect gloss on the engraving might be a passage from Erasmus's *Lingua*, where he suggests that the punished tongues of slanderers be used to create an antidote to discursive contagion: "If only pills were made of the pounded tongues of slanderers, so that they might aid by this cure those whom they harmed by their poison."[48] Here, as in many texts of the period, the fantasy of muteness and mutilation works apotropaically to ward off the very dangers it represents.

The impulse to take revenge on parts of the body is nowhere more evident than in the spectacular corporeality of the revenge drama of Elizabethan and Jacobean England. While the rupture and consequent scattering of heads, hands, and eyes can be seen to thematize multiple anxieties about integrity and fragmentation, the severing, wounding, or symbolic elaboration of the tongue is a particularly charged form of "mutilation." Recent discussions of lingual dismemberment have focused almost exclusively on the spectacle of Shakespeare's Lavinia and her classical predecessor, Philomel, that mythic figure imagined by many to embody the transcendent power of both female "voice" and poetic subjectivity itself. These arguments, emerging largely out of feminist theory of the past two decades, have tended to read the prototypical severing of female hand and tongue, instruments of self-expression, as indicative of larger strategies of patriarchal self-inscription in early modern Europe.

But while the myth of Philomel clearly influenced Renaissance poets and dramatists, it is suggestive that the grotesque spectacle of the wounded or vulnerable tongue is often relocated, in a broad range of texts, in the male mouth. George Gascoigne's *The Steel Glas* (1576), for example, represents a particularly self-reflexive appropriation of the myth of Philomel. In his text, Satyr (or Satire) turns into Satyra (Satire without a bite, or perhaps more interestingly, without a tongue).[49] The self-proclaimed "hermaphrodite" is raped and mutilated (i.e., tongue cut out) by the "Rayzor of Restraint." Some of the more memorable examples of lingual dismemberment would include the bloody spectacle of Hieronimo in Kyd's *The*

Spanish Tragedy (1586–1587); Piero in Marston's *Antonio's Revenge* (1601) with Antonio holding Piero's tongue sky high, shouting "behold!"; the reconfiguration of the dismemberment of Cicero's hands as a severing of hands and tongue in *The Tragedy of That Famous Roman Orator Marcus Tullius Cicero* (1651);[50] the Duke, with "nailed" and poisoned tongue, and Lussurioso, who expires with the words "my tongue is out of office," in *The Revenger's Tragedy* (1607).[51] Indeed, while the prototypical loss of women's tongues (from Philomel to Lavinia to Saint Christine) is often linked with a birth of "voice," with a *resistance* to the notion that agency is located in a body part, the loss of male tongues is often linked with the death of self.[52]

In many revenges, for example, violence is exacted first on the tongue, then on the heart. As Hieronimo says in the final moments of the 1602 *Spanish Tragedy*, "And now to express the rupture of my part / First take my tongue, and afterward my heart."[53] Here the "rupture of [a] part" articulates at once a condition of bodily and theatrical fragmentation; the loss of a physical organ translates, both linguistically and thematically, into the end of performativity. If, as recent critics have suggested, the heart in early modern literature and iconography was imagined as the ultimate locus of interiority,[54] it may well be true that the tongue was imagined as the ultimate locus of exteriority, as the site where the self was performed, replicated, or to return to the quotation from Abernethy's *The Poysonous Tongue*, "whereby man naturally runneth out in language the *image* of his life." When Volumnia urges Coriolanus to dissemble "with such words that are but roted in / Your tongue, though but bastards, and syllables, / Of no allowance to your bosom's truth,"[55] she is drawing on a series of conventional tropes which locate intention and action, inner and outer, in the heart and tongue respectively.[56]

The commonplace configuration of calumny as a separation of heart from tongue is often taken to a literal extreme in discourses of retaliation against liars, slanderers, scoffers, and abusers of words. Indeed, the fantasy of taking revenge with or upon the organ of speech often marks a desire (in Hieronimo's words) "to express the rupture," to articulate in the strongest possible way the way in which words (quite literally) hurt. To some men, writes Burton in *The Anatomy of Melancholy*,

> a bitter jest, a slander, a calumny, pierceth deeper then any losse, danger, bodily paine, or injury whatsoever; *leviter enim volat,* as *Bernard* of an arrow, *sed graviter vulnerat,* especially if it shall proceed from a virulent tongue, it cuts (saith *David*) *like a two edged sword. They shoot bitter words as arrowes, Psal. 64.3. And they smote with their tongues, Jer. 18.18.* and that so hard, that they leave an incurable wound behind them. Many

men are undone by this meanes, moped, dejected, that they are never to be recovered.[57]

The loss exacted by such a tongue can be revenged, it often seems, only by destroying the physical organ responsible. In *The Taming of the Tongue*, Thomas Adams suggests that "if the depopulation of Countries, if the consuming fires of contention, if the land manured with blood, had a tongue to speake; they would all accuse the *Tongue* for the originall cause of their woe."[58] *All* tragic and inarticulate marks of loss and violation point mutely, according to Adams, to the guilty organ itself.

If the tongue is imagined as the site where discursive and moral contagion begins and ends, it seems logical to detach it in the act of punishing transgression. Not only does the spectacle of the dismembered lingua figure in a range of textual and iconographic warnings against sins of the tongue (following *Proverbs* 10:31, "The mouth of the just bringeth forth wisdom: but the froward tongue shall be cut out"), but representations of these sins tend inevitably to encode a logic of revenge. Despite Erasmus's warning that "it is not Christian to retaliate against evil with evil," his own responses to sins of the tongue are endlessly literal, punitive, retaliatory.[59] He invokes Deuteronomy to justify acts of revenge against the slanderer: "If you loathe the fruit as deadly," he writes in a discussion of blasphemy, "cut away the root."[60] The urge to locate the root of discursive instability in the tongue itself is a way of rendering vulnerable that which is threatening, of rendering concrete, singular, and detachable that which is elusive, abstract, and capable of endless multiplication. The localization of discourse in the organ of speech, in other words, enables the fantasy of location, excision, and—however paradoxically—the fantasy of control.

Deciphering Symptoms

> Symptom (for example, a slip of the tongue) causes discomfort and displeasure when it occurs, but we embrace its interpretation with pleasure; we gladly explain to others the meaning of our slips.
> —Slavoj Žižek, *The Sublime Object of Ideology*

Early modern medical and religious assessments of both the individual and the community often looked to the tongue for symptoms of the condition of the body as a whole. As William Gearing writes in *A Bridle for the Tongue* (1663), "*Physitians take great notice of the tongue, judging thereby of the health or sickness of the body: so our words shew plainly the quality of our souls.*"[61] Or as Erasmus put it, "Doctors infer the symptoms of sickness not only from a man's appearance but also from his tongue. Surely the most reliable symptoms of a sick or healthy mind are in the tongue, which is the appearance of the mind."[62] While a symptom might be described in psychoanalytic terms as "a cyphered, coded message which can be dissolved through interpretation," this particular symptom, at once corporeal and ideological, was endlessly fetishized in ways that seemed to inhibit the very process of interpretation.[63] The energy and attention devoted to the praising and the blaming of this member, I want to argue, is itself symptomatic of broader anxieties about language and representation in the period.

The spectre of monstrous orality haunts a range of early modern texts precisely when questions about the instability of reference seem to be moving, as Jonathan Goldberg and others have argued, from mouth to hand, or more precisely, from tongue to pen to press.[64] The fetishization of the organ of speech in discourses about discourse is perhaps nowhere more explicitly thematized than in Thomas Tomkis's *Lingua, or the Combat of the Tongue and the Five Senses for Superiority* (1607).[65] For this learned and self-reflexive university play not only explores the way in which the "combative" tongue disrupts the symmetries and hierarchies of "Microcosmus" (the body of man in which the play is set) but ultimately reveals the way in which the very member that threatens to steal the show is—in every sense —*made* to steal the show.

As Tomkis's title suggests, the play is about the necessarily combative activities of Lingua, who thrives on pushing others around (this is appropriate enough, given that *verbum*, meaning both word and verb, was often thought to derive from *verberato*, air that has been whipped by the motion of the tongue).[66] The plot hinges on the fact that Lingua (a body part) wants to be granted the title, the privileges, and "the dignitie of a sense" (sig. F3). As the prologue makes clear, however, the play sets out to "*give displeas'd ambitious* Tongue *her due*" (sig. A2) and Lingua's efforts to expand the pentarchy are doomed from the first. Lingua, lacking the sense to know that she does not "have the nature of a sense" (sig. F3), sets out to reconfigure the hierarchy of bodily organization in Microcosmus. Though she hopes to be declared (like hearing, sight, touch, taste, and smell) a sense, she can exist only as a non-sense, as that which defies the logic of body, community, and world.

Indeed, of all the inhabitants of Microcosmus, Lingua is the one who does not seem to know her *place*. While her very first words in the play, "*Auditus,* doe but heare me speak," position her as a vehicle for language and communication, the visual spectacle created by her entrance "*appar-relled in a Crimson Satten gowne*," and by her physical movements dashing in, out, and around the cosmic mouth, continually calls attention to her status as a flamboyant and unruly bodily organ. Always fluctuating between somatic, linguistic, and theatrical "parts," Lingua is endlessly protean, as are fantasies about her generative potential. When Auditus claims, "Words are thy Children, but of my begetting," Lingua, clinging to fantasies of virgin (or parthenogenetic) linguistic births, responds, "Cal'st my unspotted chastity in Question?" (sig. A3) The truth, as she admits in a gesture not unlike Erasmus's Folly, is that she is "wont to lie" (sig. A3). In a soliloquy she boasts of her ability to fascinate the senses: "With sugred words, to delude *Gustus*' taste / And . . . various Dyes, / To draw proud *Visus* . . . [w]ith Civet speach, t'entrap *Olfactus*' nose, / And . . . Silken Eloquence, / To allure the nicer touch of *Tactus* hand" (sig. A4). The flowers and colors and textures of rhetoric are transformed into erotic enticements used to captivate the members of the otherwise homo-sensory world. As the senses later accuse her, she "has made rhetoric wanton" (sig. F3). Indeed, "*Madame Lingua*," as a later university play entitled *Patho-machia* (1630) recollects, "might sue as well for the office of an Affection as of a Sence, for her garrulous, all-daring Ladiship . . . dares lye with everie Man and Woman."[67] Madame Lingua, who lies both ways, becomes the somatic personification of all that is alien and anarchic within this little world of man.

But in a curious displacement, Tomkis's Lingua is punished less for sins of the mouth and tongue than for sins of the pen, the printer, and the text. Throughout the play, the desire to take control of written or textual representation is staged as a misguided desire to take revenge upon the organ of speech. When the senses first formally "accuse *Lingua* of high treason and sacriledge" it is not, interestingly, for treasons against the sentient microcosm or for treasons of speech in particular but rather for treasons "against the most honorable Common-wealth of *letters*; for under pretence of profiting the people with *translations*, shee hath most vilye prostituted the hard misteries of unknowne Languages to the prophane eares of the vulgar" (sig. F3, italics added). Sins of the sign (the translation and dissemination of sacred "letters") are imagined as sins of the tongue, and Lingua is put, in the most literal sense, in her place. Taken out of the circuit of signification, she is reduced to a body part, "commit[ted] to close prison, in Gustus his house . . . under the custody of two strong doores . . . well garded with 30 tall watchmen, without whose licence shee shall by no meanes wagge abroad" (sig. M3). Control of language is here imagined in terms of an elaborate allegory of biting one's tongue; the mouth of the individual becomes a repository for collective anxieties about meaning and representation.

Tomkis is by no means alone in imagining the mouth as a literal prison-house of language. In early modern anatomical texts, philosophical treatises, and conduct books alike, the mouth is positioned as a war zone, with tongue and teeth locked in perennial combat.[68] "Homer implies a great deal," writes Erasmus, "when he speaks of the 'rampart of the teeth,' since the tongue can be disciplined by a bite or wound of the teeth if it disobeys reason. Nature even sets in the front rank the teeth more fitted to wound, which the Greeks call *tomeis* 'incisors' for that reason."[69] Similarly, Richard Brathwait suggests that soldiers "know for what end or purpose the *bars* and *gates* of the *lips* and *teeth* (like a double ward) were ordained to limit or restrain the *Tongue*."[70] Nature, according to Erasmus, Brathwait, and many other early modern anatomists of the word, has encoded mechanisms for censorship into the anatomical structure of man.

What is peculiar about Tomkis's orificial allegory, however, is that the fantasy of the mouth as a site of crime and punishment, of the tongue itself as always already unruly, is exposed as a kind of collective fetish. If a fetish, as Robert J. Stoller writes, "is a story masquerading as an object," then it is all the more poignant that—in the description of Lingua's punishment—the play dramatizes the communal urge in Microcosmus to masquerade the organ *as* an object.[71] For when Lingua leaves the "prison," "whensoever she obtayneth licence to walke abroad," Phantastes suggests that she be made to objectify herself, to wear a garment in the shape of herself, in the shape of a tongue:

> in token the Tongue was the cause of her offence, let her weare a velvet hood, made just in the fashion of a great Tongue, in my conceit 'tis a verye pritty Embleme of a Woman (sig. M3).

A scarlet lingua, the tongue is at once covered and revealed, a fabricated fabricator. The imagined transfiguration of the organ of speech into ladies' clothing, while somewhat tongue in cheek, may well have had analogues in early modern culture. Though one might not normally imagine the tongue as a "pritty Embleme," it was apparently pretty enough for some women to want to wear it on their heads: in *Anthropometamorphosis*, John Bulwer comments on "Our womens French-hoods (that vaine Modell of an unruly member of the Tongue) an abusive invention [that] might be derived from some unicorne-like dress of hair among the Barbarous Indian."[72] The "bar-

4.3 Tongue head-dress from John Bulwer, *Anthropometamorphosis* (London, 1653).

barous" tongue, doubly displaced onto the French and the Indian, is vividly and mimetically illustrated in Bulwer's text, draped quite elegantly over a woman's head (figure 4.3). In an even more explicit commodification of speech, the reference to "any she that wears a tongue in Florence" in Middleton's *Women Beware Women* (or Edward's offer to Isabella to "hang a golden tongue about thy neck, / Seeing thou hast pleaded with so good success," in Marlowe's *Edward II*)[73] alludes to the fact that "jewelry in the shape of tongues was popular at the time."[74] Far-fetched as the aesthetic potential of this organ may be, the equivalence between "taming" and literally clothing the tongue is suggestive. Lingua is not only dressed ("*apparrelled in a Crimson Satten gowne*") but imagined to be *redressed*, covered with a synthetic reproduction of a "great tongue." If, as convention would have it, "language is the dress of thought," one might wonder what thoughts lurk within Lingua's ever-thickening skin.[75]

The fact that Lingua is forced to wear her tongue on her sleeve, I want to suggest, reflects as much a cultural pathology as a condition of representation.[76] While Lingua may seem heavily marked by traditional associations between femininity and masquerade, she is also explicitly fashioned after her *non*-gender specific ancestors, "Rumour" in Shakespeare's *2 Henry IV*, who enters "*painted* full of tongues," and "Report" in Holinshed's *Chronicles*, who enters "apparelled in crimsin sattin full of toongs, sitting on a flieng horse."[77] Throughout the play, Tomkis positions Lingua as less the cause than the *symptom* of chaos and heteroglossia, less the little member that "defileth the whole body" than the little member forced to bear (or *wear*) the weight of a world alienated from itself. Lingua is first and foremost the site upon which anxieties about language, agency, and the articulation of selves are powerfully cathected.

For if Lingua is coded from the first as the one inhabitant of Microcosmus who doesn't seem to know her place, it is not long before we see just how illogical and unstable all forms of communication are in Microcosmus. The play stages not only the chaos of sentience (e.g., Auditus goes deaf, Memory forgets, Tactus is unable to find a girl) but also the chaos of signification. Memory has become so crowded with bits and pieces of culture that he has lost his sense of history: as he says, "A dog cannot pisse in a Noblemans shoe, but it must be sprinkled into the Chronicles, so that I never could remember my Treasure more full, & never emptier of honorable, and true heroycall actions." And Mendacio, Lingua's "page," not only claims authorship of all true history but confounds distinctions between speech and writing:

> O those two Bokes *De Vera historia*, however they go under his name, Ill be sworne I writ them every title. I must confesse I would faine have logged *Stow* and great *Hollings-head* on their elbowes, when they were about their Chronicles, and as I remember Sir *John Mandevills* travells, and a great part of the *Decads* were of my doing. But for the mirror of Knight-hood, *Bevis of Southampton, Palmerin* of *England, Amadis* of *Gaul, Huon de Burdeaux,* Sir *Guy* of *Warwick, Martin marprellate, Robin-hood, Garragantua, Gorilion* and a thousand such exquisite monuments as these, no doubt but they breath on my breath (sig. D1).

A thousand monuments breathing on the breath of a page; here textuality and orality are explicitly linked. The crowded world of Microcosmus itself, with its fragments of history, language, clothes, text, and dates, is a world in bits and pieces reconfigured, synecdochally, as a body whole and in parts. If the ambivalent signs of authorship, of history and fiction, truth and lies, seem somewhat remote from the fantasies of lingual dominance or "superiority" with which the play begins, that is precisely Tomkis' point: the play critiques the notion that, in a world marked by the circulation of written and printed words, the tongue is still the primary agent of representation. Even Phantastes, the creative force in the body of man, works not for poet but for printer: "were it not that I pitty the poore multitude of Printers, these Sonnet-mungers should starve for conceits" (sig. D2).

The fantasy of specifically oral dominance in what was now becoming a heavily textualized culture is a fantasy that marks not only *Lingua* but a range of early modern dramatic and nondramatic texts. The invocation of the mobile and independent tongue (the agent of speech) in written texts and contexts, I want to suggest, constitutes less what Walter Ong has termed "*residual* orality," the rhetorical traces and aftermaths of an oral culture,[78] but an *aggressive* orality, an anxious response to the unsettling dispersion of languages and identities in an increasingly textualized culture, a response to the movement of representation away from the body. Indeed, the circulation and multiple fabrications of tongues in fashion, on bodies, out of place, out of context, proliferate at a time when the tongue is in many senses "out of office." The tongue, paradoxically enough, seems to matter more and more when its relation to the making and destruction of culture seems to matter less and less.

Indeed, Marshall McLuhan's and Elizabeth Eisenstein's arguments about the increasing textualization of early modern culture are perhaps all the more suggestive in terms of the insistence in a broad range of early modern texts on what may be imagined as the inherent orality of textuality.[79] Many early modern writers and grammarians took pains to assert the absolute primacy of the spoken over the written. According to Ben Jonson, for example, voice precedes writing: "Grammar is the art of true and well-speaking a language: the writing is but an Accident."[80] Or even more to the point: "The one purpose of grammar is to speak correctly, nor does it require writing. For the writing is dependent on the voice, nor should we write differently from what we speak."[81] What is suggestive about these statements is the way in which the phonocentric is insistently mapped onto the graphocentric, the spoken onto the written, the fleshly onto the linguistic. In *The Paradoxical Discourses of F. M. Van Helmont, Concerning the Macrocosm and Microcosm, or the Greater and Lesser World, and their Union* (1685), the dependence of writing on the voice is carried to a literal extreme in an astonishing fantasy about the specifically *lingual* nature of all scripted text:

> The Tongue . . . is as a Spunge moving and turning itself to all parts of the Mouth, destined for the forming of all living Images and Letters, and the sounds of them in the mouth; as we may see in the printed Hebrew Letters, that they have the same figure and form as they were shaped and formed by the Tongue in the Mouth, especially when anyone is forced to speak loud to another at a distance.[82]

Here, Hebrew letters are imagined to be based upon the literal shape of the tongue in the act of speech. The imposition of orality onto textuality in many ways constitutes a resistance to the graphic, the decontextualized word, or in more broadly cultural terms, to what McLuhan has famously termed the "making of typographical man." For in this early modern text, typographical man is always already made. And it is the tongue, the "spunge moving and turning itself to all parts of the Mouth," that is at the very basis of both the form and the forming "of all living Images and Letters."

Notes

For their generous and thoughtful comments on this essay, I would like to thank Brad Epps, Marjorie Garber, Stephen Greenblatt, David Hillman, Jeffrey Masten, Susie Phillips, Linda Schlossberg, Peter Stallybrass, and Eric Wilson.

1. Erasmus, *Lingua*, 365. All references to Erasmus's *Lingua* (trans. Elaine Fantham) will be from *Collected Works of Erasmus*, ed. Elaine Fantham and Erika Rummel (Toronto: University of Toronto, 1989). Erasmus continues, "The tongue is Ate, strife personified, if it lacks a pilot. It is a horn of plenty, if you use it well. It is Eris, rouser of quarrels, but the same tongue is Grace, who wins good will.... It overthrows city-states and kingdoms, but it also founds and establishes them." See Fantham for the translation and dissemination of *Lingua* in the sixteenth and seventeenth centuries.

    Given the theoretical attention to the social encoding of bodily orifices and emissions in anthropology (Douglas, Frazer), psychoanalysis (Freud, Klein, Winnicott, Lacan), literary and cultural criticism (Elias, Bakhtin, Bataille), and in early modern studies in particular (Woodbridge, Stallybrass and White), it is curious that more attention has not been given to symbolics of the member that not only inhabits the oral cavity but is a primary participant in the production of speech, the experience of taste, and the consumption of food. My own thinking about the complex function of the tongue in the early modern period is in many ways indebted to the following articles: Peter Stallybrass, "Reading the Body and the Jacobean Theater of Consumption," in *Staging the Renaissance: Reinterpretations of Elizabethan and Jacobean Drama*, ed. David Scott Kastan and Peter Stallybrass (New York: Routledge, 1991), 210–20; J.L. Simmons, "The Tongue and its Office in *The Revenger's Tragedy*," in *PMLA* 92 (1977): 56–68; Lynda E. Boose, "Scolding Brides and Bridling Scolds: Taming the Woman's Unruly Member," in *Materialist Shakespeare: A History*, ed. Ivo Kamps (London: Verso, 1995), 239–79; and Patricia Parker, "On the Tongue: Cross Gendering, Effeminacy, and the Art of Words," *Style* 23 (1989): 445–63.

2. According to Proverbs (18:21), "Death and life *are* in the power of the tongue: and they that love it shall eat the fruit thereof."

3. In John Rider's *Bibliotheca Scholastica* (London, 1589), the words *lingua, glossa,* and *glottis* are all found under the same heading, "*A tongue: also a speach, or language.*" And in John Florio's *Queen Anna's New World of Words* (London, 1611), "Lingua" is defined as follows: "*a tongue in generall. Also a language or speach.*"

4. In early modern texts, the tongue is at once synecdochal (for personal and political bodies) and metonymic (for individual and communal discourse). While the metonymic function which associates tongue with speech or language may seem dominant in a phrase such as "my name is tost & censured by many tongues," the synecdochal function, which associates tongue with physical body, is also often powerfully invoked. In *Directions for Speech and Style* (1600), John Hoskyns offers the phrase as an example not of metonymy but of

synecdoche: "my name is tost & censured by many tongues for manye men where the part of an entire bodye goes for the whole." Cited in Sister Miriam Joseph, *Shakespeare's Use of the Arts of Language* (New York: Columbia University Press, 1944), 315.

5. Erasmus, *Lingua*, 323.

6. George Wither, *Collection of Emblemes, Ancient and Modern* (London, 1635).

7. See Claude Paradin, *Devises Heroïques* (Lyon, 1551), 62, and Georgette de Montenay, *Emblemes, ou, Devises Chrestiennes* (Lyon, 1571), 25. In contrast to the commonplace iconography of discursive misrule, the idealized dominance of hand over tongue, act over speech, is brilliantly configured in an emblem in Ottavio Scarlatini's *Homo et ejus partes figuratus et symbolicus* (Bologna, 1684), which pictures a conventionally allegorized hand of God descending from the clouds holding an astonishingly grotesque and realistically depicted dismembered tongue (185). I want to thank Peter Stallybrass for calling Scarlatini's text to my attention.

8. Thomas Adams, *The Taming of the Tongue*, in *The Workes of Tho. Adams. Being the Summe of His Sermons, Meditations, and Other Divine and Morall Discourses* (London, 1629), 143, 148.

9. Adams, *The Taming of the Tongue*, 143–44.

10. Adams, *The Taming of the Tongue*, 149.

11. On the positioning of subject and object in early modern studies, see *Subject and Object in Renaissance Culture*, ed. Margreta de Grazia, Maureen Quilligan, and Peter Stallybrass (Cambridge: Cambridge University Press, 1996). A suggestive gloss on the vexed status of the tongue as subject and object, as a primary organ of self-articulation and self-alienation, might be Augusta Bonnard's theory that the "metapsychological neglect of the tongue" in psychoanalytic considerations of the relation between the oral drive and psychic organization conceals the significance of the tongue as "the primal organizer of the self, [and] ... as a primal bridge in the combined subject-object relationship." See Bonnard, "The Primal Significance of the Tongue," *International Journal of Psychoanalysis*, Vol 6 (April 1925): 301–7.

12. Adams, *The Taming of the Tongue*, 143.

13. Adams, *The Taming of the Tongue*, 145.

14. The independent and magical properties of the tongue, common in religion, folklore and mythology of the Renaissance, have their roots in biblical and classical sources. As one critic writes in *The Encyclopedia of Religion and Ethics*, ed. James Hastings (New York: Scribner's Sons, 1928), "Since the nervous system and the minuter structure of the tissues were unknown to the ancients, the tongue was thought to possess an *inherent* faculty of speech, as something residing in it, so that the faculty or its special qualities could be transferred by acquisition or assimilation of the tongues of specially gifted animals or men" (384). Traces of ancient rituals and mythologies are present in a number of early modern texts where one's consumption of (or mere proximity to) a par-

ticularly "gifted" organ of speech is imagined to confer the gift of eloquence. See for example, *A Hermeticall Banquet, drest by a spagiricall cook for the better preservation of the microcosm* (London, 1652). I would like to thank Anne Lake Prescott for calling this text to my attention.

15. John Abernethy, *The Poysonous Tongue* (1622), italics added, quoted in John Spargo, *Juridical Folklore in England: Illustrated by the Cucking Stool* (Durham: Duke University Press, 1944), 116.

16. Richard Ward, for example, writes in *A Treatise of the Nature, Use, and Abuse of the Tongue and Speech* (London, 1673),

> God doth nothing in vaine, and therefore he would have the sons of men to anatomize the *tongue*, and to read some profitable Lecture upon every particle thereof: *e.g.*, I. The *tongue* is placed in the head, in the midst of the senses; to teach us, that our words must be wise, grave, weighty, and discreet. II. The *tongue* is hedged, or fenced in with a double wall; *viz.* of earth and of Stone; the Lips being as the earthen wall, the Teeth as a stone wall, to teach us that we must set a watch over our Lips, and keep our *tongues* as with a bridle.... III. The *tongue* is simple and undivided: men not being like *Serpents* double or cloven tongued.... IV. The *tongue* is tied below, but hath no ligaments above; to teach us, that our *tongues* must be more prone and ready to speak of heavenly and celestiall things than of terrestrial and earthly.... V. The *tongue* is of a soft, not hard ... to teach us, that our words must be mild, soft, gentle, and not proud, reproachfull, cruel, distainfull and the like ... (169–70).

This anatomizing of parts and "particles" was commonplace throughout the sixteenth and early seventeenth centuries. The anatomizing of the tongue in particular is parodied in the *Anatomy of a Woman's Tongue, Divided Into Five Parts: A Medicine, a Poison, a Serpent, Fire and Thunder* (London, 1638). On the pervasiveness of anatomical tropes in the early modern period, see Jonathan Sawday, *The Body Emblazoned: Dissection and the Human Body in Renaissance Culture* (London: Routledge, 1995) and Devon L. Hodges, *Renaissance Fictions of Anatomy* (Amherst: University of Massachusetts Press, 1985).

17. William Gearing, *A Bridle for the Tongue: or a treatise of ten Sins of the Tongue. Cursing, Swearing, Slandering, Scoffing, Filthy Speaking, Flattering, Censuring, Murmuring, Lying and Boasting, Shewing* (London, 1663). "Man hath many importers," he writes, "his ears, his eyes, and all his senses in their several employments, but only one exporter, *the Tongue,* and that finds work enough to utter all their reports" (Sig. A3).

18. Isidore of Seville, *De hominis et portentis* (On man and monsters), from *Etymologaiae XI*, trans. William D. Sharpe. *Isidore of Seville: The Medical Writings* in *Transactions of the American Philosophical Society* 54, no. 2 (1964): 41. Similarly, the seventeenth-century anatomist Alexander Read writes that, "First, [the tongue] is the instrument of tasting: Secondly, it uttereth speech: Thirdly,

it helpeth the chewing of meat, by tossing of it to and fro, and turning it down to the stomack, Fourthly, it serveth for licking, from whence in Latin, it is called *Lingua a liguendo* from licking." *Manual of the Anatomy and Dissection of the Body of Man*, 6th ed. (London, 1658), 255. Similarly, in *De Proprietatibus Rerum* (London, 1582), Stephen Batman points out that "the tongue is called Lingua in Latin and hath that name of Lingere, to lycke: for it licketh meate." Also, Leonardo da Vinci writes of "the office of the tongue," "The tongue is employed in the pronunciation and articulation of the syllables, the component parts of all words. Further, the tongue acts in the necessary turnings of the masticated food . . . " *Leonardo on the Human Body*, translations, text, and introduction by Charles D. O'Malley and J. B. de C. M. Saunders (New York: Dover, 1983), 93, 492. The very word "Lingua," for some, emphasized the sensory pleasures of enunciation (as if language and letters were a kind of food to be savored); of the letter "L" Ben Jonson writes in *The English Grammar* (1640), "Lingua, palatoque dulcescit" ("L sweetens on the tongue and palate"), ed. Alice Vinton Waite (New York: Sturgis & Walton, 1909), 41.

19. Aristotle, *De Partibus Animalum*, trans. W. Ogle (London, 1882), 53.

20. John Bulwer, *Pathomyatomia or a Dissection of the Significative muscles of the Affections of the Mind* (London, 1649), 232.

21. Gail Kern Paster, Peter Stallybrass, Stephen Greenblatt, and others have explored the somatic dimensions of early modern social topography, the extent, for example, to which "behavior manuals of the fifteenth through eighteenth centuries return again and again to codes elaborated for the management of the body's products: urine, feces, mucus, saliva, and wind." Stephen Greenblatt, "Filthy Rites," *Daedalus* 111 (1982): 2. On the relation between the classical and the grotesque body, see Mikhail Bakhtin, *Rabelais and His World*, trans. Helene Iswolsky (Bloomington: Indiana University Press, 1984). Also see Norbert Elias, *The History of Manners*, trans. Edmund Jephcott (New York: Pantheon, 1978) and *The Civilizing Process*, trans. Edmund Jephcott (New York: Pantheon, 1978).

22. Bulwer, *Pathomyatomia*, 232.

23. John Bulwer, *Anthropometamorphosis: Man Transform'd: or, The Artificial Changling* (London, 1653), 233.

24. Adams, *The Taming of the Tongue*, 152.

25. Adams, *The Taming of the Tongue*, 146.

26. Richard Allestree, *The Government of the Tongue* (Oxford, 1674), 108, 155.

27. Allestree, *The Government of the Tongue*, 11.

28. See, for example, Spenser's *Faerie Queene*, 2.9.Sts. 25–26; Sidney's *Astrophil and Stella*, 37; Shakespeare's *Coriolanus*, 1.1; Phineas Fletcher's *The Purple Island*, canto 5, st. 56.

29. Adams, *The Taming of the Tongue*, 144.

30. Phineas Fletcher, *The Purple Island* (1633), in *The Poems of Phineas Fletcher, B.D.*, ed. Alexander B. Grosart (London, 1869), Canto 2, st.31.

31. On Lingua as a "pratling wife," see the Fletcher quote that serves as one of the epigraphs to this essay. Patricia Parker and Lynda Boose have recently discussed the extent to which the shame associated with unruly and disordered speech in the early modern period was gendered feminine. The pathologized figures of the scold and the effeminate man in many ways encapsulate the commonplace link between transgressions of speech and transgressions of gender. What I would like to emphasize, however, is the way in which the location of the unruly tongue in the female or effeminate mouth was part of a broader logic of self-estrangement systematically encoded in representations of speech in the period. For a discussion of the intensified efforts to tame the female tongue in early modern England (and of the specifically feminine spaces within which all shame was inscribed), see Lynda E. Boose, "Scolding Brides and Bridling Scolds: Taming the Woman's Unruly Member." Boose argues that in social practices of early modern England, while the verbal transgressions of women were spectacularly punished, disciplinary rituals for men "did not spectacularize or carnivalize the male body so as to degrade it to nearly the same extent" (249). Also see Patricia Parker, "On the Tongue: Cross Gendering, Effeminacy, and the Art of Words."

32. Gerhard Richter, "The Monstrosity of the Body in Moscow Diary," *Modern Language Studies* 25, no. 4 (1995): 119.

33. Terence Cave, *The Cornucopian Text: Problems of Writing in the French Renaissance* (Oxford: Clarendon Press, 1979).

34. On the vernacular in early modern England as itself an "internal *émigré*," see Stephen Mullaney, "Strange Things, Gross Terms, Curious Customs: The Rehearsal of Cultures in the Late Renaissance," in *Representing the English Renaissance*, ed. Stephen Greenblatt (Berkeley: University of California Press, 1988), 65–92. On the tongue as a specifically national trope, see Carla Mazzio, "Parting Words: Language and Nation in *The Spanish Tragedy*," forthcoming in *Studies in English Literature* (Spring, 1998).

35. Erasmus, *Lingua*, 366.

36. Thomas Howell, *The Arbor of Amitie, wherin is comprised pleasant Poems and pretie Poesies* (London, 1568).

37. See also Robert Toste, "A slow soft Tongue betokens Modestie," in *The Blazon of Jealousie* (London, 1615); Thomas Drant, "Study godliness: Charme thy tongue," in *Epigrams and sentences spirituall* (London, 1568); John Lyly, "My hart and tongue were twinnes, at once conceaved," in *The Complete Works of John Lyly* (Oxford: Clarendon Press, 1902); James Yates, "A Sonnet of a slaunderous tongue," in *The Castell of Courtesie* (London, 1582); Thomas Tusser, "A sonet against a slanderous tongue," in *Five hundred pointes of good Husbandrie* (London, 1580).

38. Bulwer, *Pathomyatomia*, 231, 230. As Bulwer's text suggests, anatomists argued a great deal about the physiology of sticking out one's tongue: "[It is for] good reason," writes Bulwer in *Pathomyatomia*, "we fall to staggering when wee would know after what manner this action of the Tongue is done":

> In *Derision, Scoffing, insultation* and contumelious Despight men are seen sometimes to lill out their tongue at those they Scoff & deride.

> Concerning this significant motion of the Tongue *Averroes* is of the opinion that it is not done by the aid of the Muscles, but by a proper motion, and would prove thereby that the Nerve and not the Muscle is the first and necessary principle of motion. But *Columbus* and most Anatomists are of the contrary opinion. *Galen* indeed is very Scepticall about this motion and hath placed it among doubtfull and obscure motions which he was not well satisfied in: for sayes he, the Tonge doth not seeme when it is extended out in length to go uniformely out of the mouth, for it covers the lower Lip and descends somewhat to the Chin, and that is by reason of the Bridle which is beneath it before, we find not the cause by reason whereof the Tongue is prolix or prolonged untill it be visibly put out of the mouth (228–29).

39. Berengario, *Microcosmographia: Or, A Description of the Body of Man: Being a Practical Anatomy, Shewing The Manner of Anatomizing from Part to Part; The like hath not been set forth in the English Tongue* (London, 1664).

40. Definition from John Rider's *Bibliotheca Scholastica* (London, 1589), Scholar Press Facsimile (Menston: Scholar Press, 1970). The physical and linguistic activity of "dilation" provides a rather suggestive gloss on Iago's "close dilations." On the rhetorical and juridical senses of "dilation" in Shakespeare, see Patricia Parker, "Shakespeare and Rhetoric: 'Dilation' and 'Delation' in *Othello*," in *Shakespeare and the Question of Theory*, ed. Patricia Parker and Geoffrey Hartman (New York: Routledge, 1985), 54–74.

41. As Wayne Rebhorn has recently noted, "when the Renaissance orator speaks, his words invade and possess, impregnate and inseminate—indeed rape—an audience composed primarily of men and boys." *The Emperor of Men's Minds: Literature and the Renaissance Discourse of Rhetoric* (Ithaca: Cornell University Press, 1995), 171. The eroticized and heavily gendered *metaphorics* of discursive penetration, I hope to suggest, had as its counterpart the literal contours, homologies, and motions of the anatomical subject.

42. Jacques Guillemeau, *Child-Birth, or, the happy delivery of women* (London, 1612), 99. Quoted in Gordon Williams, *A Dictionary of Sexual Language and Imagery in Shakespearean and Stuart Literature* (London: Athlone, 1994). Gordon Williams also offers the following quote from Fletcher's *Beggars Bush* (1620), "I took him and I graspt him by the by the codds; Betwixt his tongue and his taile I left litle odds."

43. The description is from Charles Estienne's *Dissection of the Parts of the Human Body* (1546), quoted in Katharine Park, "The Rediscovery of the Clitoris: French Medicine and the *Tribade*, 1570–1620," in this volume. The gendering of the tongue in terms of genital anatomy is by no means unproblematic. Frankie Rubinstein invokes the following example under the bawdy senses of "tongue" from Oldham's *Upon the Author of a Play Call'd Sodom*: "Sure Nature made, or meant at least t'have don't, / Thy Tongue a Clytoris, thy Mouth a cunt." *A Dictionary of Shakespeare's Sexual Puns and Their Significance* (London: Macmillan, 1984), 278.

44. Erasmus, *Lingua*, 367.

45. As Judith Butler, revisiting the theories of Freud and Lacan, writes, "[I]f men are said to 'have' the phallus symbolically, their anatomy is also a site marked by having lost it; the anatomical part is never commensurable with the phallus itself." Butler, *Bodies That Matter: On the Discursive Limits of "Sex"* (New York: Routledge, 1993), 85.

46. Allestree, *The Goverment of the Tongue.*

47. For a brief description of *le sort de la langue mechante* and other works by Nicoletto da Modena, see Mark J. Zucker, *Early Italian Masters*, in *The Illustrated Bartsch*, vol. 13, Pt. 2 (New York: Abaris Books, 1984).

48. Erasmus, *Lingua*, 321.

49. George Gascoigne, *The Steele Glas: a satyre* (London, 1576).

50. *The Tragedy of That Famous Roman Orator Marcus Tullius Cicero* (London, 1651). I thank Dale Randall for calling this play to my attention.

51. *The Revenger's Tragedy* (5.3.79), ed., Brian Gibbons (New York: Norton, 1991).

52. For other failed attempts to locate discursive agency in the female organ of speech, see *A Hertfordshire Miracle* (London, 1606), in which a woman who witnesses a murder has her tongue cut out, but who four years later manages to "perfectly speaketh, revealing the Murther, having no tongue to be seen ... " Also see Christine de Pizan's *Cité des Dames*, in which Saint Christine is tortured, mutilated, and though her tongue is cut, she not only continues to speak, scolding her torturer, but *blinds* him by spitting the remains of her tongue in his eye. And on the powerful resistance of the brutally anatomized organ, see *The Anatomy of A Woman's Tongue, Divided Into Five Parts: A Medicine, a Poison, a Serpent, Fire, and Thunder* (London, 1638).

53. Thomas Kyd, *The Spanish Tragedy*, ed. J. R. Mulryne (London: A & C Black, 1989).

54. See, for example, Eric Jager, "The Book of the Heart: Reading and Writing the Medieval Subject," *Speculum* 71 (1996): 1–26; Jacques Le Goff, "Head or Heart? The Political Use of Body Metaphors in the Middle Ages," *Fragments for a History of the Human Body*, ed, Michel Feher with Ramona Naddaff and Nadia Tazi, 3 (1989): 12–27; Peter Stallybrass, "Dismemberments and Re-Memberments: Rewriting the *Decameron*, 4.1, in the English Renaissance," *Studi Sul Bocaccio*, 20 (1991): 299–323;

55. Shakespeare, *Coriolanus* (3.2.53–57), *The Riverside Shakespeare*, ed. G. Blakemore Evans (New York: Houghton Mifflin, 1974).

56. On the trope of the heart and tongue, see John L. Harrison's "The Convention of Heart and Tongue and the Meaning of *Measure for Measure*," *Shakespeare Quarterly* 5 (1954): 1–10.

57. Robert Burton, *The Anatomy of Melancholy* (Oxford: Clarendon Press, 1989), 339.

58. Adams, *The Taming of the Tongue*, 148.

59. Erasmus, *Lingua,* 335.

60. Ibid., 333.

61. Gearing. *A Bridle for the Tongue* (sig. A4). Similarly, in *The Ladies Calling* (Oxford, 1673), Richard Brathwait reads the "great indecency of loquacity ... [as] a symptom of a loose, impotent soul, a kind of incontinence of the mind." *The Whole Duty of a Woman: Female Writers in Seventeenth-Century England,* ed. Angeline Goreau (New York: Doubleday, 1985), 11.

62. Erasmus, *Lingua,* 326.

63 Slavoj Žižek, *The Sublime Object of Ideology* (London: Verso, 1989), 73.

64. Jonathan Goldberg, *Writing Matter: From the Hands of the English Renaissance* (Stanford: Stanford University Press, 1990).

65. Thomas Tomkis, *Lingua. or the Combat of the Tongue and the five Senses for Superiority* (London, 1607), ed. John Farmer (Amersham: Tudor Facsimile Reprints, 1913). This academic play seems to have been popular, notes Farmer, because other editions surfaced in 1610, 1617, 1622, 1632, and 1657.

66. Jane Donawerth refers to this etymology in Marius Servius' *Commentarius.* See her discussion of the material origins of language in sixteenth century thought in *Shakespeare and the Sixteenth Century Study of Language* (Chicago: University of Illinois Press, 1984), 16–17.

67. *Pathomachia Or, The Battell of Affections. Shadowed by a Faigned Siedge of the Citie Pathopolis* (London, 1630). Also published as *Loves Loade-Stone* (London, 1616), 31.

68. In a suggestive gender coding of the dental guards, Isidore of Seville notes, "Gender determines the number of teeth, for they are thought to be more numerous in men, fewer in women" (*De hominis et portentis,* 42). The implication here seems to be that all women, like Chaucer's Wife of Bath, are potentially "gap toothed."

69. Erasmus, *Lingua,* 268. Similarly, in Fletcher's *Purple Island,* Lingua is imagined to conspire against the forces of nature and creation: although the "great Creator" set "twice sixteen guarders, / Whose hardened temper could not soon be mov'd," "such strange force hath her enchanting art / That she hath made her keepers, of her part, / And they to all her flights all furtherance impart" (156–57).

70. Richard Brathwait, *The English Gentleman* (London, 1633).

71. Robert J. Stoller, *Observing the Erotic Imagination* (New Haven: Yale University Press, 1985), 155. Quoted in Marjorie Garber, *Vested Interests: Cross-Dressing and Cultural Anxiety* (New York: Routledge, 1992), 118.

72. Bulwer, *Anthropometamorphosis,* 455.

73. Christopher Marlowe, *Edward II* (1.4.330–34), in *Christopher Marlowe: The Complete Plays* (London: Penguin, 1969).

74. Roma Gill, editor of the New Mermaids edition of Middleton's *Women Beware Women* (New York: Norton, 1968). Gill reads the comment "Sir, I could give as

shrewd a lift to chastity / As any she that wears a tongue in Florence" in terms of the literal commodification of eloquence.

75. The phrase, which sums up a commonplace of classical rhetoric, comes from Neil Rhode's *The Power of Eloquence and the English Renaissance* (New York: Harvester Wheatsheaf, 1992), 184.

76. As Peter Stallybrass writes in "Worn Worlds: Clothes and Identity on the Renaissance Stage," in *Subject and Object in Renaissance Culture*, "On the Renaissance stage, the transmission of cloth figures the formation and dissolution of identity, the ways in which the subject is possessed and dispossessed, touched and haunted by the materials it inhabits" (289–320).

77. Holinshead, *Chronicles* (3.849/1) (1577–1587).

78. Walter Ong, "Oral Residue in Tudor Prose Style," *PMLA* 80 (1965): 145–54. See also his *Orality and Literacy: Technologizing of the Word* (New York: Methuen, 1982), 115.

79. See Elizabeth L. Eisenstein, *The Printing Press as an Agent of Change: Communications and Cultural Transformations in Early-Modern Europe* (Cambridge: Cambridge University Press, 1979), and Marshall McLuhan, *The Gutenberg Galaxy: The Making of Typographical Man* (Toronto: University of Toronto, 1962).

80. Jonson, *The English Grammar*, 3.

81. Ibid., 2.

82. *The Paradoxical Discourses of F. M. Van Helmont, Concerning the Macrocosm and Microcosm, or the Greater and Lesser World, and their Union* (London, 1685), 56–7. I thank David Hillman for calling this passage to my attention.

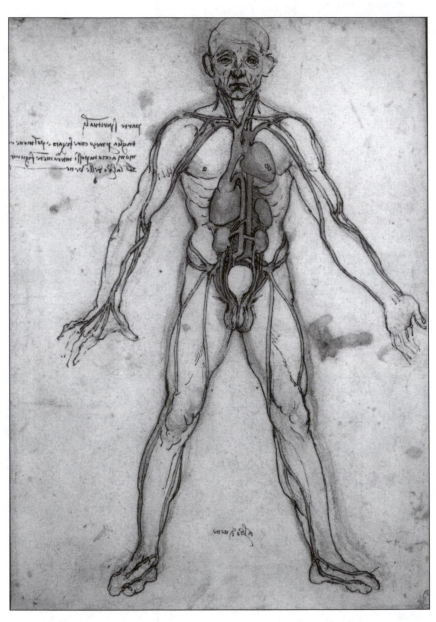

5. Anatomical figure from Leonardo da Vinci, *The Anatomy Notebooks* (circa 1500).

5

Visceral Knowledge

Shakespeare, Skepticism, and the Interior
of the Early Modern Body

DAVID HILLMAN

Othello: By heaven, I'll know thy thoughts.
Iago: You cannot, if my heart were in your hand.
—*Othello*

To begin with a simple observation: Shakespeare's plays are suffused with references to human entrails. While there are of course several plays in the Shakespearean canon in which the body's internal organs are barely mentioned, there are also in this corpus quite a few works that are preoccupied with an imagination of the visceral interior of the human body. The question of why this should be so is the point of origin, and the subject, of this essay. The plays I discuss at some length below—*Troilus and Cressida, Hamlet, The Winter's Tale*—seem to me to be important places to begin to examine Shakespeare's understanding of corporeal inwardness.[1]

As I understand it, the problem of knowledge of or access to the viscera is intimately tied in Shakespeare's plays to the skeptical problem of other minds. Skepticism—conceived of here as the motivated doubting of the possibility of knowledge of and by the other—can, I suggest, be understood in terms of one's relation to entrails.[2] For the skeptic, according to Stanley Cavell, the potential gap between the private, interior self and its external expression (in words, gestures, or actions) typically takes on spatial, corporeal dimensions: self and other are both sundered into an inside and an outside, with an ever-present potential for a breach between the two.[3] The sense of the hiddenness of the other to one's self is the source of what I take to be a central drive of skepticism—the drive to access the interior of the body of the other. If entrails are where the other's innermost truth is imagined to be located or guaranteed, the skeptic appears to be searching out this ulterior truth *within* the body, beyond the veils of its surface.[4] Several of Shakespeare's characters seem to imagine that penetrating the other's body would somehow solve the riddle of knowing the other; several of Shakespeare's plays question and problematize this notion, while at the same time allocating to the body's interior a decisive place in the comprehension of subjectivity.

The problem of other minds is, in such an account, very much a problem of other bodies. Indeed, the materialist habits of early modern thought, so well documented in recent years, must have lent a particular urgency to questions of bodily interiority. For the men and women of early modern Europe, the latter seems to have been practically inseparable from spiritual inwardness. The idea that important truths lie hidden within the body— "in [one's] *bowels*," as Donne put it, "as *gold* in a *Mine*"[5]—would have seemed entirely reasonable in this period. Virtue and sin, for example, were often imagined as literally inhabiting bodily innards, and the idea of personhood, and personality, was never far from the question of the internal composition (or "complexion") of the body: the Galenic regime of humoral physiology, as Gail Kern Paster has written, "locate[s] a form of selfhood, analogous with agency, within."[6]

The early modern understanding of physiology included detailed categorizations and interpretations of each specific internal organ.[7] Side by side with this view, however, the interior of the torso was often thought of in the early modern period as a single part, "the Arke or Chest of the spiritual members of man."[8] Indeed, Shakespeare, while to some extent differentiating heart from liver from womb from bowels (and so on), tends to treat the body's interior as a thing in and of itself, closer to the biblical idea of the "inward parts" or "hidden part" of the body than to any more detailed medical or philosophical categorization. As Katharine Eisaman Maus has recently argued about the period more generally: "In vernacular sixteenth- and early seventeenth-century speech and writing, the whole interior of the body—heart, liver, womb, bowels, kidneys, gall, blood, lymph—quite often involves itself in the production of the mental interior, of the individual's private experience."⁹

Selfhood and materiality, then, were ineluctably linked in the pre-Cartesian belief systems of the period, which preceded, for the most part, any attempt to separate the vocabulary of medical and humoral physiology from that of individual psychology.[10] When, therefore, characters on the early modern stage speak of "my heart's core, ay ... my heart of heart" (*Hamlet*, 3.2.73), or of "the heat of our livers" (*2 Henry IV* 1.2.175)—or, indeed, of being "inward search'd" (*Merchant of Venice* 3.2.86) or afflicted with "inward pinches" (*Tempest* 5.1.77)—we would do well to regard these as far from merely metaphorical referents, and to try to discover how they figure into an overall understanding of bodily—and therefore psychological—interiority in a given play.[11] For the inner world of the human frame remained very much on center stage throughout the early modern period, a period that witnessed remarkable advances in the scientific comprehension of human anatomy and physiology from Vesalius to Harvey, and at the same time saw an extraordinary level of attention directed to the body's interior by, among others, artists as different as Leonardo da Vinci and Hieronymus Bosch, writers such as Donne, Burton, and Montaigne, and even monarchs such as Elizabeth I: "I know that I have the body but of a weak and feeble woman," declared the latter, famously, "but I have the heart and stomach of a king, and a king of England, too."[12]

Writers and thinkers during the hundred or so years from the early sixteenth to the early seventeenth century were so frequently preoccupied with such imagery that we could almost go so far as to call this, only slightly hyperbolically, the visceral century. As Jonathan Sawday has recently emphasized, the period witnessed the rise of a culture in which the opening of the human body was considered a central act in the obtainment of knowledge:[13] "Some so desire to *know*," wrote John Davies of Hereford,

> that faine they would
> Breake through the *Bounde* that *humane knowledge* barres,
> To pry into His *brest* which doth infold
> *Secrets* unknowne.[14]

The rise of the protomodern science of anatomy allowed the interior of the body during these years to become the site of a rapidly growing body of "*humane knowledge.*" Beginning, more or less, with Vesalius's *De humani corporis fabrica* (1543), the body's "*Secrets* unknowne" increasingly became privileged—and accessible—objects of a reifying science, one that turned corporeal insides into a visible spectacle. In the anatomy theater and in the period's profusion of anatomical texts (as well as, we might add, on the scaffolds of disembowelment),[15] human entrails were exposed to a penetrative gaze; they were treated as "the *object* of an external knowing ... capable of being confirmed."[16] The rise of anonymous, normative models of the insides (models that, in spite of individual variations, all human bodies supposedly approach) led to a "technologizing" of the interior and a gradual move away from the location of the self *within* the body and toward a Cartesian or purely mechanistic understanding of the relation of self to standardized corpus. Such "invasions of an objectifying knowledge"[17] as Jean Starobinski puts it, made available a new vocabulary for the description of the inner layers of the human frame. These were displayed, tamed, mastered, and gradually turned into "a chartable site of scientific advance ... lending credence to larger metaphysical claims of rationality and epistemological certitude."[18]

This kind of appeal to "epistemological certitude" is one that the anatomist shares with the skeptic. It is tempting here to describe the practice of anatomy as an extremely concrete embodiment of what I have characterized as a central drive of skepticism—the desire to open up the body of the other. Skepticism with respect to other minds can manifest itself as, precisely, a desire for absolute knowledge of the body's interior, which is conceived of (by the skeptic) as a locus of truth deeper than any external manifestation of the other. Broached from this angle, the anatomist's impulse to open up the human frame begins to look like a specific embodiment of the skeptic's dream of the possibility of an "external knowing" of interiority. During this period, as Piero Camporesi has argued, "the ancient precept of 'know yourself' was taken out of its prestigious but restricted moral setting and became the symbol of the new internal panorama, the knowledge of anatomically analysed man."[19] "Anatomy is as it were a most certaine and sure guide to the admirable and most excellent knowledge of our selves, that is of our owne proper nature," wrote Helkiah Crooke early in the seventeenth century, powerfully conflating an "objective" knowledge of the human body with the understanding of subjective human nature.[20] (That such "admirable and most excellent knowledge" is attainable only in the case of a deceased other ("To know our enemies' minds," as Edgar says in *King Lear*, "we rip their hearts" [4.6.260]) is, as we shall see, not merely coincidental; nor is the fact that the practice of anatomy was thought of as transgressive well into the sixteenth century. My implication, it should be clear by now, is that the motivation to anatomy—and perhaps, by extension, to science more generally—goes beyond any simple desire for knowledge.) The anatomist seeks "certaine and sure" knowledge[21]—"specifically visual knowledge"[22]—about the insides of the human frame; the skeptic, equally, seeks proof—and, indeed, quintessentially "ocular proof"[23]—about the other's interior. The multitude of early modern anatomies, and in particular Vesalius's revolutionary book, can thus be construed as taking a not insignificant place in the history of skepticism.[24]

Such a history would have to take into account, alongside the protoscientific attention directed to corporeal insides, the no less remarkable preoccupation of religion throughout this period with the interior of the body of Christ. Perhaps we should understand this engrossment with divine entrails as something in the nature of a rearguard action in the face of science's invasions and reifications of the inner layers of the human frame, but in any event, early modern visual and verbal iconography emphasizes this interior as never before. Christ's wounds, blood, heart, and bowels become a near-obsessive topic of sermons, poems, and visual representations; everywhere, we find imagery of the divine heart, and—with remarkable regularity—references to Christ's "Bowels of pitie,"[25] or to his "bowels of compassion," which, as Donne wrote, "are so conspicuous, so manifested, as that you may see them through his wounds."[26] This absorption with Christ's entrails is similarly evidenced in, for instance, the various cults of the Sacred Heart that sprung up in the period, as well as in the numerous late medieval and early modern stories of the incorruptible innards of saints and the images literally inscribed on their hearts (or on other internal organs).[27] God himself is imagined at times to have entrails: "he speaks of himself," writes the seventeenth-century theologian Thomas Goodwin, "after the manner of Men, as of his *Heart* and *Bowels being turned within him*"; "The *Eye* that served to express God's *Omniscience*, the *Arm* his *Omnipotence*; these are *outward* Parts: but the *Bowels* are of all the most *inward*, and therefore of all other speak what is most inward in God himself."[28]

None of this is, of course, altogether new to the early modern period. Religion has always positioned the body's inner realm as the ultimate site of faith: in both Old and New Testaments, as Elaine Scarry has written, "the interior of the body carries the force of confirmation [of belief]."[29] The association of innards with belief is paradigmatically represented in the story of Doubting Thomas, where Christ's offering of access to his body's interior comes as a response to Thomas's skepticism regarding his divinity. But belief is not just a matter of human access to the divine interior: Christ's offering of himself as bread, to be incorporated physically *into* the bodies of the believers, is the central symbol in Christianity of the mutuality of access to the interior of the body of the other, whether this other is human or divine.[30] The absorption of Christ's body into ours (in the Eucharist), and vice versa—human access (as we've seen above) to the interior of the *Corpus Christi*—together obviate the problem of the other, preempting any skeptical doubt about the possibility of access to the interior: there is literally no room, no space within, for doubt.[31] And God is imagined always to have exclusive and absolute access to human innards: as the poet of Proverbs has it, "The spirit of man is the candle of the Lord, searching all the inward parts of the belly" (20:27); and of Psalms: "Behold, thou desirest truth in the inward parts: and in the hidden part thou shalt make me to know wisdom" (51:6). Whether we should think of this idea of access as preskeptical or antiskeptical is an open question, but in any event, the ascription of omniscient knowledge of the human interior to an all-seeing god—the "scrutans corda et renes Deus"[32]—renders human innards the central locus of connection with the divine. "Faith," wrote Luther, "is under the left nipple."[33]

The interior of the body, then, which (for Christianity) had always been the ontological site of belief, became, in the sixteenth century, *also* the epistemological site of rapidly growing medical and anatomical knowledge, and the two modes of understanding, incompatible in terms of the kind of access to the body's interior they deem possible, jostled against each other. Shakespeare's plays were written at a significant moment in this history, and, as we shall see, they sometimes portray this collision of an episteme of suspicion against an episteme of faith (though for the most part the latter does not seem to be, in Shakespeare, what one would call a *religious* faith);[34] they portray it in terms of a kind of battle over the access to, and the inhabiting of, the interior of the body. In so doing, they offer a challenge both to the objectivizing determinism of science and to the spiritualizing idealism of religion.

Ignorance *in physiologis*—accursed "idealism."
—Nietzsche, *Ecce Homo*

The visceral fantasies of several Shakespearean characters are intimately tied to such questions of skepticism and belief. The body's fate in Shakespeare, when subjected to the skepticism exhibited by these characters, is twofold: on the one hand, the fate of the body under the scrutiny of the skeptic; on the other, the fate of the body of the skeptic himself.[35] How these two fates are linked is a question I will come to shortly; for the moment, however, I would like to view the two separately, and to examine each in turn.

I have described the skeptic's impulse to penetrate the other's body as revealing his suspicion regarding the connection between the innermost bodily sources of the self and their external manifestations. It is in what I take to be his most skeptical play, *Troilus and Cressida*, that Shakespeare comes closer than anywhere else to simply enacting these skeptical urges, without achieving much distance or perspective upon them. The skepticism evinced by the play is in fact itself described within the play in terms of the desire to penetrate to the body's deepest layers: "Modest doubt," says Hector, "is call'd / The beacon of the wise, the tent that searches / To th'bottom of the worst" (2.2.15–17; a "tent" is a surgeon's instrument for opening and probing a wound).

Troilus and Cressida so consistently foregrounds the "Most putrefied core" (5.8.1) of the body that the idea that it evinces a general disgust with corporeality was for many years practically undisputed; and indeed, the vast majority of the play's many references to the body insist upon its diseased and utterly corruptible state. But to take this as a rejection of corporeality as such does little more than reproduce the invective of the play's most bitter character, Thersites—echoing his perspective rather than interpreting it. For the main thrust in *Troilus and Cressida* is a turn not against but back *toward* the body, an insistence on the ineradicable role of corporeality in every human endeavor. The play refuses to go along with the (self-)mythologizing tendencies of its idols and their idolizers. This "corporealization" is thus a double one, for the play's return to the body is simultaneously an undermining of the overblown, idealizing rhetoric of its own protagonists and a rejection of the disembodied, highly rhetoricized status its heroes had achieved in contemporary England. Both within the play and in the cultural milieu in which it was written, *Troilus and Cressida* enacts a restoration of language and action to their sources inside the body.[36]

This somatization constitutes a powerful countermovement to the genealogies of Tudor and Stuart mythographers who traced the ancestry of the English nation to the foundational legend of Troy.[37] That is, while these mythographers sought a heroic site of origin in the Trojan epic, Shakespeare's "skeptical satire" seeks the origins *of* the Trojan legend *in* the bodies of its heroes. Several recent critics have stressed the "massively overdetermined" citationality of the matter of Troy in the period.[38] Indeed, the story was so extraordinarily popular in England during the decade or so preceding the composition of the play that its heroes had reached the status of more or less pure rhetorical citations: "tir'd with iteration" (3.2.174), they have become by this time little more than figures of speech.[39] In his ventriloquization of the story, Shakespeare places at its core the problem of the relation between citation and source: at stake, almost inevitably, in the staging of the legend is the issue of the embodiedness of such heavily rhetoricized figures.

Troilus and Cressida reintroduces, as it were, the interior of the body into the Trojan legend, and it is this return to the body—a return to the heroically repressed, or the unveiling of what we might call the entrails of epic—that produces the play's ubiquity of corporeal images. These constitute a rebuttal both of the story's rhetoricity and of the heroes' rhetoric. On both Greek and Trojan sides, the language of the leaders is high-minded and idealistic. But their "hot and peevish vows," as Cassandra puts it, are "polluted off'rings, more abhorr'd / Than spotted livers in the sacrifice" (5.3.1618). The play undercuts their wordy idealizations by constantly reminding us of the internal physiological sources of all human activity: the various exaltations of love and war amount, in this play, to little more than the "pleasure of my spleen" (1.3.178), the "hot digestion of this cormorant war" (2.2.6), "the hot passion of distempered blood" (2.2.170), "the performance of our heaving spleens" (2.2.197), "a feverous pulse" (3.2.35), "bawdy veins" (4.1.70), "the obligation of our blood" (4.5.121), "too much blood and too little brain" (5.1.46)—the list could easily go on. Each of the play's satirized "heroes" could be described as "wear[ing] his wit in his belly and his guts in his head" (2.1.75–76).

In its simultaneous foregrounding of high-flown language and debased corporeality, then, *Troilus and Cressida* attacks the gap between the words and actions of its heroes and their corporeal sources. Within the play, the character who embodies this skeptical impulse most prominently is, of course, Thersites, whose bilious invective consistently empties the other characters' words of all pretension, attacking their rhetoric and collapsing it back into the putrefying matter of the body:

> Now the rotten diseases of the south, the guts-griping, ruptures, catarrhs, loads o' gravel i'th'back, lethargies, cold palsies, raw eyes, dirt-rotten livers, whissing lungs, bladders full of impostume, sciaticas, lime-kilns i'th'palm, incurable bone-ache, and the rivelled fee-simple of the tetter, take again and again such preposterous discoveries! (5.1.16–24)

While the content of this outburst brandishes the body's diseased interior, the excessive manner of Thersites' rhetoric might remind us that he himself had become, by this time, a proverbial figure of speech—"the standard rhyparographer."[40] Indeed, with his first words in the play, Thersites points punningly to the gap between the substance or matter of the body and the argument or matter of words: "Agamemnon—how if he had boils, full, all over, generally? ... And those boils did run—say so—did not the general run then? Were not that a botchy core? ... Then would come some matter from him: I see none now" (2.1.2–9). His announcement of a lack of "matter" at the "core" of Agamemnon hints not only at the absence of anything of substance in the Greek general's words but also, perhaps, at the insubstantiality—or pure citationality—of the character of Agamemnon himself. We could in fact say that all of these post-Homeric heroes have become, by the time Shakespeare receives the story, "Words, words, mere words, no matter from the heart" (5.3.108).

Indeed, the very word "matter," often associated in Shakespeare with the interior of the body, recurs no less than twenty-five times in the play: Shakespeare's genealogy of the Iliadic legend reintroduces, as it were, the substance or "matter" of the body to the "Matter of Troy."[41] And this genealogical return to the body is, as it happens, simultaneously an etymological return, since the very name "Ilium" meant, in Latin (in the plural form of *ile*): intestines, guts. And in case Shakespeare's "small Latine" didn't extend this far, I note that "Ilium" and "Ilion"—the two forms of the Homeric designation for Troy used alternately in the play—are (and were in the sixteenth century) alternate anatomical names for the longest part of the intestinal tract.[42]

Troilus and Cressida's relinking of words, and the ideals and values constructed out of them, to the body's matter is in many ways analogous to the enterprise that lies close to the heart of the philosophy of Friedrich Nietzsche, and it may be helpful here to see briefly what Nietzsche—the "physiologist of morals"[43]—tells us about the relations between human consciousness and the body's interior. Like *Troilus and Cressida*, Nietzsche often refers to corporeal innards as a way of undercutting idealizations of every kind—above all, the haughtiness of the human intellect and its claims to knowledge. "It is in order to contrast an abominable truth to the surface of the ideal," writes Eric Blondel, "that Nietzsche speaks of entrails."[44] "All virtues," insists Nietzsche, "[are] physiological *conditions*";[45] a certain manner of excavating the body thus becomes, for him, a central act of philosophy. One meaning of the subtitle of *Twilight of the Idols*—"*How One Philosophizes with a Hammer*"—is that the philosopher can (and must) *listen* to the interior of the body, using the hammer as a tuning fork: "*Sounding out idols....* For once to pose questions here with a *hammer*, and, perhaps, to hear as a reply that famous hollow sound which speaks of bloated entrails—what a delight!"[46] Nietzsche is always reminding us that physiology and subjectivity are ineluctably linked, and that, therefore, in any interpretation of human endeavor "we must start from the *body* and employ it as a guide."[47] "Your entrails," he writes, "are what is strongest in you."[48]

The access to one's entrails, however, is a matter for listening, or for belief—and *not* for visual or scientific knowledge: nature, writes Nietzsche, "threw away the key" to this kind of knowledge: "What, indeed, does man know of himself! Can he even once perceive himself completely, laid out as if in an illuminated glass case? Does not nature keep much the most from him, even about his body, to spellbind and confine him in a proud, deceptive consciousness, far from the coils of the intestines, the quick current of the blood stream, and the involved tremors of the fibers?"[49] Nietzsche is very clear about the limits of the epistemological inquiry into the interior of the body: "However far a man may go in self-knowledge, nothing however can be more incomplete than his image of the totality of *drives* which constitute his being. He can scarcely name even the cruder ones: their number and strength, their ebb and flood, their play and counterplay among one another, and above all the laws of their *nutriment* remain wholly unknown to him.... [O]ur moral judgements and evaluations too are only images and fantasies based on a physiological process unknown to us, a kind of acquired language for designating nervous stimuli."[50]

Like *Troilus and Cressida*, however, Nietzsche is uncompromising when it comes to revealing the distance between our proudly "acquired language" and the body's internal reality: "Verily, you fill your mouth with noble words; and are we to believe that your heart is overflowing, you liars?"[51]

> What is found inwardly is also found outwardly, and *vice-versa.*
> —Hegel, *Encyclopedia*

Troilus's angry contempt for the gap between "words, words, mere words" and the "matter from the heart" is echoed (with a difference) in Hamlet's repeated worry about the relation between "words, words, words" (2.2.192; Polonius's response is "What is the matter?") and the "heart's core" (3.2.73). As it does in *Troilus and Cressida*, the skeptical impulse to access the interior of the body takes center stage in *Hamlet*, though here there is far more distance from this desire. Near the opening of the play, Hamlet makes a famous declaration about the absolute, unbridgeable gap between internal reality and its external manifestations: "I have that within which passes show" (1.2.85). In the context of his preoccupation elsewhere in the play with bodily innards, Hamlet's statement can be taken to point to a realm of specifically *corporeal* interiority contrasted with mere outward signs. Certainly, the question of what lies "within"—within his own as well as others' bodies—is one that Hamlet harps upon repeatedly. For him, clearly, the problem of other minds is inseparably a problem of other bodies: these bodies have their own truths, and access to these truths is to a remarkable extent equated by Hamlet with access to "the pith and marrow" (1.4.22) of "the inward man" (2.2.26).

The play opens, however, under the pall of the felt absence of Hamlet's father. And it is his innards, perverted from their normal healthfulness by Claudius's "leperous distilment," that we hear about in detail first. The poison

> Holds such an enmity with blood of man
> That swift as quicksilver it courses through
> The natural gates and alleys of the body,
> And with a sudden vigour it doth posset
> And curd, like eager droppings into milk,
> The thin and wholesome blood. So did it mine,
> And a most instant tetter bark'd about,
> Most lazar-like, with vile and loathsome crust
> All my smooth body.
>
> (1.5.65-73)

The Ghost's account strikingly depicts the dual effect of the poison upon his body: an internal thickening, followed immediately by a hardening of the body's boundaries. This founding narrative leaves Hamlet, as we know, in a state of excruciating doubt; the play invites us to understand this doubt as born of what Hamlet perceives to be a denial of access to the interiors of others' bodies. Throughout the play, Hamlet thinks of the closed body as one *within* which the truth is hidden. He warns Gertrude, for instance, that her avoidance of the truth

> will but skin and film the ulcerous place,
> Whiles rank corruption, mining all within,
> Infects unseen.
>
> (3.4.149-51)

And he insists: "You go not till I set you up a glass / Where you may see the inmost part of you" (3.4.18–19); later in the same scene, he says to his mother:

> Peace, sit you down,
> And let me wring your heart; for so I shall
> If it be made of penetrable stuff,
> If damned custom have not braz'd it so,
> That it be proof and bulwark against sense.
>
> (3.4.34–38)

It is in this scene, of course, that Hamlet turns in frustration from his mother and stabs Polonius's body, then "lug[s] the guts into the neighbor room," actions I take to be representative of Hamlet's aggressive desire for access to the interior of the body and of his angry preoccupation with entrails. From his avowal to feed "all the region kites" with Claudius's "offal" (2.2.575–76) to his disquisitions upon the "worm that hath eat of a king" and the progress of an emperor "through the guts of a beggar" (4.3.27–31), from his declaration about having "that within which passes show" to his insistence that "though I am not splenative and rash, / Yet have I in me something dangerous" (5.1.254–55), Hamlet again and again displays his sense of the importance of corporeal insides. This, coupled with his bodily (and psychological) solitude, and his sense of being denied access to the interior by the bodies around him, leads to an urge to open these bodies. When Hamlet thinks of catching the conscience of the king, for example, he thinks in terms of penetrating to the very center of his body: "I'll tent him to the quick" (2.2.593), he says, as he plans the staging of "The Mousetrap."

What Hamlet eventually finds, however, is that the central truth hidden within the body, his fantasies and desires notwithstanding, is not the other's truth—not by any means "the quick"—but simply death. In the graveyard scene, within the "womb of earth," the fragments of bodies thrown about reveal only that the "fine of . . . fines"—the end result—is always "to have [one's] fine pate full of fine dirt" (5.1.104–6). All, it seems, that one can ever know of the living interior of the human body is that it is destined for death and decay; and, Hamlet discovers, mortality stinks: "Dost thou think Alexander looked o' this fashion i'th'earth? . . . And smelt so? Pah!" (191–94). Real entrails (for all our fantasies about them) have, as Nietzsche repeatedly points out, a rather unsavoury reality: "What offends aesthetic meaning in inner man—beneath the skin: bloody masses, full intestines, viscera, all those sucking, pumping monsters—formless or ugly or grotesque, and unpleasant to smell on top of that!"[52] What Hamlet finds in the graveyard is that there is no access to thought, emotion, or living knowledge through access to the interior of the human frame: neither "th'exterior nor the inward man" (2.2.6) are irrefutably able to express these. What had begun, for Hamlet, as an insistence on the insufficiency of the external, has turned by the end of the play into an understanding of the insufficiency of the internal. What is inside is neither more nor less revealing than what lies on the surface.

Yet it is from within Hamlet's own body—through listening to his own entrails—that the acknowledgment of this reality comes. Hamlet's visceral reaction to the body parts in the graveyard precisely encompasses the ambiguous place of the interior of the body in the play. His very "bones," he says, "ache to think on't" (5.1.90–91)—on, that is, the truth of mortality; and later: "my gorge rises at it" (181). And it is the smell ("And smelt so? Pah!") of the rotting interior of another's body that Hamlet takes in: it is only upon entering his own body, and noting *its* reactions, that Hamlet can finally acknowledge the reality of death, for it is within the body, in these various versions of skepticism in Shakespeare's plays, that such acknowledgments take place.

> Would that you dared to believe yourselves—yourselves and your entrails.
> —Nietzsche, *Thus Spoke Zarathustra*

By the end of the play, then, Hamlet can be seen to acknowledge the truths revealed within his own body, and to relinquish the fantasy of attaining knowledge of the interior of the other. This is something like an inversion of the position with which he began the play—with a refusal to acknowledge the expressibility of his own interior, coupled with a desire to access the interior of the other—the position of the skeptic. This latter is portrayed as a kind of internal hardening of his own body, an image representative of the skeptic's physical refusal to incorporate knowledge: "My fate cries out / And makes each petty artire [artery] in this body / As hardy as the Nemean lion's nerve" (1.4.81–83); "Hold, hold, my heart, / And you, my sinews, grow not instant old, / But bear me stiffly up" (1.5.93–95). There is here a stiffening of Hamlet's own body, as if to withstand its propensity to "burst in ignorance" (1.4.45).[53]

Skepticism, according to Cavell, is "a failure of acknowledgment,"[54] a refusal to take in certain truths (e.g., the human condition of being separate from the other, or of being subject to death, or never in a position to achieve certain knowledge). What the skeptic appears to reveal is above all a desire for irrefutable knowledge about the other, but this, according to Cavell, is merely a cover story, a *refusal* to acknowledge the other—the defensive conversion of an unacknowledged "metaphysical finitude" into "an intellectual difficulty, a riddle."[55] Hamlet's ultimate "ignorance" regarding the entire Danish court—his refusal to take anyone into his "heart of heart" (3.2.73)—is portrayed in terms of the stiffening of his own body; there are several striking instances in Shakespeare's plays of similar corporeal hardenings—versions of the skeptic more or less physically steeling the interior of his body against the coming in of an unbearable thought. At key moments in a number of plays, a point is reached where one of two alternatives must be chosen: either to acknowledge what needs to be acknowledged, which is to say to take something (some existential knowledge) into one's corporeal interior; or to deny this knowledge, to deny it access to one's body—and (by way of a cover story) to project the denial of access upon the other.

Shakespeare's most concise portrayal of this kind of denial of access occurs in *The Winter's Tale*, a play that repeatedly thematizes the desire not to know, or not to "dare to know that which I know" (4.4.452)—not to dare, as Nietzsche put it, to believe one's own entrails. Leontes' sudden jealousy of Hermione can be taken to be just such a denial of knowledge:[56]

> Alack, for lesser knowledge! how accurs'd
> In being so blest! There may be in the cup
> A spider steep'd, and one may drink; depart,
> And yet partake no venom (for his knowledge
> Is not infected), but if one present
> Th'abhorr'd ingredient to his eye, make known
> How he hath drunk, he cracks his gorge, his sides,
> With violent hefts. I have drunk, and seen the spider.
>
> (2.1.38–45)

Caught in the web of his skepticism, Leontes construes knowledge as something mortally dangerous—dangerous to "his gorge, his sides"; his skepticism is founded precisely upon a refusal to incorporate this knowledge physically into his own body. Such an incorporation is seen by him as holding the potential to "crack" his interior "[w]ith violent hefts." The "clearer knowledge" (2.1.97) that Leontes refuses to take in is repeatedly associated by him with internal corporeal distress. Upon his first apprehension of Hermione's supposed faithlessness, Leontes announces: "I have *tremor cordis* on me; my heart dances, / But not for joy; not joy" (1.2.110–11); and then: "My bosom likes [it] not" (l. 119); his condition is contrasted by him

with that of "heartiness ... bounty, fertile bosom" (l. 113). Indeed, he repeatedly makes clear that it is the thoracic cavity of his body that is
afflicted: "Whiles [Hermione] lives," he declares, "My heart will be a burthen to me" (2.3.205–6); "This sessions"—her trial—"Even pushes 'gainst
our heart" (3.2.1–2). Such a reading gives a quite localized inflection to the
notoriously difficult line, "Affection! thy intention stabs the centre"
(1.2.138). However we are to understand "Affection" (as passion, or desire,
or natural propensity), it is clear that the relation to the other that it
describes is felt by Leontes as menacing the innermost recesses—the "centre"—of his very body;[57] this is one meaning of his later, "The centre is not
big enough to bear / A schoolboy's top" (2.1.102). Given this interpretation
of Leontes' bodily imagination, perhaps it would not be going too far to
take his lines about "Sir Smile" as inadvertently revealing something about
his relation to his own corporeal interior:

>   Nay, there's comfort in't,
> Whiles other men have gates, and those gates open'd,
> As mine, against their will ...
> ....
>   ... Be it concluded,
> No barricado for a belly. Know't,
> It will let in and out the enemy,
> With bag and baggage. Many thousand on's
> Have the disease, and feel't not.

>   (1.2.196–207)

Whose belly is it, we can now ask, that needs barricading? Hermione's, or
Leontes' own? And is this a wish or a fear?

Leontes' refusal to acknowledge his wife's integrity is akin to a repudiation of his own interior, a visceral response to knowledge that leaves him
feeling that the "centre" of his body is in need of protection from encroaching knowledge. This leads me to a speculation about the possibility that
Hermione's conspicuous pregnancy at the play's opening may be a rather
precise figuration of what is troubling Leontes.[58] If Hermione's "burthen,"
her "fertile bosom," is "past doubt" (1.2.268) an image of a physical interior
that cannot but let in the other, Leontes' own interior is, exactly, steeled
against this kind of inhabitation of one body by another. (And the recovery
from skepticism is imagined, in *The Winter's Tale*, as a reincorporation of
the other: the trajectory of Leontes' restoration of faith allows him finally to
accept the existence of Hermione as other, and to imagine the incorporation of the other into his own body: "O, she's warm! / If this be magic, let it

be an art / Lawful as eating"—[5.3.109–11].[59]) If Leontes' skepticism is a disavowing of unbearable knowledge of the other, his refusal is a refusal to be physically inhabited by this knowledge—by the other. And whether Hermione's pregnancy bodies forth Leontes' wish or his fear is perhaps a moot point: at some (crisis) point, there comes to be no "great difference" (1.1.3) between the two.

Similar moments, of a refusal to allow some encroaching knowledge of the other to inhabit the body, recur at a number of points in Shakespeare's plays, and in several of them it is hard to miss the echo of Leontes' repudiation of the matrix.[60] Most notable, of course, is Lear's "O how this mother swells up toward my heart! /*Hysterica passio*, down, thou climbing sorrow" (2.4.56–57)—one such attempt to quell a knowledge (of the other) that is unbearable and threatens to burst one's insides. (Lear's and Leontes' Latinisms—*hysterica passio, tremor cordis*—appear at moments of great pressure, and may be taken to signify a kind of desperate turn to a medical or scientific register that lends a certain grounding to their skeptical refusals to take in the other.) We could add to this Lady Macbeth's "anti–hysterical" quelling or steeling of her own interior ("unsex me here, / And fill me from the crown to the toe topful / Of direst cruelty! Make thick my blood, / Stop up th' access and passage to remorse"—[1.5.41–44]); and, indeed, Hamlet's own "O heart, lose not thy nature. Let not ever / The soul of Nero enter this firm bosom" (3.2.384–85): Nero's vexed relation to his mother's womb, as well as his status as a forerunner of modern anatomy— topics of great interest throughout the Renaissance—are deeply relevant to Hamlet's simultaneous attempt to seal off his "firm bosom" to inhabitation by the other.[61]

Entrails, then, are *the* place in Shakespeare where the other is taken in, is acknowledged in his or her otherness. A primary narcissism that refuses acknowledgment of the other as other is in these instances akin to a steeling of the body, a refusal to take something or someone into it; accepting the fact of the outside world is imagined as taking that world (and in particular, its inhabitants) into one's body. (We might here ask whether Cartesian skepticism is not always akin to a refusal to be corporeally inhabited by knowledge; whether, in fact, this dynamic lies somewhere about the heart of Cartesian mind-body dualism. In other words, if Descartes's radical skepticism about the existence of the external world—and of other minds in it— can be traced to a refusal to acknowledge the external world [the other], this refusal is, as I'm describing it, a repudiation of the truth of his own entrails; hence the need to separate, ontologically, spirit from body.)

This refusal to acknowledge the other amounts to something like a quelling of one's own corporeal interior. One way of partially accounting for the peculiarly *merciless* nature of the Shakespearean skeptic, the relent-lessness with which he pursues his revenge upon the world, is to point out that in the sixteenth century the bowels are almost invariably thought of as the locus of "mercie" or compassion. God, writes Thomas Goodwin, "planted the Inwards of us Men, and Bowels of Mercy and Pity in them," and from thence spring the possibility of "forbearing one another, and forgiving one another"; God's own mercifulness is "represented by Bowels and Heart."[62] Goodwin—like several other early modern writers—traces the Hebrew etymology of the word *Racham* to both mercy and bowels—or womb. The place of mercy is the bowels exactly because this is where the other is taken in, introjected, acknowledged; and quelling one's entrails is precisely a denial of entry to the other—a refusal of "th' access and passage of remorse"—hence a refusal of any need for forbearance or compassion.

❖

"Thou art not certain," Duke Vincentio reminds Claudio on the eve of the latter's execution, "For thy complexion shifts to strange effects / After the moon" (*Measure for Measure*, 3.1.23–25). If the "strange effects" of the body's shifting "complexion"—the composition of the body's internal humors—are ever-present beneath the surface of Shakespeare's plays, the possibility of real knowledge of them is always, in the end, a dream. For Shakespeare, as for Donne and for Montaigne (as well as for numerous other writers of the period), there is no certain knowledge to be found within the body—except the knowledge of doubt, disease, and ultimately death. "I wholy set forth and expose my selfe: It is a Sceletos; where at first sight appeare all the vaines, muskles, gristles, sinnewes, and tendons, each severall part in his due place. The effect of the cough produceth one part, that of palenesse or panting of the heart another, and that doubt-fully," wrote Montaigne.[63] Or as Donne put it, in a sermon preached at Whitehall:

> We know the receipt, the capacity of the ventricle, the stomach of man, how much it can hold; and wee know the receipt of all the receptacles of blood, how much blood the body can have; so wee do of all the other conduits and cisterns of the body; But this infinite Hive of honey, this insatiable whirlpoole of the covetous mind, no Anatomy, no dissection hath discovered to us.[64]

It is the body's internal finitude (in every sense of the word) that advocates against its being used as a ground of subjective truth. Shakespeare, like Donne and Montaigne, returns again and again to the body's interior, to its "conduits and cisterns"; but renounced in this return is the anatomist's fantasy of absolute legibility; abandoned is the appropriative, active knowledge of the skeptic. Subjectivity in Shakespeare, while inseparable from viscerality, is far from reducible to the body's interior. "The capacity of the ventricle, the stomach of man" may be measurable, but the capacity of the body to love, to pity, to take in the other—this is an "insatiable whirlpoole" indeed.

Notes

I warmly thank the following for their careful reading of the essay and helpful comments: Stanley Cavell, Elizabeth Freund, Marjorie Garber, Jeff Masten, Carla Mazzio, Ruth Nevo, and Alexis Susman.

1. Other plays absorbed with viscerality include *1* and *2 Henry IV, Twelfth Night, Measure for Measure, King Lear, Othello, Macbeth,* and *Coriolanus.* When I speak in this chapter of "Shakespeare's" understanding of viscerality, I refer to these plays in particular; they seem to me to share certain ways of thinking about the interior of the body, as well as, in relation to this matter, a profound attentiveness to problems of knowing and acknowledging the other.

2. In speaking of "skepticism," I refer not to any overtly philosophical stance but to the human impulse to lose one's faith in the world outside the self, to deny the possibility of knowing the other; "the skeptic" embodies an extreme version of this impulse. On the carnality of this kind of suspicion of the other, see Jean Starobinski, "The Inside and the Outside," *Hudson Review* 28, no. 3 (autumn 1975): 333–51.

3. Here (and throughout this essay) I am relying on Stanley Cavell's work on skepticism and "the imagination of the body's fate under skepticism." Cavell's *Disowning Knowledge: In Six Plays of Shakespeare* (Cambridge: Cambridge University Press, 1987), and his *The Claim of Reason* (Oxford: Oxford University Press, 1979), in particular, have deeply influenced my thinking; the quotation above is from *Disowning Knowledge,* 125.

4. Psychoanalysts such as Sándor Ferenczi, Melanie Klein, and D. W. Winnicott have concerned themselves in great detail with (in particular, children's) fantasies about one's own and others' bodily internality; their writings have colored my thinking about these issues. On the constructedness of such fantasies of internal essentiality, see for example Jean-Luc Nancy, "Corpus," in *Thinking*

Bodies, ed. Juliet Flower MacCannell and Laura Zakarin (Stanford: Stanford University Press, 1994), 17–31 (esp. 19–20), and Judith Butler, *Gender Trouble: Feminism and the Subversion of Identity* (New York: Routledge, 1990), 132–37.

5. John Donne, *Devotions Upon Emergent Occasions*, ed. Anthony Raspa (New York: Oxford University Press, 1987), 87.

6. Gail Kern Paster, *The Body Embarrassed: Drama and the Disciplines of Shame in Early Modern England* (Ithaca: Cornell University Press, 1993), 12.

7. Almost all categorizations retained the traditional Galenic distinction between the thoracic cavity, ruled by the heart, the abdominal cavity, dominated by the liver, and the head, sphere of the brain; more detailed understandings of particular organs were similarly often derived from Greek and Roman systems. See R. B. Onians, *The Origins of European Thought: About the Body, the Mind, the Soul, the World, Time, and Fate* (Cambridge: Cambridge University Press, 1951), esp. 23–43, 62–70, 84–89, 505–6.

8. Thomas Vicary's description of the thoracic cavity; in *The Anatomie of the Bodie of Man* (London, 1548; reprint (London: Early English Text Society, 1888), 54.

9. Katharine Eisaman Maus, *Inwardness and Theater in the English Renaissance* (Chicago: University of Chicago Press, 1995), 195. Maus discusses at some length the prevalence in the early modern period of what she calls the "inwardness *topos*" (15).

10. Cf. Michael Schoenfeldt's comments on this ontology in "The Matter of Inwardness: Shakespeare's *Sonnets*" (paper given at the Shakespeare Association of America, April 1996). On a highly speculative note, I would say that it is possible, indeed plausible, that the people of early modern Europe may have quite concretely *felt* the interiors of their bodies differently from the way we post-Cartesian moderns sense "our ascetic guts" (as Louis MacNeice has called them. ("Postscript to Iceland for W. H. Auden," in *Collected Poems, 1925–1948* [London: Faber & Faber, 1949].)

11. Citations from *Hamlet, Troilus and Cressida,* and *The Winter's Tale* are from the Arden editions, ed. Harold Jenkins (London: Routledge, 1982); ed. Kenneth Palmer (London: Routledge, 1982); ed. J. H. P. Pafford (London: Routledge, 1963), respectively; all other Shakespeare citations are from *The Riverside Shakespeare*, ed. G. Blakemore Evans (Boston: Houghton Mifflin, 1974).

12. Quoted in Paul Johnson, *Elizabeth I: A Study in Power and Intellect* (London: Weidenfeld & Nicolson, 1974), 320. The phrase "heart and bowels" (or "heart and stomach") is extraordinarily common in the period, in a wide variety of contexts.

13. See Jonathan Sawday, *The Body Emblazoned: Dissection and the Human Body in Renaissance Culture* (London: Routledge, 1995).

14. John Davies of Hereford, *Microcosmos. The Discovery of the Little World, with the government thereof* (Oxford, 1603), 88; emphases in original.

15. Detailed descriptions of various forms of disembowelment as punishment or torture abound throughout the period. On the centrality of the interior of the body to spectacles of royal power—the public display of heart and bowels as "proof" of guilt—see, for example, Peter Stallybrass, "Dismemberments and Re-memberments: Rewriting the *Decameron*, 4.1, in the English Renaissance," *Studi sul Boccaccio* 20 (1991): 299–324, esp. 318–21.

16. Jean Starobinski, "The Body's Moment," in *Montaigne: Essays in Reading*, ed. Gérard Defaux, *Yale French Studies* 64 (1983): 273–305, at 276.

17. Starobinski, "The Body's Movement," 277.

18. The quote is from Timothy Murray, "Philosophical Antibodies: Grotesque Fantasy in a French Stoic Fiction," in *Corps Mystique, Corps Sacré*, ed. Françoise Jaouën and Benjamin Semple, *Yale French Studies* 86 (1994): 143–63, at 145. On the centrality of the practice of anatomy in the period, see especially Devon L. Hodges, *Renaissance Fictions of Anatomy* (Amherst: University of Massachusettes Press, 1985), and Sawday's recent *The Body Emblazoned*.

19. Piero Camporesi, *The Anatomy of the Senses: Natural Symbols in Medieval and Early Modern Italy*, trans. Allan Cameron (Cambridge: Polity Press, 1994), 99.

20. Helkiah Crooke, *Microcosmographia, A Description of the Body of Man* (London, 1615), 14. The passage continues: "And therefore we reade, that valiant courageous Princes, worthy and renowned Nobles, yea, and invincible Emperors, being mooved and incited with this desire of the knowledge of themselves, did most studiously practice this worke of Anatomy." Crooke's rhetoric, like that of many other anatomists of the sixteenth and seventeenth centuries, suggests that the anatomist's penetrative urges cannot be attributed to an uncomplicated desire for "scientific" knowledge.

21. "The anatomists elevated observation into a form of certain knowledge," writes Andrew Wear: "Medicine in Early Modern Europe, 1500–1700," in Lawrence I. Conrad et al., *The European Medical Tradition, 800 BC to AD 1800* (Cambridge: Cambridge University Press, 1995), 285.

22. Luke Wilson, "William Harvey's *Prelectiones*: The Performance of the Body in the Renaissance Theater of Anatomy," *Representations* 17 (winter 1987): 62–95, at 62.

23. *Othello*, 3.3.360. On *Othello* as a depiction of the problem of other minds, see Cavell, *The Claim of Reason*, 481–96.

24. Richard Popkin (*The History of Scepticism from Erasmus to Descartes* [Assen, Netherlands: Van Gorcum, 1960]); Don Cameron Allen (*Doubt's Boundless Sea: Skepticism and Faith in the Renaissance* [Baltimore: Johns Hopkins University Press, 1964]), and Victoria Kahn (*Rhetoric, Prudence, and Skepticism in the Renaissance* [Ithaca: Cornell University Press, 1985]), among others, have written extensively about the resurgence of classical forms of skepticism in the period. These relate primarily to knowledge of the material world rather than of other minds—the specific form of skepticism I discuss here. On the relation between the two, see Cavell, *The Claim of Reason*, especially 451–53.

25. George Herbert, "Longing," in *The Works of George Herbert*, ed. F. E. Hutchinson (Oxford: Clarendon Press, 1941), l:19. Cf. the references to "Mercie's Bowels" in Davies, *Microcosmos*, 70.

26. John Donne, "Death's Duell," in *The Complete Poetry and Selected Prose of John Donne*, ed. Charles Coffin (New York: Modern Library, 1952), 593. These references are based on Philippians 1:8: "For God is my record, how greatly I long after you all in the bowels of Jesus Christ."

27. See Johannes Behm, "Koilia" and "Kardia" in *Theological Dictionary of the New Testament*, ed. Gerhard Kittel, trans. Geoffrey Bromiley, 10 vols. (Grand Rapids, Mich.: 1964–1976), 3:605–14; Caroline Thomas Bynum, *Fragmentation and Redemption: Essays on Gender and the Human Body in Medieval Religion* (New York: Zone Books, 1992), 13, 84, 88; Piero Camporesi, *The Incorruptible Flesh: Bodily Mutation and Mortification in Religion and Folklore*, trans. T. Croft-Murray and H. Elsom (Cambridge: Cambridge University Press, 1988); Eric Jager, "The Book of the Heart: Reading and Writing the Medieval Subject," *Speculum* 71 (1996): 1–26.

28. Thomas Goodwin, *Of the Object and Acts of Justifying Faith*, in *The Works of Thomas Goodwin* (London, 1697), 4:88.

29. Elaine Scarry, *The Body in Pain: The Making and Unmaking of the World* (Oxford: Oxford University Press, 1985), 215; elsewhere she speaks of "the mining of the ultimate substance, the ultimate source of substantiation, the extraction of the physical basis of reality from its dark hiding place in the body out into the light of day, the making available of the precious ore of confirmation, the interior content of human bodies, lungs, arteries, blood, brains" (137).

30. The arrival of the "second Adam" in this sense inverts the original fall of the first Adam, brought about by, precisely, the incorporation of forbidden knowledge.

31. Cavell, in *The Claim of Reason*, 470, proposes "understanding the philosophical problem of the other as the trace or scar of the departure of God"; cf. 482–83.

32. John Foxe, *Acts and Monuments of these latter and perilous days* ... (New York: AMS Press, 1965), 8:238, cited in Maus, *Inwardness*, 10. Maus adds: "God's immediate, superhuman knowledge of the hidden interior of persons is one of the primary qualities for which he is admired and feared by many early modern Christians."

33. Cited by Ludwig Wittgenstein, *Philosophical Investigations* trans. G. E. M. Anscombe (New York: Macmillan, 1958), sec. 589. It is interesting to note, in this context, the significance attributed to anatomy by Protestant theologians in particular. Luther "was reported to have said that anatomy was almost as important as religion in imparting morality"; Melanchthon wrote that "the soul cannot be properly understood without a knowledge of the workings of the body"; Calvin was similarly enthusiastic. (The citations are from Wear, "Medicine in Early Modern Europe," 288–89.) What, then, are we to make of

the conjunction between Protestantism's move away from the Eucharistic incorporation of Christ's body and the approximately contemporaneous rise of the "culture of dissection" (Sawday, *The Body Emblazoned*, viii) in the sixteenth century? It seems to me at least imaginable that there is a link between the emergence of new modes of access to human innards and the (very gradual) attenuation of a religious frame of reference predisposed to conceiving of a divinity in direct corporeal contact with the interior of the human body. While the practice of anatomy reduces the self to an objectivized, mechanistic picture of the body, the Protestant rejection of the Eucharist attempts to spirit away, so to speak, the body as such. But the apparent split between the two is only superficial: both, I suggest, have something to do with the attempt, ultimately, to reduce or escape the mystery of human embodiedness.

34. My grasp of the "irreligiousness" of Shakespeare's plays is indebted to C. L. Barber's interpretation of their "post-Christian" nature; see especially his "The Family in Shakespeare's Development: Tragedy and Sacredness," in *Representing Shakespeare: New Psychoanalytic Essays,* ed. Murray M. Schwartz and Coppélia Kahn (Baltimore: Johns Hopkins University Press, 1980), 188–202. See also Stephen Greenblatt's "Shakespeare and the Exorcists," in his *Shakespearean Negotiations: The Circulation of Social Energy in Renaissance England* (Berkeley: University of California Press, 1988), 94–128.

35. I use the masculine pronoun, here and throughout this essay, advisedly; in Shakespeare and elsewhere, the skeptic is almost invariably gendered male. See below, 17–18, and 44 n. 58, and Cavell, *Disowning Knowledge*, 34–37, esp. n. 3.

36. For an extended discussion of the relation between language and the interior of the body in this play, see my "The Gastric Epic: *Troilus and Cressida*," forthcoming in *Shakespeare Quarterly.*

37. Cf. Matthew Greenfield's comment, in "Undoing National Identity: Shakespeare's *Troilus and Cressida*" (paper presented at the Shakespeare Association of America, March 1995), 5: "The work of *Troilus and Cressida* is not to provide England or Elizabeth with a genealogy but rather to undo the genealogies created by other myth-makers."

38. The phrase is Linda Charnes's, in "'So Unsecret to Ourselves': Notorious Identity and the Material Subject in Shakespeare's *Troilus and Cressida*," *Shakespeare Quarterly* 48, no. 4 (winter 1989), 413–40, at 418; on the play's citationality, see esp. Elizabeth Freund, "'Ariachne's Broken Woof': The Rhetoric of Citationality in *Troilus and Cressida*," in *Shakespeare and the Question of Theory,* ed. Patricia Parker and Geoffrey Hartmann (New York: Methuen, 1985), 19–36, and Carol Cook, "Unbodied Figures of Desire," *Theater Journal* 38, no. 1 (1986): 34–52.

39. On the stunning popularity of the story of Troy in the decades preceding Shakespeare's play, see, e.g., J. S. P. Tatlock, "The Siege of Troy in Elizabethan Literature, Especially in Shakespeare and Heywood," *PMLA* 30 (December 1915): 676: "no traditional story was so popular in the Elizabethan Age as that of the siege of Troy and some of its episodes." On the characters as proverbial

figures, see Rosalie Colie, *Shakespeare's Living Art* (Princeton: Princeton University Press, 1975), 343–44.

40. Colie, *Shakespeare's Living Art,* 326; she describes Thersites as having become a "rhetorical and proverbial figure" (343).

41. On "matter" as bodily substance, see Alexander Schmidt, *Shakespeare Lexicon and Quotation Dictionary*, 3d. ed. (New York: Dover, 1971), 1:700–701, and Elaine Scarry, Introduction to *Literature and the Body: Essays on Populations and Persons* (Baltimore: Johns Hopkins University Press, 1988), xxii.

42. For the etymology, see the *OED*, s.v. "Ileum," "Ilion," and "Ilium," and A. Ernout and A. Meillet, *Dictionnaire Étymologique de la Langue Latine* (Paris: Klincksieck, 1959), 308 ("ilia, -ium ... parties latérales du ventre"); for the anatomical data, see for example Vicary, *The Anatomie of the Bodie of Man*, 65.

43. The phrase is taken from Georg Stauth and Bryan S. Turner, *Nietzsche's Dance* (Oxford: Basil Blackwell, 1988), 17.

44. Eric Blondel, *Nietzsche: The Body and Culture* (Stanford: Stanford University Press, 1991), 220. On Nietzsche's physiological brand of philosophy, see especially Elizabeth Grosz, "Nietzsche and the Stomach for Knowledge," in *Nietzsche, Feminism, and Political Theory*, ed. Paul Patton (London: Routledge, 1993), 49–70, and her *Volatile Bodies: Toward a Corporeal Feminism* (Bloomington: Indiana University Press, 1994), 115–37.

45. Friedrich Nietzsche, *The Will to Power*, trans. Walter Kaufmann & R. J. Hollingdale (New York: Vintage Books, 1968), 148.

46. Friedrich Nietzsche, *Twilight of the Idols or, How One Philosophizes with a Hammer*, in *The Portable Nietzsche*, ed. and trans. Walter Kaufmann (New York: Penguin Books, 1976), 465; emphasis in the original. Nietzsche repeatedly speaks of the "hard, unwanted, inescapable task" of philosophy as a kind of vivisection; Socrates, for example, is "the old physician and plebeian who cut ruthlessly into his own flesh, as he did into the flesh and heart of the 'noble.'" (*Beyond Good and Evil: Prelude to a Philosophy of the Future*, trans. Walter Kaufmann [New York: Vintage Books, 1989], 137–39 [sec. 212].)

47. Nietzsche, *The Will to Power*, 289; emphasis in the original.

48. Friedrich Nietzsche, *Thus Spoke Zarathustra*, in *The Portable Nietzsche*, 234.

49. Friedrich Nietzsche, "On Truth and Lie in the Extra-Moral Sense," in *The Portable Nietzsche*, 44.

50. Friedrich Nietzsche, *Daybreak: Thoughts on the Prejudices of Morality*, trans. R. J. Hollingdale (Cambridge: Cambridge University Press, 1982), 74–76 (sec. 119).

51. Nietzsche, *Thus Spoke Zarathustra*, 235.

52. Friedrich Nietzsche, *Werke, Kritische Gesamtausgabe*, 7:2, 25; cited in Blondel, *Nietzsche*, 220.

53. The fact that the main threat to the body in *Hamlet* is portrayed as a threat to the ears is not irrelevant here: "The ear," wrote Voltaire, "is the road to the

heart." As Cavell puts it, "our access to belief is fundamentally through the ear" (*The Claim of Reason*, 391): the fear or refusal of such access can be imagined as a fear of what may enter one through the ear. The skeptic's distrust of the connection between language and the body pertains not only to what emanates from the other but also, and concomitantly, to what enters the skeptic himself.

54. Cavell, *Disowning Knowledge*, 206.

55. Ibid., 138.

56. Cavell calls act I of *The Winter's Tale* "a portrait of the skeptic at the moment of the world's withdrawal from his grasp" (*Disowning Knowledge*, 206).

57. The Arden editor, J. H. P. Pafford, interprets line 166 as "your intensity penetrates to the very heart and soul of man," and adds a Ben Jonson description of "Affection ... in her hand a flaming heart." Cf. Romeo's "Can I go forward when my heart is here? / Turn back, dull earth, and find thy centre out" (*Rom.*, 2.1.1–2).

58. Hermione's pregnancy has been discussed by many critics of the play; of these, Janet Adelman's comments are of greatest relevance to my thesis. Adelman writes in *Suffocating Mothers: Fantasies of Maternal Origin in Shakespeare's Plays, "Hamlet" to "The Tempest"* (New York: Routledge, 1992), that "in its very fullness, [Hermione's] body becomes the register of male emptiness" (221). My description of Leontes' expulsion of the other could be seen as the other side of "the trauma of contamination at the site of origin" (226) described by Adelman. The former can be understood as a form of revenge (or ressentiment) for one's originary separateness from the interior of the maternal body.

59. We could also read this as more problematic than I imply here, along the lines of Nicolas Abraham and Maria Torok's description of incorporation of the other as something in the nature of failed introjection. See *The Shell and the Kernel*, vol. 1, ed. and trans. Nicholas T. Rand (Chicago: University of Chicago Press, 1994), 125–38.

60. In terms of the possibility of being corporeally inhabited by the other, the woman's womb as an (at least potential) space for such inhabitation may play no small role in this gender gap. On the womb as the place of woman's knowledge, see Catherine Clément, *Opera, or the Undoing of Women*, trans. Betsy Wing, foreword by Susan McClary (Minneapolis: University of Minneapolis Press, 1988), 175–77; and Stanley Cavell's comments on this passage in *A Pitch of Philosophy: Autobiographical Exercises* (Cambridge: Harvard University Press, 1994), 169.

61. Hamlet's soliloquy continues: "Let me be cruel, not unnatural; / I will speak daggers to her, but use none" (3.2.386–87), which I construe as Hamlet's refusal to be *just* a skeptical anatomist. For more on this passage, see my "*Hamlet*, Nietzsche, and Visceral Knowledge," in *The Incorporated Self: Interdisciplinary Perspectives on Embodiment*, ed. Michael O'Donovan-Anderson (Lanham, MD: Rowman & Littlefield, 1996), 93–110.

62. Goodwin, *Works*, 4:87; cf. the references to Christ's "bowels of pitie" and "bowels of compassion" above, p. 85.

63. *The Essays of Montaigne, done into English by John Florio* (London: Davis Nutt, 1893), 2:vi (p. 60).

64. Sermon preached at Whitehall, April 8, 1621; cited in Donne, *Complete Poetry and Selected Prose*, 479.

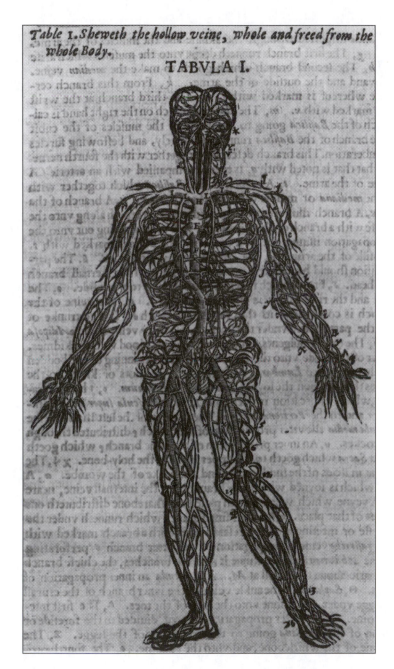

6. Illustration of the vessel and arteris from Helkiah Crooke's
Microcosmographia (London, 1631).

6

Nervous Tension

Networks of Blood and Spirit in the Early Modern Body

GAIL KERN PASTER

First, a riddle about the body from the mental world of the early seventeenth century: What do wrestling, leaping, exploding gunpowder, and playing division on the lute have in common?

This riddle is concocted from Section 30 of Francis Bacon's strange book of physiological investigation, *Sylva Sylvarum, or a Natural History in Ten Centuries* (1626). My reason for posing it includes but goes well beyond piquing curiosity about what follows in this chapter, because responding to its conjunction of terms, puzzling through to the answer, draws us deep into early modern habits of bodily thought and sensation at a time—just before Harvey's discovery of the circulation of the blood in 1628—when those habits were under challenge. In Section 30, entitled "Experiment Solitary touching the *Commixture* of *Flame* and *Aire*, and the *great Force* therof," Bacon meditates upon the properties of fire and air in an attempt at scientific explanation of various kinds of force. (We should understand "force" here to mean the explosion, under compression, of air and fire.) For Bacon, human motion is one form of elemental explosion; indeed, in sudden or concentrated displays of force and velocity by the human body, he finds the combination of air and fire most beautifully expressed.[1] But it is

Bacon's terms of human motion that make his meditation seem so unfamiliar to modern readers because he discovers categorical affinities, where we would not, between the properties and characteristic behaviors of unlike bodies.

It is popular misunderstandings of the nature of explosive force that most concern Bacon here, especially the idea that explosions occur simply as a result of the "Rarefaction" of a combustible element into flame without the intervention of air. He begins with the following proposition: "*Flame* and *Aire* doe not Mingle, except it be in an *Instant;* Or in the *vitall Spiritts* of *vegetables*, and *liuing Creatures*." Bacon then focuses upon how air and fire interact when they are compressed and distinguishes between compressions occurring within animate or inanimate bodies. Unlike the solid elements of earth and water, which easily and freely cohere, the two higher elements on their own, "being free," will fly apart. But fire and air, if brought together inside a hard, inelastic container like a gun barrel, will produce an explosion ("Mingle . . . in an *Instant*"): "wee knowe that simple *Aire*, being preternaturally attenuated by *Heate*, will make it self Roome, and breake and blowe vp that which resisteth it."

Bacon's experimental imagination is caught by the variety of explosive materials: "wee see that *Brimstone, Pitch, Camphire, Wilde-Fire*, and diuers other Inflammable Matters, though they burne cruelly, and are hard to quench; Yet they make no such fiery winde, as *Gunpowder* doth." He is intrigued by the diversity in the physical properties of combustibles; and he finds quicksilver especially puzzling because, despite being liquid ("a most Crude and Watry *Body*"), it explodes with a ferocity like that of gunpowder. Such differences in the explosive properties of combustible minerals matter most for Bacon, however, when he compares their force to the behavior of fire and air within the containing vessels of a living body:

> As for *liuing Creatures*, it is certaine, their *Vitall Spiritts* are a Substance Compounded of an *Airy* and *Flamy* Matter, And though *Aire* and *Flame* being free, will not well mingle; yet bound in by a *Body* that hath some fixing, they will. For that you may best see in those two Bodies, (which are their *Aliments*), *Water* and *Oyle;* For they likewise will not well mingle of themselues, but in the Bodies of *Plants*, and *liuing Creatures*, they will.

Bacon has no doubt that a union of fire and air occurs in animate life forms and makes them move. He identifies the product of this union as "Vital Spiritt," the adjective functioning here to mark the separation of the active properties of animate life forms from the active properties of mineral entities. His understanding of spirit is philosophically orthodox and distinctly premodern, conforming in essentials to that of his predecessors, including, for instance, Thomas Elyot: "Spirite," wrote Elyot in 1541, "is an ayry substance subtyll, styrynge the powers of the body to perfourme theyr operations."[2] Eighty-five years later, with the hierarchical scale of elements still in place, it remains logical even for an antischolastic like Bacon to suppose that the forceful behaviors of minerals would compare, analogically, with forceful behaviors in animate life. This means that like the explosions of air, fire, and gunpowder in the containing barrel of a gun, so growth, motion and other life-sustaining operations would result from explosions of air and fire within the body's dense liquidity.

Thus it is finally, after the cross-comparisons among combustibles, that we discover Bacon's goal in this passage—to explain the force released by the combustion of different materials in terms that demystify, indeed desanctify the glories of human movement:

> It is no maruaile therfore, that a small *Quantity* of *Spiritts*, in the Cells of the Braine, and Canales of the Sinewes [i.e., nerves], are able to moue the whole Body, (which is of so great Masse,) both with so great Force, as in Wrestling, Leaping; And with so great Swiftnes, As in playing Diuision vpon the *Lute*. Such is the force of these two Natures, *Aire* and *Flame*, when they incorporate.

Here Bacon's train of thought about explosions of air and fire finds its completion in human motion, implied images of the human body—purposeful, vigorous, highly skilled—in action. He thinks first of large motor movements, athletic displays of force, and adds, seemingly as an afterthought, the swift movement of fingers up and down the neck of the lute.

In part, what is dazzling about the structure of his imagery is that, in the space of less than a page, he has traveled with air and fire up the scale of nature from gunpowder to the hands of the lutenist, from mining saltpeter to making music. But the character of his thought in the passage and the structure of his transitions, which are my focus here, matter most where he seems to be engaging dialectically with an unseen interlocutor, a representative voice of theological physiology against which he will define what is and is not "marvelous" about the nature of human motion.[3] For Bacon, what undergirds the analogy between the forceful movement of a muscle and the forceful movement of a bullet through a gun barrel is the assumption, fundamental to Aristotelian natural science and Galenic medicine alike, that living things are kept alive and in motion by the action of spirit, variously composed of heat and air, coursing through vessels within them.[4] Since the materiality of spirit is a given (an assumption he shares with his silent opponent), explaining the force of that spirit to move an animate body with a solid, stable form—a body with "some fixing"—is categorically little different from technical explanations of gunpowder's reaction to flame. The compressed force of the lively fluid in the "Cells of the Braine, and Canales of the Sinewes" is able to account even for the most intense and vivid displays of muscular force and skill. Recourse to the supernatural, the "marvelous," Bacon insists, is not explanatory.

But, for modern readers, the effect of such comparisons may be just the opposite of what Bacon has in view: his meditation does not dispel marvel but rather effects it with an image of human movement in an alienated, or strangely literalized mode. For Bacon, movement is explosion not because of the possibilities of figuration in discourse but because of the most elemental of physical facts: "Such is the force of these two Natures, *Aire* and *Flame*, when they incorporate." His rhetorical energy is dedicated to opposing the voice of theological physiology, but our imaginations are caught by the strangeness of seeing neural pathways as gun barrels, by the strangeness of imagining wrestling, leaping, music making as actions of a stream of heated, liquefied air on muscle. We are struck, in sum, by the marvel of understanding human movement *literally* as a series of explosions.

The short answer to my opening riddle, then, about what exploding gunpowder, wrestling, and lute playing have in common (in the mind of one famous seventeenth-century questioner) is "spirit": all four are similar actions of matter brought about by the compression of incorporated air and fire moving along the liquid streams of containing vessels. The reason I begin an essay about the early modern body with Bacon's speculations about air and fire is as a reminder, first of all to myself, that the most basic physiological references in early modern texts, certainly those before and even well after Harvey's discovery of the circulation of the blood, begin from a different set of elementary bodily facts than our own. And this is true even when the early modern investigator is, like Bacon, determined to subvert inherited intellectual paradigms.

In this essay, I will concentrate on the early modern body's vessels, which I define here, as seventeenth-century physiologists would have done, to include not only the vascular system of arteries and veins but the neural pathways as well—the three anatomical networks held responsible for the flesh's animating penetration by "spirit." Arteries, veins, and nerve fibers, I want to argue, are bodily systems where semantic differences between past and present discourses of the body may work most powerfully to occlude early modern habits of bodily sensation and self-experience and may lead us to substitute figurative where literal meanings ought to remain. One reason for confusion is that, despite our own lack of belief in the actual material presence of bodily spirits, modern discourses of the body remain pervaded by residues of that earlier physiological lexicon, locutions such as high- or low-spiritedness, which we employ routinely to describe behavior or inner emotional states. ("High" or "low" measured in relation to what bodily or affective center? we might ask deconstructively.) That which is bodily or emotional figuration for us, preserved metaphors of somatic consciousness, was the literal stuff of physiological theory for early modern scriptors of the body. For us, an interpretive literalism is especially necessary in understanding physiological discourse of the vessels' function and meaning because, despite the effects of the "new," post-Vesalian anatomy in subverting Galenic thought, early modern physiology was still profoundly indebted to classical paradigms.[5]

Discourses of the body are never truly literal, of course, since, as with any other discourse, they cannot escape the slippages and deferrals of the signifying chain, the tropings to which even narrowly referential language is subject. As we'll see, to engage in physiological description of the spirits' operations in the vessels of the early modern body was, inevitably, to reproduce master tropes of early modern social narratives. Because the physical and the social—symptomatology and ideology—shared a discursive environment, they worked to demonstrate each other's dominant truths. The master tropes of most interest to me here are those belonging to the history of manners or what Norbert Elias has called "the civilizing process." What Elias meant by "civilizing," says Roger Chartier, was "the pacification of behaviour and control of emotions" characteristic of the history of the early modern subject.[6] For Elias, European court society's explicit goal of disciplining and controlling boorishness (i.e., the aggression and impulsiveness valued by feudal elites) took place through the gradual promotion and inculcation of a set of bodily refinements including table manners, posture, gesture, and expression. At least in theory, internalization of these social demands worked a gradual physical and social transformation, producing not only greater refinement in behavior and regulation of affect but also the heightening of a naturalized self-consciousness about the body's capacity to offend.

What these social regulations on the body have in common with physiological theory of the vessels and spirits is an intense focus upon impulsivity and bodily force, a focus on those energetic faculties—those "spirits" —that make the body move and feel. Physiological explanation, as with Bacon's images of movement, produces a narrative in which the vessels, conceptualized hierarchically, replicate, naturalize, and work to displace the struggles of the civilizing process. In this dynamic, it is the vessels that, in the mode of Bacon's gun barrels, contain the body's internal mechanisms of force and seek to regulate them. Their conduits sustain the body's characteristic temperature and hence are primarily responsible for producing its temperament.[7] Their hierarchical integration of function turns the movements that Bacon visualizes as a series of explosions differing in force and velocity into the sequential, self-contained behaviors of the "civilized" person. Hence the vessels become in effect the body's internal distribution systems of early modern subjectivity, functioning (in the ideal) to bring unique human "essences" suitably refined and moderated out to the limbs and the parts. Along the vessels is transmitted that vocabulary of gesture that enacts the richly nuanced performativity of social embodiment to the world. By bringing order and connection to bodily substance, their networks help to constitute what we might call the early modern subject's imagined physiology of self.

What endows the vessels of the early modern body with this symbolic centrality is, in the first place, a product of anatomical classification. Thus Helkiah Crooke devotes all of Book Eleven of *Microcosmographia*, his massive 1615 description of the body of "man," to the vessels: "Vnder the name of vessels we vnderstand three kinds, Veines, Arteries and Sinewes, because out of these as out of riuers, doe flow into all the parts of the body Blood, Heate, Spirits, Life, Motion and Sense."[8] For Crooke, as for other authorities of the body before Harvey's proof that blood moves in a circle, the veins, arteries, and nerves are recognizably discrete bodily systems carrying out autonomous functions. But they constitute a logical unit of anatomical and physiological thought and description. In the body's complex topography, they are its "riuers," nourishing, irrigating, connecting, and endowing its flesh with life. More important for the body's status as object of knowledge, the vessels seem to Crooke, as anatomical topographer, like the welcome appearance of rivers to an explorer lost in difficult and wooded terrain: they rescue him from the threatening undifference and unknowability of an interior journey through the "dark" substance of flesh.

> Hauing wrought our way through the darke and shady groue of the Muscles *Nulli penetrabilis astro*, into the secret whereof I thinke no wit of man is able to reach: ... we are now ariued in these medowes, where the vessels like so many brookes do water and refresh this pleasant Paradise or modell of heauen and earth; I meane the body of man. And surely by these streames doe grow many pleasant flowers of learning to entertaine and delight our mindes beside the maine profit arising there-from vnto the perfection of that Art we haue in hand. (825)

Like rivers issuing from invisible sources, each network of vessels was thought to arise from one of the body's principal organs—veins from the liver, arteries from the heart, nerves from the brain. And the fluids each system delivered were, like all assimilated fluids of the early modern body, hierarchically interrelated but essentially alike as increasingly pure, increasingly spirit-filled products of blood and inspired air.[9] In the conceptual linking of blood flow, both arterial and venous, with neural transmission, blood, spirit, and sensation become nearly indistinguishable in action and properties.[10] "Blood" becomes related integrally to "sense," and blood vessels become, in effect, sites of production and dissemination for the lower reaches of somatic consciousness.

Thus for Crooke, as for Bacon, explanation of the body's ability to move at all—let alone to accomplish the multitude of physical and mental tasks involved in playing division on the lute—builds upon the *fact* of the body as a container of spirit, which Crooke defines early in the *Microcosmographia* as "a subtile and thinne body alwayes moouable, engendred of blood and vapour, and the vehicle or carriage of the Faculties of the soule" (173–74). This key somatic endowment of flesh by spirit proceeded from fundamental classical and Christian dualisms of body and soul. Of the two writers I am concerned with here, however, only Crooke, being the more conventional and theologically accommodating, feels obliged to begin his discussion of the vessels' structure and function by mentioning the soul. But, just as soul by itself could have no connection with medical practice, it had no explanatory force in physiological description: "Whatever a doctor's innermost religious convictions might be," John Henry points out, "his role was to treat all sickness as a purely natural phenomenon."[11] By definition, soul could not be found in anatomical dissection. For anatomy and for physiology, however, the spirits in their "middle Nature" (824) could not be so readily dismissed, either logically or practically. As properties animating, even defining the living body, they, like soul, eluded the anatomist; but, unlike soul, they mattered to his work because they were thought responsible for some of the body's most important structures of visible and behavioral difference, inside and out. Indeed in anatomy's largest structures, they constituted a class all by themselves, being one of the seven *res naturales,* or the "natural" things basic to Galenic thought.[12] Early in his text, Crooke cites Hippocrates' division of the body "into *Continentia, contenta, and impetum facientia,* that is, into parts conteining, conteined, and such as moue with a kinde of impetuous violence" (174). Impetuous violence was the propulsive action of spirit in the body's containing vessels.

Indeed, spirit was thought to be so crucial to the understanding of vessels that, instead of beginning his book describing the vessel systems with an overview of the vessels themselves or even with a summary retrospective of the anatomical journey that his book has thus far accomplished, Crooke begins with a preface devoted to an explanation of the body's three sorts of spirits:

> As in the Heauens the Angels are the Messengers of God, carrying downe his commandements vnto men whome also they guard and defend; so in this *Microcosme* the dull Flesh being of too slow a kind to ensue the noble motions of the Soule, ... our wise Creator ordained spirites of a middle Nature betweene the Soule and the Body, which like quicke Postes, like Purseuants or Heralds might trauell betweene them, and communicate their commission to the particular partes which they receiue eyther at the first hande from the Soule it selfe in the Brayne, or haue it sealed in the Heart or the Liuer, as in her subordinate Officers.[13] (824)

These figures of spirit-messengers traversing a powerfully centralized body/state emphatically presuppose the soul's command and control functions. But Crooke's figuration of the spirits as "Purseuants or Heralds" traveling along the body's vessel networks requires him to personify as well the soul's "subordinate Officers," the heart and liver, and hence to elide the difference between soul and brain. Soul does not go far, in other words, to explain how spirit arises *naturally* in the microcosm of "dull Flesh." And, within the frame of nature, spirit offers itself to the anatomical scriptor as a wilder, less tractable body than Crooke's metaphorical designation of it as soul's obedient herald might suggest. Being material but invisible, hence dangerously hybrid, the ensouled body's spirits can be described only in figures of action, through metonymy (what they effect), or simile:

> [T]heir motion is sudden and momentanie like the lightning, which in the twinkling of an eye shooteth through the whole cope of Heauen; ... or they are like the winde which whiskes about in euery corner and turnes the heauy saile of a Wind-mill, yet can wee not see that which transports it. (824)

Like Bacon's metallurgy, Crooke's meteorology constructs a natural explanation of spirit less as a material substance created by the body and comfortably housed therein than as an flyaway natural force barely held within the bodily frame. Crooke's troping of spirit as lightning or wind aligns the body's forces with wild and unpredictable motions of air, pulled from outside by a needy intake of breath, drawn into the body and retained with difficulty. Unconfined spirit, free as the air and fire of which it is made, uses itself up, breaks out: "How necessary therefore was it that such subtile and vndertaking or actiue Creatures should be confined as well to guide their motion which otherwise would bee inordinate, as also to keepe them from exhaling or vanishing away" (824).

But, we might argue, what has really vanished in these powerful images of the spirits' dispersal and dissolution at the tenuous outer edges of the bodily frame is an idea of spirit controlled discursively by soul or even figuratively by metaphor: what remains in the body is a paradoxical hybrid— spirit obedient as lightning, tractable as wind. For Crooke, such metaphoric displacements of spirit seem unproblematic, doing the work of Bacon's gun barrel to dispel the body's motion as a marvel of theology in order to make it an object of knowledge. Furthermore, by beginning his description of the vessels with an articulation of spirits and, implicitly, a celebration of *pneuma*'s breakaway force, Crooke makes the spirits responsible for the vessels' internal organization and behaviors rather than the reverse: "Nature therefore because the Spirites are of three sorts, Naturall, Vitall and Animall, hath prepared three kindes of Vesselles for their transportation, Veines, Arteries, and Sinewes" (824). The inductive circularity here is manifest only across an epistemic gulf. Features of gross anatomy, especially those of great structural complexity, produce a comforting teleology, reassuring Crooke as to the existence within us of impetuous, constantly moving agents he cannot see or describe except, like Bacon, through imagining the active field of human bodies as something else. He nevertheless remains convinced:

> That there is an Animall spirit . . . many reasons do euict. For to what purpose else was the braine hollowed or bowed into so many arches? To what purpose are those intricate mazes and labyrynthes of small Arteries. . . . And why are the sinewes propagated into so many branches? (174–75).

What the differential force and nature of the spirits account for, in fact, is not only the tripartite structure of the vessels themselves but the visible differences between them, as, for example, their differences in tensile strength and density:

> The Veines because their guest is not so subtile but a more cloudy and thicke spirit, generated immediately out of the purer substance of the blood, haue but a single coate, as being sufficient to conteine a more quiet spirit. The Arteries because their spirits are more sprightfull and impetuous, moouing alwayes with a subsultation, and perpetually playing up & down, are made (as some thinke) sixefould as thicke as the Veines, the safer to immure the vnruly Inmate. (824)

Here as before, *Microcosmographia*'s most suggestive ideological tracery is to be glimpsed in its tropings, whereby bodily substances enact relations of hospitality or discipline, undergo differential bodily protocols of assimilation and refinement. Tropes of hospitality, alternating with tropes of discipline and confinement, replace tropes of nature; meteorological forces are brought within doors, into the body's implied domestic culture and means of production. Veins and arteries enact the sanctions of patriarchal physiology, separating the spirits as if by caste in order to make them useful to the dull, hungry flesh.

The interrelations of the spirits and of the vessel systems that transport them, I want to suggest, read out a familiar patriarchal narrative of social productivity by means of hierarchical differentiation. The "cloudy and thicke" spirit-guests of the veins, quietly confined and slowly moving, contrast sharply with the "unruly inmates" of the arteries, which beat against the tough containing fibers in their swift, violent passage through the bodily habitus. Even more telling in this essentially Galenic narrative of human physiology is that bodily substances and fluids acquire privilege by means of their duration within the social field of the body and their distance from the site of bodily origin. Complexity and elaboration of structure, self-evidently good, affirm the details of anatomy's teleological design: "Nature no where in all the body hath made any web or complication of vesselles but onely for a newe coction and elaboration" (283). The successive "coctions" of food and air—from chyle to venous blood to more serous arterial blood to cerebrospinal fluid—enact a physiology under the aegis of romance. In this narrative, dilation and delay, whether anatomical or physiological, are tokens of the human body's privileged place in the order of things.[14] The narrative of physiology is one of assimilation of nature's raw matter—its food and water and air—into the stuff in which consciousness must lodge, the bodily stuff of self, but distillation's change occurs through time-in-the-body and distance along the network of passageways.

Physiological process enacts its own disciplining through refinement of substance. Thus because venous blood is made first, "generated immediately" by the liver, it is cruder than its arterial counterpart, produced later by the greater heat of the heart and cruder still than the even purer concoction of the brain. Over against the purer distillation (read greater worth) of the vital spirits, the natural spirits and the inborn natural faculty that they sustain display a kind of subjection and need for inspirational discipline: "the heate and naturall spirit of the parts wherein this inbredde faculty doth consist is but vncertaine like a fugitiue, and dull or stupid; it standeth in neede of another influent yet like vnto it selfe, whereby it might be stirred vp, established, and from a potentiall vertue brought into an opera ue act" (175). And, in this forgiving but nonetheless strictly differential economy, the lesser natural spirits are due less from the body's work of respiration: "this thicke and cloudy spirit needeth but a little ayre for his refection" (175). As the blood, so the person. And as the structure of the veins, so the structure of the whole body. Thanks to the technology of venesection and early modern medicine's great reliance on phlebotomy, the veins had a particular privilege since they offered a multitude of bodily sites for cultural semiotics to take hold:

> [B]ecause the blood through the veines is diuided into the whole body, wee may well make estimation of the plenty and temper of the bloode by the amplitude and straytness of the Veynes. They that haue much blood are esteemed hot, for their veynes are large. (827)

But this picture of vital process implies the likelihood of excess or instability. The motility of the vital spirits, manifested in the incessant beating or "subsultation" of the arteries, would threaten to produce too great, too explosive a set of impulses unless it were ballasted. For early physiologists, this need for ballast in the blood offered a function for the otherwise somewhat mysterious spleen, to produce the black bile whose weight could help to stabilize the lightness and even violent impetuosity of arterial blood:

> A part also happely of this humour thus altered is drawne into the next adioyning arteries, and so conueyed into the great Artery, to contemperate the intense and sharp heat of the bloud in the left ventricle of the heart, and to establish and settle the nimble & quick motions of the vitall spirits, which are a very great cause why some mens wits are so giddy and vnconstant. (128)

But the spleen's contribution, because it affected only blood vessels, could moderate only blood itself. Smoothing out and gentling the otherwise explosive movements produced by the lower spirits was the task and movement of the animal spirits, which were neither sluggish and stable like natural spirits, nor jumpy and incessantly playful like vital spirits. As with other analogies between spirit and the structures that contain them, the membranous structure of the brain follows from the character of the spirits it is intended to administer. These "do rather Beame then are transported" (824), being irradiated along the neural pathways rather than propelled; they contributed refinement and continuity to the otherwise crude and jerky commotions of the limbs:

> The Nerves are nothing else but productions of the marrowy and slimy
> substance of the Brayne, through which the Animall spirits do rather
> beame then are transported, ... And this substance is indeede more fit for
> Irradiation then a conspicuous or open cauity, which would haue made
> our motions and Sensations more sudden, commotiue, violent and dis-
> turbed, whereas now the members receiuing a gentle and successiue illu-
> mination are better commaunded by our Will and moderated by our
> Reason. (824)

Here, Crooke's physiology meets and improves upon Bacon's. Human
motion does not arise from successive tiny explosions along neural pathways but from a luminescent force operating continually within the human
frame to move the muscles and—by an easily recognizable though silent
progression from physiology to psychology—to produce the consistency of
behaviors ideally characteristic of the human "essence" knowable to its self-
conscious possessors as "Will" and "Reason."

But both these explanations of human motion display how easily physiological knowledge intersects with early modern behavioral thought to produce somatically based theories of desire and affect. The penetration of
flesh by spirit that was accomplished by the vessels had the effect of distrib-
uting needs and affects outward to every part, of radically decentralizing
what might be called the body's intentionality or even the physiology of its
ensoulment. Thus for Crooke, the sensation of hunger does not arise merely
from a bilateral communication of stomach and brain but is produced,
rather, by an experience of lack distributed everywhere in hungry, mortal,
subjected flesh:

> [O]ur substance is in perpetuall wasting and decay; the inbred heate con-
> tinually feeding vpon the Radicall moysture. But now it is otherwise,
> because the naturall hunger that is setled in euery particular part, hath
> with it adioyned a sence of discontent, which is onely appeased by assimu-
> lation of fresh nourishment. (122)

This fresh nourishment is the blood transported by the veins to the members and there consumed. Bodily behaviors result from the interactions of
bodily substances that the vessels bring about. Just as black bile stabilizes
arterial blood's potential to produce giddy impulsiveness or even violence
(symbolized by the continous "subsultation" of the arteries), so the dead
weight of flesh is enlivened by the diverse actions of the spirits conducted
outward by veins, arteries, and nerves from the tripartite organic center of
liver, heart, and brain. The importance of the vessels, especially the veins
and arteries, is not only as the distribution network of vital bodily goods

but also as one of the physiological body's most powerful ordering and uni-fying principles: "by the veynes," says Crooke, "the whole body hath a kind of connexion or coherence" (827).

Crooke's correlations of bodily substances and bodily behaviors are particularly revealing of early modern materialist psychology because he intends a complete description of the human corpus. Unlike theorists of the passions or the complexions, such as the English Jesuit Thomas Wright or the Belgian physician Levinus Lemnius, Crooke seems uninterested in the possibilities of humoral typology to classify human behaviors or personali-ties. Correlations between structure and ethos occur in his text as after-thoughts, as the obviousness of cultural commonplace. And because the properties of human psychological difference are not his theme, they can function instead as a readily available body of evidence for corroborating otherwise unknowable physiological process. To describe the actions of the vessels and the spirits carried within them is to qualify and naturalize the behaviors that those spirits generate—behaviors that, in turn, act heuristi-cally to express the quality of the inner movements of "Blood, Heate, Spirits, Life, Motion, and Sense" (825) within the bodily frame.

Crooke's account of the spirit-containing vessels, taken together with Bacon's theory of muscle physiology as a stream of small explosions, pro-duces an image of physical behavior understood as a powerful tension. It is a tension between the impetuous violence of the three sorts of spirits—con-stantly moving, "playing vp & down" (824), continually threatening to exhale or vanish away—and the moderating work of the vessels to bring connectedness and fluidity to the body's movements in social space and time. The vessels, issuing from deep within the body's organic core out to its readable surfaces, mediate and naturalize contradictory demands between the propulsive force of the spirits and the regulatory regimes of the civilizing process. Without the work of the vessels, as Crooke presents it, human movement would be disturbed, violent, unsequential, impulsive. It would, in other words, resemble the wild, ungoverned, perpetually moving bodies of adolescent boys, the first and most obvious targets for elite culture's "pacifi-cation of behaviours and the control of emotions." In the canonical text of the civilizing process, Erasmus's *De ciuilitate morum puerilium*, the aristo-cratic boy is enjoined to still his body and to refine his movements lest in his physical impulsiveness he be mistaken for a rustic or madman:

> Continuous eating should be interrupted now and again with stories. Some people eat or drink without stopping not because they are hungry or thirsty but because they cannot otherwise moderate their gestures,

unless they scratch their head, or pick their teeth, or gesticulate with their
hands, or play with their dinner knife, or cough, or clear their throat, or
spit. Such habits, even if originating in a sort of rustic shyness, have the
appearance of insanity about them.[15]

To read Crooke's physiology alongside prescriptions of manners like
these is to glimpse the contours of ideological terrain, the space that ostensibly disinterested physical description shares with social prescription in
early modern England. The texts of Bacon and Crooke offer up images of
bodies moved by natural, vital, or animal spirits at a time when spirits,
motion, and impulse are themselves important signifiers of social difference—the signs, as Erasmus suggests, of rusticity or even insanity for those
who do not recognize the social necessity of physical composure or cannot
achieve it. Using the vascular system, early modern physiological theory
naturalizes an etiology of gesture and movement that reproduces the regulatory procedures of the civilizing process at their most self-contradictory.
For, it is the paradox of civility to celebrate the possession of higher spirits
as the birthright of finer natures but, at the same time, to discourage impulsiveness and uncontrolled aggression and reward consistency, staying
power, predictability, and the control of aggression.

As is often the case with forms of early modern agency poised semantically between figurative and literal meaning, references to the significant
actions of the nerves and vessels are so widely distributed in discourse as to
be almost illegible except under an intensely focused (not to say overdetermined or potentially reductive) scrutiny. I do not have space here to trace in
detail the discursive pathways of the vessels and spirits in canonical literary
texts. Nor can I show, except very briefly, how physiological discourse intersects with the major forms of social representation to yield powerfully naturalized constructions of class and gender difference located within the
body's organic core and distributed by its spirit-bearing vessels. I will try,
by way of conclusion, to sketch out some textual relations between the
motions and emotions privileged by the civilizing process since these
motions and emotions were, on one hand, explicitly prescribed in the manuals of socialization and, on the other, seen as unequally distributed in the
"natural" social hierarchy of bodies. Thus, in the passage from *De civilitate*
quoted above, it is hard to tell whether Erasmus's threat of confusing aristocratic boys, rustics, and madmen is a crude rhetorical strategy of limited
believability or points to a newly felt form of difference. The ability to make
themselves physically and socially distinct, as well as the obligation to do so,
belong in any case to the boys.

What I am suggesting, then, is that physiological discourse of the spirit-bearing vessels, as it appears in dramatic or romantic narratives, provides a historically specific rationale for strong, ethically loaded contrasts between paired traits like impulsiveness versus self-containment, spontaneity versus calculation or strategic thinking. In traditional idealist criticism, such behavioral and emotional contrasts were treated as transhistorical and ethically constitutive, even if moral labels did not attach automatically to the different traits. Contemporary historians of bodies and emotions ought to resist the moral labeling of any represented behaviors, or at least to question the interests always at stake in such representations. In early modern texts, ethical oppositions often work to reveal the historically specific regulatory reforms of the civilizing process and to display the kind of newly moderated, emotionally continuous, and socially distinct subject those reforms were meant to produce. Thus characters, whether male or female, represented in fictions as impulsive, inconsistent, or unable to sustain a mood or action are also likely to bear an imprint of social backwardness, rusticity, or archaism.

The examples of Hotspur and Sir Andrew Aguecheek, two Shakespearean characters who rarely get to inhabit the same sentence, will have to suffice. Thus, in *1 Henry IV*, the complex characterological entity that is nicknamed Hotspur is conspicuously marked by traits of high spiritedness—by vigorous strength, athleticism, spontaneity, hot-bloodedness. Wrestling and leaping—Bacon's metonymies for human explosiveness—are the very motions to which Hotspur attaches his identity: "By heaven, methinks it were an easy leap, / To pluck bright honor from the pale-fac'd moon" (1.3.201–2). His aristocratic spiritedness is directly opposed to Hal's initial languor and forms the core of what the beleaguered king finds to praise when he describes Hotspur as "a son who is the theme of honor's tongue, / Amongst a grove the very straightest plant" (1.1.81–82). But these traits also help to mark Hotspur as socially archaic and determine his relegation to a nostalgically remembered but nonetheless outmoded feudal past when, in the scenes with Lady Percy, they are recoded as adolescent, becoming emotional and physical impulsiveness, restlessness, and finally a kind of aristocratic rusticity. Hotspur, unable and/or unwilling to calibrate his behavior to his social environment, cannot lie still in his wife's lap and listen to the Welsh lady's song.[16]

In *Twelfth Night*, characterization organizes itself around the possession and display of behavioral traits more or less acceptable to the new domestic civility.[17] In Sir Andrew Aguecheek, a comic constellation of conspicuously archaic, socially outmoded traits converge: he is poorly educated, incapable of socially attractive display (like the civilized spiritedness of dancing), and given to provoking quarrels without being able to conclude them. "For besides that he's a fool, he's a great quarreller," says Maria, "and but that he hath the gift of a coward to allay the gust he hath in quarrelling, 'tis thought among the prudent he would quickly have the gift of a grave" (1.3.29–33).[18] In the wordplay of "allay the gust" we hear echoes of Crooke's meteorological figuration of the spirits. And it is a deficit of spirit, or a lack of the blood that carries it, from which Sir Andrew conspicuously suffers. Sir Toby offers a contemptuous diagnosis: "[I]f he were open'd and you find so much blood in his liver as will clog the foot of a flea, I'll eat the rest of the anatomy" (3.2.60–63). Aguecheek's deficiency plays off against Orsino's: self-described as "unstaid and skittish in all motions else, / Save in the constant image of the creature / That is belov'd" (2.4.18–20), Orsino's most consistent action in the play is his relinquishing of erotic agency to Cesario and Sebastian. The dis-spirited passivity of Aguecheek and Orsino also sets off Malvolio's unacceptable behavioral prepossession, his too-calculated summoning up of "prescribed" behaviors that bear no demonstrable relation to the "natural" character of his physical core: "Thy Fates open their hands," the forged letter exhorts him, "Let thy blood and spirit embrace them, and to inure thyself to what thou art like to be, cast thy humble slough and appear fresh" (2.5.146–49). Because Malvolio's preening, unspontaneous behaviors threaten the social distinction that it was Erasmus's task to enjoin, he is punished with the same fate as the aristocratic boy unable to keep still at table: being mistaken for a madman, one possessed by the spirits of others.

Discursive evidence from Shakespearean playtexts or from learned theory, like the texts of Bacon and Crooke, cannot of course provide even indirect access to the lived bodily experiences of early modern men and women or the collectively imagined bodily experiences of representations. Nor by interrogating the tropings of such texts can we presume to have pressured them into revealing the ideological texture of early modern somatic experiences. What such texts and their tropings do offer us, however, are textually recoverable occasions of somatic alterity, images of bodies *epistemically* though not *biologically* different from our own. My point here in linking these playtexts to Bacon and Crooke is not to suggest that Crooke's physiology of the vessels, or for that matter Bacon's account of motion as explosion through the neural pathways, offers the basis for any new hermeneutic of "the" body, or even "the" early modern body. On the contrary, it seems to me that their tropings of bodily workings offer evidence of almost the reverse: one means of reading early modern bodies otherwise than essentially, of producing a history of affects and behaviors resistant to the seductive evasions and erasures of essentialism. The boys enjoined into mannerliness who kept their bodies still at table and their vital spirits under control would not be mistaken for their impulsive social inferiors, restless rustics or jumpy madmen. And in the social privilege accorded to the motions of wrestling, leaping, or playing division on the lute the controlled violence of their impetuous bodies was—or so the prescriptive theory of behaviors would have us believe—fully on view.

Notes

1. *Sylva Sylvarum: Or a Naturall Historie in Ten Centuries* (London, 1626). All the material quoted occurs on p. 10. For a characterization of *Sylva Sylvarum* as an "often despised work," see Kenneth D. Keele, "Physiology," in *Medicine in Seventeenth-Century England*, ed. Allen G. Debus (Berkeley: University of California Press, 1974), 151.

2. Sir Thomas Elyot, *The Castel of Helth* (London, 1541), 11.

3. See, for example, the theological physiology of Aquinas: "The members do not move themselves but are moved through the powers of the soul," in *The Summa theologica*, quoted in Keele, "Physiology," 147. Elaine Scarry talks about other consequences of the "rather glacial change from a religious to a secular and scientific world" in relation to Donne in "Donne: 'But yet the body is his booke,'" in *Literature and the Body*, ed. Elaine Scarry (Baltimore: Johns Hopkins University Press, 1988), 77.

4. Theological and philosophical controversies about the nature of soul and the relations of soul to spirit are plentiful in the seventeenth century; see John Henry, "The matter of souls: medical theory and theology in seventeenth-century England," in *The medical revolution of the seventeenth century*, ed. Roger French and Andrew Wear (Cambridge: Cambridge University Press, 1989), 87-113.

5. "Though Vesalius in presenting his new human anatomy claimed to have exposed therein some two hundred Galenic errors, deep respect for Galen's physiology remained untouched," says Keele in "Physiology," "for lack of any better physiological concepts to replace it" (148). In *The Advancement of Learning* (2.10.4), Bacon complains about the energy expended on anatomy compared to that on physiology: "they inquire of the parts, . . . but they inquire not of the diversities of the parts, the secrecies of the passages, and the seats or nestling of the humours"; see *The Advancement of Learning*, ed. Arthur Johnston (Oxford: Clarendon Press, 1974), 109.

6. Norbert Elias, *The Civilizing Process,* trans. Edmund Jephcott (New York: Pantheon, 1989); I quote Chartier here from the preface to the new French edition of Elias's *The Court Society* (vol. 2 of *The Civilizing Process*), reprinted as "Social Figuration and Habitus: Reading Elias," in *Cultural History: Between Practices and Representations,* trans. Lydia Cochrane (Ithaca: Cornell University Press, 1988), 74. See also Pierre Bourdieu on societies' "implicit pedagogy" of the body in *Outline of a Theory of Practice,* trans. Richard Nice (Cambridge: Cambridge University Press, 1977), 94.

7. As Lester S. King explains, "The Galenists were fundamentally concerned with the dynamic aspects of reality, with function and activity.... How did objects produce their effects? Quite obviously the effects depended largely upon the qualities that inhered therein; for example, an object would be hot because of the primary quality *hot* present in the appropriate elements. The properties or *vires* bore a direct relation to the proportionality or balance of the qualities. This balance represented their *temperamentum* or *temperies.*" See "The Transformation of Galenism" in Debus, *Medicine in Seventeenth-Century England,* 19.

8. Helkiah Crooke, *Microcosmographia, A Description of the Body of Man* (London, 1615), 825. All further quotations from Crooke will be cited parenthetically. Crooke's statement could not be made after Harvey's demonstration, because the venous system could no longer be thought of as effluent, bringing life-sustaining humors and spirits contained in the blood out to the parts. See Gweneth Whitteridge, *William Harvey and the Circulation of the Blood* (London: Macdonald; and New York: American Elsevier, 1971), 210–35.

9. For a discussion of the "free-trade economy of bodily fluids," see Thomas Laqueur, *Making Sex: Body and Gender from the Greeks to Freud* (Cambridge: Harvard University Press, 1990), 35–43. While accepting Laqueur's emphasis on the fungibility of bodily fluids for the early moderns, I (and others) have resisted his further claim that this "corporeal flux" produces an ungendered, implicitly male body. See my critique of Laqueur in *The Body Embarrassed: Drama and the Disciplines of Shame in Early Modern England* (Ithaca: Cornell University Press, 1993), 16–17.

10. This was certainly the case even for Harvey himself after the discovery of the circulation; see Henry, "The Matter of Souls," 92.

11. Henry, "The Matter of Souls," 88-89.

12. The other six were the elements, the temperaments, the humors, the parts, the faculties and functions, and human generation. For a basic presentation of this material, see King, "Transformation of Galenism," 8–9.

13. The location of soul continued to be a matter of controversy, which Crooke ignores here; late in the seventeenth century, according to John Henry, J. B. Van Helmont wanted to locate it in the pylorus "because of its extreme sensitivity and behaviour, which he took to be evidence of emotions, deliberations, and decision-making"; see "The Matter of Souls," 101.

14. Compare Bacon's assessment of the complexity of the human constitution based, in part, on the variety of human nourishment: "[O]f all substances which

nature hath produced, that of man's body is the most extremely compounded" (2, 10.2) in *The Advancement of Learning,* 105. On the privileging of "dilation," as meaning both "to delay" and "to expound at large," see Patricia Parker, "Shakespeare and Rhetoric: 'dilation' and 'delation' in *Othello,*" in *Shakespeare and the Question of Theory,* ed. Patricia Parker and Geoffrey Hartman (New York and London: Methuen, 1985), 54–58. *In Literary Fat Ladies: Rhetoric, Gender, Property* (London: Methuen, 1985), Parker demonstrates links between rhetorical dilatio and the figure of the feminine (10). Here the dilation of the vessels seems to occlude the question of gender altogether, producing a reification of "the" body entirely characteristic of humanism.

15. From "On Good Manners for Boys/*De civilitate morum puerilium,*" trans. Brian McGregor, in *The Collected Works of Erasmus,* vol. 25, ed. J. K. Sowards (Toronto: University of Toronto Press, 1985), 284.

16. This coding of Hotspur's body complicates and enriches the gendered contrast between bodies in Valerie Traub's brilliant, Bakhtinian reading of the play; see "Prince Hal's Falstaff: Positioning Psychoanalysis and the Female Reproductive Body," *Shakespeare Quarterly* 40 (1989): 456–74.

17. For an account of the play in terms of new norms for domestic civility, see Keir Elam, "The Fertile Eunuch: *Twelfth Night,* Early Modern Intercourse, and the Fruits of Castration," *Shakespeare Quarterly* 47 (1996): 1–36.

18. All quotations from Shakespeare refer to G. Blakemore Evans, gen. ed., *The Riverside Shakespeare* (Boston: Houghton Mifflin, 1974).

Part II

❖

Sexing the Part

7. Anal musculature, Julius Casserius plate from Adriaan van de Speigel's *De humani corporis fabrica* (Venice, 1627).

7

Is the Fundament a Grave?

❖

JEFFREY MASTEN

Let's begin with some anatomical considerations. Human bodies are constructed in such a way that it is, or at least has been, almost impossible not to associate mastery and subordination with the experience of our most intense pleasures. This is first of all a question of positioning.

—Leo Bersani, "Is the Rectum a Grave?"

I haue had a most rare vision. I had a dreame, past the wit of man, to say, what dreame it was. . . . Me-thought I was, and me-thought I had. But man is but a patch'd foole, if he will offer to say, what me-thought I had. The eye of man hath not heard, the eare of man hath not seen, mans hand is not able to taste, his tongue to conceiue, nor his heart to report, what my dreame was. I will get *Peter Quince* to write a ballet of this dreame, it shall be called *Bottomes Dreame*, because it hath no bottome.

—*A Midsommer Night's Dreame* (1623 edition)

I

In a widely cited essay, Leo Bersani has recently asked whether the rectum is a grave—the grave of the self, the burial of "proud subjectivity" he sees literalized in, or at least exacerbated by responses to, the AIDS epidemic.[1] The present essay seeks in part to ask whether the rectum—or, as it will be my habit to write for the next few pages, the *fundament*—was, as inescapably as it seems to be for Bersani, a grave, a loss of subjectivity, in early modern England as well. I want to make explicit at the outset that—in what I see as merely preliminary to a broader investigation—my discussion will focus largely on men. But, following a number of important treatments of sexuality in the early modern period, I mean explicitly not to restrict the range of this discussion to "homosexuals"; it will be a contention of this essay that, in an era before the invention of the homo/hetero divide,[2] a consideration of the fundament is relevant to the bodily structures and practices of men generally.

Was the fundament a grave in early modern England? A review of some familiar examples would seem to confirm that this was the case. We could begin for instance at the "back-gate" to Spenser's castle of Alma, a structure "cleped . . . *Port Esquiline*."[3] The passage thus associates the body part with the gate near Rome's Esquiline Hill, used as a pauper's cemetery in antiquity. Likewise, the Red Cross knight's exit from the House of Pride is via a "priuie Posterne," a "fowle way," strewn with "many corses . . . / Which all through that great Princesse pride did fall / And came *to shamefull end*." [4] We could add to this list Hamlet's "Imagination" tracing the "dust" of Alexander the Great in the graveyard, "till he find it stopping a bunghole."[5]

The end of Edward II is another important site for this conjunction of fundament and grave, at least in the famous Holinshed passage now routinely also used to gloss the absence of any stage direction for the "same" scene in Marlowe's play:

> [T]hey came sodenly one night into the chamber where hee lay in bed fast asleepe, and with heavie feather beddes, (or a table as some write) being cast upon him, they kept him downe, and withall put into his fundament an horne, and through the same they thrust up into his bodie a hote spitte, (or as other have through the pype of a Trumpet, a Plumbers instrument of yron made verie hote) the which passing up into his intrayles, and being rolled to and fro, burnt the same, but so as no appearance of any wounde or hurt outwardly might bee once perceyved.[6]

In Holinshed's account the fundament becomes, almost literally, the unmarked grave of Edward; a variety of the historical accounts remark the unmarked nature of Edward's death.

In a less torturous but no less fatal instance, Aston Cokaine's description of the double burial of playwrights John Fletcher and Philip Massinger might seem to activate a similar punning conjunction of fundament and grave:

> In the same Grave *Fletcher* was buried here
> Lies the Stage-Poet *Philip Massinger*.
> Playes they did write together, were great friends,
> And now one Grave includes them at their ends.[7]

In one sense the text seems unambiguous: Cokaine says that Massinger and Fletcher are buried together at the ends *of their lives*, which, as it turns out, ended fifteen years apart: *these* ends, at least, are not coterminous. At the same time, however, the poem also reads sodomitically (we might say *sodometrically*[8]) in its positioning of the two men: laid end to end, lying end to end, the two playwrights seem to find (the text suggests, even in apparently valorizing them) that their ends are at an end, that the fundament has become a grave, two ends in one end. The line between sodomy and friendship is easily crossed, as Alan Bray has helped us to see;[9] here, separated by only a poetic line, sodomy and friendship rhyme: friends at ends; sodomy as fatal attraction.

Such a reading of the conjunction of fundament and grave in early modern England is persuasive, not least for the ways in which the death penalty for sodomy under the laws of the Tudors and Stuarts, itself a version of the conjunction of sodomy and death in Leviticus 20:13, might thus become a default cultural equation played out in less determinedly lethal contexts, like Cokaine's poem—that is to say, even in a context that seems to approve of and publicize homoerotic union.[10] Massinger and Fletcher's lying together might be said to anticipate and preclude the Levitican punishment: lying together in their abominable state, there is no need to kill them: they're already at an end.[11]

But you know from my borrowing of Bersani's question, my re-citing of it *as* an open question, that this cannot be the end of my discussion, and I want here to resist—if only in the form of brief and speculative prolegomena—the seemingly easy early modern connection between the fundament and the grave, the site of sodomy and the end of subjectivity. Or to give a less determinedly literal but no less critical reading to Bersani's essay: the idea that "the rectum" has any single definitive meaning. This is to ask another question, one that engages issues of genealogy and philology that increasingly occupy and enable cultural analyses of sex/gender in the classical, medieval, and early modern periods: what if we do not simply translate, as I have in repeating Bersani's question, the modern *rectum* into the early modern *fundament*? What is lost in translation? What if, instead, we read the rhetoric of the *fundament* itself more critically? "This is first of all," to reiterate Bersani, "a question of positioning." But what position?

II

Bottome ... thou art translated.
　　　　　—*A Midsommer Night's Dreame* (1623)

If *sodometries* are, in Jonathan Goldberg's definition, "relational structures precariously available to prevailing discourses," the prevailing sodometry of the early modern period has been horizontal, the structuring of front and back—more linearly, the beginning and the end. Goldberg and Patricia Parker have both detailed the anality and circulation of the rhetorical trope *histeron proteron*, translated by Puttenham as the "preposterous," a disordering trope that (as Parker writes) "connotes here the reversal of *post* for *pre*, back for front, after for before, posterior for prior, end or sequel for beginning."[12] The sodomitical meanings of this prominent trope come more fully into view when we recall with Parker that John Barret's 1580 dictionary glosses *preposterous* as "arsieversie: contrary to al good order";[13] *preposterous*, as both Goldberg and Parker note, is a period term for sodomy.[14]

Parker makes clear that this horizontal structure of the preposterous—that which is, in Barret's phrase, "contrary to al good order"—is linked to the overturning of traditional bodily and social hierarchies, top for bottom, head for posterior, the raising of the Bakhtinian lower bodily strata. Gail Kern Paster has emphasized this structure of anal rhetorics in her readings of bodily purgation and the reversals of Bottom and Titania's relation in *A Midsummer Night's Dream*. For Paster too, these structures are related to more general bodily and political structures, "Titania's mastery and Bottom's passivity."[15]

These readings of early modern anal rhetorics are utterly convincing: there in the text to be analyzed once—alerted by Parker's and Goldberg's tracing of these complex webs of etymology, rhetoric, and what we would call "wordplay"—one begins to see them.[16] But I want to suggest that this structure that has seemed always to characterize the rhetoric of the anus (whether that's front and back, beginning and end, top and bottom, head and ass) is not the only rhetoric of the anus in early modern culture: there is at least another rhetoric that is related to but does not structure itself along the same axes as the *histeron proteron, preposterous, arsieversie*. A different "positioning" or sodometry; a sodometry of the fundament.

For *fundament*, of course, does not precisely mean "arse," or "posterior," or "behind"—does not mean these things if we take seriously its etymology and the rhetorical surround of related terms, in the sixteenth and seventeenth centuries in England. *Fundament*, also spelled *foundament* and *foundment* (to name only two of many other forms), is closely related to a set of words that have remained in circulation in English: *foundation*, to *found*, and a bit later, *fund*. One of *fundament*'s meanings, in fact, is "[t]he foundation or base of a wall, building, etc."[17] Indeed, the word *fundament*, in its three primary meanings of "foundation," "buttocks," and "anus," seems to exist in English for a century before *foundation*, the word that, after several centuries of overlap, eventually takes its place. Or more precisely: *one* of its places. It is worth noticing, however, that, through the end of the seventeenth century, *fundament* means "foundation," and *foundation* is used to refer to the body part. Not only can we not give *fundament* and *foundment* distinct histories, as the *OED* notes, but the fundament seems always to be inseparably foundational.[18]

This inseparability is supported by the kinds of hard-word lists and translation dictionaries from the period that the *OED* does not cite. In Minsheu's 1617 *Ductor in Linguas*, for example, the entry for "to *founde*, or cause to bee built"[19] overlaps significantly in its translations with the entries for *fundament*. The entries for *fundament* itself translate the word into a group of meanings around *foundation* (German *Grundt*, Greek *Basis*) and then around *seat* (Latin *sedes*, French *siege*, German *gesesz*, etc.).

Such a history will seem obvious to anyone who has contemplated the etymology of the word still with us, *fundamental*. Yet it is important to notice the way in which even the word *fundamental* in this period has not yet been transfigured into dead metaphoricity; at the same time that *fundament* is circulating as "buttocks" and "anus,"[20] the word *fundamental* is being used as we would use, in its most literal sense, *foundational* (meaning "of a foundation"). Texts speak of a building's "fundamentall walls," the "first fundamental stone" of a foundation.[21] John Florio's 1598 *Worlde of Words* translates the Italian "Fondamentale, [as] *fundamentall, that hath or is a ground or foundation.*"[22] Many uses of this set of related terms seem to have a religious valence: in a 1650 text cited by the *OED*, for example, Christ is described as the church's "fundamental stone." Again, this is perhaps not surprising to those who have considered modern religious fundamentalism's relation to an ostensible textual foundation; what *is* striking in this context is the coexistence of the ass(hole) and the church's foundation in a complexly interimplicated rhetoric.[23]

What interests me in these texts is the way in which the *fundament* resists what have been the normative ways of talking about the anus—ways that may begin to suggest, at least in certain contexts, the alterity of this culture's conception of the anus and of the body attached to and articulated around it. Or, to be more attentive to the discourse: the body constructed *upon* it. I have already suggested the way in which the rhetoric of the fundament is not preposterous, not bassackwards, or arsieversie. But notice too that the fundament is not always necessarily imagined in this cultural context as a passive recipient or receptacle of dominating penetration. Instead, it is "a grounde, a foundation, a building"[24]—it "hath *or is* a ground or foundation."[25] Or, as Florio also translates, "Also an offspring, beginning, or groundworke."[26] This is not a language of passivity; in fact, it seems largely outside or unengaged with an active/passive binary. At the same time, the fundament is imagined as originary: an offspring, beginning— and thus at some distance from the preposterous ends of the other anal rhetorics. Consider Thomas Elyot's description of the function of the fundament in *The Castel of Helth* (1541), in his chapter "Of Euacuation":

> [T]here be two sortes of ordure, that is to saye, one digested, which passeth by siege [a word we have seen above, in Minsheu: from *seat*, but also meaning "stool" and thus "shit"], the other vndigested, which is expellyd by vomyte. Where I saye digested, I meane, that it is passed the stomake, and tourned in to another fygure.[27]

For Elyot, the mouth and the fundament are equally salubrious sites of evacuation; like the mouth, the fundament produces health through purgation. And perhaps in this sense it is seen as more productive: what the fundament passes has been "tourned in to another fygure."

This is what is perhaps most striking about the rhetoric of the fundament, especially when juxtaposed with the more familiar Bakhtinian model of the bottom, the lower bodily strata; while the fundament, as foundation and seat, may participate in the rhetoric of the low, this is lowliness with a positive valence—the foundational is hardly a negative rhetoric in this culture. Consider, for example, Florio's 1611 translation of the Italian "Fondataménte, [meaning] from the very foundation, groundedly, vpon good ground or foundation. Also deeply, or profoundly."[28] (At this point, it is probably unnecessary to point out pro*fund*ity's etymological relation to *fund*ament.)

One might easily extend this hypothesis too far, but I want nevertheless to advance it as an observation that has some explanatory power. First, however, I want to articulate what is at stake theoretically in this observation, and to do so by noting that part of the impetus for a rethinking of what we call the anus emerges from the work of two modern theorists. Lee Edelman has suggested the importance of reviewing the binarism that places in opposition a valued activity and a derogated passivity, in a way that is ultimately tied to the formation and articulation of the subject in culture: within the modern regime Edelman is critiquing, "the civic authority of subject status" is thought to be "purchased through the projective refusal of the luxurious 'passivity,' . . . that signifies the erotic indulgence of the self that always threatens to undo the 'self.'"[29] Edelman shows in particular how the modern use of an active/passive rhetoric by gay men urging other gay men to activism reenacts and reinscribes the familiar binary that has done the work of oppression (usually from the "outside") in prior cultural moments. Thinking about the early modern rhetoric of the fundament might be another (historical) way of resisting that binary, for as I have been suggesting, the fundament lies productively in a strangely active-passive position: it is the ground but also the groundwork; the seat but also the offspring; the founding and the foundation. The fundamental is that which "hath *or is* a ground or foundation."[30]

As I hope to show in more detail near the end of this essay, my hypothesis is also a historicist attempt to address Guy Hocquenghem's theorization of the anus as the seat of a privately owned subjectivity: "[I]t forms," he says, activating the etymologies at the base of my argument, "the subsoil of the individual, his 'fundamental' core."[31] To think in this way might be to emerge from the Freudian model Hocquenghem's text itself works to resist, in which (he argues) "the homosexual can only be a degenerate, for he does not generate—he is only the artistic end to a species."[32] The fundament—if not, in Hocquenghem's term, "the homosexual"—might be said to found, to generate, to merge in a (to us) strangely active-passive, object-subject position.

We might indeed take this to be the meaning of another of Thomas Elyot's evocations of the fundament, this time not in the *Castel of Helth* (itself an edifice with a fundament) but instead in his 1538 Latin/English dictionary. There, as the other dictionaries have taught us to anticipate, Elyot defines Latin "Fundamen, & fundamentum [as] *a fundacion,*" related closely (etymologically and on the page) to "Fundo . . . , to founde, to make stable," and to "Fundus, that whyche is vsed to be callyd lande or soyle."[33] In the dictionary's "additions," however, "Fundus, is somtyme taken for a foundation, also for the chiefe authour of a thynge."[34] *Author:* itself from Latin *augere* ("to make to grow, originate, promote, increase") and meaning, in period English, to generate, to father, also a Creator, a writer, a cause.[35] Elyot's "chiefe authour" is probably closer to "authority" than to modern "authorship," but to read his startling conjunction of fundament and author, and to entertain the possibility that others in this culture might likewise have seen it, is to ask Foucault's familiar question once again, in an unaccustomed position: "What is an author, that it is related to a fundament?"[36]

Obviously, I am indulging in some speculation here, tracing some possible positionings made available by an early modern discourse of the fundament, but I do at the same time want to show that such a discourse may indeed have been available in the sixteenth and seventeenth centuries, and that, furthermore, it might have some relevance not simply for thinking about bodies in their particular members (and the uses and functions of bodies) but also for excavating other discursive strata. Take, of all unexpected anatomical sites, the following passage from the preface to the reader of James I's *Works* (1616), a discussion of precedents for James's royal authorship:

> [God] wrote, and the writing was the writing, saith *Moses*, of God; . . . the matter was in Stone cut into two Tables, and the Tables were the worke of God written on both sides. *Diuines* hold, that the Heart is the principall Seate of the Soule; which Soule of ours is the immediate worke of God, as these Tables were the immediate worke of his owne fingers. . . . And certainely from this little *Library*, that God hath erected within vs, is the foundation of all our Learning layd.[37]

Is this passage, concluding as it does at the foundation, "about" the early modern anus? Probably not, although as my quotation marks around *about* suggest, I think it is a theoretical problem of some complexity to extricate the body from the building this prose erects.

Does the passage, however, engage the rhetoric of foundationalism that informs the articulation and experience of the anus in early modern England? In this passage, the heart is the "Seate" of the soul; the soul is the work and groundwork of an authorial god, writer of the Decalogue; the Decalogue, a "little *Library*" within us, situated in the seate/soul, is a foundation—the productive foundment of "all our Learning." The body is figured here as a building; indeed, the passage is itself a rhetorical edifice related to the trope of *gradatio*,[38] culminating in a foundation: heart = soul; soul = God's commandments; commandments = foundation. Or perhaps not "culminating" but *delving down to* the foundation, and building up the religious subject from this groundwork: to the extent that the passage encodes an early modern notion of readerly interiority or subjectivity, that space is both fundamentally situated and textually articulated. Reading is fundamental.

The edifice of knowledge built upon the fundament is not to be found only in quasi-religious contexts. Consider the following series of medical procedures, detailed in *A treatise of the Fistulae in the fundament,* a 1588 translation and publication of a fourteenth-century text by John Arderne:

> Let the pacient be decently layde vppon a bed against a faire light window. . . . Which done, let the chirurgian put the fore finger of the left hand into his fundament, and with his other hand, put the head of the instrument called *Sequere me,* into the hole of the Fistulae that is next to the fundament. If there be many holes, proue with your instrument diligently in euery hole, your finger remaning in the fundament.
>
> Let ye paciêt be laid vpon a bed against a light window, and his legges raised vp with a towell or a corde, which being done, lette the fundament be opened with a paire of Tonges made in such order, that when ye presse the one end together, the other may open, or with some other conuenuent instrument, at your discrecion.
>
> The fundament being opened, and the griefe diligentlie seene, let the hole be filled with [the following medicines].[39]

These passages (and there are more, not for the squeamish) resonate strikingly with the author-surgeon's description of his own project, the opening and publication of medical knowledge:

> [I]n hard things students and practicioners should be more busie to seeke out the secrets of nature. . . . Therefore to the honour of almightie God, that *opened knowledge to mee,* that I should *finde treasure within the fielde of knowledge,* that with longe time and panting breast, I haue sweat and trauailed, and full busilie indeuored my selfe as my facultie suffiseth, to *sette foorth* this woorke faithfullie.[40]

In this text, the fundament is assuredly not a grave (the writer claims to have cured the fistulae of nineteen patients, "with many other which it were to long to set downe"[41]); it becomes the foundation or seat of knowledge, which is *set* forth and *set* down (as a foundation, basis, groundwork), and, following the cure, the foundation of a castle of health for its patients. Likewise, in the descriptions of medical procedure, we see an emergent language of knowledge: "*proue* with your instrument diligently." In a culture where knowledge is figured as depth, the fundament may be fundamental.

We are witnessing here, in a specifically fundamental form, an important resemblance, articulated in many other locations in early modern culture, between the rhetoric of the body and the rhetoric of bodily knowledge, its pursuit, and its setting forth. This conjunction is most famously on display in the title page to Vesalius's *Fabrica,* a book that makes opening the body analogical to opening the book that displays the opened body.[42] This equation of bodily knowledge and the opened book of bodily knowledge is made in another form in a later English anatomical atlas of 1695, *A Survey of the Microcosme: Or, The Anatomy of the Bodies of Man and Woman*. In this remarkable book, several plates (called "Visions") of male and female bodies can literally be opened by the reader: paper flaps representing the skin and layers of organs can be pulled back to reveal other layers—still more bodily knowledge. In Vision II, Figure H (this flap "[r]epresents the Intestines"): "a. the *Anus*, or Fundament." The Fundament here is inside, to be opened out.

III

It is perhaps obvious, as I move further astray from any text that has a homoerotic or sodomitical valence, that the discourse of the fundament I have sought here to uncover may hold no great liberatory erotic potential.[43] After allegorizing the fundament's excretory function, Phineas Fletcher's *The Purple Island, Or, The Isle of Man* suggests obliquely and without further explanation that it is a "gate endow'd with many properties"[44] but does so in the context of a volume that is also explicitly antisodomitical.[45] I do nevertheless think that there is something to be learned from these materials about (1) the placement of the fundament within mappings of the (male) body and the cultural resonances of those mappings, and (2) a sodometry that somehow accounts for the foundationalism of the anus, that is to say: an analysis of eroticism that engages with this alternative understanding of the anus-as-foundation in early modern culture.

Reading the rhetoric of the fundament—that is, an asshole that is not the derogated bottom of the lower bodily strata, not the backside of what should "rightfully" be front-sided—may alert us to other unusual sodomitical positionings, sodometries, that we would not otherwise see. Reading Marlowe's *Edward II*, I had always assumed—and my assumption seems, on the basis of Derek Jarman's film version and several recent stage versions, to be widely shared—that Edward ends face down, overthrown, arsieversie, bottoms up. But consider a 1626 verse version of Edward's end, published as Francis Hubert's in 1628, quoted here from the manuscript at the Folger:

> 583
> But being ouer watcht and wearie too
> Nature asmuch desirous of some rest
> Which gave them opportunitie to doe

What they desir'd .' for being wth sleep opprest
They clapt a massie table on my breast
    And wth great waight, so kept me downe wthal
    That breathe I could not, muchles crie or call;

      584
And then into my fundament they thrust,
A litle horne, as I did groueling lie . . . [46]

Do I need to go on?—you know how this one ends up. Or do you? It does end up, in one sense: Edward ends face up, ass down, the table on his *breast*. But it also does not quite end there either. For strange as it may seem, Edward goes on to narrate another stanza, a kind of moral conclusion or end to his story, and with it, there comes the reader's realization that this whole text—spoken in the first person singular, as these excerpts have suggested—emerges *after*, or on the basis of, his end. The fundament again seems no grave here, at least in a narratological or discursive sense. It seems to produce a long narrative poem, ending in its 584th stanza, then ending finally again a stanza later, with a final "Finis infortunis," an unfortunate end.

We might, finally, think about what subject positionings could be imagined out of the material circumstances of writing, copying, tracing out, reading, the manuscript of this poem, the 585 stanzas of the first-person discourse of a sodomite, and then of setting all those stanzas in print two years later, to be read more widely. For the persons in this culture who performed these acts of literacy and inscription, what might have been the subjectivity effects of *this* "little Library"—of articulating (copying, reading out, setting forth in type) that resilient "I" for more than four thousand lines? Reading such a text might be foundational, founding, fundamental in quite another way; the fundament may be turned into another figure.

IV

This essay has not engaged the question of early modern psychic structures, and I think a larger consideration of the issues raised here would ultimately want to do so, for it is a central assumption of my argument that what I have been calling "the rhetoric of the fundament" is not *merely* rhetoric; rather, it participates in the structuring of everyday social and psychic life, the experience of the body (at least "a body"), by which I mean the experience of the body-in-culture.[47] This is of course to contest Bersani's assertion, articulated in my epigraph and elsewhere, that "[h]uman bodies are constructed in such a way that it is, or at least has been, almost impossible not to associate mastery and subordination with the experience of our most intense pleasures."[48] Dwelling on the foundment has, I hope, at least troubled the notion of "bodies constructed [only] in such a way." But what—to follow this sentence further—are "*our* most intense pleasures," and are they the same as those experienced by the early moderns? In this passage, Bersani is writing about (heterosexual) penetration, but we should notice that "our" pleasures, even our "most intense" ones, shift around, apparently, even in modernity. Elsewhere, in the context of sadomasochism, Bersani cites "the powerful appeal of those ["authoritarian"] structures, their harmony with the body's most intense pleasures" and—still elsewhere, in a context that becomes but has not yet been articulated as "the experience of masturbation"—he echoes these citations by citing "a man's most intense experience of his body's vulnerability."[49] Is the rectum, even in Bersani's texts, the site of definitive, superlative pleasure?

To dislodge the rectum or anus from any definitive and transcultural meaning—to acknowledge that the fundament might be turned into another and different figure—may be analogically to experience *Bottomes Dreame*, or at least to read the experience it encodes seriously. Speaking as a historian of the experience of his own body, Bottom reviews his "most rare vision," an experience legible only as a dream that troubles the meaning of subjectivity ("Me-thought I was") and of the body ("me-thought I had"), and that imagines (if only in a negative fantasy) a body in parts set loose from their customary meanings and functions: hearing eyes, seeing ears, tasting hands, conceiving tongues, reporting hearts.[50] What is a fundament in this context? What does a bottom do? *Bottomes Dreame* is of course ultimately antifundamentalist; its vision sees no stable ground or groundwork of bodily meaning, no definitive answer to such questions: "it hath no bottome." The rectum—we have seen Phineas Fletcher note, in his less explicitly synaesthetic, if no less phantasmatic, description of *The Isle of Man*—is "endow'd with many properties."[51]

NOTES

1. Leo Bersani, "Is the Rectum a Grave?" in *AIDS: Cultural Analysis/Cultural Activism*, ed. Douglas Crimp (Cambridge: M.I.T. Press, 1988), 222. Subsequent citations will appear parenthetically.

2. On this, see Alan Bray, *Homosexuality in Renaissance England* (London: Gay Men's Press, 1982); Bray, "Homosexuality and the Signs of Male Friendship in

Elizabethan England" in *Queering the Renaissance*, ed. Jonathan Goldberg (Durham: Duke University Press, 1993), 40–61; Jonathan Goldberg, *Sodometries: Renaissance Texts, Modern Sexualities* (Stanford: Stanford University Press, 1992).

3. Edmund Spenser, *The Faerie Queene*, ed. Thomas P. Roche, Jr. (New Haven: Yale University Press, 1978), II.9.32.7–8.

4. Ibid., I.5.52–53, my emphasis. In the context of his topographical, quasi-Spenserian surveying of the body as an *island*, Phineas Fletcher likewise figures the anus as a "port *Esquiline*" that "between two hills, in darkest valley lies." (P.F., *The Purple Island, Or The Isle of Man: Together with Piscatorie Eclogs and Other Poeticall Miscellanies* (Cambridge: by the Printers to the Universitie, 1633), 27 (canto 2.43).

5. *The Tragedie of Hamlet, Prince of Denmarke*, in *Mr. William Shakespeares Comedies, Histories, & Tragedies* (London: by Isaac Iaggard, and Ed. Blount, 1623), as reproduced in *The Norton Facsimile: The First Folio of Shakespeare*, prepared by Charlton Hinman (New York: Norton, 1968), TLN 3390–92, (5.1.202–4). *OED* gives a 1611 usage of *bung-hole* as "anus" and a late-seventeenth-century use of *bung* as "bum" (see *bung* [*n*. 1], meanings 5 and 6). Hamlet's description of "stopping a bunghole" as a "base vse" I take to be resonant both with the explicit sense of the passage (to associate "Noble" Alexander with beer barrels is ignobling) and with sodomy as a "base" practice (also sometimes associated with class transgression and usury).

6. Holinshed's *Chronicles* 2:883, as quoted in Bruce R. Smith, *Homosexual Desire in Shakespeare's England* (Chicago: University of Chicago Press, 1991), 220. My "same" is in quotation marks, for, as Stephen Orgel has recently pointed out, critics have not been fully attentive to the difference this lack of direction (at least in the printed text) might make for the meaning of the scene; see *Impersonations: The Performance of Gender in Shakespeare's England* (Cambridge: Cambridge University Press, 1996), 47–48. A notable exception to this critical blindness is Derek Jarman's film version (British Screen & BBC Films, Fine Line Features, 1992), which stages Edward's death à la Holinshed as (only) a dream/fantasy. Orgel's certainty that the hot spit was *not* used in early modern performance seems to me to occlude some other possibilities: that, like many other stage directions, it doesn't appear in the printed text (technically speaking, Edward doesn't die either); or that a stage direction used in performance was (for whatever reason, perhaps including censorship) left out of the printed version.

7. Sir Aston Cokain, Epigram 100, *Small Poems of Divers sorts* (London: by Wil. Godbid, 1658), 186.

8. As I make clear below, I take this term from Jonathan Goldberg's *Sodometries*; I mean to engage at least two of its meanings outlined there: structures and positions of sodomy, and the argument whose logic seems illogical.

9. Alan Bray, "Homosexuality and the Signs of Male Friendship," 40–61.

10. On Tudor/Stuart sodomy laws, see Bruce Smith, *Homosexual Desire in Shakespeare's England: A Cultural Poetics* (Chicago: University of Chicago Press,

1991), 41–53. Also Gregory W. Bredbeck, *Sodomy and Interpretation: Marlowe to Milton* (Ithaca: Cornell University Press, 1991) 5–10, 18–20; Goldberg, *Sodometries*, 3, 7, (cf. also 238–42 on America); Janet E. Halley, "*Bowers v. Hardwick* in the Renaissance," in *Queering the Renaissance*, 15–39. A number of contemporary sodomy prosecutions are discussed in Bray, *Homosexuality in Renaissance England.*

11. I read the collaborative homoerotics of this poem in more detail in the introduction to *Textual Intercourse: Collaboration, Authorship, and Sexualities in Renaissance Drama* (Cambridge: Cambridge University Press, 1997), 1–4.

12. Patricia Parker, "Preposterous Reversals: *Love's Labor's Lost*," *Modern Language Quarterly* 54, no. 5 (1993): 435–36.

13. Quoted in Parker, "Preposterous Reversals," 436.

14. Goldberg, *Sodometries*, esp. 180–81; Parker, "Preposterous Reversals," 479. I also want to acknowledge the influence throughout this essay of Goldberg's "The Anus in *Coriolanus*" (paper delivered at the Shakespeare Association of America meeting, Albuquerque, April 1994).

15. Gail Kern Paster, *The Body Embarrassed: Drama and the Disciplines of Shame in Early Modern England* (Ithaca: Cornell University Press, 1993), 138.

16. On this kind of linguistic activity as structuring early modern English rather than as linguisitic excess or (merely) intentional "wordplay," see Margreta de Grazia, "Homonyms Before and After Lexical Standardization," *Shakespeare Jahrbuch* (1990), 143–56.

17. Definitions and citations are from the *OED* (2d ed.) except where otherwise noted.

18. The *OED* writes (in a somewhat anachronistic view of the idea of discrete words) that the "form *fundament* is directly from the Lat., and is therefore strictly a distinct word from *foundment*, but it is convenient to treat them together on account of the occurrence of mixed forms." On *foundation* as *fundament*, see *foundation* 5b.

19. Iohn Minsheu, *Ductor in Linguas, The Guide into the tongues* (London: for Iohn Browne, 1617), 204. Roman type here indicates blackletter in the original.

20. Both of these terms were also in use in the period, though *anus* seems to have been restricted to more learned and medical use.

21. *OED, fundamental* 1.

22. Iohn Florio, *A Worlde of Wordes, Or Most copious, and exact Dictionarie in Italian and English* (London: by Arnold Hatfield for Edw. Blount, 1598), 135.

23. A different but related positioning of God (Christ?), fundament, and church is mapped in Richard Rambuss's important rereading of the Donne sonnet "Batter my heart," in "Pleasure and Devotion," in Goldberg, *Queering the Renaissance*, 271–74. It is not irrelevant that many anatomy texts in the period refer to the coccyx as "The Holy-bone, called *Os sacrum*, . . . not because it containeth in it any sacred and hidden mystery, as some haue fondly imagined, but because of his greatnesse, for it is the greatest of all the bones of the Spine";

Helkiah Crooke, *Microcosmographia, A Description of the Body of Man* (London: by W. Iaggard, 1616), 978.

24. Florio, A WORLDE of Wordes, 135.

25. Ibid., my (de)emphasis.

26. Iohn Florio, *Qveen Anna's New Worlds of Words, Or Dictionarie of the Italian and English tongues* (London: by Melch. Bradwood, for Edw. Blount and William Barret, 1611), 192.

27. Thomas Elyot, *The Castel of Helth Corrected and in some places augmented, by the fyrste authour therof. syr Thomas Elyot knyght* (1541), 53r.

28. Florio, *Qveen Anna's New World of Words*, 192.

29. Lee Edelman, "The Mirror and the Tank: 'AIDS,' Subjectivity, and the Rhetoric of Activism," in *Homographesis: Essays in Gay Literary and Cultural Theory* (New York: Routledge, 1994), 110. Edelman's essay has been a foundational influence on the present essay; see also his commentary on Bersani's "Is the Rectum a Grave?" 98–99.

30. The fundament as a site of subject-producing activity is articulated by Crooke, in his chapter "Of the muscles of the Fundament, the Bladder, the Testicles and the Yard":

> Because Man was a politique creature, made for Action and contemplation, it was not fit that he should either receiue his nourishment, or auoyde his excrements perpetually as plants doe, but at his owne choyce. As therefore in the Chops there are muscles seruing for diglutition or swallowing, so in the end of the guts and the outlet of the vrine, there are muscles set as porters to interclude the passage vnlesse we list to open it. (*Microcosmographia*, 803)

31. Guy Hocquenghem, *Homosexual Desire*, trans. Daniella Dangoor, preface by Jeffrey Weeks, new introduction by Michael Moon (Durham: Duke University Press, 1993), 100.

32. Ibid., 107.

33. *The Dictionary of syr Thomas Eliot knyght* (Londini: Thomae Bertheleti, [1538]) n.p. My italics signify blackletter (normative) type in the original.

34. Ibid., "The additions," n.p.

35. Quotation and summary of the *OED*'s entries for *author*. See also the frontispiece to this essay, which seems to register a body, as well as a tree, growing up from the fundament.

36. Michel Foucault, "What Is an Author?" in *The Foucault Reader*, ed. Paul Rabinow, (New York: Pantheon, 1984), 101–20. On the relation of early modern *author* to modern authorship, see Masten, *Textual Intercourse*, 64–73.

37. *The Workes of the Most High and Mightie Prince, Iames* (London: Iames, Bishop of Winton, 1616), sig. b3, original emphasis.

38. On *gradatio*, see Thomas Wilson, *The Arte of Rhetorique* (London: by George Robinson, 1585); reprint, ed. G. H. Mahr (Oxford: Clarendon Press, 1909), 204; Patricia Parker, *Literary Fat Ladies: Rhetoric, Gender, Property* (London and New York: Methuen, 1987), 96.

39. The treatise is printed as a part of *A most excellent and Compendiovs Method of curing woundes in the head, and in other partes of the body, with other precepts of the same Arte, practised and written by that famous man Franciscvs Arcevs, Doctor in Phisicke & Chirurgery: and translated into English by Iohn Read, Chirurgion. Whervnto Is Added The exact cure of the Caruncle, neuer before set foorth in the English toung. With a treatise of the Fistulae in the fundament, and other places of the body, translated out of Iohannes Ardern* (London: by Thomas East, for Thomas Cadman, 1588), 85v–86v, 89v. (The text is printed in blackletter; the emphases here signify the original's roman.) The Arderne text is internally dated 1349; on Arderne and this text (including illustrations from the MS version), see D'Arcy Power, ed., *Treatises of Fistula in Ano, Haemorrhoids, and Clysters by John Arderne, from an Early Fifteeth-Century Manuscript Translation* (London: Oxford University Press for the Early English Text Society, 1910).

40. Arderne, *A Treatise*, 82, my emphases.

41. Ibid.

42. My thinking about the relation of the book to dissection in Vesalius is indebted to an unpublished lecture by Katherine Park, "Nero dissects his mother" (Harvard Unversity, March 7, 1996); an ensuing exchange with Marjorie Garber about the production of medical knowledge; and Wendy Wall's consideration of "'violent enlargement' and the voyeuristic text" in *The Imprint of Gender: Authorship and Publication in the English Renaissance* (Ithaca: Cornell University Press, 1993), 169–72, 202–3.

    The linking (or substitution) of open book/body is made strikingly graphic in Alexander Read's tiny anatomical handbook, *The Manvuall of the Anatomy or dissection of the body of Man, Which usually are shewed in the publike Anatomicall exercises* (1638), in which the typical title-page cartouche reveals itself to be an opened up human skin, with hands and feet at the borders, and a decorative head at the top; the entire text of the title page is inscribed upon this corpus, as if the book were discovered (literally) in the body.

43. For men (whether engaged in hetero- or homoerotic practices) and/or for women. I want to note that my lack of examples of the fundament gendered female may be either the fault of my research or possibly the property of the discourse: to what extent did medical or religious discourses, for example, conceive of women as having "foundational" body parts? Nancy J. Vickers cites a French "'Blason du Q [Cul]' ('Blason of the Ass[hole]')" published in 1539: "The unauthored 1539 volume in which is printed the *Hecatomphile, The Flowers of French Poetry,* and *Other Soothing Things,*" in *Subject and Object in Renaissance Culture,* ed. Margreta de Grazia, Maureen Quilligan, and Peter Stallybrass (Cambridge: Cambridge University Press, 1996), 171.

44. Fletcher, *The Purple Island*, 27.

45. Ibid., 90 (canto 7.21–22), where the allegorical figure "Sodomie" is described in specifically pederastical terms, "lean[ing]" upon one boy, and accompanied by and "toy[ing]" with others.

46. *The historie of the troublesome Raigne of King Edward the second with the liues and deaths of the greate Duke of Cornwall & Sr Hugh Spencer the youngest, the two greate Minions of his time, togither wthe the Conspiracie of the Queene & Mortimer against the Deposinge of the Kinge. 1626 Neuer printed. written by* [name obliterated]; Folger MS V.a. 234. I am indebted to Laetitia Yaendle of the Folger Library for assistance in puzzling out the occasional difficulties of the handwriting. The Folger MS is interesting not least for the possible context(s) of transgression, censorship, controversy, and perhaps even "the closet" that might be read out of the seemingly intentional obliteration of the writer's name. Bredbeck discusses the printed version of this text in *Sodomy and Interpretation*, chap. 2, passim. The MS stanza quoted above concludes:

> And that my violent death might shune mistrust
> Through that same horne; a red hot spitt whereby
> They made my gutts and bowells for to frie
> And soe continued, till at last they found
> That I was dead, yet seem'd to haue noe wound

47. On this question, see Judith Butler, *Bodies That Matter* (New York: Routledge, 1993), esp. 67–68. By connecting the body-in-culture with "psychic structures," I mean not to disavow psychoanalysis as a methodological tool for the analysis of early modern culture but, rather, to stress, as my argument above suggests, that the normative structures and understandings of the body (including "rhetorics") available to such an analysis will change over time. One place to begin: What would "anality" mean—would it exist—as a psychoanalytic structure within the rhetoric I sketch here? On the problematics of "Psychoanalysis and Renaissance Culture," see Stephen Greenblatt's essay of that title in *Literary Theory/Renaissance Texts*, ed. Patricia Parker and David Quint (Baltimore: Johns Hopkins University Press, 1986), 210–24.

48. Bersani, "Is the Rectum a Grave?" 216.

49. Leo Bersani, *Homos* (Cambridge: Harvard University Press, 1995), 90, 102.

50. As many have noted, the passage is a rewriting of I Corinthians 2:9–10, especially in the Geneva version, which culminates in a *bottom*: "the Spirite searcheth all thinges, ye the botome of Goddes secretes." For an interpretation that makes use of this resonance, see Jan Kott, *The Bottom Translation: Marlowe and Shakespeare and the Carnival Tradition* (Evanston: Northwestern University Press, 1987), 31.

51. Fletcher, *The Purple Island*, 27 n. For another, related reading of Bottom's Dream, see Paster, *The Body Embarrassed*, 142; on Bottom as somatic "pun," see ibid., 125–26.

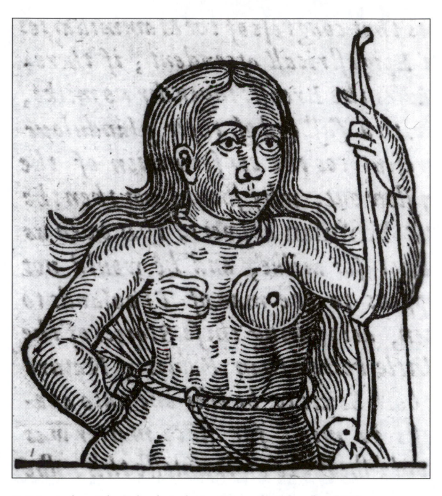

8. Amazon from John Bulwer's *Anthropometamorphosis* (London, 1653).

8

Missing the Breast

Desire, Disease, and the Singular Effect of Amazons

KATHRYN SCHWARZ

Again and again in the medical, social, and more explicitly fictional narratives of the English Renaissance, representations of the female breast reify the logic that puts women in their place. Presented in a causal relationship to domestic convention, breasts demonstrate the processes through which social constructions of the feminine and physical qualities of the female become precisely coextensive. The breast identifies women, distinguishing them from men both visually and functionally: men, too, have "paps," but women's breasts impose a necessarily gendered performance. Thomas Vicary, in *The Anatomie of the Bodie of Man*, writes, "But I fynde certayne profitablenes in the creation of the Paps, aswel in man as in woman: for in man it defendeth the spirituals from annoyannce outwardly: and another, by their thicknes they comfort the natural heate in defence of the spirites. And in women there is the generation of milke."[1] Accounts of generation that define woman as matter, man as spirit, find material proof in the production of milk, in the image of the woman acting as a vessel in the most literal possible sense. And even if, as in the Galenic model, women's genitals are imagined to mirror those of men, producing some degree of reproductive mutuality, the maternal breast is an inescapable site of difference: whatever may be said of the genitals—or, for that matter, of the arms, legs, hands, or feet—women's breasts neither look nor act like those of men.[2]

The breast comes to summarize the implications of gender difference. Breasts provide a physical referent for domestic categories, displaying the sense in which women are vulnerable to disease and to desire, implicated in generation, more demonstrably embodied than men. Functionally defined, the female body imposes a causality of acts as women play the social parts to which their body parts confine them. The very insistence of this causal logic suggests its potential fragility; the investment in a normative femininity that can be referred to the body, and specifically to the breast, is at once most visible and most vulnerable when the terms of that body prove subject to change. Such preoccupations explain—in part—the peculiar fascination of Amazons: Amazons, who according to myth make a deliberate monomastic choice, illuminate as they destabilize the categoric processes of reading through the breast.

Everyone knows that the Amazon is missing a breast. This is a fact that, perhaps somewhat oddly, becomes more self-evident when it is most evidently not true: in pictorial instances ranging from Athenian black figure vases to Wonder Woman, the Amazon breast isn't missing at all. Yet its absence, even when contested, defines the Amazons of English Renaissance texts, in which physical lack provides a logic for performative excess; thus in *Hakluytus Posthumus: or, Purchas his Pilgrimes*, Samuel Purchas offers a suggestive marginal comment on one explorer's Amazon quest. "Re Amazons why so called. Note the truth of that which hath mocked men touching Amazons in Asia, Africa, and America. None other have yet by credible reports beene found but warlike wives, and not solitary unimammians."[3] At first glance, this might seem to be the same logic that refers always to the elusiveness of the Amazon encounter, as in the chapter heading of Hakluyt's narrative of Prester John that reads, "Of the kingdom of Damute, and of the great quantity of gold there is in it, and how it is collected; and to the south of this are the Amazons—if they are there," or Purchas's own reference to "Amazonian Dreames."[4] However, the logic that points to the absence of "solitary unimammians" is in fact quite different; it suggests, not that there is no there there, but that whatever might be there, it isn't Amazons. The question of why monomasty should be the hallmark of the genuine Amazon—rather than, for example, weaponry or sexual self-sufficiency or violence against men, all of which can apparently also be attributes of "warlike wives"—returns to the larger question of what is at stake in the image of the absent breast.

The much-mythologized amazonian body, imagined through the absence of the breast, focuses concerns surrounding women's bodies more generally, inspiring a range of theories involving sexuality, reproductive practice, aesthetics, and violence. These theories are at once polemical and contradictory, reflecting the problematic status of the referent: it is not, in a sense, *logical* to look for a missing breast on a body that cannot be found, and Amazons complicate interpretation even as they frustrate more literal discovery. In a doubled metonymy, the absent breast signifies the deferring and displacing processes of the explorer's quest; amazonian self-mutilation, producing a body that is missing something, becomes a figure for the narratives that are always (just) missing the Amazons. And this doubling of the function of metonymy—metonymy as the part that defines the whole, and metonymy as a process that leads always *away*—gestures toward the far more general sense in which the breast as a legible text is at once complicated and evasive. Metonymy is a figure not only of definition but of association, displacement, and excess, suggesting that the body or its parts might signify beyond any bounded interpretive space. Thus women's roles as read through their bodies threaten always to shift, to expose the contingency of their terms: if the breast is a metonymic icon that puts women in their place, it is also, like Amazon myth itself, always implicated in the process that Lacan describes as "being caught in the rails—eternally stretching forth towards the *desire for something else*."[5]

English Renaissance representations of the breast suggest a whole constellation of desires: defined erotically, iconographically, aesthetically, or maternally, the breast is, as I have suggested, a metonym for the feminine, a text that proves the equation between sex and gender, body and act. Yet, as amazonian narratives suggest, this metonymic function is not invulnerable to the potential excesses of the body itself; in contexts ranging from Petrarchism to medicine, a complicated relationship between body and text intervenes in the reading of body *as* text. Thus when, in Middleton's *Women Beware Women*, Fabritio asks, "How like you her breast now, my lord?" the answer is not confined by the space of the question. "Breast" might, in this period, be an ungendered term meaning "voice"—a meaning that is in itself metonymically derived—but the synonym is already somewhat archaic, and Bianca's response refuses the signifier in favor of a referent:

> Her breast!
> He talks as if his daughter had given suck

Before she were married, as her betters have;
The next he praises sure will be her nipples.[6]

The associations of maternity and sexuality exceed the space of metaphor, and it is a possibility that lies beneath any definition of the breast as icon or text. Amazonian self-mutilation only makes explicit a tension that is always present in appropriations of the breast as a categoric signifier. Invoked to confine women to specific erotic, domestic, iconographic, and maternal roles, the breast must function both as trope and as material proof; and, as this complicated simultaneity suggests, the evasions of metonymy cannot be entirely subdued.

Iconographically, exposure of the breast represents qualities ranging from chastity to agricultural bounty, and the eroticism implicit in such representations becomes explicit in Petrarchan contexts, in which the breast is often the last labeled item in the catalogue. While the entire body of the Petrarchan object is eroticized and desired, the progress from hair to brow to eyes to nose to lips to breast is often precluded by discretion from going farther. Robert Burton, in *The Anatomy of Melancholy*, describes "Love Melancholy. Beauty a Cause" in terms that echo the blazon: "A white and round neck, that *via lactea*, dimple in the chin, black eye-brows, *Cupidinis arcus*, sweet breath, white and even teeth, which some call the sale-piece, a fine soft round pap, gives an excellent grace, *Quale decus tumidis Pario de marmore mammis!* and make a pleasant valley *lacteum sinum*, between two chalky hills, *Sororiantes papillulas, et ad pruritum frigidos amatores solo aspectu excitantes. Unde is, Forma papillarum quam fuit apta premi!* — Again *Urebant oculos durae stantesque mamillae.*"[7] The moment of reaching the breast inspires an extravagance of Latin, suggesting an eroticism that can be pursued only in another language, by another semiotic route. For Petrarchan poetry itself, the space beyond the breast imposes silence, as in Andrew Marvell's "To His Coy Mistress":

An hundred years should go to praise
Thine eyes, and on thy forehead gaze;
Two hundred to adore each breast,
But thirty thousand to the rest.

(lines 13–16)

In this gesture downward that mirrors a displacement upward, Marvell, like other poets, inscribes his desired conclusion through the metonymy of the breast. As Nancy Vickers has shown, there is a powerful claim to poetic agency in this progress through pieces; and at the end of the catalogue, in a sort of synecdochic extravagance, to name the breast is to have the rest.[8]

For all the self-evidence of this objectification, the breast is not un-complicated in its relationship to the gaze. If the breast marks a limit to what can properly be mentioned, it also, in the rhetoric surrounding early-seventeenth-century fashion, transgresses the boundaries of what can prop-erly be *seen*. In *The Masque of Beauty* Ben Jonson describes the figure of "Splendor" "in a robe of flame color, naked-breasted, her bright hair loose-flowing. She was drawn in a circle of clouds, her face and body breaking through; and in her hand a branch with two roses, a white and a red."[9] Iconography, patriotism, and eroticism converge in this figure of the woman "naked-breasted," and the exposed or only transparently concealed breasts of Jacobean masquers reflect a larger trend in fashion that leaves the breasts partially or even totally exposed to view. The gesture of display is related to agency in ways not fully contained by the logic of the Petrarchan catalogue; although those who condemn such display imply that it is appro-priate only to the sexually promiscuous, exposing a woman's character as well as her breasts, it is in fact a practice that crosses the boundaries of rank and complicates the terms of aesthetic evaluation. James T. Henke, in *Gutter Life and Language in the Early 'Street' Literature of England*, suggests in his entry "Naked paps" that the custom is popular not only with masquers and prostitutes but with "a variety of 'honest' madams."[10] Like the queen/quean homonym that runs throughout the language of this period, the naked breast conflates high and low, implicating women in a rhetoric of sexual excess that shows no regard for social status. The author of *Hic Mulier* urges women, "for those things which belong to this wanton and lasciuious delight and pleasure: as eyes wandring, lips bylling, tongue inticing, bared brests seducing, and naked armes imbracing: O hide them, for shame hide them in the closest prisons of your strictest gouernment."[11] Breasts, then, are used to define women as erotic objects, to assign them a value in the economy of desire; at the same time, they are erotic to the point of excess, threatening always to signify not the desire of the spectator but that of the woman herself. Reading the erotic breast requires a complicated logic of possession, in which agency derived from embodiment is pitted against the poet's power to define.

In a sort of extension of Petrarchan logic, breasts are imagined to be medically as well as erotically legible in this period, again transforming the body into text. The visible condition of a woman's breast reveals a variety of kinds of information to the informed reader, including the sex and health of the child she carries and the health and even the virtue of the mother. A firm right breast promises a male child; sudden softening of the breasts suggests the death of the child in the womb; and the color of the nipple tells a great deal more. Jane Sharp, in *The Compleat Midwife's Companion*, writes, "The Nipples are red after Copulation, red (I say) as a Strawberry, and that is their Natural colour: But Nurses Nipples, when they give Suck, are blue, and they grow black when they are old."[12] And, as in the blazon, the breast in medical discourse offers an index to the rest of the body, particularly the body below. According to Sharp, "The consent of the Womb with the Breast is most observable, the Humours passing ordinarily from one to the other, whereby we may know the affections of the Womb, and how to cure them, and of the State of the Child contained in it."[13] The womb in these texts is represented as the center of disease and madness as well as of pregnancy; its close connection to the breast implicates phenomena ranging from cancer and hysteria to the conviction that breast milk is a translation of menstrual blood.

Representations of the breast, and particularly of the maternal breast, are always at least as concerned with morality as with medicine, and the question of what obligation a mother has to nurse her child is based in a range of beliefs concerning the effects of nursing itself.[14] Most simply expressed, such beliefs assume that similarity is better than difference, that the infant should continue as it has begun; thus the early midwives' manual *The Birth of Mankynde* advises, "[T]he mothers mylk is more conuenient and agreeable to the Infante, then anye other womans, and more doth it noryshe it, for because that in the mothers belly it was wont to the same, and fed with it, and therefore also it doth more desyrouslye couet the same, as that with the which it is best acquaynted."[15] This notion of "acquaintance," not much different from our own cultural notions of the relationship between nursing mother and child, finds its logical extreme in the idea that the milk makes the child *like* the nurse; that, in fact, the process of nursing is at least as powerful as the moment of generation. In sixteenth- and seventeenth-century England, for the authors of midwives' manuals and other texts that theorize maternity, breast milk, connecting mother—or wet nurse—to infant, signifies beyond nutrition, and contact with the breast forms and even transforms the child. James Guillimeau, in *The Nursing of Children*, writes, "We may be assured, that the Milke (wherewith the child is nourish'd two yeares together) hath as much power to make the children like the Nurses, both in bodie and mind; as the seed of the Parents hath to make the children like them."[16] Stories of children who gain martial valor through being nursed by

Spartan women recur throughout these texts, recalling Volumnia's claim to Coriolanus: "Thy valiantness was mine, thou suck'st it from me."[17] In such narratives the breast has more power than the womb or even the seed, excluding men from the child's formation; whether exposed for the sake of nursing or of fashion, the breast threatens always to signify an excess of female control.

In giving nursing this extraordinary formative efficacy, medical texts and midwives' manuals suggest that mothers who send their children to wet nurses risk not only the child's health but its hereditary identity. Guillimeau reads this as an act of violence: "Avlvs Gellius (in my opinion) did not amisse in putting no difference betweene a woman that refuses to nurse her owne childe; and one that kills her child, as soone as she hath conceiued; that shee may not bee troubled with bearing it nine moneths in her wombe."[18] This notion that the denial of maternal milk is equivalent to murder goes far beyond any literal concern with sufficient food. The metonymic progression in which Lady Macbeth first plucks her nipple from her infant's "boneless gums" and then dashes its brains out suggests the deadly causality that begins in maternal rejection (1.7.54–58); in the rhetoric surrounding nursing, the dead child and the child displaced are equally vulnerable, the mother equally culpable in her unnaturally willful act. Guillimeau lists four consequences of disrupting the absolute relationship between mother and child, beginning, "First there is danger least the child be changed and an other put in his place," and concluding, "And lastly, the Nurse may communicate some imperfection of her body into the child."[19] The anxiety of changing structures this catalogue; the first, literal fear that the child might be exchanged is not qualitatively different from its exposure to "some bad conditions or inclinations," and disease comes a poor fourth in the list of imaginable transformations. Through nursing, the child becomes like the mother; there is real danger in displacing the maternal breast.

There is also an implicit danger in retaining it. The maternal breast presents a disruptive synthesis of eroticism and control; the rhetoric of nursing, with its insistence on an exclusively maternal act of determination, gives the mother extraordinary imaginative power. It is a power that must at best produce ambivalence, as in Melanie Klein's description of the infant's relationship to the breast and, by extension, to the mother: "The child's libidinal fixation to the breast develops into feelings towards her as a person. Thus feelings both of a destructive and of a loving nature are experiences towards one and the same object and this gives rise to deep and disturbing conflicts in the child's mind."[20] Janet Adelman reads this conflicted relationship in the specific context of the English Renaissance: "What we know of the actual conditions that shape infantile fantasy suggests, that is, that many would have experienced a prolonged period of infantile dependency, during which they were subject to pleasures and dangers especially associated with nursing and the maternal body."[21] In a culture that imagines the breast as at once a summary of erotic desire and a site of potential violence, such ambivalence is not unique to the nursing child, and the image of the overeroticized, and thus dangerous, maternal breast is a recurring trope.[22] The erotic maternal body is at once frightening and irresistible not only to infants but to men; Suffolk's speech to Margaret in *2 Henry VI* suggests the sense in which this conflation of father and child leads inevitably to violence.

> If I depart from thee, I cannot live,
> And in thy sight to die, what were it else
> But like a pleasant slumber in thy lap?
> Here could I breathe my soul into the air,
> As mild and gentle as the cradle-babe
> Dying with mother's dug between its lips.
>
> (3.2.388–93)

Margaret's interpretation of sexual and maternal relationships enables her to cuckold and finally banish her husband, appropriate his armies, and claim control over the hereditary destiny of his son; in the third part of *Henry VI*, York will call her "Amazonian trull" just before she kills him. But for Suffolk, her maternal breast figures not her agency but his own sexual desire. The success of this metonymy might best be summarized in the stage direction, "Enter the King with a supplication, and the Queen with Suffolk's head."[23]

Such violence is in a sense already implicit in the association of milk with blood; the act of nursing is always potentially an unnatural act. Eccles cites Paré on the aesthetic crises that lies just beneath the surface of idealized maternity: "Paré considered it a great dispensation of nature that the blood turned white, otherwise people would be shocked by 'so grievous and terrible a spectacle of the childes mouth so imbrued and besmeared with blood.'"[24] The nursing child smeared with blood, recalling Lady Macbeth's subjunctive act of violence, suggests the sense in which the breast is necessarily implicated in excess. And that excess is bound up with eroticism, with the complicated relationship between nursing and desire; as Gail Kern Paster writes, "[T]he culture's heightened erotic investment in and signification of the female breast contained within it the specter of autonomous female desire. Worse, it suggested the possibility of female control of erotic practices, even an autoeroticism using suckling as its modality."[25] Men are doubly excluded, from the formative process that supersedes generation and from the erotic dyad of mother and child; still more disruptively, the eroticized maternal breast might always prove to be *self*-satisfying, self-contained in its economy of desire. *The Problems of Aristotle*, a collection of popular beliefs concerning the body, suggests that even the child might find itself excluded from or deprived by the mother's erotic response: in the section titled "Of the Paps and Dugs," the question "Why is the milk naught for the child, if the woman uses carnal copulation?" elicits this reply. "Because in time of carnal copulation, the subtilest and best part of the milk goeth to the vessels of the seed, and to the womb, and the worst remains in the paps, which doth hurt the child."[26] Again the child might be "hurt," might be implicated without agency in the mother's excessive desires. In the speculations of some authors, those desires can produce the effects of nursing itself in the absence of both infants and men; *Aristotle's Masterpiece* reports, "*Lascivious Virgins*, and *Widows* wholly intent to Lustfull *Cogitations*, and much in thinking of *Breasts, Milk,* and their Suckling, wantonly rubbing, tickling, or Sucking thereof, may have got *Milk* in them ... yet that is most rare."[27] Even as it is invoked to prove the embodied logic of feminine roles, the eroticized maternal breast might have nothing to do with desires imposed from without; it is a possibility that endangers the causalities that keep women in their place.

Inevitably the maternal breast is dangerous to women as well. *The Womans Doctour* warns, "Nurses are tormented with sore breasts, painfull Swellings, Ulcers, and Cancers, and the like cruell diseases," and *The Complete Midwife's Practice* lists eight "inflammations of the breast" among the diseases of women, most of which are associated in one way or another with maternity.[28] Guillimeau, too, describes the risk of breast disease from nursing, offering a range of precautions and cures "to the end then that her breasts after her deliuery, be neither too big and puft vp, nor yet hanging downe like bags, and to preuent the danger that might happen vnto her, by the too great quantity of bloud, that is turned into milke, (which may be curdled, and so suppurate, and putrifie)."[29] Here his rhetoric symptomatically conflates the medical and the aesthetic; the breasts that are "too big and puft up" or "hanging downe like bags" are at risk for infection and even cancer, but they are also, inescapably, ugly. Women who nurse their children risk the loss of the idealized breast, and midwives' manuals are full of advice for keeping maternal breasts smooth and small.[30] At least one author blames the class-based economy of wet nursing not on a desire to avoid disease or produce another child quickly but on aesthetic preoccupations: "Women at this daie are so curious of their comlinesse, or rather of their vanitie, that they hadde rather pervert the nature of their Children, then chaunge the fourme of their firme, harde, and round pappes."[31] The language of eroticized description intervenes in the moralized discourse of nursing; in a peculiar rhetorical turn, the Petrarchan object displaces her child to defend her place in the blazon.[32]

Underlying this concern with the loss of a conceit is the possibility of a more literal loss. The catalogues of treatment for diseased breasts often end with veiled references to mastectomy; thus *The Complete Midwife's Practice*, having recommended changes in diet, oral medicines to adjust the humors, letting of blood in the feet, topical decoctions applied to the breast, and friction, concludes, "You must at length, when all other waies do fail, use the operation of the hand to take away the root of the disease; but this is not to be done, till you have used all other means to soften and dispell the humour."[33] In this text as in others, narrative becomes oddly elusive at the moment of surgical intervention, referring to "the operation of the hand" or to the bringing in of instruments, but showing little of the zest for detail that characterizes descriptions of other operations. Diseases of the breast threaten to literalize the Petrarchan process of fragmentation, displacing the tropes of aestheticized desire with a horrific actuality. In midwives' manuals and anatomical texts, loss of the breast seems to inspire a horror matched only by loss of the womb; aesthetic and medical preoccupations converge in the certainty that such a mutilation can produce only monstrosity.

Nursing is idealized as a sign of connection and devotion but threatens always to become grotesque; the language of rejection, disease, and excess is never far from the maternal breast. Sharp suggests that the breast is beyond prediction or control: "[S]trange things have come forth of the Breasts, and sometimes the menstrual Blood unchanged runs forth this way at certain Seasons. *Hippocrates* writes that when the Blood comes out of the Nipples, those Women are Mad."[34] Again nursing threatens to produce the image of the bloody child, and the maternal breast, again like the womb, might become a source of horror and even of madness. In an extraordinary moment from a New World text, it might even become a weapon; Diego Durán, in *The History of the Indies of New Spain*, tells this story of one nation's last stand against the conquering Aztecs. "The women, naked, with their private parts revealed and their breasts uncovered, came upon them slapping their bellies, showing their breasts and squirting milk at the

Aztecs.... The Aztecs, dismayed by such crudity, were ordered by King Axayacatl not to harm any of the women but to take them prisoners together with the children."[35] The maternal breast is imagined as a weapon that might be used against men, and the Aztecs, if they are not defeated or deterred, are symptomatically "dismayed." The breast is always potentially something crude, something that must be feared or shunned or contained rather than desired; even as it is used to reify social convention, it signifies the anxieties of excess. Women who refuse to nurse their children, women who nurse children too much or too long, women who are paralyzingly beautiful or paralyzingly ugly, women who have too many breasts or too few or breasts that are too large or too small figure repeatedly in the narratives that attempt to define a normative feminine space. The aesthetic cannot be detached from the monstrous, and again medical and aesthetic discourses are difficult to separate; the diseased and deformed breast is the other side of the Petrarchan mirror. Thomas Laqueur, characterizing the relationship between blazons and antiblazons, says, "The beautiful breast—ivory, rose, a fruit—poetically confronts the ugly breast—black, sagging, stinking, shapeless—in this discourse between men."[36]

If we return, then, to the notion of the "solitary unimammian," and in particular to the ways in which "solitary" not only designates separatism but doubly modifies the singleness of the breast, the kinds of definitional crisis produced by amazonian self-mutilation begin to emerge. If the breast is used to represent categories—iconographic, aesthetic, erotic, maternal, domestic—and to articulate the logic through which women are confined to certain spaces, then the willed absence of the breast, like the fear of excess that surrounds maternity and female desire, challenges that spatial logic. In Amazon myth, the breast is removed in the service of a specifically violent utility: Diodorus Siculus writes, "If they be women children, they sere of theire brestes with an hote iron, playnely affermyng how they shuld els be grevously annoyed and gretely it shuld hyndre theym in tyme of theire warres."[37] This narrative of self-mutilation, like the medical rhetoric concerning mastectomy, again literalizes the fragmenting Petrarchan trope and disrupts the terms of erotic, aesthetic, and maternal convention. Here, though, the Amazon body is deliberately revised in the name of agency, an agency that extends to the process of naming itself; the most common etymology given for "Amazon" is "without breast."[38]

What effect does this deliberate and efficient monomasty have on the integrity of the breast as a referent for social logic? Louis Montrose describes amazonian practice as inversion: "The Amazonian anticulture precisely inverts European norms of political authority, sexual license, marriage and child-rearing practices, and inheritance rules."[39] Amazons disrupt patriarchal logic; I would like to suggest that at least in the case of the social structures implicated in representations of the breast, they do so precisely by taking that logic to its extreme. Despite Purchas's wistful nostalgia for solitary unimammians, the Amazons of English Renaissance texts are aggressively implicated in social structures; in narrative after narrative they are not lesbian separatists or ritualized descendants of goddesses but mothers, lovers, and in some cases wives. Stories ranging from Ralegh's "discovery" of Guiana to Theseus's conquest of Hippolyta threaten to bring the Amazon home, and amazonian excess is less unimaginably other than it is a fulfillment of variously socialized anxieties and desires. Categories of the domestic, constructed to defend against or repudiate female excess, are inevitably implicated in that excess, and, seen in this light, the strangeness of Amazons looks curiously familiar. Metonymically represented through the breast in discourses ranging from Petrarchism to fashion critiques, the eroticized female body is always potentially excessive or disruptive; Amazon myth plays out the fear that the object of desire, the body looked at or, in the case of the Amazon quest, looked *for*, may itself possess sexual agency: that all women might be sexually voracious, given half a chance. Thus Radigund's eroticized enslavement of Artegall in the *Faerie Queene*, like a range of New World narratives, insists that amazonian violence is causally related to sex; Amazons endanger not only men's lives but their relationship to sexual agency. In a culture inclined to read female masculinity as an excess of heterosexual desire—as Phyllis Rackin writes, "In life as on the stage, masculine women were regarded as whores"—the Amazon's implication in sexual aggression is an inevitable consequence of the disruption of gender roles.[40]

This is not the only version of amazonian sexual excess. Penthesilea, perhaps the most frequently invoked Amazon in the English Renaissance and certainly the most accessible to patriotic appropriations, is notoriously virginal, and her body reifies her distance from any violation but violence itself; according to the *Aeneid*, she displays her unmutilated breasts in battle, recalling the iconographic convention that reads the exposed virginal breast as a signifier of chastity. Penthesilea stands behind the tradition of Camilla, Belphoebe, and the Virgin Queen, a tradition that sharply divides female martial valor from any sexual causality. Yet even Penthesilea, visibly double-breasted, much-cited by conduct manuals as a "good Amazon," is not uncomplicated as a social ideal, for chastity itself does a certain violence to social logic. Admired as a temporary condition of unmarried women or metaphorized as constancy in marriage, chastity conveniently circumscribes the potential excesses of female reproductive agency; literalized as a permanent state, it can only get in the way. William Blake Tyrrell's description of Penthesilea's death suggests the sense in which idealized virginity is always a narrative of loss: "The Argives long for a wife like Penthesilea, and Achilles wants her as his wife, only *after she is dead*."[41] Penthesilea's exposed breast may displace the horrific scar of the solitary unimammian, may guarantee her place in the iconography of chastity; but, imagined on the body of the Amazon, both the present and the absent breast display an assertion of sexual agency and signify a violent escape from patriarchal structures of generation and desire.

The amazonian body implicates maternity as it complicates the agency of sexual determination. The doubleness of the maternal breast, represented as at once ideal and monstrous, is played out in the spectacle of the amazonian mother. Definitions of Amazons as mothers rest largely on what they do to their boy children; in various accounts they kill them, mutilate and enslave them, or send them to fathers who, having been seduced in the dark, have to guess which child belongs to whom based on accidents of resemblance. Within patriarchal logic, it would be difficult to say which of these options is to be preferred, and for these amazonian sons the missing breast seems almost inevitable as a reification of maternal loss. The ambivalence proposed by object relations theory, what Klein describes as "the internalization of an injured and therefore dreaded breast on the one hand, and of a satisfying and helpful breast on the other,"[42] seems inescapably to refer to the self-mutilating Amazon body. Paster, referring to this good breast/bad breast structure, reads the amazonian body in terms of "a certain emotional distance from or refusal to become absorbed into the personal and maternal gratifications, the social rewards, of nurture."[43] And Tyrrell reaches the same conclusion: "Why, in analyzing the name ["Amazon"], did single-breastedness seem appropriate? One reason is movement—not only movement as freedom to hurl the javelin but movement as freedom from nursing.... As much as possible, Amazons are released from maternal attachments."[44]

This structure of maternal rejection, whether defined in terms of the mother's experience or that of the child, begs the question of the daughter, the incipient mirror-image so often defined by negation: unlike the notorious amazonian boy babies, she is *not* killed or mutilated or given away. Helen Diner insists that to nurse even these future Amazons would itself be deplorably unamazonian: "Amazon babies never drank out of their mothers' breasts but suckled on the breasts of their totem mothers, the mares."[45] Diner clearly assumes that nursing would compromise amazonian identity, that it cannot be part of the martial woman's relationship to her child. Yet the maternal utility of the Amazon breast remains as a site of contention: some readers of the myth insist that the Amazons *do* in fact nurse their children, and others share Diner's conviction that such a sign of maternity has no place on the Amazon body. Thomas Heywood describes that body as a synthesis of maternal and martial pragmatism, writing of the Amazons, "[O]ne of their brestes they reserue safe and vntouched, with which they giue sucke to their infants; the right brest they burne off, that with the more facilitie they may draw a Bowe, thrill a Dart, or charge a Launce."[46] Heywood, like Diner, finds the amazonian body eminently legible; for Heywood, however, the sight of the unimammian's scar does not preclude but merely focuses maternal response.

What is, to me, most interesting about this difference of opinion is its various assertions of certainty; in the absence of actual Amazons, each commentator on Amazon myth nonetheless claims to reach the only possible conclusion. Amazons are not conventionally feminine, therefore they *must not* nurse; Amazons have female, albeit customized, bodies, therefore they *must* nurse.[47] But within the terms of Amazon myth the breast neither precludes nor requires the maternal function of nursing, despite the recurring fascination with questions of *how, when, whether,* and *with which.* Whether the Amazon nurses or not, whether she has a right breast, a left breast, neither or both, only one act is explicitly and repeatedly defined by Amazon myth as an act of nurturing maternity: the mutilation of the breast itself. Thus William Painter writes in *The Palace of Pleasure*, "And for as mutch as these Amazons defended themselues so valiantly in the warres with bowe, and arowes, and perceyued that their breastes did very mutch impech the vse of that weapon, and other exercises of armes, they seared vp the right breasts of their yonge daughters."[48] The mutilation of the breast is not *self*-mutilation but an act performed by the mother upon her child; Amazon maternity reproduces the transformed female body that enables sexual, martial, and reproductive agency. If, in that popular Renaissance causality, the child draws its image from the mother's breast, this is another conceit that finds its unexpectedly logical extreme in Amazon myth.

Amazons are never, at least so far as Hakluyt and Purchas and Richard Eden can tell, actually *found,* and within the elusive space of amazonian representation the breast functions with a peculiar simultaneity of literalism and abstraction, fictionality and material proof. This simultaneity, like polemical appropriations of the breast more generally, exposes the tension within the term "figure"—"figure" as body, "figure" as trope—and the female body, the masculine female *amazonian* body, becomes perhaps most representationally complicated when it appears onstage. Definitions of the breast, like representations of the Amazon body, are in some sense inescapably theatrical, invoking the possibilities of the supplement and the prosthesis, engaging the gap between what can be seen and what can be recognized, and multiplying the causal relationships between body and act. When, in *The Devil's Law Case*, Leonora says, "Ile be a fury to him—like an Amazon lady, / Ide cut off this right pap, that gave him sucke, / To shoot him dead," she at once recalls the violence of amazonian maternity and suggests the mutability not only of the Amazon body but of the body onstage (3.3.289–91). And plays such as *Antonio and Mellida* and *Swetnam the Woman-Hater*, in which a man conspires with the audience to disguise himself as an Amazon, suggest the sense in which Amazon myth mirrors theatrical production. The Amazon disguise plot performed on a transvestite stage, with its image of the man who dresses as a man who dresses as a woman who acts too much like a man, reflects the peculiar synthesis of essentialism and performativity that is always an element of Amazon myth. In that myth the female body, apparently veiled or displaced by masculine acts, returns through the insistence on maternity, eroticism, and sexual violence; Amazon myth at once eludes and insists on the specificity of the physical. And if, in the conceit of exploration narratives, Amazon myth is a myth that at any moment might produce a body, on stage it *must* produce a body, and that body must beg the question of the missing breast. I have in fact seen one production of *A Midsummer Night's Dream* in which Hippolyta appeared single-breasted, and it becomes tempting to ask the question, of modern as well as of Renaissance stages: How many breasts does an actor put on to play an Amazon? For the majority of productions the answer, perhaps disappointingly, seems to be two.

A different answer might be displacement. The references to breasts, whether amazonian or otherwise, which I have taken from drama have tended to displace the literalism of the body in favor of its power to signify; neither Volumnia's nor Lady Macbeth's reference to nursing produces the maternal breast onstage, any more than York's description of Margaret as an "Amazonian trull" transforms her into a solitary unimammian. However, when in *3 Henry VI* Edward says of Margaret, "Belike she minds to play the Amazon," he suggests the extent to which theatricality and Amazon agency have converged, and it is difficult to imagine that an actor's reference to breasts does not cause the audience to look for them—or, in the case of the Amazon, perhaps to look for it. As Peter Stallybrass has pointed out, breasts present an interesting—and, again, a doubled—problem for the transvestite productions of the English Renaissance. In "Transvestism and the 'body beneath,'" Stallybrass speculates about a tension between "the clothes which embodied and determined a particular sexual identity and contradictory fantasies of the 'body beneath'—the body of a woman, the body of a boy; a body with and without breasts."[49] The Amazon is always in that position of neither-and-both, embodying the impossible simultaneity that the transvestite stage requires its audience to imagine; the Amazon's is always "a body with and without breasts."

Mythographically, Amazons are variously represented with both breasts concealed by armor, with one breast mutilated, and with one breast exposed. It is an excess of narratives in which the breast might be there or not there or, most uncannily, both, and the etymology of the name suggests the range of possibilities and the impossibility of certainty. Although "without breast" is the most popular reading of "Amazon," the name, like the body, complicates any singularity of definition; thus Thevét, in his *New Founde Worlde*, acknowledges the etymological popularity of monomasty but does not believe that its referent is medically likely. "If it were so, I would thinke that for one that escapeth death, there died a hundreth." He considers "A maza" ("without bread") but finds it almost equally implausible. It is "as absurde as the others: for in that time they might call many that lived without bread *Amazones*, as the *Troglodites*." Finally he returns to his point of beginning, but with a suggestive functional difference, deciding in favor of "the others of A. privative & *Mazos*, as those that have bene norished w'out womans milke, the which is most likeliest to be true."[50] Thevét here detaches the breast from the milk: not, in the literal amazonian sense, by removing the breast itself but by suggesting that the female body is no guarantee of the maternal act, that form and function may be anything but coextensive. I find Thevet's to be a peculiarly *amazonian* reading of "Amazon," but there are a number of alternatives; contemporary theorists refer the name to qualities as diverse as religion and armor, and this does not yet anticipate such later readers as Mary Daly, for whom "A-mazing Amazons" are successful escapees from the patriarchal maze.[51]

Such overdetermination refuses even the anxious certainty of absence: the Amazon breast, exposed, removed, or concealed beneath armor, is a peculiar mirror for the breast as an emblem of chastity, disease, and desire. Again the mirror at once reflects and inverts, and again, as always with Amazons, the effect produced is the singular effect of double vision. Thus Penthesilea appears in the *Aeneid* "in armour girt, her pappe set out with lace of golden bandes."[52] But George Sandys's translation of this passage, in his commentary on the ninth book of the *Metamorphoses*, renders this line as: "Her *seared* brest bound with a golden Bend." In an extraordinary misreading, Sandys translates *exsertae* ("thrust out," or, regarding body parts, "bare, uncovered") as meaning "seared," literalizing the conflation of absence and presence.[53] The Amazon, who simultaneously acts *as* a woman and *like* a man, who might have one or two or none at all, asserts control over the terms of possession, performance, and display. And the possibility that having, not having, and not being *seen* to have might all be part of the same structure of signification radically destabilizes any phallic economy of possession and lack. If amazonian use of the conventionally phallic sword problematizes the sexual referentiality of that weapon, the question of breasts threatens to dismantle referentiality altogether.

The idea that Amazons embody maternal and erotic excess might have a salutary effect, might define the boundaries of social logic by locating the Amazon firmly beyond them. But the problem, as so often in Amazon myth, is telling the difference, for Amazons, again, are mothers, daughters, icons, wives, and the line between such figures and "normally" or even ideally socialized women is far from clear. The amazonian body might be Penthesilea's, that of the idealized virgin with one breast exposed; it might be the horrific unimammian, with or without a girl child at the remaining breast; it might be armed and armored, denying the possibility of knowing at all. And, at least in the strong misreading of Sandys, Penthesilea herself might either display or conceal not a breast but a scar. The desire to *know* about the Amazons is rendered as the desire to *know* about the Amazon breast; so Ralegh, who returns from his voyage having found neither cannibals nor gold, having acquired neither Guiana nor royal patronage, having, for that matter, not seen any Amazons at all, asserts, "But that they cut of the right dug of the breast I do not find to be true."[54]

Ralegh's "findings" notwithstanding, the absence of the Amazon breast recurs as a preoccupation throughout the narratives of exploration; Purchas, in another editorial aside, refers to "Amazons, not a one-breasted Nation, but warlike women," and says, "The Amazons are still further off: I doubt beyond the region of Truth; if the title be properly meant of such as are described. For warlike wives living in societie with men, are many."[55]

The possibility of finding the Amazons, of confronting material proof of their simultaneously social and unsocializable practice, requires rhetorical displacement: claims concerning "warlike wives"; impostors; even, in one memorable instance, nuns, displace the Amazons who are "discovered" and thus perpetuate the quest. In a seemingly inexhaustible series of substitutions, exploration narratives recount a pursuit that cannot, by definition, reach its conclusion. The Amazon breast, as a partial figuration, metonymically represents a desired object that itself always recedes through the processes of metonymy; the part that might or might not be there articulates the elusiveness of the whole. In amazonian quests as in polemical figurations of women's bodies, metonymy is the synecdoche of desire, and desire, again, is a process that leads always *away*. The breast, defined through and defining the logic of social structures, might always signify beyond those structures to suggest the peculiar effects of bringing the Amazon too close to home.

Notes

1. Thomas Vicary, *The Anatomie of the Bodie of Man*, issue of 1548 as reissued by the Surgeons of St. Bartholomews in 1577, ed. Fredk. J. Furnivall and Percy Furnivall (London: Early English Texts Society, 1888), 55.

2. For an extended discussion of the "one sex" model of reproduction, see Thomas Laqueur, *Making Sex: Body and Gender from the Greeks to Freud* (Cambridge: Harvard University Press, 1990); see also Stephen Greenblatt, "Fiction and Friction," in *Reconstructing Individualism: Autonomy, Individuality, and the Self in Western Thought*, ed. Thomas C. Heller, Morton Sosna, and David E. Wellbery (Stanford: Stanford University Press, 1986), 30–52.

3. Samuel Purchas, *Hakluytus Posthumus, or Purchas his Pilgrimes: Contayning a History of the World in Sea Voyages and Lande Travells by Englishmen and others* (1625). I here cite the modern edition, 20 vols. (Glasgow: James MacLehose and Sons, 1905); for the quotation, see 17:261.

4. *The Prester John of the Indies: A True Relation of the Lands of the Prester John: being the narrative of the Portuguese Embassy to Ethiopia in 1520, written by Father Francisco Alvarez*, the translation of Lord Stanley of Alderley (1881), revised and edited with additional material by C. P. Beckingham and G. W. B. Huntingford (Cambridge: Published for the Hakluyt Society at the University Press, 1961), 455.

5. Jacques Lacan, "The Agency of the Letter in the Unconscious," in *Ecrits: A Selection*, trans. Alan Sheridan (New York: W. W. Norton, 1977), 167.

6. I quote from the Revels Plays edition, ed. J. R. Mulryne (London: Methuen, 1975), 3.3.157–60. The notion that the voice *comes from* the breast, and that to have a good breast is thus to have a good voice, seems to be behind Fabritio's question; see the similar reference to Feste's "breast" in *Twelfth Night* 2.3.19–20. However, a footnote to Bianca's speech suggests that the word "breast" is already incongruous in this context: "Bianca's exclamation perhaps indicates that even in the 1620's 'breast' meaning 'voice' was obsolescent, regarded as odd or affected" (3.3.157 n).

7. Robert Burton, *The Anatomy of Melancholy. What it is. With all the Kindes, Causes, Sympathies, Prognostickes, and seuerall cvres of it. By Demetrius Iunior* (Oxford, 1621), 3.2.2.2.

8. See Nancy Vickers, "Diana Described: Scattered Women and Scattered Rhyme," in *Writing and Sexual Difference*, ed. Elizabeth Abel (Chicago: University of Chicago Press, 1982).

9. Ben Jonson, *The Masque of Beauty* (1608), in *The Complete Masques*, ed. Stephen Orgel (New Haven: Yale University Press, 1969), lines 159–61. Such exposure is not uncommon in the Jacobean masque, as Ellen Chirelstein suggests: "In his [Inigo Jones's] designs for women's costumes, the full contours of breasts and nipples are frequently revealed beneath a veil of transparent fabric, and the costume itself is drawn to suggest movement" ("Lady Elizabeth Pope: The Heraldic Body," in *Renaissance Bodies: The Human Figure in English Culture, c. 1540–1660*, ed. Lucy Gent and Nigel Llewellyn [London: Reaktion Books, 1990], 56).

10. James T. Henke, *Gutter Life and Language in the Early 'Street' Literature of England* (West Cornwall, Conn.: Locust Hill Press, 1988), 170. See also Donald Foster's brief discussion of this historical practice in "'Shall I Die' Post Mortem: Defining *Shakespeare*," *Shakespeare Quarterly* 38, no. 1 (spring 1987): 71, esp.

11. *Hic Mulier: or, The Man-Woman: Being a Medicine to cure the Coltish Disease of the Staggers in the Masculine-Feminines of our Times* (London, 1620), sig. B3v–B4.

12. Jane Sharp, *The Compleat Midwife's Companion, Or the Art of Midwifry Improv'd*, 3d ed. (London: Printed for John Marshall, 1724), 217.

13. Sharp, *Compleat Midwife's Companion*, 81.

14. For an extended discussion of breast-feeding, in the English Renaissance and in a more extensive historical and cultural context, see Valerie A. Fildes, *Breasts, Bottles and Babies: A History of Infant Feeding* (Edinburgh: Edinburgh University Press, 1986).

15. *The Birth of Mankynde, otherwyse named the womans booke, by Thomas Raynalde, Phisition*. Audrey Eccles describes the first (1540) translation of this

text as "the earliest English textbook for midwives in print," and points out that Raynald was the second to translate the German original (*Der swangern Frauwen und Hebammen Roszgarten*, published in 1513 by Eucharius Rösslin) into English. According to Eccles, Raynalde's revised translation appeared in thirteen editions from 1545 to 1654; I quote here from the 1565 edition. For a more detailed discussion of this textual history, see Eccles, *Obstetrics and Gynaecology in Tudor and Stuart England* (Ohio: Kent State University Press, 1982), 11–12.

16. James Guillimeau, *The Nursing of Children. Wherein is set downe, the ordering and gouernment of them, from their birth*; this is bound with his *Childbirth, or the Happie Deliuerie of Women* (London, 1612); for the quotation, see sig. Ii4.

17. William Shakespeare, *Coriolanus*, 3.2.129; all quotations from Shakespeare's plays are taken from the *Riverside Shakespeare*, ed. G. Blakemore Evans (Boston: Houghton Mifflin, 1974). Eccles points out the danger of giving too much valiantness to the wrong kind of child, quoting a contemporary text: "One had to be careful to choose a nurse whose own child was of the same sex, 'For the milk of a male child will make a female nursery more spritely, and a man-like Virago; and the milk of a girl will make a boy the more effeminate'" (98).

18. Guillimeau, *The Nursing of Children*, sig. Ii2.

19. Guillimeau, *The Nursing of Children*, sig. Ii2–Ii2v.

20. Melanie Klein, "The Psychogenesis of Manic-Depressive States," in *The Selected Melanie Klein*, ed. Juliet Mitchell (New York: Free Press, 1986), 141.

21. Janet Adelman, *Suffocating Mothers: Fantasies of Maternal Origin in Shakespeare's Plays, "Hamlet" to "The Tempest"* (New York: Routledge, 1992), 5.

22. Gail Kern Paster discusses this at length, in the specific context of drama and in English Renaissance culture more generally, in her chapters "Complying with the Dug" and "Quarrelling with the Dug," in *The Body Embarrassed: Drama and the Disciplines of Shame in Early Modern England* (Ithaca: Cornell University Press, 1993), 163–280.

23. *2 Henry VI*, 4.4.s.d. Phyllis Rackin analyzes the conditions of power set up by Suffolk's speech in terms of Margaret's simultaneously excessive sexuality and masculinity; see her essay "Historical Difference/Sexual Difference," in *Privileging Gender in Early Modern England*, ed. Jean R. Brink, Sixteenth-Century Essays and Studies, vol 23 (Kirksville, Mo.: Sixteenth-Century Journal Publishers, 1993), 42. Adelman describes the inexorable progress toward violence that begins in this moment: "Death and the mother's body coalesce in his image of union; and the grim image of Margaret parading around the stage with his head in her arms (4.4) suggests what happens to the men who succumb to its allure" (*Suffocating Mothers*, 8).

24. Eccles, *Obstetrics and Gynaecology*, 51.

25. Paster, *The Body Embarrassed*, 233–34.

26. *The Problems of Aristotle, with other Philosophers and Physitians, wherein are contained, Divers Questions with their Answers, Touching the Estate of Mans Body* (London, 1670), sig. C3v.

27. Quoted in Eccles, *Obstetrics and Gynaecology*, 53.

28. Nicholas Fontanus, *The Womans Doctour, or, An exact and distinct Explanation of all such Diseases as are peculiar to that Sex* (London, 1652), 8.

29. Guillimeau, *Childbirth, or the Happie Deliuery of Women*, 27–28.

30. For one such catalogue of remedies, and the specifically class-based reasons that make them not only desirable but necessary, see Guillimeau, *Childbirth*, 204.

31. *The ciuile Conuersation of Mr. Stephen Guazzo, written first in Italian, divided into foure bookes, the first three translated out of French by G. Pettie* (London: Thomas East, 1586), 143–143v.

32. Paster, *the Body Embarrassed,* discusses this impulse to "preserve" the idealized breast in terms that usefully synthesize medical, aesthetic, and social concerns; see especially 208.

33. *The Complete Midwife's Practice Enlarged, In the most weighty and high concernments of the Birth of Man* (London, 1680), 168. Eccles writes, "Operative treatment was sometimes advised, not for cancers in the womb or vagina, which were generally treated by medical means, but for breast cancers, and for the king's evil in the breasts. Sometimes it was proposed to extirpate only the obviously affected glands, but even this was often understandably more than the patient could face . . . in most cases, perhaps more realistically, palliation of the pain only was attempted" (*Obstetrics and Gynaecology*, 84–85).

34. Sharp, *The Compleat Midwife's Companion*, 216.

35. Fray Diego Durán, *The Aztecs: The History of the Indies of New Spain* (1581), ed. and trans. Doris Heyden and Fernando Horcasitas (New York: Orion Press, 1964), 159.

36. Laqueur, *Making Sex,* 130.

37. Diodorus Siculus, *The Bibliotheca Historica*, trans. John Skelton, Early English Text Society (London: Oxford University Press, 1956), 288.

38. This meaning derives from a reading of "Amazon" as a version of the Greek *a mazos*, literally "without breast." It is a contested etymology at best, in which the causal relationship between the name and the practice of mutilation is far from clear. For a discussion of this etymology, see William Blake Tyrrell, *Amazons: A Study in Athenian Myth-Making* (Baltimore: Johns Hopkins University Press, 1984), esp. 48–49.

39. Louis Adrian Montrose, "The Work of Gender in the Discourse of Discovery," *Representations* 33 (winter 1991): 26.

40. Rackin, "Historical Difference/Sexual Difference," 43.

41. Tyrrell, *Amazons,* 81; emphasis in text.

42. Klein, "The Psycho-Analytic Play Technique," in *The Selected Melanie Klein,* ed. Juliet Mitchell (New York: Free Press, 1986), 50–51.

43. Paster, *The Body Embarrassed,* 236. For a detailed reading of the implications of the missing Amazon breast for the social conventions surrounding breast-feeding, see 234–38.

44. Tyrrell, *Amazons,* 49.

45. Helen Diner, *Mothers and Amazons: The First Feminine History of Culture,* ed. and trans. John Philip Lunden (New York: Julian Press, 1965), 101.

46. Thomas Heywood, *Nine Bookes of Variovs Historie, Onelie concerning Women: Inscribed by the names of the nine Muses* (1624), 223; for the continued influence of this reading, see for example Paster's assertion that "unlike European society, Amazon society did not designate a class of nurses, and all the Amazons presumably continued to offer babies milk from one breast" (*The Body Embarrassed,* 237).

47. Such claims, as they read the idiosyncratic amazonian body in terms of socialized maternal convention, recall a medieval tradition that decides which breast the Amazons sacrifice according to their rank: thus Christine de Pizan writes, "[T]hey had a custom whereby the nobles among them, when they were little girls, burned off their left breast through some technique so that it would not hinder them from carrying a shield, and they removed the right breast of commoners to make it easier for them to shoot a bow" (*The Book of the City of Ladies,* trans. Earl Jeffrey Richards [New York: Persea Books, 1982], 1.16.1). For a similar account of this practice, see chapter 14 of *The Voiage and Travaile of Sir John Maundevile.* Described simultaneously in terms of social status and biological utility, this version of the amazonian practice of breast mutilation might provocatively be juxtaposed to the social structures that underlie wet-nursing.

48. William Painter, "The First Nouell: The hardinesse and conquests of diuers stout, and aduenturous women, called Amazones," *The Second Tome of the Palace of Pleasure, Containing Store of Goodly Histories, Tragical Matters, and Other Moral Arguments, Very requisite for Delight and Profit, Chosen and Selected out of Divers Good and Commendable Authors* (1575) (London: Reprinted for Robert Triphook by Harding and Wright, 1813), 1–7.

49. Peter Stallybrass, "Transvestism and the 'body beneath': Speculating on the Boy Actor," in *Erotic Politics: Desire on the Renaissance Stage,* ed. Susan Zimmerman (New York: Routledge, 1992), 76.

50. Andrewe Thevét, *The New Founde Worlde* (London, 1568), 102.

51. *Gyn/Ecology: The Metaethics of Radical Feminism* (Boston: Beacon Press, 1978, 1990); see esp. 2, xvii.

52. Vergil, *The Aeneid,* trans. Thomas Phaer and Thomas Twyne (1573), in *The "Aeneid" of Thomas Phaer and Thomas Twyne: A Critical Edition Introducing*

Renaissance Metrical Typography, ed. Steven Lally (New York: Garland, 1987), l. 468.

53. George Sandys, *Ovids Metamorphosis Englished, Mythologized, and Represented in Figures* (Oxford, 1632); reprint, ed. Stephen Orgel (New York: Garland, 1976), 334; italics added.

54. Ralegh, *Discoverie,* 367.

55. Purchas, *Purchas his Pilgrimes,* 16:225; 17:35.

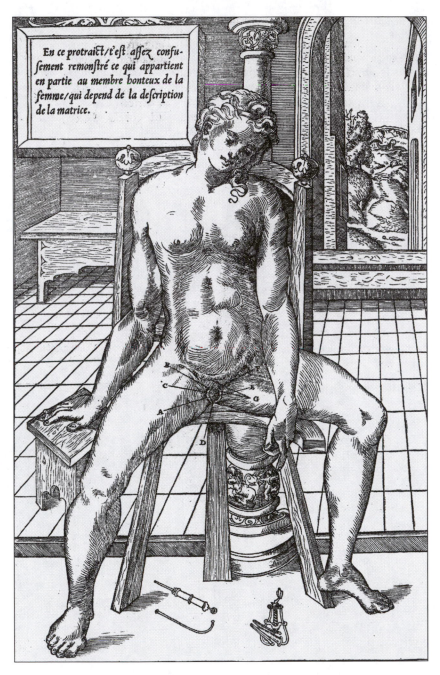

En ce protraict/t'eſt aſſez confu-
ſement remonſtré ce qui appartient
en partie au membre bonteux de la
femme/qui depend de la deſcription
de la matrice.

9. From Charles Estienne, *De la dissection des parties du corps humain* (Paris: Simon de Colines, 1546).

9

The Rediscovery of the Clitoris

French Medicine and the Tribade, 1570–1620

KATHARINE PARK

In his treatise *Des monstres et prodiges* (On monsters and prodigies), first published in 1573, the French surgeon Ambroise Paré concluded his chapter on hermaphrodites with a detailed description of the female genitals under the rubric "Extremely monstrous thing that occurs in the labia [*nimphes*] of some women." On occasion, he wrote, these are so developed that they can erect when stimulated, "like the male penis, so that they can be used to play with other women."[1] In the second edition (1575), he expanded this discussion with a detailed account of the activities of the female diviners of Fez, in Mauritania, taken almost verbatim from the French translation of Leo Africanus's *Historical Description of Africa* (1556). These were supposedly called in by other women, who pretended to be ill or possessed in order to enjoy the diviners' sexual services and who even used their own gullible husbands as go-betweens. Some of these, however, "having perceptively recognized the ruse, exorcize the bodies of their wives with fine blows and beatings," as Paré put it. "This is described by Leo Africanus, who indicates elsewhere that there are people in Africa who go around the city like our [livestock] castrators and make a career of cutting off those excrescences."[2]

Paré's projection of sexual irregularity onto the exoticized bodies of women of another race and continent was a familiar trope in early modern

European topographical literature.[3] Nonetheless, some contemporaries found his inclusion of this material ill advised. Taken to task by the physicians of the Parisian Faculty of Medicine for detailing a "dangerous example of sodomy"—especially in a book written in the vernacular and hence accessible to a female audience—Paré protested that he was only following ancient medical authorities: Hippocrates, Galen, Aetius, and Paul of Aegina.[4] In 1579, however, he capitulated to the faculty on this one point, replacing most of the African material with a brief reference to the trial of two French women, from the section on "abominable lust" in Jean Papon's *Receuil d'arrestes notables des cours souvereins de France* (Collection of notable rulings of the sovereign courts of France of 1565).[5]

As Thomas Laqueur has pointed out, Paré's discussion, in both its original form and its subsequent revision, is remarkable for the slippages that structure it.[6] Having begun with hermaphrodites, defined as beings with "two genitals [*sexes*] in a single body,"[7] Paré moved without discernible transition first to women with enlarged labia, as ostensibly described by Greek medical authors, then to Leo Africanus's diviners of Fez and their clients, to whom Leo had attributed no genital irregularity, and finally to an apparent recommendation for clitoridectomy, taken from another section entirely of Leo's work. This loose set of associations, between hermaphrodites, women with enlarged external genitals, female homoeroticism, and clitoridectomy was not idiosyncratic but figured in a number of French medical works both before and after Paré's, receiving what was perhaps its most extreme formulation in the *Discours sur les hermaphrodits* (Discourse on hermaphrodites) (1614) of the Parisian anatomist Jean Riolan the younger; there the author argued, apropos of yet another legal case involving two French women, that most so-called hermaphrodites were in fact women with clitorises as large as fingers. Riolan noted that the ancient Greeks called such women *tribades* (from the Greek word "to rub"), "insofar as they take on both sexual roles and would rather have sex with women than with men."[8]

The great interest of these French sources lies in the fact that they were the first postclassical European medical texts to accord significant visibility to sexual contacts and sexual desire between women; whereas men occasionally figured in medieval medical discussions of what was construed as the "unnatural" sexual habits and anatomy that led men to seek out sex with other men, and such discussions tended to deemphasize women or elide them altogether.[9] In the works of these sixteenth-century French writers, however, the situation dramatically reversed itself, and accounts of sex between women assumed a much greater prominence than those of sex between men. Furthermore, they did so in a very specific context: the rediscovery of the clitoris. Although the clitoris as an anatomical organ (rather than a general locus of female sexual pleasure) had been well known to late Greek writers on medicine and surgery, that knowledge had been lost to medieval European medical authors.[10] Misled by the linguistic imprecision of their Arabic sources, exacerbated by the uncertain terminology of Latin translators, they tended either to identify it with the labia minora or, following the eleventh-century Persian medical authority Avicenna, to think of it as a pathological growth found in only a few women.[11] In the middle decades of the sixteenth century, however, European anatomists rediscovered the clitoris through a rereading of the ancient Greek works, supplemented by their own anatomical researches on female cadavers. As the texts of Paré and Riolan suggest, this rediscovery proved explosive, triggering a host of contemporary cultural concerns about female sexuality.

In the rest of this chapter, I will explore the complicated nature and meanings of the clitoris, the *tribade,* and female genital hypertrophy in early modern French medical literature. I will show that this complex of themes was connected with certain specific mid-sixteenth-century changes in medical and anatomical thought concerning sex and sex difference, but I will also argue that these changes carried the emotional charge and elicited the popular interest they did because they ultimately reflected deeper and broader contemporary concerns related to male privilege and the status of women. Paré's own treatment of the diviners of Fez can stand as emblematic of this point. What appears initially as a story about sex between women reveals itself eventually as a story about male authority in the household, challenged by a female conspiracy but happily restored by physical force. A story about anatomical monstrosity, located in the transgressive female body, reveals itself as a story about political monstrosity, located in the household and, by association, I will argue, in the French realm. In this period, if male sodomy was a crime of divine *lèse-majesté*, as Alan Bray has shown, then sex between women—or at least certain kinds of sex between women—was a crime of what Marie-Jo Bonnet has called *lèse-patriarcat.*[12]

In focusing on medical writing, I do not intend to suggest that medicine functioned as a "master discourse" in sixteenth-century France in the way that it does to a large degree today; gender was produced and maintained in many different sites in early modern Europe.[13] But it is important not to underestimate the degree to which medical treatises, particularly vernacular medical treatises, both reflected and shaped literate lay views. Furthermore, in France—at least in urban middle-class and aristocratic circles—doctors were generally recognized as the relevant authorities in cases of sexual ambiguity and the apparently sodomitical liaisons that could ensue. Families or judges faced with problematic situations regarding sex difference regularly deferred to the judgment of physicians and surgeons, rather than leaving the decision up to the individual in question, as (wishfully) argued by Foucault.[14] Thus medical opinion could and did dramatically alter the lives of individuals, forcing them to change their gender, leave their marriages, or submit to dangerous surgery, and sometimes condemning them to punishment, exile, or imprisonment.[15]

Finally, early modern medical writing on the clitoris reveals a persistent inclination to reduce what was considered deviant female sexual behavior to deviant genital anatomy: to use what Valerie Traub has called "a paradigm of bodily structure" where we would use a "paradigm of desire."[16] This strategy had precedents: Joan Cadden has recently analyzed the attempt of Pietro d'Abano, a fourteenth-century Italian physician, to relate some men's pleasure in passive anal intercourse to a malformation in the passages that were thought to carry the spermatic fluid to the penis.[17] But, as Traub and Laqueur have both emphasized, the association of the clitoris with female sexual "deviance" has had a much longer and more influential history than Pietro's theory and has significantly shaped Freudian and post-Freudian debates on female sexuality and the modern construction of "lesbianism."

I hope that this chapter, paired with Traub's important piece, will illustrate the advantages to be gained from an alliance of theoretical and historical approaches to material of this sort. In it I aim to expand the archival and empirical base available to scholars, with special emphasis on the Latin medical tradition. But I hope to show in addition the importance of untangling not only individual positions in early modern anatomical writing but also national schools and specific intellectual traditions, emphasizing in this case the "Frenchness" of the earliest sixteenth- and early-seventeenth-century discussions of the clitoris from which other European treatments derived.[18]

Thus I have tried above all to preserve the complexities, confusions, and controversies of the early modern medical tradition. In so doing, I wish specifically to underscore the impossibility of reducing contemporary ideas to a "one-sex body," in the phrase of Laqueur, or indeed to a single model of any kind. Such heuristic simplifications can perform a useful initial role in staking out problems and issues in a nascent field like the history of sexuality, but their accuracy and utility is limited.[19] The topography of medical thought and writing on sexual difference was as complicated and contested in the sixteenth and seventeenth centuries as it is today (and as it had been for millennia), molded by the crosscurrents of professionalization, personal rivalry, and national tradition, as well as by the impact of new methods of inquiry and the rereading of ancient texts. It is these crosscurrents and fault lines, far more than any retrospectively constructed consensus, that reveal the complicated relationships between sex and gender in the early modern period.

Constructing the Tribade: the Rediscovery of the Clitoris

As I have already indicated, Paré's description of the female diviners of Fez was not original. He took both his account of their activities and his term for such women (*fricatrices*, the Latin counterpart of the Greek *tribades*, meaning women who rub one another) from the recent French translation of Leo Africanus. But his description of their putative anatomical peculiarity came almost verbatim from a closer source: the *Chirurgie françoise* (French surgery) (1570) of Jacques Daléchamps, erstwhile professor of medicine at the University of Montpellier. Written in the vernacular for "journeymen and master surgeons, who have not been educated in Greek and Latin,"[20] this work was intended to make broadly accessible the surgical knowledge of medieval and, especially, ancient authorities. Structured as a translation of and commentary on the *Surgery* of the Greek writer Paul of Aegina (fl. 640), it also included observations from Aetius (early sixth century) and Caelius Aurelianus (a fifth-century Latin medical compiler, whose work Daléchamps had edited), in addition to traditional Arabic authorities such as Avicenna and Albucasis.

Like Paré, Daléchamps first introduced the issue of sex between women in his chapter on hermaphrodites, noting that some writers thought that the women called *tribades* by Caelius Aurelianus were "female hermaphrodites, who abuse human nature" (422). In the following chapter, he took up Paul's discussion of "nymphotomia," the operation to amputate an unusually large *nymphe*; according to Daléchamps, this unusual anatomical feature occurred in almost all Egyptian women, as well as "some of ours, so that when they find themselves in the company of other women, or their clothes rub them while they walk, or their husbands wish to approach them, it erects like a male penis, and indeed they use it to play with other women, as their husbands would do." Thus, Daléchamps wrote, the Egyptians cut off this part, as described in both Aetius and (pseudo) Galen's *Introduction* (425).

There are two things to note about the latter passage. First, Daléchamps was obviously unclear about exactly which part of the female genitals Paul of Aegina, Aetius, and pseudo-Galen were describing; although he used the word *nymphe* (a French version of *nympha*, one of the Greek words for clitoris), he seems to have identified it with the labia minora (usually called *nymphes* in French), thus perpetuating the medieval confusion concerning the organ I have described above. In the second place, despite Daléchamps's copious citation of Greek, Latin, and Arabic medical authors in support of his account of the anatomical peculiarities of the *tribade*, none of these authors in fact connected an enlarged clitoris (or labia) with female homoerotic desire or behavior. Paul of Aegina, Aetius, and pseudo-Galen referred to the operation to be performed on a hypertrophied clitoris—and Aetius and pseudo-Galen described this operation as particularly common in Egypt—but neither indicated that the structure allowed or encouraged women to have sex with other women.[21] Caelius Aurelianus, on the other hand, in the chapter of his *De acutis morbis / De diuturnis* (On chronic diseases) devoted largely to male sex role inversion, described the activities of *tribades* (women who "practice both kinds of sex and desire women more than men") without any reference to anatomy at all.[22] Thus Daléchamps seems to have fabricated the connection between clitoral hypertrophy and female homoeroticism by consolidating what were in fact two separate topics in his ancient texts and then to have authorized his construction by projecting it back onto those texts.[23] The amalgamation of these two separate ideas became standard in French (and eventually other European) medical writing after Daléchamps, as is clear from both Paré's *Des monstres et prodiges* written shortly after Daléchamps's *Chirurgie françoise*, and Jean Liébault's *Trois libres appartenant aux infirmitez et maladies des femme* (Three books relating to women's infirmities and illnesses), first published in 1582.[24]

Daléchamps constructed this preliminary version of the *tribade* on the basis of Greek and Roman anatomical texts, newly translated or edited as part of the initiative by humanist medical writers to purify and render accessible the works of ancient authorities. But the definitive *tribade*, in all her phallic glory, was a product of a second set of developments in sixteenth-century medicine: the explosion of anatomical knowledge based on systematic human dissection by Andreas Vesalius and his contemporaries and the anatomical debates surrounding the newly rediscovered clitoris. Although contemporaries generally attributed this rediscovery to Gabriele Falloppia, professor of anatomy at Pisa and Padua, the first early modern writer clearly to identify the clitoris in a work of anatomy based on human dissection seems in fact to have been the Parisian Charles Estienne. In his *La dissection des parties du corps humain* (Dissection of the parts of the human body), published in Latin in 1545 and in French translation in 1546, Estienne described the clitoris as part of woman's "shameful member" (*membre honteux*)—"a little tongue [*languette*] ... at the place of the neck of the bladder"—and included it in one of his highly eroticized woodcuts of female reproductive anatomy, where it is indicated by the letter F (Fig. 9).[25] Estienne related the function of the clitoris to urination rather than sexual response; perhaps as a result, his observation made no discernible impact, for Falloppia celebrated what he considered his own rediscovery of the clitoris in his *Observations anatomicae* (Anatomical observations), written around 1550 though not published until 1561. "Modern anatomists have entirely neglected it," he wrote, "and do not say a word about it.... And if others have spoken of it, know that they have taken it from me or my students."[26]

Falloppia's discovery caused an immediate stir in the European medical community. At Padua, Realdo Colombo tried to appropriate it, staking his own claim in his treatise *De re anatomica* (On anatomy), which he brought out two years before his rival's work, in 1559. While later writers generally discounted Colombo's assertions of priority, they nonetheless acknowledged him as the first to emphasize its role in female sexual pleasure. "It is the principal seat of women's enjoyment in intercourse," he wrote, "so that if you not only rub it with your penis, but even touch it with your little finger, the pleasure causes their seed to flow forth in all directions, swifter than the wind, even if they don't want it to."[27] But not all of Falloppia's contemporaries were equally impressed with his discovery. In particular, Andreas Vesalius, éminence grise of the new anatomy, explicitly rejected it, reasserting the traditional opinion that the clitoris was a pathological structure found only in what he called "women hermaphrodites." He chided Falloppia,

> It is unreasonable to blame others for incompetence on the basis of some sport of nature [*naturae lusum*] you have observed in some woman, and you can hardly ascribe this new and useless part, as if it were an organ, to healthy [*integris*] women. I think that such a structure appears in hermaphrodites who otherwise have well formed female genitals, as Paul of Aegina describes, but I have never once seen in any woman a penis (which Avicenna called albathara and the Greeks called an enlarged nympha and classed as an illness) or even the rudiments of a tiny phallus.[28]

As Vesalius's strenuous resistance indicates, the anatomical rediscovery of the clitoris carried a special charge. For Vesalius and many of his contemporaries, a large part of this charge lay not only in Colombo's identification of the clitoris as the locus of female sexual pleasure, as Laqueur rightly emphasized, but also in the fact that Falloppia and his followers emphasized its exact structural analogies with the male penis.[29] The finding was momentous because it was generally acknowledged that women already had a full set of genitals corresponding in general terms to their male counterparts: ovaries to testicles, uterus to scrotum, vagina to penis. If they possessed in addition a miniature penis, lacking only a perforation, this meant that all women were in some sense hermaphrodites, bearing both female and male organs. The corollary, drawn by some Italian writers, most notably Constantino Varolio, professor of anatomy at Bologna, was that most hermaphrodites were really women with enlarged genitals.[30] In this way, the discovery of the clitoris, far from being easily absorbed into the resilient earlier model of male and female as occupying different points on a vertically continuous hierarchy of complexional heat, as Laqueur has argued, seems rather to have contributed to its dissolution.[31]

But the anatomical rediscovery of the clitoris as a normal structure in women, rather than as an illness or anatomical peculiarity, had even more powerful and troubling implications for the view of female sexuality, in the context of the now newly visible *tribade*. In particular, it suggested that many more women than previously thought—indeed perhaps every woman —could potentially penetrate and give pleasure to another woman. Paré, writing without reference to the clitoris, had reassured his critics in the Faculty of Medicine that the deformity that allowed a woman to have sex with another woman was extremely rare—so much so, he wrote, "that for every woman that has it, there are ten thousand who don't."[32] His successors had no such consolation.

Writing in the 1570s, Paré, like Daléchamps, seems still to have been confused about the relationship between the labia and the clitoris.[33] Twenty years later, however, the confusion between the clitoris and the labia in French medical circles seems to have been resolved. André Du Laurens clearly distinguished the two in his *Historia anatomica humani corporis* (Anatomical history of the human body), first published in 1593,[34] and Séverin Pineau underscored the point in his *De integritate et corruptionis virginum notis* (Notes on the integrity and corruption of virgins) of 1597, describing the clitoris as "that part with which imprudent and lustful women, aroused by a more than brutal passion, abuse one another with vigorous rubbings [*confricationibus*], whence they are called *confricatrices*. [They do not do this] by inserting their labia into one another's vaginas, as some imagine, since the body of the labia ... is unfitted to erecting, and is much less suitable for rubbing and titillation on account of its softness."[35]

Jean Riolan's chapter on the clitoris in his *Anthropographia* (first edition 1618) was the most explicit of all. After an elaborate account of the various names given to it by ancient and contemporary authors, he described the enormous size it could attain, describing one as large as a "goose's neck" and two—one of which he had seen personally—as "as long and thick as my little finger."[36] He concluded his discussion by citing in considerable detail a wide range of ancient and modern authorities, from Saint Paul to Lucian and Martial to Leo Africanus, who had described (and for the most part roundly condemned) sex between women. Both the escalating size of the clitoris and the increasing prominence of accounts of female homoeroticism in medical discussions of it indicate its importance as a cultural construct in late-sixteenth- and early-seventeenth-century France.

Tribades and Hermaphrodites: The Duval-Riolan Debate

Thus by 1600, the phallic *tribade* was no longer confined primarily to the African periphery, as she had been for Paré and his contemporaries; she had moved from the margins to the European center, ultimately taking up residence in France itself. With this change came a new emphasis in French medical writing: whereas sixteenth-century discussions of the subject dealt mainly in abstractions—establishing the norms and exceptions of female sexual behavior and anatomy—seventeenth-century treatments dealt increasingly with particular cases involving identifiable individuals and, in consequence, with more pressing and specific issues of gender and sex.

One of the most famous of such cases was that of Marie le Marcis, a young chambermaid from Rouen, who in 1601 had defended herself against charges of sodomy with her female lover on grounds that she was in fact a man with a hidden penis.[37] Condemned to death after visual inspection by two commissions of doctors, who failed to corroborate her claim, she appealed to the Parlement of Rouen. A third medical commission, composed of six physicians, two surgeons, and two sworn midwives, was on the verge of confirming the opinion of the two previous, when one of its members, a physician from Rouen named Jacques Duval, inserted his finger into Marie's vagina, found the hidden member, and filed a dissenting opinion declaring her a predominantly male hermaphrodite. A decade later, when Marie (now Marin) was living as a bearded male tailor, Duval published an extended account of the story, as the centerpiece of his *Traité des hermaphrodits, partis génital, accouchemens des femmes, etc.* (Treatise on hermaphrodites, female genitals, and childbirth) (1612). Duval's work was rebutted two years later by no less than Jean Riolan, professor of anatomy at the University of Paris, in his *Discours sur les hermaphrodits* (1614), which Duval answered shortly afterward in his *Responce au discours ... contre l'histoire de l'hermaphrodit de Rouen* (Reply to the Discourse ... against the

Story of the Hermaphrodite of Rouen) (n.d.). Duval and Riolan took opposing positions on the case of Marie le Marcis. Duval held that she was a male-dominated hermaphrodite and hence innocent of sodomy; Riolan argued that she was a woman and hence guilty. In his treatise, Riolan denied the existence of true hermaphrodites; he argued that most people identified as such—though not Marie, to whom he attributed a prolapsed uterus[38]—were in fact *tribades*, with enlarged clitorises.

Duval's and Riolan's opinions in the matter of Marie le Marcis reflected their commitment to two different theories of sex difference, with radically different sexual, and ultimately social and political, implications.[39] Duval subscribed generally to the theory of generation associated with Galen and Hippocrates, which interpreted hermaphrodites as beings of genuinely intermediate sex.[40] According to this tradition, the sex of the fetus was determined by two important oppositions: between the male and female principles in the maternal and paternal seed and between the left and right sides of the uterus. Depending on which seed from which parent was dominant and the position of the fetus in the womb, the offspring would occupy one of a number of discrete points on a sexual spectrum, ranging from unambiguously male to wholly female. Intermediate points corresponded to offspring of intermediate sexual nature: fragile and effeminate males, strong and masculine viragos, and—in the rare event of perfectly or nearly perfectly balanced male and female factors—the occasional hermaphrodite, fertile in both sexes.[41] The tradition subscribed to by Duval, in other words, gave equal emphasis to both the maternal and paternal seed in generation and admitted a wide range of variation between the poles of male and female.

Riolan, on the other hand, aligned himself specifically with Aristotle, who had treated hermaphrodites not as intersexual beings but as a special case of twins. In *The Generation of Animals*, Aristotle had devoted a passage to beings with doubled or redundant genitalia, explaining that these developed when the matter contributed by the mother at conception was more than enough for one fetus but not enough for two. If located on the foot, for example, the extra matter would produce a sixth toe; if in the groin, a second set of genitals.[42] Even in this latter case, however, Aristotle emphasized that the sex of the hermaphrodite was never more than apparently ambiguous, since the operative genital, like the sex of the whole fetus, was always determined by the heat of the heart. A local "cold spot" in the doubled groin of a hot-hearted body might produce a female genital alongside a male one, for example, but the temperature of the heart ensured that only the corresponding male genital would be operative.[43] Thus Aristotle, like his medieval and early modern followers, was already a believer in what

Foucault called "true sex."[44] For them, there were no true hermaphrodites; the heart was always hot or cold, the animal was always effectively male or female, and the inoperative set of genitals was attached, as Aristotle put it, "like a growth."[45]

Riolan subscribed to Aristotle's highly dichotomized model of sex difference, which emphasized the absolute incommensurability of male and female. In Riolan's words,

> The male genitals are different from the female genitals in species, ... and their temperament is also dissimilar. For men are hotter than women; thus a single person cannot have both the genitals and temperaments of both man and woman together, so as to be able to use both—insomuch as the male is defined by Aristotle as that which can engender in another, and the female, as that which receives from outside to engender in herself. Furthermore, the two principles of human generation are different and cannot be supplied by the same person: the woman contributes matter, and the man gives the active and shaping seed of the child.[46]

According to this theory, women were not only radically different from men but also inferior: as Riolan put it, echoing Aristotle's famous formula, the female was an "imperfect male."[47] For this reason, the "vice of hermaphroditism is more common in women than men"; according to Riolan, most so-called hermaphrodites were in fact simply women with enlarged clitorises, which "in the lascivious can grow and thicken to the size of a finger, [so that they] can abuse it to give themselves pleasure, by having sex [*habitant*] with each other" (79).

What was at stake in this early-seventeenth-century anatomical and physiological debate? On the one hand, it involved issues of professional authority and prestige. Like Paré before him, Duval found himself, as a relative outsider, locked in conflict with a highly placed representative of the Parisian medical establishment; Riolan was a professor of anatomy and botany at the University of Paris, while Duval was only a provincial physician, unversed in any but the most basic anatomy, as Riolan did not hesitate to point out (46–47). Whereas Riolan wrote primarily in Latin, for an audience of students and professors of anatomy, Duval professed to have composed his vernacular *Traité* to inform (presumably female) patients and to help young surgeons and midwives in their obstetrical practice and their legal testimony.[48] From this point of view, his embrace of Hippocratism represented an attempt both to reassert the authority of a more traditional medical position regarding sex difference, in the face of the radical Aristotelianism of some medical academicians, and to align himself with the fashionable new Hippocratism being promoted by other scholars.[49] From this point of view, the debate between Duval and Riolan shows the ways in which the activities of sixteenth-century medical humanists like Dalé-champs, dedicated to recuperating the original meanings of ancient medical texts, forced a kind of clarification of classical positions and issues that had been obscured by the syncretizing tendencies of medieval medical thought.

But Duval's Hippocratism also involved a more specific set of ideological commitments concerning sex and gender, one no doubt intended to appeal to his lay audience of both women and men. Unlike Riolan, Duval presented a highly positive view of women; after a paean to the uterus ("a lovable temple, august, holy, venerable, and wonderful"), he concluded that "woman is not a failed male or imperfect animal, as maintained by Aristotle, who did not realize that she was formed by God the Creator, who makes nothing that is not whole and perfect."[50] For Riolan's stern suspicion of human lustfulness and irrationality, he substituted what might be termed a "sex-positive" reading of the Biblical injunction "Be fruitful and multiply," praising the "natural inclination, needlings of the flesh, and curious will" bestowed by God on humans to help them follow his command.[51]

Finally, Duval rejected Riolan's Aristotelian commitment to a starkly binary model of sex difference. Not only did he accept the existence of a spectrum of people whose temperament and conformation—each unique—made them genuinely intermediate between male and female; he celebrated that diversity as a manifestation of natural variety and divine creativity: "Thus we should consider diligently the excellent work of Nature here represented to us, admiring more and more her divine effects."[52] In particular, Marie/Marin le Marcis, formed by nature "of doubtful sex," was an ornament of creation. Whereas the ancients might have tried to destroy her/him, Duval argued, we should keep her/him just as she/he was born.[53]

It is tempting to see Duval as representing a general premodern tolerance of transgendering and intersexuality and an acceptance of sex difference as artificial and unstable, along the lines proposed first by Foucault. But the situation is more complex. For one thing, Duval was hardly representative of European medical orthodoxy (even French medical orthodoxy): not only is it impossible to identify an orthodox position on these matters but the specific issues Duval raised were hotly contested—by Riolan among many others—and his position was in some respects idiosyncratic and extreme. For another, neither he nor Riolan believed that people should be left alone to determine their own sexual preferences: both concurred with the courts that those preferences should follow the individual's sexual anatomy, as determined by medical experts (and neither believed that people *ever* spontaneously changed their sex).[54] It was only because Duval had concluded on the basis of a thorough medical examination that Marie/ Marin was a predominantly *male* hermaphrodite that he rejected the court's finding of sodomy in her/his liaison with her/his lover, Jeanne. The free choice fantasized by Foucault existed only for the "perfect" or "true" hermaphrodite, functional in both sexes—a quasi-mythical being thought to be either nonexistent or, at best, extremely rare. Doctors continued, as they had for centuries, to be the gatekeepers of a functionally dichotomous sexual world.[55]

A striking sign of this general commitment to sexual binarism was the early modern French medical writers' promotion of clitoridectomy as a feasible remedy for clitoral hypertrophy and its inconvenients, not just in faraway Africa but in Europe itself. Medieval surgical authors, following Albucasis and Avicenna, had described the operation,[56] which was further detailed in the newly edited works of Paul of Aegina and Aetius, as well as those of Daléchamps and his followers. Writing in mid-sixteenth-century Italy, Realdo Colombo was uncertain about its safety; asked by an "Ethiopian" to perform it, so she could have sex "like a woman," he demurred.[57] But the operation may have been more current in France: Duval cited a legal case from the 1560s in Anjou, where the judge had annulled a marriage at the request of the husband, after the wife refused to have her one-to-two-inch clitoris removed, and he relayed the testimony of a medical colleague, who had been asked by Guillaume Frerot of Honfleur to "cut" (*tailler*) his six-year-old daughter. The same doctor had also examined the fourteen-year-old daughter of the sieur de Blangues from Caux, and having pronounced her female, despite a clitoris as large as a man's index finger, saw her successfully married, unaltered, to another local notable.[58]

Such cases, if Duval is to be believed, suggest not only that clitoridectomy was not unknown but also that this impulse to police sexual boundaries was not imposed by medical or legal authorities alone, as is often suggested;[59] rather, it seems also to have been initiated by individuals and their families, moved by the desire to contract durable marriages, as well as by what Duval called "shame" and fear of being "a popular tale."[60] The accounts testify to the varying ways in which people in early modern French society navigated the ambiguities of sex and gender, occasionally engaging surgeons to make that passage easier, but more often, as with the daughter of the sieur de Blangues, trusting to the flexibility of contemporary sexual practice.

Writing several years later in his *Anthropographia*, however, Jean Riolan proposed another use entirely for clitoridectomy. Where Duval, like ancient and medieval surgical writers, presented the operation as a remedy of last resort for an unusually large clitoris, Riolan suggested that it might be performed on *all* contemporary women, as a way of disciplining unbridled female sexuality. Noting that "Ethiopians" not only regularly amputated the clitorises of their women but also sewed up the entrance to their vaginas, he described this custom as "cruel" but "perhaps not without its utility in this depraved period, when the modesty of virgins is easily overcome by gold, flattery, and licentiousness, and when virgins allow themselves to be conquered by either the weakness of their minds or an almost masculine jealousy."[61] Although doubtless partly facetious, Riolan's comment, with its clear verbal echoes of Caelius Aurelianus's discussion of female homoeroticism, suggests that the clitoris and clitoridectomy had acquired a broader cultural meaning than in the work of Duval or even of Paré.

From Dildo to Clitoris: Penetrating Women

The phallic *tribade* was not confined to medical works, as I have already mentioned, but fascinated and preoccupied French writers in other genres. In their works the sexual concerns that lay beneath the often more neutral surface of the medical texts took clearer form, crystallized in an increasing preoccupation with sex roles and penetration. This issue had a special resonance in late-sixteenth-century France, where it formed part of a virulent and escalating political polemic that swirled around the French monarch Henry III, and his mother and regent, Catherine de' Medici. During the two decades after Henry's accession in 1573, he became a target first of Protestant and then of Catholic invective, both of which played upon the themes of sodomy, hermaphroditism, and sexual inversion.[62]

A few examples suffice to convey the general tone and content of this invective. Thus when Henry founded a penitential order of flagellants in 1583 and led them together with his favorites, in a procession on Holy Thursday, the diarist Pierre de l'Estoille recorded a verse that read: "Favorites who carry behind you [*en croupe*] the French king, beat not only your backs but also your offending arses." Another, in the same vein, described the group as "coupled side by side in a devout enough manner, but I find them full of vice when they take each other from behind."[63] Other polemicists condemned Henry and his circle as "hermaphrodites" fond of passive anal intercourse and elaborate dress.[64] Catherine received analogous treatment. In *Les tragiques*, the Huguenot writer Agrippa d'Aubigné lamented France's current rulers as "hermaphrodites" and "effeminate monsters,"[65] but he reserved his most virulent polemic for the king's mother, whom he described in 270 violent verses couched in the language of monstrosity and sexual inversion (1:89–109). "Happy the Romans," he wrote, "who had for tyrants the Caesars, lovers of arms and art, but unhappy he who lives as an infamous slave under a manlike woman and a female man" (2:53–54).

Political polemics of this sort used the trope of sodomy to brand Henry and his mother as sinners not only against French laws and customs but also against the natural order instituted by God.[66] Penetration was a central topos in these, for the ultimate figures of unnatural sodomy were the penetrating woman and the penetrated man. It was in this charged rhetorical context that even relatively apolitical medical writers such as Daléchamps and Paré first constructed their fantasies of female genital hypertrophy. Paré used the *tribade* to represent the inversion of household order and the expropriation of the husband's authority, but she also came to stand for contemporary French concerns about the perceived subversion of the state by female political authority, which fed contemporary debates on female succession and Salic law.[67]

In addition to these specific political associations, however, the rediscovery of the clitoris raised more general social and sexual concerns. As Lilian Faderman has argued, sixteenth- and seventeenth-century French writers made a clear distinction between female homoerotic behavior that involved rubbing the genitals—the etymology of the word *tribade*—and any activity that involved the penetration of one woman by another. The former was seen as regrettable but fundamentally benign because it hardly counted as sex in the phallocentric world of the Renaissance male writer.[68] The latter, in contrast, was a serious transgression. As a true sex act, it was the only form of sexual behavior between women to qualify as sodomy, a mortal sin and (at least in theory) a capital crime, threatening both the natural/theological and the social order.[69]

In the mid-sixteenth century, before the rediscovery of the clitoris—or before knowledge of the clitoris was widespread outside the medical community—legal authorities and lay writers could conceive of penetration of one woman by another only as involving a dildo, as appears in a story told by the humanist Henri Estienne in his *Apologie pour Hérodote* (Apology for Herodotus) (1566). A young woman from the town of Fontaines assumed male dress and took a position as a stableboy in an inn in the faubourg of Foye. After seven years, she married a local girl and worked as a vinedresser. Two years later, according to Estienne, "the wickedness that she used to imitate the role of husband was discovered," and she was arrested, convicted, and burned alive.[70] The very language used by Estienne—as well as by Montaigne, who several decades later described a similar case—betrays the charged nature of the topic. Neither could bring himself to use the word *godemiché* (dildo) itself, employing instead cumbersome circumlocutions: "the wickedness that she used to imitate the role of a husband," in Estienne's words; "illicit inventions to remedy the defects of her sex," in Montaigne's.[71] And even the generally tolerant Pierre Bourdeille de Brantôme, approving chronicler of the sexual foibles of the Valois court, made do with the elliptical abbreviation "g......"; according to Brantôme, the form of "female loving" that involved only rubbing the external genitals "does no harm," but the use of dildos is "very dangerous," since it "engenders sores in the womb by unnatural motions and frictions."[72]

Like Daléchamps, Brantôme knew nothing of the clitoris and associated naturally enlarged labia mainly with the women of distant Persia.[73] But his uneasy reflections on penetrative female sex, like those of Estienne and Montaigne, testify to a preexisting cultural space that the clitoris would come to fill. By the early seventeenth century, the correspondence of clitoris to dildo was enshrined in vernacular terminology; according to Duval, French prostitutes called it the *gaude mihi* or *godemiché*.[74]

What was the cultural meaning of these stories, and what contemporary concerns did they reflect? On the most obvious legal and theological level, the fact that a woman was newly imagined as being able to penetrate another woman with her clitoris meant that at least one kind of sex between women qualified unambiguously as sodomy, which was generally defined as the insertion of an inappropriate organ into an inappropriate orifice. In addition, however, the concern had to do with sexual and social usurpation, as is clear from Brantôme's discussion. If a woman could penetrate another woman, they could give each other real pleasure, as opposed to what Brantôme considered the pale imitation produced by rubbing. This might awake in them a generalized promiscuity, but, more disturbing, they might choose to forgo sex with men altogether, thereby avoiding the dangers and inconveniences of pregnancy.[75] In this way, sex between women might no longer function merely as a preparation or inferior substitute for heterosexual sex: Brantôme specifically envisaged the possibility of women interested exclusively in sex with one another and "unwilling to suffer men" (10:195). Another of the other vernacular names of the clitoris, according to Duval, was *le mespris des hommes*.[76]

Sex between women, removed from a heteronormalizing context, became significant as a social as well as a sexual threat; it imperiled not only marriage and reproduction, but also the "natural" position of men as heads of household. Of certain "very great ladies" who "loved other ladies, honored them, served them more than men, and made love to them like a man to his mistress," Brantôme wrote that they "maintained [their favorites] in hearth and home and gave them whatever they wished."[77] Thus penetrative female sex, with dildo, clitoris, or labia, as in the case of Paré's diviners, represented in a more abstract sense an unacceptable usurpation of male status, especially when accompanied by other forms of pretension to male identity, including transvestism and certain kinds of work. It was in this context that Jean Riolan called for wholesale clitoridectomy to control the new tide of female licentiousness he perceived as menacing French society as a whole.[78]

The prominence of the clitoris, tribadism, and clitoridectomy in French medical discourse runs counter to Laqueur's description of these issues as of relatively little concern in the world of the putative one-sex body. According to Laqueur,

> [T]he problem ... well into the seventeenth century was not finding the organic signs of sexual opposition but understanding heterosexual desire in the world of one sex. Being sure that "jackdaw did not seek jackdaw," that "like did not seek like," as Aristotle had put it, took tremendous cultural resources.... But the clitoris was only a very small part of the problem, if a problem at all, when the entire female genitalia were construed as a version of the male's.[79]

Laqueur is surely right to stress the "social problem of the clitoris"—of "making sure that women engage in sexual intercourse as befits their station and not as befits men." But he is wrong to dismiss the anatomical significance of the clitoris and of medical discussions of tribadism. French medical writers recognized analogies between the genitals of men and women, but they did not by that token deny the fundamental anatomical reality of sex difference—a difference in degree so great as to be a difference in kind. It was not male homoeroticism that worried them in the first instance, but female: their concerns focused not on the naturalness of heterosexuality (about which none expressed any doubts), but on the perversity of women, as embodied in the penetrating *tribade*.

Notes

Versions of the paper on which this article is based were presented at the 1990 meeting of the History of Science Society and most recently at a session on early modern "lesbianisms" at the 1994 conference Attending to Women in Early Modern Europe, together with papers by Valerie Traub, Patricia Simons, and Harriette Andreadis. I am very grateful to Vernon Rosario, Geeta Patel, Joan Cadden, Paula Findlen, and Lorraine Daston for their helpful comments on earlier drafts of this paper and to Nancy Siraisi for advice on translating Vesalius.

1. Ambroise Paré, *Des monstres et prodiges*, ed. Jean Céard (Geneva: Droz, 1971), 26.

2. Ibid., 27, citing Leo Africanus, *Historiale Description de l'Afrique*, 2 vols. (Lyon: Jean Temporal, 1556), 1:161–62.

3. See, for example, Patricia Parker, "Fantasies of 'Race' and 'Gender': Africa, *Othello*, and Bringing to Light," in *Women, "Race," and Writing in the Early Modern Period*, ed. Margo Hendricks and Patricia Parker (New York: Routledge, 1994), 84–100; and Valerie Traub, "The Psychomorphology of the Clitoris," *GLQ* 2 (1995): 85–89, esp.

4. Ambroise Paré, *Responce de M. Ambroise Paré, premier chirurgien du Roy, aux calomnies d'aucuns médecins et chirurgiens, touchant ses oeuvres*, in Le Paulmier, *Ambroise Paré d'après de nouveaux documents* (Paris: Charavay Frères, 1884), 232. For background to the controversy, see Le Paulmier, *Ambroise Paré*, 87–93, and Alison Klairmont Lingo, "Print's Role in the Politics of Women's Health Care in Early Modern France," in *Culture and Identity in Early Modern Europe (1500–1800): Essays in Honor of Natalie Zemon Davis*, ed. Barbara Diefendorf and Carla Hesse (Ann Arbor: University of Michigan Press, 1993), 207.

5. Paré, *Des monstres*, 27; cf. Jean Papon, *Recueil d'arrests notables des cours souveraines de France* (Geneva, 1609), 1256–57. Paré claimed erroneously that the two women were burnt; in fact, according to Papon, they were ultimately released for lack of evidence.

6. Thomas Laqueur, "Amor Veneris, vel Dulcedo Appeletur," in *Fragments for a History of the Body*, ed. Michel Feher with Ramona Naddaff and Nadia Tazi, 3 vols. (New York: Zone, 1989), 3:117.

7. Paré, *Des monstres*, 24.

8. [Jean Riolan the Younger], *Discours sur les hermaphrodits, ou il est desmonstré contre l'opinion commune, qu'il n'y a point de vrays hermaphrodits* (Paris: Pierre Ramier, 1614), 79.

9. See, e.g., Danielle Jacquart and Claude Thomasset, *Sexuality and Medicine in the Middle Ages*, trans. Matthew Adamson (Princeton: Princeton University Press, 1988), 155–60; and Patricia Simons, "Lesbian (In)Visibility in Italian Renaissance Culture: Diana and Other Cases of *donna con donna*," *Journal of Homosexuality* 27 (1994): 85–87, esp.

10. This does not mean that its general location or function was unfamiliar. In addition to what I presume to have been lay knowledge, the medieval medical theorist Pietro d'Abano had noted in the early fourteenth century that rubbing the area between the vagina and the pubis could lead to orgasm; see Jacquart and Thomasset, *Sexuality*, 46, and in general 44–47. This knowledge must also have been available to midwives and other female medical practitioners, who treated women for suffocation of the uterus by masturbating them.

11. Avicenna, *Liber canonis* (Venice: Paganini, 1507), fol. 377v.

12. Alan Bray, *Homosexuality in Renaissance England* (London: Gay Men's Press, 1982), 23–26; Marie-Jo Bonnet, *Un choix sans équivoque: recherches historiques sur les relations amoureuses entre les femmes, XVIe–XXe siècle* (Paris: Denoël, 1981), 57.

13. Ann Rosalind Jones and Peter Stallybrass, "Fetishizing Gender: Constructing the Hermaphrodite in Renaissance Europe," in *Body Guards: The Cultural Politics of Gender Ambiguity*, ed. Julia Epstein and Kristina Straub (New York: Routledge, 1991), 80–92.

14. Michel Foucault, *Herculine Barbin, Being the Recently Discovered Memoirs of a Nineteenth-Century Hermaphrodite*, trans. Richard McDougall (New York: Pantheon, 1980), vii–viii.

15. Lorraine Daston and Katharine Park, "Hermaphrodites in Renaissance France," *Critical Matrix* 1, no. 5 (1985).

16. Traub, "Psychomorphology."

17. Joan Cadden, "Sciences/Silences: The Natures and Languages of 'Sodomy' in Peter of Abano's *Problemata* Commentary," in *Constructing Medieval Sexuality*, ed. K. Lochrie, J. Schultz, and P. McCracken (Minneapolis: University of Minnesota Press, forthcoming 1997).

18. For later English recapitulations of this theme, for example, see Emma Donoghue, "Imagined More than Women: Lesbians as Hermaphrodites, 1671–1766," *Women's History Review* 2 (1993): 199–216.

19. Laqueur, "Amor Veneris," 106; Laqueur, *Making Sex: Body and Gender from the Greeks to Freud* (Cambridge: Harvard University Press, 1990). A detailed critique of Laqueur's argument concerning the one-sex and the two-sex body appears in Katharine Park and Robert M. Nye, "Destiny Is Anatomy," *New Republic*, January 31, 1991: 53–57. On the importance of retaining complexity in this area, see also Estelle Cohen, "The Body as a Historical Category: Science and Imagination, 1660–1760," in *The Good Body: Asceticism in Contemporary Culture*, ed. Mary G. Winkler and Letha B. Cole (New Haven: Yale University Press, 1994), 67–90.

20. Jacques Daléchamps, *Chirurgie françoise* (Lyon: Guillaume Rouille, 1573), preface.

21. Paul of Aegina, *Chirurgie de Paul d'Egine*, ed. and trans. René Briau (Paris: Victor Masson, 1815), 292–93; Aetius of Amida, *Contractae ex veteribus medicinae tetrabiblos*, trans. Ianus Cornarius (Basel: Froben, 1549), 906; [pseudo-] Galen, *Introductio, seu Medicus*, in his *Opera . . . omnia*, ed. Conrad Gessner, 4 vols. (Lyon: Jean Frellon, 1550), 1:170.

22. Caelius Aurelianus, *De acutis morbis/De diuturnis morbis* (Lyon: Guillaume Rouille, 1567), 493. Caelius Aurelianus in fact emphasized that this disease of women, like the corresponding disease of men, was wholly nonorganic: "a passionibus corporis aliena, sed potius corruptae mentis vitia"; see p. 492.

23. The only conceivable textual justification for this move is a single clause in Caelius Aurelianus, *De diuturnis morbis*, 493: "Nam sicut foeminae Tribades

appellatae quod utranque Venerem exerceant, mulieribus magis quam viris fes-
tinant, et *easdem invidentia pene virili sectantur*" (my emphasis). It is barely
possible that Daléchamps confused the Latin *pene* and *paene*, both spelled *pene*
in standard sixteenth-century orthography; thus he may have misread this
clause as "they chase after them [with] jealousy [and] a masculine penis" rather
than "they chase after them with almost masculine jealousy."

24. Jean Liébault, *Trois libres appartenant aux infirmitez et maladies des femmes*
(Paris: Jacques du Puys, 1582), 509–11. Liébault further muddied the waters by
confusing the clitoris with uterine prolapse.

25. Charles Estienne, *La dissection des parties du corps* humain (Paris: Simon de
Colines, 1546), 312. On these illustrations and on the vexed publishing history
of Estienne's work, see C. E. Kellett, "Perino del Vaga et les illustrations pour
l'anatomie d'Estienne," *Aesculape* 37 (1955): 74–89; and Robert Herrlinger,
"Carolus Stephanus and Stephanus Riverius (1530–1545)," *Clio medica* 2
(1967): 275–87. Estienne described the instruments lying on the ground at the
front of the image as those "desquelz lon a de coustume user tant a l'apertion
de la dicte matrice, qu'au sonder et iniection que se peut faire en icelle";
Estienne, *Dissection*, 312.

26. Gabriele Falloppia, *Observationes anatomicae*, 2 vols. (Venice, 1561; reprint
Modena: S.T.E.M. Mucchi, 1964), 1: fol. 193r–v.

27. Realdo Colombo, *De re anatomica libri XV* (Venice: Niccolò Bevilacqua, 1559),
243.

28. Andreas Vesalius, *Observationum anatomicarum Gabrielis Fallopii examen*
(Venice: Francesco de' Franceschi da Siena, 1564), 143.

29. Falloppia, *Observationes*, 1: fol. 193r; see Laqueur, "Amor Veneris," 103–5.

30. Constantino Varolio, *Anatomicae, sive de resolutione corporis humani libri IIII*
(Frankfurt: Johann Wechel and Peter Rischer, 1591), 99.

31. Cf. Laqueur, "Amor Veneris," esp. 112, 119. Insofar as there was a shift between
Renaissance and modern ways of thinking about sexual differentiation, I argue
that this in fact began much earlier than the eighteenth century; one can find
strong statements of dimorphism as early as the later sixteenth century, especially in the works of Aristotelians such as Varolio and Riolan and mostly in the
context of debates of the possibility of sex transformation and of the existence
of so-called perfect hermaphrodites, fertile in both sexes. There is some evidence that the attention given to the clitoris in fact acted to promote this shift;
see, e.g., Riolan, *Discours*, esp. 67–68, 102–3.

32. Paré, *Responce*, 232.

33. Paré's discussions of the clitoris are complicated and puzzling: he described it
clearly, with appropriate references to Falloppia and Colombo, in the earlier
version of his treatise on anatomy that appeared in the editions of his *Oeuvres*
published in 1573, 1575, and 1579, although he dismissed it there as "very
obscure." In the fourth edition of the *Oeuvres* (1585), however, he dropped
these lines from the work, replacing them by the passage concerning the

enlarged labia of the female diviners of Fez that had been excised in the meantime from his treatise *Des monstres*; see 26–27.

34. André Du Laurens, *Historia anatomica humani corporis et singularum eius partium multis controversiis et observationibus novis illustrata* (Paris: Marc Orry, 1600), 356.

35. Séverin Pineau, *De integritate et corruptionis virginum notis*, in his *Opusculum physiologum [sic] et anatomicum* (Paris: Etienne Prevosteau, 1597), 62–63.

36. Jean Riolan [the Younger], *Anthropographia*, in his *Opera anatomica*, 6th ed. (Paris: Gaspard Meturas, 1650), 188.

37. We have discussed this case at length, together with other contemporary ones, in Lorraine Daston and Katharine Park, "Hermaphrodites in Renaissance France"; see also Patricia Parker, "Gender Ideology, Gender Change: The Case of Marie Germain," *Critical Inquiry* 19 (1994): 336–64. Stephen Greenblatt's analysis of this case is based on Laqueur's hypothesized "one-sex body"; see Greenblatt, "Fiction and Friction," in his *Shakespearean Negotiations: The Circulation of Social Energy in Renaissance England* (Berkeley: University of California Press, 1988), 66–93.

38. Riolan, *Discours*, 38–42.

39. For a detailed survey of ancient and medieval ideas on this topic, see Joan Cadden, *The Meanings of Sex Difference in the Middle Ages: Medicine, Science, and Culture* (Cambridge: Cambridge University Press, 1993); these issues are also discussed in Lorraine Daston and Katharine Park, "The Hermaphrodite and the Orders of Nature: Sexual Ambiguity in Early Modern France," *GLQ* 1 (1994): 419–38.

40. The core texts in this tradition were the Hippocratic works *De spermate* and *De natura pueri*, and two treatises *De spermate* attributed to Galen, one authentic and one pseudonymous. See in general Cadden, *Meanings*, 12–21, 30–37, together with the literature cited there.

41. Jacques Duval, *Traité des hermaphrodits, parties génitales, accouchemens des femmes, etc.* (Rouen, 1612; reprint, Paris: Isidore Lisieux, 1880), 297–98.

42. Aristotle, *The Generation of Animals*, trans. Arthur Platt, in *The Works of Aristotle*, ed. J. A. Smith and W. D. Ross, vol. 5 (Oxford: Clarendon Press, 1949), 772b13–29.

43. Aristotle, *The Generation of Animals*, 766b3–7.

44. Foucault, *Herculine Barbin*, vii–ix.

45. Aristotle, *Generation of Animals*, 772b30. On the complexities of medieval writing on this matter, see Cadden, *Meanings*, 198–202.

46. Riolan, *Discours*, 67–68; cf. Aristotle, *Generation of Animals*, 726a29–730b31. In his theories of sex difference, Riolan echoed the opinions of the Bolognese anatomist Constantino Varolio, who was also strongly influenced by Aristotle; see Varolio, *Anatomicae*, 88–101.

47. Riolan, *Discours*, 72.

48. Duval, *Traité*, 9.

49. There has been no comprehensive work on the meanings and uses of sixteenth-
    and seventeenth-century Hippocratism, but see, for example, Iain M. Lonie,
    "The 'Paris Hippocratics': Teaching and Research in Paris in the Second Half of
    the Sixteenth Century," in *The Medical Renaissance of the Sixteenth Century*, ed.
    Andrew Wear, R. K. French, and I. M. Lonie (Cambridge: Cambridge Univer-
    sity Press, 1985), 156–74. On the impact of Hippocratism on contemporary
    theories of generation, see Ian Maclean, *The Renaissance Notion of Woman: A
    Study in the Fortunes of Scholasticism and Medical Science in European
    Intellectual Life* (Cambridge: Cambridge University Press, 1980), chap. 3.

50. Jacques Duval, *Responce au discours fait par le sieur Riolan docteur en médecine
    et professeur en chirurgie et pharmacie à Paris, contre l'histoire de l'hermaphrodit
    de Rouen* (Rouen: Julian Courant, n.d.), 29.

51. Duval, *Responce*, 26.

52. Duval, *Traité*, 384.

53. Duval, *Traité*, 8.

54. Duval, *Traité*, 322, 342; Riolan, *Discours*, 102–3.

55. In Italy, Spain, and France, there is evidence that doctors were acting as private
    and public consultants in these matters from at least the early fourteenth cen-
    tury; see, for example, Michael R. McVaugh, *Medicine Before the Plague:
    Practitioners and Their Patients in the Crown of Aragon, 1285–1345* (Cambridge:
    Cambridge University Press, 1993), 206.

56. Guy de Chauliac, *La grande chirurgie de Guy de Chauliac . . . composée l'an 1363*,
    ed. E. Nicause (Paris: F. Alcan, 1890), 547; Albucasis, *Chirurgia*, in Pietro da
    l'Argellata, *Chirurgia Argelate cum Albucasis* (Venice: Giunta, 1520), fol. 141v;
    Avicenna, *Liber canonis*, fol. 356r.

57. Colombo, *De re anatomica*, 268–69.

58. Duval, *Traité*, 331–32.

59. See, e.g., Julia Epstein, "Either/Or-Neither/Both: Sexual Ambiguity and the
    Ideology of Gender," *Genders* 7 (1990): 102–3, esp.

60. Duval, *Traité*, 323–24.

61. Riolan, *Anthropographia*, 195.

62. David Teasley, "The Charge of Sodomy as a Political Weapon in Early Modern
    France: The Case of Henry III in Catholic League Polemic, 1585–1589,"
    Maryland Historian 18 (1987): 17–30; J.H.M. Salmon, "French Satire in the
    Late Sixteenth Century," *Sixteenth-Century Journal* 5, no. 3 (1975): 64–65.

63. Pierre de l'Estoile, *Mémoires-Journaux*, ed. P. Brunet, 10 vols. (Paris: Librairie
    de Bibliophiles, 1875), 2:113, 114.

64. [Thomas Artus], *Description de l'isle des hermaphrodits nouvellement découverte*
    (Paris: n.p., 1605); see Donald Stone, "The Sexual Outlaw in France, 1605,"
    Journal of the History of Sexuality 2 (1992): 597–608.

65. Agrippa d'Aubigné, *Les tragiques*, ed. A. Garnier and J. Plattard, 4 vols. (Paris: E. Droz, 1932), 2:46.

66. Teasley, "Charge of Sodomy," 18; cf. Bray, *Homosexuality*, 23–32.

67. Ian Maclean, *Woman Triumphant: Feminism in French Literature, 1610–1652* (Oxford: Clarendon Press, 1977), 58. On the perceived parallelisms between gender roles in the political and domestic order in early modern France, see in general Natalie Zemon Davis, "Women on Top," in her *Society and Culture in Early Modern France* (Stanford: Stanford University Press, 1975); Sarah Hanley, "Engendering the State: Family Formation and State Building in Early Modern France," *French Historical Studies* 16 (1989): 4–27; and Constance Jordan, "The Household and the State: Transformations in the Representation of an Analogy from Aristotle to James I," *Modern Languange Quarterly* 54 (1993): 307–26.

68. Lilian Faderman, *Surpassing the Love of Men: Romantic Friendship and Love between Women from the Renaissance to the Present* (New York: Morrow, 1981), 23–27.

69. Louis Crompton, "The Myth of Lesbian Impunity: Capital Laws from 1270–1591," *Journal of Homosexuality* 6, nos. 1–2 (1980–1981): 17–19. Bonnet points out that in none of the few French cases brought to court does the death penalty seem to have been applied, casting doubt on the narratives of both Estienne and Montaigne included by Crompton and mentioned below; see Bonnet, *Choix*, 55. Note that none of these statements apply to England in the late sixteenth and early seventeenth centuries, where legal definitions of sodomy excluded women: Bray, *Homosexuality*, 17.

70. Henri Estienne, *Apologie pour Hérodote*, ed. P. Ristelhuber, 2 vols. (Paris: Isidore Lisieux, 1879), 1:178.

71. Michel de Montaigne, *Journal de voyage en Italie*, in his *Oeuvres complètes*, ed. Robert Barral and Pierre Michel (Paris: Editions du Seuil, 1967), 456.

72. Pierre de Bourdeille Brantôme, *Des dames galantes*, in his *Oeuvres complètes*, 11 vols. (Paris: Jules Renouard, 1876), 10:202–3.

73. Brantôme, *Dames*, 269–70. In the same passage, Brantôme also cited medical testimony that women could produce this condition artificially by pulling and touching their own or each other's genitals.

74. Duval, *Traité*, 68.

75. Brantôme, *Dames galantes*, 10:24 .

76. Duval, *Traité*, 68.

77. Brantôme, *Dames galantes*, 10:195.

78. Riolan, *Anthropographia*, 195.

79. Laqueur, "Amor Veneris," 113.

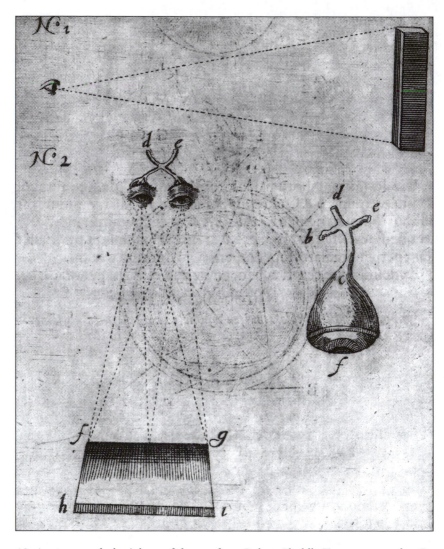

10. Anatomy and physiology of the eye from Robert Fludd's *Tractatus secundus, De natvrae simia seu Technica macrocosmi historia* (London, 1624).

10

Taming the Basilisk

S ERGEI L OBANOV - R OSTOVSKY

In his *Anatomica Methodus* (1535), the Spanish anatomist Andres de Laguna interrupts his dissection of the tissues of the eye to describe his initial discovery of its power:

> I shall not pass over in silence something that happened to me when I was a small boy. Since I did not have enough money for my childish games and had no source from which I could obtain it I followed my father who was visiting the bedside of a nobleman ill with fever and climbed up with him to the patient's bedroom. The light there was sufficiently bright but it seemed quite dark to me since I had just come in from a brighter place. After I had rested for a while I saw by chance a purse half lying upon the sick man's bed, and because I judged, plausibly enough, that the eyes of the sick man and of those around him were dimmed as mine were (falsely, however, since they had been longer in the room and had accustomed their sight to the shadows), I came up closer and began to handle the purse. But he to whom it belonged (for illness had not deprived him of speech) said: "What are you doing with my purse? Isn't it enough that the druggists have left it thin without you to empty it completely into your hands?" I blushed and was struck dumb, and began to philosophize very energetically about light and shadows.[1]

De Laguna offers this narrative to his reader as an example of the effects of strong light on vision, but his denial of an impulse to concealment ("I shall not pass over in silence") calls attention to its status as a confession. Caught in the act, de Laguna finds himself an object lesson in the duplicity of the eye: he becomes at once a philosopher of ocular proofs and the object of a shaming gaze. The incident reveals less about the eye's response to faint light than it does about its ideological power. De Laguna contemplates the old man with the anatomist's objectifying gaze. By returning the gaze, the old man destroys the boy's status as perceiving subject ("I blushed and was struck dumb"), reducing him to an object of scrutiny. De Laguna assumes that his eye's perception reflects an objective reality, "that the eyes of the sick man and of those around him were dimmed as mine were." His error exposes the eye's complexity, its status as both perceiving subject and object of study. At the same time, the boy's misperception reveals his own eye as flawed, and, more importantly, as flesh. The eye becomes not a window for the soul but a frail organ, a proper object of anatomy. De Laguna deflects the power of the old man's shaming gaze by reconstituting this perception as knowledge, beginning "to philosophize very energetically about light and shadows." The gesture allows him to deny the truth his text seems to contemplate; the eye's reduction to flesh compels him to remake its power as knowledge, affirming his status as a perceiving subject.

Narrated in an anatomical text, this anecdote reflects the ideological subtext of the period's discourses about the eye. De Laguna's dissection of the eye's seven "tunics," its crystalline and vitreous humors, has its origins in his childhood speculations on light and shadow:

> You may learn from this example how useful and necessary is philosophy, the mother of all things, not only to physicians but to thieves and murderers. For I would not have been caught so shamefully in the act if I had known then as I know now the causes of things.[2]

The study of ocular anatomy, in which the eye is dissected under the anatomist's gaze, reveals itself in de Laguna's analogy as an effort to restore a subjectivity threatened by the eye's power to objectify, to impose shame. De Laguna's study of "the causes of things" affirms the power of *his* eye to know its own nature: he sees, rather than being seen, reduces the eye that shamed him to an object of his own inquisitive gaze.

What de Laguna's text offers us, then, is a *fantasy* of the eye's power. Like the fabulous basilisk of classical bestiaries—a serpent that killed, according to Pliny, both by seeing and by *being* seen[3]—the probing, anatomical eye is a metaphor that destroys itself. In an irony of Renaissance natural philosophy, the power attributed to the basilisk's eye proved fatal not to men but to the basilisk itself: its lethal gaze could not survive the test of the period's empiricism, since, as Albertus Magnus wondered, how could the basilisk be *known* if it could not be *seen*?[4] If to know, in the Renaissance, is to see, then to see the basilisk—or, for the period's anatomists, the eye itself—is an act that destroys the eye's claim to power.

I invoke this analogy of basilisk and anatomized eye to suggest the duplicity of the eye's status in both the period's anatomical and literary texts. Recent theorizations of the gaze have suggested that the eye's claim to power is compensatory, an attempt to deflect an objectifying gaze by affirming the eye's status as viewing subject.[5] In similar terms, the period's medical and literary texts affirm the eye's sovereignty by reenacting—as if compulsively—a narrative of an eye under siege. Such metaphors, I will argue, become a device by which to reconstruct a privileged male subjectivity threatened by anatomy's reduction of the eye to flesh. In the Petrarchan conceit of the eroticized eye, the visible world is embodied as an aggressive beauty, a female eye that does not *see* but solicits the male gaze. The woman's gaze threatens to objectify the male lover, only to retreat before the power of his desire. Like the eye probing its own nature in the anatomy theater, this gesture of taming the female gaze averts the threat of a passive, effeminized eye, subject to the world it views. As metaphor, the eye reclaims the sovereignty lost to the anatomist's objectifying gaze. It *becomes* the gaze, affirming its power by effacing its own status as flesh.

During the sixteenth century, the practice of ocular anatomy made the eye visible to itself, intensifying the traditional conflict between the eye's material nature and its status as metaphor:

> An eye therefore is a member, round, whole, and hard, as the ball of a foote, or as the scowred new bason full of cleare water, set in the well of the head to minister light to the whole body, by the influence of the visible spirits, sent from the fantasticall cell by a sinew that is called *Nervus opticus*, with the helpe of a greater light ministered from without.[6]

In Philip Barrough's anatomy, the eye is at once flesh and idea, a "fantasticall cell" whose complex nature allows for such disparate images as "the ball of a foote" and a "scowred bason full of cleare water." It "ministers" external light to the body, hinting at the eye's traditional role as a privileged servant of the soul. The metaphor affirms the eye's distinct status, mediating between world and spirit, flesh and soul. The eye, in these terms, is more subject than object, more perceiving consciousness than obedient flesh. In a gesture common to the period's anatomical texts, Barrough notes the eye's inability to gaze upon itself:

> But the eye which is wont with curious inspection to pry into all other things, and to find out the nature and order of them, hath bin unable to unfoldl his owne wonderfull constitution, and hath bene alway blind in judging of it selfe, and in foreseeing the discommodities which attend upon it, or in curing them, when they have layed hold of it.[7]

As anatomists, both Barrough and de Laguna aspire to make the eye visible for study, yet they share an impulse to conceal its materiality in metaphors that deflect attention to the eye's power rather than its status as flesh, the optic rather than the optic nerve. Anatomized, the eye vanishes beneath the knife, rendering up its physiology only as evidence of its essential non-materiality. It remains an image of the soul, ruling over the visible world by the power of its gaze.

In effect, the eye emerges from the period's dissections not as flesh but as a Platonic idea, an image of itself projected upon the cave's wall. The metaphor is implicit in the classical origin of optics: Plato's theory of vision conceived of the eye as projecting an inner fire, which coalesced with day-light to extend from the eye to the object of vision.[8] In Galen's refinement of the Platonic model, the eye emits a "visual pneuma" that transforms the air into an optical instrument, illuminating the object of vision with the eye's sensory power, much as the sun transforms air into a medium of light.[9]

In Galenic theory, the eye is both sovereign and implicitly *male:* it engenders the visible world by its projection of spiritual substance, the "pneuma" that flows out through the hollow optic nerve, exciting the surrounding air and translating it into a receptive body made "sympathetic . . . with the change effected by the outflow of the pneuma into it."[10] In Plato's *Theaetetus,* the eye's emission of visual fire is explicitly an engendering of forms:

> [A]s soon . . . as an eye and something else whose structure is adjusted to the eye come within range and give birth to the whiteness together with its cognate perception . . . then it is that, as the vision from the eyes and the whiteness from the thing that joins in giving birth to the colour pass in the space between, the eye becomes filled with vision and now sees, and becomes not vision, but a seeing eye; while the other parent of the colour is saturated with whiteness and becomes, on its side, not whiteness, but a white thing.[11]

In the act of vision, the eye emits an essence that "gives birth to" the forms of the world; when the process ends, the eye is restored to itself ("and becomes not vision, but a seeing eye"), while the object of its gaze is endowed with its own essential nature ("while the other parent . . . is saturated with whiteness and becomes . . . not whiteness, but a white thing"). The eye imposes form on the visible world, much as the male endows the flesh with spiritual form in classical theories of the act of sexual generation:

> [T]he female always provides the material, the male that which fashions it, for this is the power we say they each possess, and this is what it is for them to be male and female. . . . While the body is from the female, it is the soul that is from the male.[12]

The eye conceives the visible world upon itself, disseminating forms by its projection of visual pneuma.

The rival theory of vision in the early history of European optics, based on Aristotle's rejection of the emanation of spiritual fire, envisions the eye as a vulnerable orifice, a passive receiver of light:

> In general it is unreasonable to suppose that seeing occurs by something issuing from the eye; that the ray of vision reaches as far as the stars, or goes to a certain point and there coalesces with the object, as some think. It would be better to suppose that coalescence occurs in the very heart of the eye.[13]

In Aristotle's terms, the eye becomes a matrix, in which light implants its substance. Where Plato's eye emits fire, Aristotle's is composed of water, which assumes the form of the object that stimulates it to vision.[14] Aristotle's eye is a womb of light, conceiving the world within itself in passive acceptance of its forms.

This gendering of the eye frames the debate over ocular anatomy—and shapes the imagery of the eye's power that flourished in metaphors of erotic desire—as late as the seventeenth century.[15] While the practice of ocular anatomy offered increasing evidence for an Aristotelian view of the eye as a passive receptor during the period, the stubborn persistence of the Platonic theory of an active, penetrating eye suggests its ideological power. Indeed, as the eye surrendered its secrets to the anatomist's knife, what replaced the emission of Platonic "fire" as a cultural model of the masculine eye's power was ideology in its purest form: the gaze.

The Renaissance practice of anatomy may be defined as a process of transforming flesh into knowledge:

> In medicine, anatomization takes place so that, in lieu of a formerly complete "body", a new "body" of knowledge and understanding can be created. As the physical body is fragmented, so the body of understanding is held to be shaped and formed.[16]

Yet, as de Laguna's meditation on the powers of the eye suggests, what is created by this process of dissecting the body is *not* knowledge but a gaze that affirms the anatomist's subjectivity. Anatomy solicits the gaze, constitutes it as a form of language—Foucault's "speaking eye," which seeks to transform the clinician's observations of the material body into signs.[17] In its multiple meanings, anatomy suggests at once the process, subject, and product of dissection: the act of probing the flesh, the corpse itself, and the body of learning that may be derived. It is the anatomist's gaze that mediates between the corpse and its reconstitution as language. In effect, the gaze is anatomy's most important product, a catalyst that reduces flesh to empirical truth:

> [T]he clinician's gaze becomes the functional equivalent of fire in chemical combustion; it is through it that the essential purity of phenomena can emerge: it is the separating agent of truths.... The clinical gaze is a gaze that burns things to their furthest truth.[18]

In Foucault's analogy, the clinician's gaze reveals itself as a form of Plato's "inner fire," searing its perceptions into the anatomized body.

Yet, the anatomical gaze is, paradoxically, less an act of seeing than a *refusal* to see the self mirrored in the dissected corpse. Anatomy's role as the foundation of medical education derives from its role as both a source of concrete knowledge and a method for conditioning the mind to "necessary Inhumanity," the objectivity that allows a surgeon to cut into flesh with clinical detachment.[19] As it opens the flesh to the probing mind, the anatomical gaze asserts a difference between the materiality of the dissected body and the eye that transforms that flesh into knowledge. The anatomist's gaze lays claim to the status of pure empiricism, even as it derives from an aversive gesture, a looking away. It is from this gesture that the eye's ideological power derives. In its capacity to gaze into the dissected body, the eye makes the anatomist—at once—both less human and *more*: the objectivity implied by this gaze (a "necessary Inhumanity") affirms the anatomist's subjectivity, makes him a perceiving mind, not objectified flesh.[20]

The empirical gaze—the eye as pure ideology—reduces the world to a series of objects on which it inscribes meaning; by the mediation of the eye, the self views itself as both distinct from these objects of view and sovereign over them. In the illustration that dominates the title page of Helkiah Crooke's 1655 *Microcosmographia*—to cite but one example of a common trope in the period—the eye transcends the anatomized body to become an image of the sovereign gaze; both anatomists and corpses look out at the reader, as if to affirm a common subjectivity—based on anatomical knowledge—by the power of this shared gaze. As the reader's eye moves up the page, it finds its own likeness inscribed there as an image of God. The illustration imagines the eye not as flesh but as divine similitude, distinguished from the anatomized bodies below by the power of its gaze. Throughout the Renaissance, the eye assists—and implicitly *embodies*—the soul in its vigilant rule over both body and world.[21] The eye serves, in the period's metaphors of the body politic, as both watchman and judge.[22] In Leonardo's close examination of ocular function, the eye becomes "the universal judge," from whose gaze nothing is excluded.[23] In the House of Alma, Spenser expands this idea of the eye's vigilance to include the projection of effective rule: the eyes are "goodly beacons, set in watches stead" (bk. 2, canto, 9, st. 46), suggesting both illumination and judicious surveillance of the body's domain.[24] The eyes project light, as well as consume it, affirming the soul's governance over both the body and the world that lies beyond its walls. In his *Discourse of the Preservation of the Sight*, André Du Laurens assigns heroic status to the christalline humor of the eye as it engages with both the outward and inward light, world and soul:

> This is that icelike humour, which is the principall instrument of the sight, the soule of the eye, the inward spectacle: this is that humour which alone is altered by colours, & receiueth whatsoeuer formes of the things that are to be seene. This is that christalline humour, which in more hardie wise then *Hercules*, dares to encounter two at once, namely, the outward and the inward light. This is that only christalline humour, which all the other parts of the eye acknowledge their soueraigne, and themselues the vassals thereof: for the hornie tunicle doth the office of a glasse vnto it: the apple, the office of a window: the grapelike coate is as a fayre flowring garden, to cheare and reoiyce the same after wearisome labour: the cobweblike coate serueth as lead to retaine such formes as are offered: the waterish humour as a warlike foreward, to intercept and breake off the first charge of the objects thereof, assaying all vpon the sudden, and with headlong violence to make breach and entrance: the vitreous humor is his cooke, dressing and setting forth in most fit sort his daily repast: the nerve opticke, one of his ordinary messengers, carrying from the braine thereto, commandement and power to see, and conueying backe againe with all speede whatsoeuer hath been seene.[25]

In Du Laurens's metaphor, the "christalline humor" reigns as the eye's warrior king, "the soule of the eye," whose power derives from its defense against the "headlong violence" by which the world tries to make "breach and entrance" into the brain. Yet, the eye's role in the metaphor is not simply defensive; in his elaborate metaphor, the eye is itself a world, which reflects the images it captures from the realm of the visible. What the brain sees, Du Laurens implies, is not the world itself but a devil in crystal; the eye offers, in his pun, an "inward spectacle," a mimetic reenactment of the world, which the brain accepts as a true image of the world. Given the brain's "commandement and power to see," the eye deflects the world's attack but retains its forms; what it returns to the brain is an image of itself. If the eye engages in Herculean "encounters" with the objects of the visible world, it does the same with the "inward light" of the soul. The eye becomes, in effect, a third realm, distinct from both world and soul, a realm much like London's liberties, which originated as a defensive barrier but became a site of spectacle and temptation.

What such metaphors produce within the culture is a potent metonymy: the eye stands in for the mind in the perceiving consciousness, then supplants it, as the act of perception comes to define the self to itself. Consciousness, manifested as an act of self-conception—*idea* (from *idein*, "to see")—begins in the act of visual perception.[26] Eye becomes "I," the self perched at the edge of the body. If these metaphors reflect a need to *limit* the eye's power, it is because the analogy exposes the self to the many threats implicit in the eye's engagement with the world, its vulnerability to disease, deception, and the objectifying power of another's gaze.

Such an anxiety dominates the era's erotic poetry. In part, the urge to tame the female gaze common to Petrarchan love imagery derives from the convention that the male lover's eye is a vulnerable orifice, wounded by beauty:

> [T]he eyes are the harbingers of love and the first step of love is sight, ...
> they as two sluices let in the influence of that divine, powerful, soul-
> ravishing and captivating beauty, which, as one saith, "is sharper than
> any dart or needle, wounds deeper into the heart and opens a gap through
> our eyes to that lovely wound which pierceth the soul itself."[27]

Beauty is a weapon that solicits the eye, then strikes through it to pierce the soul. In Philip Sidney's *Astrophil and Stella*, the eye is a traitor, whose weakness allows the violent conquest of the lover's heart:[28]

> *Stella*, whence doth this new assault arise,
> A conquerd, yelden, ransackt heart to winne?

Whereto long since, through my long battered eyes,
Whole armies of thy beauties entred in.

(Sonnet 36)

While Astrophil acknowledges in Sonnet 5 that "eyes are formed to serve / The inward light," his own eyes quickly submit to Stella's beauty. In Sonnet 16, her beauty is a poison that enters through the eye; in Sonnet 7, Astrophil reasons that Nature made Stella's eyes black "To honor all their deaths, who for her bleed." The initial effect of his submission to Stella's beauty is the loss of his status as a privileged male subject. In Sonnet 53, the eye's weakness emasculates, as Stella's beauty, which had inspired his successful guidance of horse, hand, and lance in Sonnet 41, now subverts his hand's rule:

I look'd, and *Stella* spide,
Who hard by made a window send forth light.
My heart then quak'd, then dazled were mine eyes,
One hand forgott to rule, th'other to fight.
Nor trumpets' sound I heard, nor friendly cries;
My Foe came on, and beat the aire for me,
Till that her blush taught me my shame to see.

The eye, dazzled by Stella's beauty, becomes more than a source of shame; its vulnerability subverts the will, reducing both the inspired horsemanship of Sonnet 41 and the dazed immobility of Sonnet 53 to effects of Stella's gaze. Astrophil surrenders his subjectivity, becomes not himself but an image meant to seduce her own eye to tears: "I am not I; pity the tale of me" (Sonnet 45).

Yet his surrender to her eye's power is not passive, as it initially seems. As Burton notes, the eye's role in love is not simply to be the object of love's darts; it seeks out love, exchanges wounds with the object of its gaze: "[T]he Eye betrays the soul and is both Active and Passive in this business; it wounds and is wounded, is an especial cause and instrument, both in the subject and in the object."[29] The lovers' gaze becomes a combat; as the eye suffers wounds, it also strikes. In Petrarchan tradition, these roles are strictly gendered, but not as one might expect: the male lover's eye is a passive victim, wounded by the beloved's gaze:[30]

His mother dear, Cupid offended late
Because that Mars, grown slacker in her love,
With pricking shot he did not th'roughly move
To keep the pace of their first loving state.

> The boy refus'd, for fear of Mars's hate
> Who threatened stripes if he his wrath did prove;
> But she, in chafe, him from her lap did shove,
> Brake bow, brake shafts, while Cupid weeping sate;
> Till that his grandam Nature, pitying it,
> Of Stella's brows made him two better bows,
> And in her eyes of arrows infinite.
> O how for joy he leaps! O how he crows!
> And straight therewith, like wags new got to play,
> Falls to shrewd turns! And I was in his way.
>
> (Sidney, Sonnet 17)

The poem attributes no desire to Stella's wounding gaze; her beauty is Nature's cruel gift to mischievous Cupid. Nevertheless, the source of her eye's violence is female desire: Venus, frustrated by Mars's failure of passion, breaks her son's bow, forcing him to use Stella's eyes for his weapon. The conceit imagines maleness as militant disinterest; the slackening of Mars's desire (and, we must assume, his flesh) becomes—paradoxically—an image of his *power*, as he frightens Cupid into a promise of immunity from love's arrows. By contrast, the poem figures Astrophil's desire as a wound. The metaphor reverses the structure of male desire, making Astrophil the victim of an aggressive—and effeminizing—female gaze.[31]

Yet the apparent weakness of the lover's eye reveals itself as a snare. The power of Stella's eye gives way in Sonnet 66 to a male gaze that claims the power to impose contingency:

> *Stella's* eyes sent to me the beames of blisse,
> Looking on me, while I lookt the other way;
> But when mine eyes backe to their heav'n did move,
> They fled with blush, which guiltie seem'd of love.

The woman's eye, which was capable of engraving Astrophil's soul with its "blacke beames" as late as Sonnet 44, is here figured as in retreat from the male gaze. By the last sonnets of the sequence, it is Astrophil's eye that is "famished" (Sonnet 106) by Stella's absence, reducing Stella's beauty to the "nectar" (Sonnet 105) that it feeds upon. The lover's eye has evolved from wound to gaping mouth, which consumes her beauty. But an even more empowered—and consuming—gaze makes its appearance in Sonnet 81, where Astrophil coerces kisses from Stella by threatening to expose her desire "to all men's eyes." The threat reflects the poet's strategy: in his praise of the woman's beauty, his eye becomes her subject, but only as a means to entrap the woman's desire, reproducing it as poetry for consumption by an audience of male readers. The poet's "speaking eye" masters the female gaze, affirming the power of the masculine eye to disseminate the woman's form in verse. The woman's "aggressive eye" becomes a figure for the poet's gaze; his eye is revealed not as a wound but as a weapon. The Petrarchan conceit of the eye as wound gives way to a projective, masculine gaze—the eye as phallus.[32]

At one level, as Nancy Vickers has shown, the violence implicit in the Petrarchan poet's gaze represents a reaction to the objectifying power of the beloved's beauty.[33] Yet, this metaphor demands closer examination as a response to the materialization of the eye in the period's medical discourses. By locating the beloved's power to objectify in an aggressive female eye, the Petrarchan poet reenacts de Laguna's entrapment by the gaze, and so becomes subject to the same duplicity in the eye's status; even as he tames the female gaze, the lover concedes the eye's double role as gazing subject and objectified flesh. To unravel the implications of this gesture, we must return for a moment to the basilisk.

The crucial element in this impulse to tame the female gaze is the objectifying power of desire. The poet imagines the woman's eye as a basilisk, fatal in its power to penetrate the male lover's body and poison his soul:[34]

> Fair cruell, why are ye so fierce and cruell?
> Is it because your eyes have powre to kill?
> Then know, that mercy is the mighties jewell,
> And greater glory thinke to save, then spill.
> But if it be your pleasure and proud will,
> To shew the powre of your imperious eyes:
> Then not on him that never thought you ill,
> But bend your force against your enemyes.
> Let them feele th'utmost of your crueltyes,
> And kill with looks, as Cockatrices doo.
>
> (*Amoretti* 49)[35]

Like the Platonic eye, the basilisk fell victim during this period to the empirical gaze. The last "documented appearance" of a basilisk was recorded in Warsaw in 1587, and within a few decades, Sir Thomas Browne had confidently assigned it to the realm of the fabulous: "Nor is this Cockatrice onlly unlike the Basilisk, but of no real shape in Nature; and rather an Hieroglyphical fansie."[36] Yet, if the basilisk disappeared from the period's natural philosophy, it survived in the period's poetry as an image for the eye's projection of desire. Crucially, it is not female desire that the image of the basilisk invokes but a male fear of the woman's gaze, which threatens to solicit or destroy male desire.[37] "Cockatrice" was Elizabethan slang for a prostitute. While the analogy may originate in an aggressive eye that solicits male desire, the prostitute's trade is based upon her status as not one who looks but one who is looked at: prostitution, by its Latin etymology, means to set or place (*statuere*) in public (*pro*), available to all eyes.[38]

In part, this association of the basilisk's gaze with a threatening female desire may derive from a common myth of its origin: Lucan notes that the basilisk was born from Medusa's blood, inheriting her power to turn men to stone.[39] In these terms, the basilisk's lineage invokes the connection between an excess of male desire (Medusa's rape by Poseidon, the stiffening of male flesh) and the fear of an objectifying female gaze. The metaphor, like Perseus's shield, protects the power of the male eye by displacing it onto the woman. When Lady Anne wishes for the basilisk's venom during the seduction scene in *Richard III*, she provides the defining metaphor for Richard's desire:

> Anne: Out of my sight! Thou dost infect mine eyes.
> Richard: Thine eyes, sweet lady, have infected mine.
> Anne: Would they were basilisks to strike thee dead!
> Richard: I would they were, that I might die at once;
>   For now they kill me with a living death.
>   Those eyes of thine from mine have drawn salt tears,
>   Shamed their aspects with store of childish drops
>
>   (1.2.148-154)[40]

Like Sidney's Sonnet 17, Richard's seduction opposes the integrity of the warrior's eye with her beauty's power to penetrate, poison and blind his eye with tears. Yet, the power that he assigns to her eyes simply reflects the power he *claims* in *Henry VI, Part 3* ("I'll slay more gazers than the basilisk" [3.2.187]). In *The Changeling*, Beatrice-Joanna's hatred for De Flores is an explicitly visual antipathy: "Such to mine eyes is that same fellow there, / The same that report speaks of the basilisk" (1.1.110-111).[41] De Flores, with his "foul chops," is a sight that threatens to poison her eye. While she assigns the fatal gaze to De Flores, her accusation reflects her own eye's desire: "I know she had / Rather see me dead than living, and yet / She knows no cause for't but a peevish will" (101-3). De Flores attributes an active malevolence to Beatrice-Joanna's gaze; she would *see* him dead, making her eyes the source of the basilisk's poison, not its victim. Yet, even here, the image retains its Petrarchan resonance. Within her antipathy, we find the imagery of desire. He is her "infirmity," the equivalent of the roses, oil, and wine that Alsemero cites to support his observation that "There's scarce a thing but is both lov'd and loath'd" (121). The play implicates Beatrice-Joanna in the Petrarchan structure of desire: De Flores's desire is met with cruelty, and both are figured as poison that enters through the eye. In these terms, it is Beatrice-Joanna who plays the basilisk's part, De Flores who tames her gaze through the following acts by shaping her hatred into an image of his desire. As a metaphor for desire, the basilisk is an equivocal figure: it poisons, as Pliny notes, both by the power of its gaze and by attracting the gaze of its victim. The duplicity of this figure calls into question the terms on which the period's poetry genders the gaze. It suspends the lover's eye between subject and object, active and passive, male and female. For example, the Neoplatonic conceit of the lovers' gaze in Donne's "The Ecstasy" begins in an image of the eye as a medium of ungendered sexual exchange:

> Our eye-beams twisted, and did thread
>   Our eyes, upon one double string;
> So to' intergraft our hands, as yet
>   Was all our means to make us one,
> And pictures in our eyes to get
>   Was all our propagation.[42]

Donne's metaphor makes the sexual nature of the gaze explicit, as the lovers "get" their own images in each other's eyes. The image constructs the eye as both male and female at once: it projects each lover's image into the other's eye and serves as the womb that may be impregnated with the beloved's image. In one sense, this imagery of the eye as doubly sexed simply reflects the poem's Neoplatonic conceit of the union of souls into a single "abler soul" that comprehends both their natures:

> This ecstasy doth unperplex
>   (We said) and tell us what we love,
> We see by this, it was not sex,
>   We see, we saw not what did move:
> But as all several souls contain
>   Mixture of things, they know not what,
> Love, these mixed souls doth mix again,
>   And makes both one, each this and that.
>
>   (29–36)

In these terms, the lovers' gaze is unsexed, Platonic, the poem's initial figure for a union of souls. Yet, what results from this union is not an unsexed soul, but a sovereign *maleness*—the "great prince" whose freedom may only be won, the poet insists, by sexual union:

> So must pure lovers' souls descend
>   T' affections, and to faculties,
> Which sense may reach and apprehend,
>   Else a great prince in prison lies.
> (65–68)

The sexual imperative that concludes the poem ("to our bodies turn we then"), while argued as the means by which souls may achieve union, serves instead to affirm the speaker's maleness. Their blood labors to create not souls but "spirits, as like souls as it can" (62); semen replaces the ideal of an unsexed soul in the poet's substitution of bodily for spiritual forms.[43] The power to "get" forms in the male eye that the initial stanzas grant the woman's gaze vanishes as the poet sexualizes their union. The poem effaces the female gaze, returning the eye to an image of male subjectivity:

> To our bodies turn we then, that so
>   Weak men on love revealed may look;
> Love's mysteries in souls do grow,
>   But yet the body is his book.
>
> And if some lover, such as we,
>   Have heard this dialogue of one,
> Let him still mark us, he shall see
>   Small change, when we'are to bodies gone.
>
> (69–76)

The implied voyeurism of the final stanzas marks the eye's transformation from its complex, doubly-sexed status in the initial stanzas to its traditional role as the vehicle for an analytical male gaze. The poem evokes the image of the eye as womb only to exclude it, replacing it with an image of male subjectivity, an eye that scrutinizes the female body for meaning. Yet, in the process the probing male eye begins to look remarkably like the image it seeks to efface: the eye as wound, as womb, the site where the masculine subject is conceived.

What this ambiguity reveals is an impulse to restore the eye's threatened power by dematerializing it, moving it—like the basilisk—from the realm of flesh to status of pure idea. As metaphor, the eye retains its power to affirm the male subject, not so much by projecting its gaze upon the visual world as by imposing its *form* on the gaze that it solicits. It is this gesture that Phoebe reveals in her critique of her lover's Petrachan tropes in *As You Like It:*

> Thou tell'st me there is murder in mine eye:
> 'Tis pretty, sure, and very probable,
> That eyes, that are the frail'st and softest things,
> Who shut their coward gates on atomies,
> Should be called tyrants, butchers, murtherers!
> Now I do frown on thee with all my heart,
> And if mine eyes can wound, now let them kill thee.
> Now counterfeit to swound; why, now fall down,
> Or if thou canst not, O, for shame, for shame,
> Lie not, to say mine eyes are murtherers!
> Now show the wound mine eye hath made in thee,
> Scratch thee but with a pin, and there remains
> Some scar of it; lean upon a rush,
> The cicatrice and capable impressure
> Thy palm some moment keeps; but now mine eyes,
> Which I have darted at thee, hurt thee not,
> Nor I am sure there is no force in eyes
> That can do hurt.
> (3.4.10–27)

In response to Silvius's metaphors, Phoebe insists on the eye's material reality, its frailty. Like the patient in de Laguna's anecdote, she catches him in the act, imposes shame by making his deception visible to the eye. Silvius's crime is an accusation that objectifies by empowering, attempts to impose his own eye's aggressive desire on her gaze. Significantly, she reinscribes the eye in terms that suggest frailty, even femininity, discarding the masculine forms ("tyrants, butchers, murtherers") of Silvius's accusation. The eye she imagines is the one that emerges in the period's anatomies, not subject but frail object. Her own eye will prove itself easily deceived, but she has tamed the basilisk concealed within Silvius's metaphor by making it *visible*. The power of such metaphors, like the eye's itself, is self-consuming. What Phoebe's demystification of the eye reveals is the same paradox that confronts the period's anatomists: that the eye's only power—and it is tenuous, at that—is to conceal its nature from its own probing gaze.

Notes

1. Andres de Laguna, *Anatomica Methodus, seu de Sectione Humani Corporis Contemplatio* (Paris, 1535), fol. 57, trans. L. R. Lind, in Lind, *Studies in Pre-Vesalian Anatomy: Biography, Translations, Documents* (Philadelphia: American Philosophical Society, 1975), 291.

2. Laguna, *Anatomica Methodus*.

3. Pliny notes that "the basilisk serpent also has the same power [whoever sees its eyes dies at once].... [It] is said to be fatal to a man if it only looks at him." *Natural History*, trans. H. Rackam et al., 10 vols. (Cambridge: Harvard University Press, 1938–1962), 8:33, 29:19. A twelfth-century Latin manuscript describes the basilisk's power in similar terms: "Even if it looks at a man, it destroys him. At the mere sight of a Basilisk, any bird which is flying past cannot get across unhurt." *The Beastiary: A Book of Beasts, Being a Translation from A Latin Bestiary of the Twelfth Century*, trans. T. H. White (New York: Capricorn Books, 1954), 168.

4. Albertus Magnus, *De animalibus*, in *Opera Omnia*, vol. 6, lib. 25 (Lyons, 1651).

5. See, for example, Jacques Lacan, "The Split between the Eye and the Gaze," in *The Four Fundamental Concepts of Psycho-Analysis*, ed. Jacques-Alain Miller, trans. Alan Sheridan (New York: Norton, 1981), 73–74; Laura Mulvey, "Visual Pleasure and Narrative Cinema," *Screen* 16 (1975): 6–18; and Barbara Freedman, *Staging the Gaze: Post-Modernism, Psychoanalysis, and Shakespearean Comedy* (Ithaca: Cornell University Press, 1991).

6. Philip Barrough, *The Method of Physicke, containing causes, signes and cures of inward diseases in mans body, from the head to the foote* (London: 1590), 49.

7. Barrough, *The Method of Physicke*. De Laguna's anatomy renders the eye strangely invisible, displaying most clearly what cannot be seen:

> Thus the eyes (to return to my discussion) like the keenest watchman of the soul have been allotted the highest position. They do not see themselves, although they are quite bright and shining and seem to sparkle, but the soul sees through them as if through windows.

See Lind, *Studies in Pre-Vesalian Anatomy*, 257. Dissecting the tissues of the eye, de Laguna peers through it to the soul. The eye has no presence in itself but acts as a servant ("like the keenest watchman of the soul") or medium for the sovereign soul ("but the soul sees through them as if through windows"). This limitation on the eye's power is repeated throughout the period's discourses on vision. It seems a curious convention in texts devoted to ocular anatomy that allow the eye to penetrate its own nature, removing this final barrier from its gaze. The repetition of this claim in so many texts during the period suggests a discomfort with the eye's power, an impulse to restore its status as a tributary power to the soul.

8. De Laguna adopts a Platonic theory of vision, in which vision derives from the union of "the forms of things to be seen, an inner fire, and an external light or glow, as with a rare felicity and beyond controversy the most worthy Plato seems to indicate in the *Timaeus*." See Lind, *Studies in Pre-Vesalian Anatomy*, 291. De Laguna's attempt to conform his knowledge of ocular physiology with his readings of classical texts is a common gesture during the period. Chalcidius's translation of the first half of Plato's *Timaeus* in the early fourth century, with a commentary that appended an anatomical description of the optic nerves and membranes of the eyes, offered the "evidence" of the anatomist's probing eye in support of the text's claim of a penetrating gaze. Similarly, the practice of anatomy in medical education prior to the sixteenth century had traditionally served as a means of affirming the authority of Galen's theories. Yet, this assumption of the text's veracity had come under increasing stress as evidence of disagreement between text and body mounted. The evidence of the eye threatened to supplant the Galenic text as the primary means of ascertaining truth in the anatomy theater. See K. B. Roberts and J. D. W. Tomlinson, *The Fabric of the Body: European Traditions of Anatomical Illustration* (Oxford: Clarendon Press, 1992), 6–7. By 1535, Laguna's explicit defense of the Platonic theory of vision had become a rarity in anatomical texts. While Plato's conception of the eye's emission of "inner fire" in the *Timaeus* had a profound influence on Galen, and thus on medieval medical theory, the Aristotelian tradition, which conceived of vision as the influx of light into the eye, had become the dominant ocular theory after the thirteenth century. Despite efforts by such medieval scholars as Robert Grosseteste, Roger Bacon, and John Pecham to synthesize the conflicting positions into a single optical theory, the textual tradition inherited by sixteenth-century anatomists had become primarily Aristotelian. With the publication of Felix Platter's *De corporis humani structura et usa . . . libri III* (1583), the modern conception of ocular structure, which located the power of vision in the retina and ocular nerve, began to take shape. It was this new understanding of the eye's anatomy that provided the foundation for Kepler's theory of the retinal image in the *Ad Vitellionem paralipomena* (1604). For a brief history of the development of optical theory, see David C. Lindberg, *Theories of Vision from Al-Kindi to Kepler* (Chicago: University of Chicago Press, 1976). For an account of early modern responses to the eye's power, see Martin Jay, *Downcast Eyes: The Denigration of Vision in Twentieth-Century French Thought* (Berkeley: University of California Press, 1993), 21–82.

9. *De placitis Hippocratis et Platonis* 7.5, trans. Philip De Lacy, in Lindberg, *Theories of Vision*, 10.

10. *De placitis*, 7.7.

11. Plato, *Theaetetus* 156d–e, in *Plato's Theory of Knowledge: The Theaetetus and the Sophist of Plato*, trans. Francis M. Cornford (London: Routledge & Kegan Paul, 1935), 47.

12. Aristotle, *Generation of Animals* (Cambridge: Harvard University Press, 1958), 2.4.738b20–23, quoted in Thomas Laqueur, *Making Sex: Body and Gender from the Greeks to Freud* (Cambridge: Harvard University Press, 1990), 30.

13. Aristotle, *De sensu* 2.438ᵃ26–438ᵇ2, trans. W. S. Hett (London: Loeb Classical Library, 1957), 225; cited in Lindberg, *Theories of Vision*, 8.

14. Aristotle, *De sensu*, 2.438ᵇ19–24, trans. J. I. Beare, in *Works* (Chicago: University of Chicago Press, 1952), 1:675.

15. For a summary of the classical roots of this "aggressive eye" topos, see Lance K. Donaldson-Evans, *Love's Fatal Glance: A Study of Eye Imagery in the Poets of the Ecole Lyonnaise* (University, Mississippi: Romance Monographs, 1980), 9–49. Leone Ebreo, in his *Dialoghi d'Amore*, sought to give a theoretical foundation to the erotic metaphor of the aggressive eye by reconciling the Platonic theory of vision with its Aristotelian rival:

> I hold that both the transmission of rays from the eye to apprehend and illumine the object and the representation of the form of the object in the pupil are necessary to sight; and further, these two contrary are not sufficient without a third and final notion, namely that the eye directs its rays for a second time on to the object to make the form (impressed on the pupil) tally in every respect with the external object. And in this third action consists the true essence of vision . . . and my purpose is to prove . . . that the eye not only sees but first illumines what it sees.

See Leone Ebreo, *The Philosophy of Love*, trans. F. Friedeberg-Seeley and Jean H. Barnes (London: Soncino Press, 1937), 215.

16. Jonathan Sawday, *The Body Emblazoned: Dissection and the Human Body in Renaissance Culture* (London: Routledge, 1995), 2.

17. Michel Foucault, *The Birth of the Clinic: An Archaeology of Medical Perception*, trans. A. M. Sheridan Smith (New York: Pantheon Books), 114.

18. Foucault, *The Birth of the Clinic*, 120.

19. William Hunter, introductory lecture to students, c. 1780, St. Thomas's Hospital Manuscript 55, 182 verso, quoted in Ruth Richardson, *Death, Dissection and the Destitute* (London: Routledge, 1987), 30–31: "Anatomy . . . informs the Head, guides the hand, and familiarizes the heart to a kind of necessary Inhumanity."

20. The mannerism of Valverde's "self-demonstrating" figures in the *Historia de la composicion del cuerpo humano* (1556) offers an obvious exception to this claim. As his figures hold the flesh open to the eye or contemplate their own internal organs, they reflect the viewer's gaze, refuting the fiction of an objectifying gaze. In one figure, the anatomist stands above the corpse, hands opening the chest cavity to display the internal organs, his own chest open for our

inspection. Yet, both corpse and anatomist look away, not consuming the image of the dissected body but displaying it. See Roberts and Tomlinson, *The Fabric of the Body*, 214; and Jonathan Sawday, "The Fate of Marsyas: Dissecting the Renaissance Body," in *Renaissance Bodies: The Human Figure in English Culture, c. 1540–1660*, ed. Lucy Gent and Nigel Llewellyn (London: Reaktion Books, 1990), 124–26.

21. In Sir John Davies' "Nosce Teipsum," the eye serves as an image of the mind, as it projects its gaze—like Plato's "inner fire"—into the visible world:

> Is it because the mind is like the eye,
> Through which it gathers knowledge by degrees,
> Whose rays reflect not, but spread outwardly,
> Not seeing itself when other things it sees?

Davies, "Nosce Teipsum," in *Silver Poets of the Sixteenth Century*, ed. Gerald Bullett (London: J. M. Dent & Sons, 1947), 348. The image defines the mind's consciousness by the eye's perception. The mind's "power to know all things" is contingent upon—and thus, limited by—this analogy to the eye, which can see all of creation but is unable to see itself.

22. Leonard Barkan credits John of Salisbury with the first sustained anatomy of the political body, in *Policraticus*, where the eye serves as part of a triumvirate of official power: "the duties of eyes, ears, and tongue are claimed by the judges and the governors of provinces." See *The Statesman's Book of John of Salisbury*, trans. J. Dickinson (New York: Knopf, 1927), 5.2, 65; quoted in Barkan, *Nature's Work of Art: The Human Body As Image of the World* (New Haven: Yale University Press, 1975), 72. In *Coriolanus*, Menenius assigns the eye a central role within the governing consciousness of the state in his association of surveillance and rule: "the kingly crowned head, the vigilant eye" (1.1.118).

23. Leonardo da Vinci, *Literary Works*, trans. Jean Paul Richter (London, 1939; reprint, New York: Phaidon, 1970), 1:131.

24. Edmund Spenser, *The Faerie Queene*, ed. Thomas P. Roche, Jr. (New Haven: Yale University Press, 1978), 323.

25. André Du Laurens, *A Discourse of the Preservation of the Sight: of Melancholike Diseases; of Rheumes, and of Old Age*, trans. Richard Surphlet (London, 1599; reprint, London: Shakespeare Association Facsimiles, 1938), 32.

26. Joel Fineman, *Shakespeare's Perjured Eye: The Invention of Poetic Subjectivity in the Sonnets* (Berkeley: University of California Press, 1986), 12.

27. Robert Burton, *The Anatomy of Melancholy*, ed. Holbrook Jackson (New York: Vintage Books, 1977), pt. 3, sec. 2, Mem. 2, Sub. 2, p. 65. See also Castiglione's observation that beauty "draweth unto it mens eyes with pleasure, and pearcing

through them, imprinteth himself in the soule." *The Book of the Courtier*, trans. Sir Thomas Hoby (London: J. M. Dent & Sons, 1974), 304.

28. *Sir Philip Sidney: Selected Prose and Poetry*, ed. Robert Kimbrough (Madison: University of Wisconsin Press, 1983), 182–83.

29. Burton, *The Anatomy of Melancholy*, 76.

30. Donaldson-Evans, *Love's Fatal Glance*, 48. See also Petrarch's Sonnet 87, where the shot passes from the beloved's eyes into the lover's heart, which causes the wound to flow with tears:

> similemente il colpo de' vostr'occhi,
> Donna, sentiste a le mie parti interne
> dritto passare, onde conven ch' eterne
> lagrime per la piaga il cor trabocchi.

Petrarch's Lyric Poems, ed. and trans. Robert M. Durling (Cambridge: Harvard University Press, 1976), 321. In Sonnet VI, Ariosto uses the same image of the eyebrow as a bow and the lady's glance an arrow that wounds the lover:

> La rete fu di queste fila d'oro,
> In che il mio pensier vago intricò l'ale
> E queste ciglia l'arco, e 'l guardo strale
> E 'l feritor questi begli occhi foro.

See Ariosto, *Opere*, ed. A. Racheli (Trieste, 1857), Sonnet VI; quoted in Donaldson-Evans, *Love's Fatal Glance*, 42.

31. Linda Woodbridge's recent discussion of this trope notes the gender reversal, relating it to the tradition of the evil eye, in which images of the eye—or poetic descriptions of its power—were required as defenses against its effeminizing power. See *The Scythe of Saturn: Shakespeare and Magical Thinking* (Urbana: University of Illinois Press, 1994), 219–21.

32. As Joel Fineman notes, the Petrarchan poet's praise for the beloved's beauty reflects an act of self-conception. See *Shakespeare's Perjured Eye*, 12–15. In Fineman's terms, the eye's *idea* is an engendering of forms: as Thomas Laqueur has suggested, the theory of sexual conception that the Renaissance inherited from classical texts is of "the male having an idea in the woman's body." The eye, in these terms, becomes an explicitly sexual organ, the source of the male idea that becomes the "efficient cause" required in conception. See *Making Sex*, 59.

33. Nancy Vickers's influential discussion of the Petrarchan trope of Actaeon's gaze, which fragments the beloved's body in his "scattered rhymes" to deflect the threat of dismemberment implied in his visual pleasure, informs my reading of

these compensatory objectifications by a vulnerable male eye. See "Diana Described: Scattered Woman and Scattered Rhyme," *Critical Inquiry* 8 (1981): 265–79.

34. Stafano Protonotaro da Messina makes the analogy explicit:

> Poi che m'appe ligato,
> co li occhi sorrise,
> si ch'a morte mi mise
> como lo badalisco.

See *Poeti del Duecento*, ed. G. Contini (Milano, no date), 2:138; quoted in Donaldson-Evans, *Love's Fatal Glance*, 35.

35. See *English Sixteenth-Century Verse: An Anthology*, ed. Richard S. Sylvester (New York: Norton, 1984), 368–69.

36. Peter Lum, *Fabulous Beasts* (New York: Pantheon, 1951), 42–43; *The Works of Sir Thomas Browne*, ed. Geoffrey Keynes (Chicago: University of Chicago Press, 1964), 175. While the cockatrice (a chimerical monster, related to the crocodile) and the basilisk were distinct animals in classical bestiaries, English usage tended to conflate the two, using the term "cockatrice" to describe a winged basilisk, born of a cock's egg. See Laurence A. Breiner, "The Basilisk" in *Mythical Beasts and Fabulous Creatures: A Source Book and Research Guide*, ed. Malcolm South (New York: Greenwood Press, 1987), 115.

37. See Woodbridge, *The Scythe of Saturn*, 220–25, who also notes that "the phallus was often represented on amulets against the evil eye" (218), along with phallic gestures (*fica*) and the sixteenth-century wedding ritual of urinating through the wedding ring as a protection against both the evil eye and impotence (226). Such attributions of power to the female gaze are common in the period's source texts: Gaius Julius Solinus claims that Scythian women "have two pupils in each eye and kill people by sight if they happen to look at them when angry." See *Collectanea rerum memorabilium*, ed. Theodore Mommsen (Berlin, 1895), 26. Pliny makes the same claim in his *Natural History* 7.2.16–18. Both are quoted by Roger Bacon in *Opus maius*, pt. 5.2, dist. 1, chap. 3, ed. John Henry Bridges (Oxford: Clarendon Press, 1897), 2:91; see Lind, *Studies in Pre-Vesalian Anatomy*, 88, 246 n.12. Joannes Versoris offers support for a theory of projective vision by comparing a menstruating woman looking in a mirror to a basilisk gazing at a man, as both mirror and man are harmed. See *Questiones super parva naturalia cum textu Aristotelis* (Cologne, 1493), qu. 4, fols. 3v–4r,; quoted in Lind, *Studies in Pre-Vesalian Anatomy*, 138.

On the Jacobean stage, the basilisk frequently embodies the power of female desire as reflected in male jealousy. In *The Winter's Tale*, Camillo describes Leontes's jealousy to Polixenes as a "disease and it is caught of you, that yet are well":

> Polixenes: How caught of me?
> Make me not sighted like the basilisk.
> I have looked on thousands, who have sped the better
> By my regard, but killed none so.

(1.2.387–90)

Leontes' jealousy, which originates in his perception of the warmth of Hermione's courtesies, becomes a metaphoric poison caught from Polixenes' eye. While Leontes *is* infected through the eye, watching the exchange of courtesies, his jealousy conceives desire where none exists; by denying the role of basilisk, Polixenes denies the desire attributed to him. In Leontes' case, his jealous gaze reveals him as the play's true Basilisk, with the power to turn Hermione to stone.

38. Charles Bernheimer, *Figures of Ill Repute: Representing Prostitution in Nineteenth-Century France* (Cambridge: Harvard University Press, 1989), 1.

39. Lucan, *The Civil War*, trans. J. D. Duff (Cambridge: Harvard University Press, 1928), 9.696ff. Petrarch, Sonnet 197, compares Laura's glance to Medusa's:

> L'aura celeste che 'n quel verde lauro ...
> po quello in me che nel gran vecchio mauro
> Medusa quando in selce transformollo ...
> L'ombra sua sola fa 'l mio cor un ghiaccio
> et di bianca paura il viso tinge,
> ma gli occhi ànno vertù di farne un marmo.

Pietro Bembo makes same comparison:

> Medusa s'egli è ver, che tu di noi
> Facevi pietra, assai fosti men dura
> Di tal, che m'arde, strugge, agghiaccia, e' ndura.

Opere, vol 2. *Rime* (Venezia, 1729), Sonnet 72, quoted in Donaldson-Evans, *Love's Fatal Glance*, 43.

40. All quotations are from *The Riverside Shakespeare*, ed. G. Blakemore Evans (Boston: Houghton Mifflin, 1974): hereafter cited in text.

41. Thomas Middleton and William Rowley, *The Changeling*, ed. George Walton Williams (Lincoln: University of Nebraska Press, 1966), 8.

42. John Donne, *The Complete English Poems*, ed. A. J. Smith (Middlesex: Penguin Books), 53.

43. In Galenic theory, semen was the product of both male and female blood, refined by the excess heat of intercourse. "Spirit" was a common term for male ejaculate during the period, as in Shakespeare's Sonnet 129 ("The expense of

spirit in a waste of shame / Is lust in action") or Bacon's comment that "much use of Venus doth dim the sight.... The cause of dimness of sight ... is the expense of spirits"; see *Sylva Sylvarum; Or A Natural History In Ten Centuries*, Century VII, 693, in *The Works of Francis Bacon*, ed. James Spedding, Robert Leslie Ellis, and Douglas Denon Heath (Cambridge: Riverside Press, 1863), 4:468. Semen, then, was a "spirit" produced by the blood's labor, that could, in Thomas Laqueur's terms, "impart movement to matter"—a vital force, like the soul. See Laqueur, *Making Sex,* 40–46. Bacon's remark is interesting in our context because it suggests that the transition to sexual union in Donne's poem diminishes the eye's power to conceive, taming the gaze.

Part III

❖

Divining the Part

11. Frontispiece to John Bulwer's *Anthropometamorphosis* (London, 1653).

11

Mutilation and Meaning

❖

S T E P H E N   G R E E N B L A T T

I want to begin by recalling a conversation I had some years ago at a dinner party in honor of a celebrated anthropologist. We were talking about grandparents, and I asked the anthropologist whether he had been much influenced by his grandfather, a distinguished rabbi. Not at all, he replied; he was the spiritual heir to Chateaubriand, the nineteenth-century auto-biographer and author of *The Genius of Christianity*, and not to Moses Mendelssohn, the advocate of Jewish emancipation and enlightened reform. Since we had earlier been speaking about ritual scarification and since the anthropologist had done some of his most brilliant work on tattooing, I ventured to ask him if his own sons had been circumcised, in accordance with Jewish law. Yes, he replied, but quite by accident. By accident? In the case of his younger son, the circumcision had been performed routinely and, as far as the anthropologist could remember, without parental consent, in a New York hospital just after the Second World War. As for his older son, the circumstances were less routine. German troops had occupied Paris, and the anthropologist and his wife had fled to his rabbinical grand-father's house in the south of France. It was there that his child was born and, in compliance with the religious sensibilities of the grandparents, had been circumcised.

The term "accident" seems rather strange as a description of either of these cases.[1] But the anthropologist's odd characterization of the deliberate mutilation of his children as an accident serves to point us to the peculiar way in which marks on the body, like marks on paper, may be distinguished from the particular explanations, justifications, and chains of historical causality that led them to be made.[2] The local accounts—hygiene, aesthetics, family feeling, tribal custom, institutional procedure, fantasies of propitiation or fertility—are crucially important, but the mark or mutilation is detachable from these accounts, in the way that an image is detachable from even the most scrupulous and circumstantial textual interpretation of the image. In the case of male circumcision, which appears to have been a widespread practice throughout the ancient Middle East, Judaism provided a myth of origin that is in effect the expression of this detachability. Without narrative rationalization or doctrinal justification, God simply commands it of Abraham and his descendants: "This is my covenant, which ye shall keep, between me and you and thy seed after thee; Every man child among you shall be circumcised. And ye shall circumcise the flesh of your foreskin; and it shall be a token of the covenant betwixt me and you" (Genesis 17:10–11).

An awareness that the practice extends beyond the boundaries of a single tribe, however, complicates even this absolute and absolutist command, if only by exciting the desire to grasp the underlying logic, the secret code, registered in the bodily mark. For the Hebrew prophets and for the author or authors of Deuteronomy, that code seems to have been moral: circumcision serves as a metaphor of cleansing or repentance. "Circumcise therefore the foreskin of your heart," says Deuteronomy, "and be no more stiff-necked" (10:16).[3] The similar Pauline moralization of circumcision—"For he is not a Jew, which is one outwardly; neither is that circumcision, which is outward in the flesh: But he is a Jew, which is one inwardly; and circumcision is that of the heart, in the spirit, and not in the letter; whose praise is not of men, but of God" (Romans 2:28–29)[4]—is a gesture toward this logic, and it has the advantage, from the male infant's point of view inestimable, of obviating the cut itself.

But, though its Hellenistic allegorization of circumcision enabled it to abandon circumcision as an actual practice, Christianity did not thereby abjure the language of wounds. On the contrary, for Saint Paul it is in the body, in the visible sign, that meaning must continue to reside if it is to cross the boundaries of radically distinct cultures. Circumcision ceases to be the sign of the exclusive, tribal covenant with God—"For in Jesus Christ neither circumcision availeth any thing, nor uncircumcision; but faith which worketh by love" (Galatians 5:6)—but the savior invoked here is an incarnate God, a God made flesh. And that flesh was repeatedly, spectacularly, and, as it were, crucially wounded. The root perception, and it is one that Christians embraced far more than Jews, is that there is a link between mutilation, as a universal emblem of corporeal vulnerability and abjection, and holiness. Pauline Christianity saw the physical marks on Jesus' body, from his circumcision to his scourging, piercing, and crucifixion, as the signs of an exalted sanctity, the salvific manifestations of a divine love that willingly embraces mortal vulnerability. What looks at first like a move away from the ritual shedding of blood—the metaphorization of circumcision—is intertwined in fact with a more radical, literalizing insistence on the meaningfulness of sacrificial wounds.

For Jews, God manifested himself principally in a text, the Torah, but for Christians God's flesh was itself a text written upon with universal characters, inscribed with a language that all men could understand since it was a language in and of the body itself, independent of any particular forms of speech. An early-sixteenth-century sermon by John Fisher, bishop of Rochester, eloquently rehearses this widespread medieval way of understanding Christ's wounds. For Fisher, Saint Francis's stigmata vividly demonstrate that the saint has been reading that most sacred of books, the crucified body of Christ: the "two boards of this booke is the two partes of the crosse, for when the booke is opened & spread ... the leaves of this booke be the armes, the handes, legges, and feete...." This is, to be sure, an unusual book, not so much because it is flesh but because it has no blank spaces: "[T]here was no margent lefte in all thys booke, there was no voyd place, but every where it was eyther drawne with lynes, or els wrytten with letters, for these scourges fylled not onely his most precyous bodie with lynes drawne everie where, but also left many small Letters, some blacke, some blewe, some reade.... And for bycause no parte of thys booke shoulde bee unwritten, hys head also was pearsed with sharpe thornes."[5] The text thus written in the flesh, Fisher makes clear, is for everyone to read with ecstatic pleasure: who "may not be ravished to hope and confidence" at the sight of "all his bodie stretched, forcesing him selfe to give it wholly unto us."

Pious men and women in the Middle Ages were not content only to read the sacred book of Christ's wounded body; they longed for Christ to inscribe his truth on their own bodies and in particular on their hearts. According to the *Golden Legend*, the name of Christ was found written in golden letters on the heart of the martyred Ignatius of Antioch, and the nuns who cut open the body of Clare of Montefalco in 1308 found precisely figured in her massively enlarged heart not only the cross but also the scourge, the pillar, the crown of thorns, the three nails, the spear and the pole with the sponge.[6] The intensity of the longing expressed in these stories is conveyed by the action of the Dominican monk Heinrich Seuse (c. 1295–1366):

> He pushed back his scapular, bared his bosom, took a sharp stylus, and called on God to help him saying: "Almighty God, give me strength this day to carry out my desire, for thou must be chiseled into the core of my heart." Then stabbing the stylus backwards and forwards, in and out of the flesh, he engraved the name of Jesus (IHS) over his heart. Blood gushed out of the jagged wounds and saturated his clothing. The bliss he experienced in having a visible pledge of *oneness* with his truelove made the very pain seem like a sweet delight.[7]

The self-inscription had its desired effect: "When the wounds that he had made were healed, the sacred name still remained above his heart in letters the width of a cornstalk and the length of the joint of his little finger." But, as a modern scholar wryly remarks, Seuse risked discovering for himself the truth of the warning that the letter kills.[8]

Such a belief in the universal grammar of sacred wounds had a powerful effect on Christian attempts to understand other cultures and their ritual practices. Thus, for example, Odoric of Pordenone, like Marco Polo before him, mentions that the body of Saint Thomas, the apostle whose doubt drove him to put his hand into Christ's wound, is buried in the province of Maabar or Mobar in India. The Christians of Mobar, Odoric reports, are Nestorians, "that is to say Christians, but vile and pestilent heretics," and their churches are full of idols.[9] He then turns to the description of one such idol, a gold and jewel-encrusted figure "as big as St. Christopher is commonly represented by the painters" (142), to whom Indians go on pilgrimage, "just as Christian folk go far on pilgrimage to St. Peter's" (143). Some of these pilgrims arrive, he reports, "with a halter round their necks, and some with their hands upon a board, which is tied to their necks; others with a knife stuck in the arm, which they never remove until they arrive before the idol" (143).

What is happening in effect is that Indian religious practice, or rather a fantastic vision of such practice, is being processed as at once a continuation and a reversal of Christian observance. The temples are churches, the priests bear some relation to Christianity, and the images resemble familiar saints, but where Christian worshipers go to seek health, the Indian pilgrims welcome disease. Indeed some of these pilgrims go further in their single-minded pursuit of holiness:

One will come saying: "I desire to sacrifice myself for my God!" And then his friends and kinsfolk, and all the players of the country, assemble together to make a feast for him who is determined to die for his God. And they hang round his neck five sharp knives, and lead him thus to the presence of the idol with loud songs. Then he takes one of those sharp knives and calls out with a loud voice: "Thus I cut my flesh for my God"; and cutting a piece of flesh wherever he may choose, he casteth it in the face of the idol; and saying again: "I devote myself to die for my God," he endeth by slaying himself there. And straightway they take his body and burn it, for they look on him as a saint, having thus slain himself for his idol. (145)

Such a ceremony is, Odoric makes clear, "detestable"—a perverse and damnable worship in the service of a false god—and yet its sacrificial character echoes and evidently derives from the worship of a god who sacrificed himself for mankind.[10] So too is there a resemblance between the annual procession of religious images with which Odoric must have been familiar in Italy and the monstrous procession he describes in the same Indian city:

[T]he king and queen and all the pilgrims, and the whole body of the people, join together and draw it forth from the church with loud singing of songs and all kinds of music; and many maidens go before it two by two chaunting in a mavellous manner. And many pilgrims who have come to this feast cast themselves under the chariot, so that its wheels may go over them, saying that they desire to die for their God. And the car passes over them, and crushes and cuts them in sunder, and so they perish on the spot. And after this fashion they drag the idol to a certain customary place, and then they drag him back to where he was formerly, with singing and playing as before. And thus not a year passes but there perish more than five hundred men in this manner; and their bodies they burn, declaring that they are holy, having thus devoted themselves to death for their God.

This passage may be the earliest European description of the procession that came to be known as the Juggernaut, the emblem of all that was strangest, most incomprehensible, and horrible in the religion of the East, the sign of a fundamental lack of respect for life, a crushing (here literal) of the individual, a fanatically misguided devotion of art, wealth, and existence itself to the service of a false god who delights in mutilations.[11]

Whether or not this is an even remotely accurate representation of the Juggernaut procession in the period, what is important for our purposes is that Odoric's report (or invention) is an account of worship that is built out of the language of holy wounds.[12] It is this origin that enables the most influential travel book of the Middle Ages, *Mandeville's Travels*, to rehearse

Odoric's vision of a horrendous perversion of Christian devotion as an indictment of the weakness of Christian devotion. Mandeville characteristically elaborates upon and exaggerates the gruesomeness of his source—for example, the pilgrims now slay their own children and sprinkle their blood upon the image; so great is the desire to die beneath the wheels of the chariot that "two or three hundred in a single day will kill themselves for love of that idol." He also characteristically intensifies its exoticism: the Juggernaut is the custom of those who live on the earth's margins in a bizarre world of deformity and inversion. But at the same time Mandeville intensifies the resemblances to Christian worship: people approach the idol with great devotion, "as frequently as Christian folk come to Saint James"; the devout "bring with them incense and other sweet-smelling things to cense that image, as here we do the Host"; "[a]nd just as among us a man would think it honorable if among his kindred a confessor or holy martyr was canonized, and his virtues and miracles written in books, even so it seems to them a great honour when any of their cousins or friends kill themselves for love of that idol."

The echoes of Christian belief are most striking in the speech that Mandeville says that his friends and kinsmen make when presenting the martyr's body to the god:

> Behold what thy loyal servant has done for thee! He has forsaken wife and children and all the riches and pleasures of this world, and his own life, for love of thee. He has made sacrifice unto thee of his own flesh and blood. Wherefore, we pray thee, set him beside thee among thy dear friends in the joy of Paradise, for he has well deserved it.[13]

In light of this devotional language, it is not surprising that Mandeville observes that "they suffer so much pain and mortification of their bodies for love of that idol that hardly would any Christian man suffer the half—nay, not a tenth—for the love of Our Lord Jesus Christ." As so often in *Mandeville's Travels*, what begins as a reassuring vision of the centrality, reasonableness, and truth of Christian belief threatens to become a humbling vision of the strangely moving piety of others.

The powerful, destabilizing account of holy self-mutilation begun by Odoric and expanded by Mandeville reaches its climax in *The Travels of Mendes Pinto*. The great Portuguese traveler provides the most extensive early description of the Juggernaut festival which he locates in the kingdom of Calaminhan (identified by modern scholars as the Laotian territory of Luang Prabang) in a pagoda called Tinagogo, "god of a thousand gods." It is not at all clear that Mendes Pinto actually saw anything resembling what he describes—the location, the recycling of Odoric and Mandeville, and other improbable details should provoke skepticism—but he characteristically gives what he claims to be an eyewitness account based on a twenty-eight-day stay in the company of an ambassador. Combining Odoric's horror and Mandeville's sly moralism, Mendes Pinto writes that he offers his account "in order to show the Christians—and I am including myself among them—who are as careless about their lives as I am, how little we do to save our souls, in comparison with all that these blind wretches do to lose theirs."[14] Mendes Pinto then is reflecting the moral vision of his medieval sources, but, as I hope to show, his version, in its elaborateness and wealth of phantasmagoric detail, marks the early stages of a new way of conceptualizing what I have called the universal language of wounds.

Mendes Pinto's understanding of the alien ritual is deeply shaped by the language and symbols of Christian belief. The idol is accompanied by priests in vestments, accompanied by people with censers and thuribles; those who pull the carts by the long silk-covered ropes are "granted plenary remission of their sins," and the faithful crowd forward in order to receive "absolution" and "indulgence"; the streets of the procession are adorned, as they would have been in Mendes Pinto's native country, with palm fronds, woven branches of myrtle, and silken flags and banners; people make offerings in the fulfillment of vows and purchase religious souvenirs "much the same way as among us it is the custom of the pilgrims returning from Santiago to bring back those trinkets of jet" (345). There are performances of religious interludes and a charitable distribution of food and clothing. As in a jubilee year (to which Mendes Pinto likens the event), feuds are reconciled and debts forgiven, "and many other pious deeds were performed, so much in keeping with Christian ethics that had they been done with faith and baptism in the name of Christ our Lord, without the intrusion of worldly matters, it seems to me that they would have been acceptable to him" (342).

But, of course, these pious deeds were not done with faith and baptism—"the best was wanting in them," he writes, "for their sins, and for ours"—and, with a horrifying clamor of music and shouts, the procession lurches toward an orgy of self-slaughter. Mendes Pinto further increases the grisly statistic already augmented by Mandeville—"well over six hundred" threw themselves under the chariot wheels, he reports—and he adds baroque details of ritualized self-mutilation. Those who cut off pieces of their own flesh shoot the pieces from bows toward heaven in honor of various of their kin; the frenzied crowd rushes forward to seize what they regard as holy relics, while in the meantime the "poor wretches would go staggering about, dripping with blood, without noses, or ears, or the semblance of men, until they finally fell to the ground dead" (343). Other penitents involve the bystanders in a different way: they threaten to kill themselves if they are not given alms, and if the alms are not produced quickly enough they slit their throats or disembowel themselves. Still others go about holding copper pots filled with a mixture of human urine and feces. "Quick, give me some alms," they say, "or I will eat the devil's food and spray you with it so that you will be as accursed as the devil himself." If the bystander does not immediately comply, the horrible penitents make good on their threat.

The mention of the devil here is not for Mendes Pinto an accident, since these and similar acts of grotesque penitence and piety are in his view the consequence of the lack in this part of the world of true belief. He recognizes that the people he is encountering in many cases have good judgment and wit, but their "blind spots and brutish customs ... are so far beyond all reason and human understanding," he writes, "that they serve as a great motive for us to offer thanks continually for the infinite mercy and goodness He has shown us, by giving us the light of true faith wherewith to save our souls" (343). Without this light, all of the observances Mendes Pinto describes seem to him either "humbug" or service to the devil. He ends his account with a further reflection on the lesson he wants his readers to draw: "So that all these people who practice these different forms of terribly harsh penitence become martyrs of the devil, who rewards them with everlasting hell, and it is indeed an extremely pitiful and painful thing to see how much these poor wretches do to lose their souls and how little most of us Christians do to save ours" (347).

The last remark, which closely resembles a similar observation that I have already quoted from *Mandeville's Travels*, could be taken as evidence to support Rebecca Catz's thesis that *The Travels of Mendes Pinto* is a satire. "How can the Portuguese, whom Pinto paints in the darkest colors," Catz writes, "hope to convert the Asians who live in accordance with God's laws and who are prepared to go to greater lengths, to make greater sacrifices— as in the case of the heathens of Calaminhan—than the greatest Catholic saint of his time, in an effort to apprehend the eternal?"[15] But, though there are unmistakable currents of Mandevillian irony in Mendes Pinto, his account of the Juggernaut hardly holds up the hideous self-mutilators of the Juggernaut ceremony as a model for Christians to follow.[16] On the contrary, they are, in his view, losing their souls, and their filthy, wounded, defiled bodies are in vivid contrast to the miracle of Saint Francis Xavier's incorruptible body with which Mendes Pinto brings his long peregrination to a close: "They found the body completely intact, with no sign of decomposition or defect of any kind, so much so, that not even the shroud and the cassock he wore were found to have any spots or blemishes, for both were as clean and white as if they had just been washed, with an extremely sweet smell about them" (498).

This contrast would seem to locate Mendes Pinto securely within the medieval conceptual framework that mapped cultural difference along the axis of the sacred and the demonic. But the problem is first that his graphic description of the demonic rites seems to leave very little space for the traditional Christian valorization of penitential wounds—that is, the perception of resemblance is continually undermined by the horror of the ceremonies described—and second that his imaginative investment in the Asian peoples and their customs seems to bespeak not piety alone (or even principally) but rather what medieval writers condemned as curiosity.[17] In short, Mendes Pinto is on a border between the medieval travelers' tales and something else. That something else, in my view, is not so much satire as what we might call, borrowing a term from Michel de Certeau, heterology.

Early modern heterology is constructed, I propose, out of what appear to be contradictory impulses, even obsessions: a fascination with particular, distinctive bodily customs and a fascination with the universal meanings that are disclosed in those same customs. The focus is principally (though not exclusively) on *bodily* customs for two reasons: first, the body in its malleability, its inability to remain fixed and unchanging, its equally intense beauty and grotesqueness, is the site of what we might call an intractable theoretical otherness, and second, the body of strangers, of all those peoples whom Europeans in the wake of 1492 encountered at the outermost edges of their known world, is the site of a recalcitrant practical otherness. Possessing for the most part little or no grasp of the language, the society, or the beliefs of those whose lands they invaded, Europeans focused their often formidably intense attention on scars, ornaments, skin color, hair, clothing and other expressive details of physical existence. Travelers like Thevét, Hariot, or Ralegh dwell obsessively on what Thevét calls the "singularities" of the peoples they have observed, and at the same time they repeatedly construct overarching theories that knit together what at first seem like intractable individual practices into the shared fabric of all humankind. These dual impulses—the drive to the irreducibly particular and the drive to the universal—are particularly marked in discourses of bodily mutilation, such as Mendes Pinto's description of the Juggernaut.

While in Mendes Pinto the contradictory forces are still largely contained within the overarching framework of somatic sacredness that governed the accounts of Odoric or Mandeville, in the late sixteenth and seventeenth centuries this framework begins to crumble. The forces at work in its gradual weakening or dissolution are many, but Protestantism, in its various strains, is clearly among the most important. Hence, for example, in 1532 Luther's great associate Philipp Melanchton, commenting on Romans 12:1—"present your bodies a living sacrifice, holy, and acceptable to God"—urges his readers to "think that we always stand bound and garlanded at the altar, reaching our necks out to enemies who strike us." But, Melanchton quickly adds, though Saint Paul commands us to be sacrifices for Christ's sake, "it is not because we injure or destroy ourselves but because others injure us." For the Reformer, Catholic self-mortification is one of a range of practices that are neither holy nor acceptable to God:

> For God does not approve of sacrifices like those of Manasseh, who killed his sons, or those of the gentiles: the sacrifice of Iphigenia and Polyxena and the suicidal vow of the Decii. The priests of Baal also mutilate their bodies, and I hear that Turkish priests still continue this practice. In the past, some monks killed themselves by fasting, self-flagellation, cold, and other vile practices. But it is clear enough in the gospel that all rites either against or without divine command are to be condemned. [18]

A footnote to the passage on the Turkish priests cites Luther's observation that the holy men among the Turks "show the reality of their patience in the various stigmata and wounds burned or cut into their bodies. For if one of them wished to prove [himself], he used fire or cut his flesh with a sword, all which he felt only as if you burned a stone or cut a piece of wood with a sword." A marginalium to this passage oddly echoes the accounts of the Juggernaut that we have been analyzing: "If strict observance, as they call it, makes one holy, these certainly of all men are the most saintly and saintlier than the Carthusians themselves."[19] But, of course, Luther does not regard strict observance, either among the Turks or the Christians, as a sign of holiness. The delicate balance of horror and admiration that extended from Odoric to Mendes Pinto has collapsed, and the example of the Turkish holy men is not meant to lead the reader to emulate the Carthusians but to understand that the Carthusians are no better than Turks.

For the Reformers, self-inflicted wounds and other signs of somatic holiness are deeply suspect, bespeaking fraud, credulity, vain superstition, and, worst of all, a fall into pagan or demonic worship. Such an account leaves the axis of sacred and demonic intact, though it moves what was formerly viewed as ambiguously sacred into the zone of the demonic. But the sixteenth and seventeenth centuries also saw the beginning of a gradual shift away from the axis of sacred and demonic and toward an axis of natural and unnatural. I want to sketch briefly the emergence of this new conceptualization of heterology by considering the work of a little-known English savant, John Bulwer. As we will see, Bulwer is fascinated by wounds, but this fascination arises in the context of a lifelong investigation not of the meaning of the tears and scars and violations of the body but rather of the meaning of the muscles. In 1649 Bulwer published in London a book called *Pathomyotomia, or A dissection of the significative muscles of the affections of the minde.*[20] The author was a physician, and the title might suggest a medical text, but Bulwer's "dissection" is figurative rather than literal. His concern is with somatic signification. How does the body naturally convey meanings? How are commands conveyed from the spirit to the muscles? How do "affections"—passions, ideas, responses, projects—pass from the silent and inaccessible inner reaches of the mind to the world? The obvious passageways, of course, are speech and writing, but central to Bulwer's inquiry is his conviction that speech and writing are only part of the signifying resources of human beings, and not the most reliable part at that, for language is notoriously slippery, deceptive, and unstable—notoriously, from the point of view of both theology and science.

The Hebrew Bible relates the fall of language in the wake of the attempt to build a tower that would reach to heaven. "The whole earth was of one language, and of one speech," the Bible says, when the tower was undertaken; its builders proposed to "make us a name, lest we be scattered abroad upon the face of the whole earth" (Genesis 11:1, 4). God's response is to shatter humankind and scatter the fragments across the face of the earth. The tower gets a name, but the name signifies the splits, gaps, opacities, and multiplicities in language and in human culture: "Therefore is the name of it called Babel; because the Lord did there confound the language of all the earth: and from thence did the Lord scatter them abroad upon the face of all the earth" (Genesis 11:9).

To this melancholy account of the fracturing of human unity through the confounding of language was added in the late sixteenth and early seventeenth centuries the searching epistemological skepticism of Montaigne and Bacon. The problem was not, Montaigne recognized, simply the multiplicity of languages; a single, familiar, apparently shared language is in fact deeply unreliable: "Our speech has its weaknesses and its defects, like all the rest," he writes in "The Apology for Raymond Sebond," "Most of the occasions for the troubles of the world are grammatical."[21] For Montaigne, the acknowledgment of the defects of language leads to an acceptance of human limitation, an awareness of all that will remain unstable, unresolved, imperfect, incomplete. To grasp the inherent weaknesses of speech is to give up the grand ambitions of the human mind, the dreams of perfection and certainty, and to accept the pervasive, shaping force of custom. For Bacon, by contrast, a skeptical critique of language is the necessary precondition of a programmatic advancement of learning. Only by liberating oneself from the fraudulence and sloppiness and myth making of ordinary language can one begin to acquire a genuine and well-founded knowledge of things, a knowledge that will initiate the long road back to the unity and the power possessed fully in Eden and lost definitively at Babel.

With Bacon we return to the obscure John Bulwer, for Bulwer was a Baconian, not one of those followers who refined the experimental methods or who pondered the epistemological problems of the emerging science but one who responded to the utopian element implicit in Bacon's program, the dream of recovering the primal power whose key was the primordial language spoken before the confounding of tongues. The revolutionary ferment of the mid-seventeenth century sparked many searchers for this ur-language or at least enabled their ambitious projects to surface in print. Often their hopes led them to Hebrew or to some version of Hebrew cleansed of its post-Babel corruptions. Hence, in 1655, Thomas (TheaurauJohn) Tany informed the world that he had received a revelation of "the pure language."[22] Tany's response to his revelation was to circumcise himself. Others similarly sought not only the primordial spoken language but also the root and origin of writing, the so-called Real Characters that would not merely represent things but express in direct and unmediated form the essence of reality itself.

Bulwer's project in the *Pathomyotomia* and other works is clearly related to this search, but there is a significant difference. Where Tany and others were searching for the universal language in speech and in writing (including a kind of writing directly on the body), Bulwer had the idea of looking elsewhere in what, following Aristotle, he takes to be the highest perfection of a living creature: *motion*. The qualities and attainments that characterize human identity depend on the muscles; without them man "would be left destitute of the grace of elocution, and his mind would be enforced to dwel in perpetual silence, as in a wooden extasie or congelation; nay his Soul which is onely known by Action, being otherwise very obscure, would utterly lose the benefit of explaning it self, by the innumerable almost *motions* of the Affections & passions which outwardly appear by the operation of the *Muscles*" (3).

The muscles, then, are the link between the soul—"being otherwise very obscure"—and the known world. Human expression demands motion, and for Bulwer the principal sites of significant motion are the head and the hands. In 1644, he published *Chirologia; or the Naturall Language of the Hand*, an achievement that prompted him thereafter to wish to be known as "the Chirosopher." Words are conventional, slow, and often misleading, but the signs made by the hands are "part of the unalterable laws and institutes of nature" (16). The natural language of the hand, Bulwer writes, "had the happiness to escape the curse at the confusion of Babel" (19).[23] Bulwer's passionate interest in what he called "manual rhetoric" led him to a singular achievement: in 1648, in a book called *Philocophus: Or, the Deafe and Dumbe Mans Friend*, he published what appears to be the first English hand alphabet for the deaf.

But if this accomplishment would seem from our vantage point to be the triumph of Bulwer's career, he himself would no doubt have regarded it as a minor bypath on the road to what the *Pathomyotomia* calls the "universall and naturall Language" (55), now not of the hand but of the head. That is, Bulwer does not consider facial expressions to be merely conventional; they are voluntary—that is, the product of muscular movements under the guidance of the soul—but the expressive system they articulate is not bound by the particular will of either individuals or cultures. After all, Bulwer observes, we do not actually think about most of our facial expressions, nor are we generally aware of commanding them (though they are not, in his view, less voluntary for that). But we are able to read those facial expressions; indeed, we count on doing so as part of understanding our social interactions. A face condemned to one fixed posture "would be like a Cabinet lockt up, whose key was lost" (40). There would be no access then to the subjectivity of the other, "no certaine way of entrance into his mind."

The *Pathomyotomia* intends to systematize this entrance by performing what it calls "dissections"—isolating, analyzing, and naming the muscles of the head that govern the range of human expressions. Hence, for example, "When we would bow low, as in *assenting with reverence*, or to *adore, worship*, or *profess a submissive respect*, the whole Neck with the Head is inclined and lowly bent forward" (51–52). This motion is performed, Bulwer writes, by two pairs of muscles, the first called *Longus* and the second called *Triangulare*. After describing these in some technical detail, he proposes to rename them in keeping with "the naturall Philosophy of Gesture": "The first long Muscles which so appeare active in these Declarations of the Mind might by our scope of Denomination be called *Par reverentiale*, the Reverentiall paire; The other commonly called *Triangulare*, for distinction, *Par adorans*, the Muscle of Worship or Adoration, or the Muscles of the yoke of submissive obedience" (53). This is the basic form for dozens of "dissections," from the "Muscles of Rejection," to the

"Muscles of Supplication," to "the Arrogant paire or the Muscles of Disdainfull Confidence" that work in tandem with "the Insulting or Bragging paire or the Muscles of Insolent Pride, and fierce Audacity"—that is, the proud stiffening of the neck and elevation of the head produced "when all the hinder Muscles of the Neck and Head and that confused Chaos and heape of Muscles in the Back, which are like a Labyrinth of many waies, work together" (78).

As Bulwer is fascinated by the movements of the head, he is equally fascinated by the subtlety and range of facial expressions: "the pleasant Muscle of Loves pretty Dimple" (109), "the Severe and Threatning Muscles" (148) that cause the brows to contract; "the Muscles of Wonder or Admiration" that lift the eyebrows; "the Muscle of Staring Impudence" that "draws the superior Eye-lid upwards" (158), "the Dastard Muscle, or the Ranke cowards Sphincter" that causes "the affrighted *Eyes* to twinkle, that is to open and incontinently to shut more than is convenient" (159). No movement—the pursing of the lips, the twitching of the ears, the slight rounding of the eyes—is too small for his attention, but he is particularly taken with that exuberant, convulsive spectacle unique to humans, laughter. Bulwer conceives of laughter as a great "Dance of the Muscles performed . . . upon the Theater of Mirth, the Countenance" (106), and he analyzes its component parts for many pages. What particularly strikes him is the extent to which laughter is not only an effect of the mind or the heart or the body but "of *totius conjuncti*, of the whole man" (128). Accordingly, "in laughter the Face swells; for, the whole Countenance is powred out and spread with the Spirits that then swell the Muscles" (110).

If laughter is the very heart of the universal and natural language of the head, it is also the limit case of the claim that this language is essentially voluntary. For Bulwer himself recognizes that by his own account laughter resembles the experience that had, at least since Saint Augustine, been recognized as the very emblem of the involuntary, the male erection: "So that the Muscles of the Face are filled with Spirits after the same manner as a certaine member directly opposite unto it which importunately sometimes lookes us in the Face, which being filled with Spirits growes stiff and is extended" (110). The only reason that the laughing face—"at the highest pitch and scrued up to the very Ecla of mirth"—does not actually stand erect is that the facial muscles "adhere most firmly to the bone and skin." Why then does Bulwer continue to insist on the principle of voluntary motion—not only in the case of laughter but even of sleepwalking? The answer seems to lie in the utopian impulse with which we began: Bulwer is determined to recover and to analyze the pure and unfallen communicative system of humankind, and this system must by definition enhance the power of the human will.

Bulwer's analysis of the signifying power of the muscles then is haunted by two demons that he must hold at bay. The first is the demon of involuntary or nonsignificant movement: all of the twitches, tics, swellings, and contractions that do not seem to express meanings or that cannot be performed at will. And the second is the demon of culture, the possibility that the expressive motions of the muscles are not primordial, pure, pre-Babel, but, rather, like any other language, determined by the varied and changing customs of peoples. The possibility surfaces on occasion in his books on the hands and the head, as when he writes that the Cretans make the sign of refusal or denial by moving their heads straight backward "not as we *refuse* and *denie*, who drive the head about him a circumduction" (*Pathomyotomia*, 54). But somehow such observations never compel Bulwer to abandon or even substantially modify his conviction that the muscles speak the true language of nature.

There is some indirect evidence, however, that he was aware of the problem and troubled by it. In 1650, he published yet another study of the body, but this time his point was not that the body did not lie. The work's full title in the expanded 1653 edition sketches its principal argument: *Anthropometamorphosis: Man Transform'd: or, The Artificial Changling Historically presented, In the mad and cruell Gallantry, foolish Bravery, ridiculous Beauty, filthy Finenesse, and loathsome Loveliness of most Nations, fashioning and altering their Bodies from the mould intended by Nature; With Figures of those Transfigurations To which artificiall and affected Deformations are added, all the Native and Nationall Monstrosities that have appeared to disfigure the Humane Fabrick. With a Vindication of the Regular Beauty and Honesty of Nature.* The body in its natural state is impeccably "honest," but as Bulwer makes clear, in more than five hundred pages of closely packed and often zany citations, there is virtually no culture in the world that does not fashion and alter the body "artificially." Bulwer's obsession with the body's natural language has, in effect, generated a counterobsession with all of the things that cultures do to change the body from its natural state. In this classic of heterology—a strange precursor of ethnography written out of loathing and disgust—he comes close to imagining the virtually limitless malleability of the body: heads drastically change shape, the genitals are cut and resewn, the skin is made into a canvas, lips, ears, nose, and nipples are pierced, the thighs are artificially fattened or thinned, breasts are enlarged or reduced or removed altogether, feet are crushed or elongated. Bulwer recognizes that many of the motives for these transformations of the body are religious, but approximations or departures from Christianity are no longer the way in which his observations are organized. The *Anthropometamorphosis* regards all attempts to reach the sacred through the mutilation or reshaping of the body as instances of what it calls "tampering with Nature" (1650 ed., 218). There is no place in Bulwer for the pious contemplation of Christ's wounds, the celebration of the stigmata, or the mystical interpretation of circumcision. On the contrary, there is nothing unique about Jewish circumcision—"The *Colchians, Ethiopians, Trogloditians, Egyptians, Syrians,* and *Phoenicians,* were wont to circumcise their new-born infants" (1650 ed., 209)—and Bulwer's account of the practice incorporates it into a larger discussion of genital mutilation, including castration in Turkey, female circumcision in Africa, artificial attempts in Guinea to lengthen or enlarge the penis, and the piercing of the male genitals in Siam in order to insert jewels or bells.[24]

For Bulwer, then, the search for the sacred has been displaced by an investigation of the natural and the unnatural, but the natural is not to be found, or at least not reliably found, among primitive or uncivilized peoples. On the contrary, it is precisely those peoples who tamper the most systematically with their bodies and make themselves into "artificial changelings." The stage is set for the self-congratulatory conclusion that European culture, and English culture in particular, is at once the most civilized and the most natural. But that is not the conclusion that Bulwer draws. In an appendix that seems less an afterthought than the disclosure of the work's hidden agenda, Bulwer gives what he calls "the Pedigree of the English Gallant." He argues that contemporary English clothing at its most fashionable actually reproduces many of the transformations that are carried out in other cultures on the flesh itself. Hence, for example, sugarloaf hats express "the same conceit that the *Macrones* of *Pontus,* and the *Macrocephali* once had, among whom they were esteemed the best Gentlmen who had the highest head" (531); "the slashing, pinking, and cutting of our Doublets, is but the same phansie and affectation with those barbarous Gallants who slash and carbonado their bodies" (537); and codpieces are "the shadowed imitation of the reall bulke of the great Privy Membred *Guineans*" (539), and the ribbons that "our modern Gallants hang at their Cod-piece, want nothing but Bells instead of Tags, to be allied in their Phansie to the yard-balls" (540) of the Siamese.

Bulwer then is one of the first to give an anthropological account of dress as well as of the body: like Mendes Pinto he draws upon classical and medieval accounts of distant peoples, but his work no longer conceptualizes the body's transformations in the mythic terms encouraged by Ovid and his followers or in the terms of folk belief sanctioned in the trials of witches or in the theological terms developed by the Christian discourse of sacred wounds. He wants to understand what is actually done systematically and culture by culture to change the body's shapes. But he can have this perception only in the mode of horror: after all, he longs for the body in its natural state, a state he imagines precisely as a single, universal norm from which virtually all cultures have fallen away. He stands, then, in some sense for a turning away from the multiplicity of the languages of the body, even at the moment that this multiplicity is first powerfully acknowledged, precisely *because* it is the moment in which it is first powerfully acknowledged.

Notes

1. "Accident" was meant, I suppose, to convey the absence of a personal religious intention, a willed identification with the tribal practice and its traditional meanings. But, though such voluntary and self-conscious choice is unquestionably important and was immediately relevant to our conversation—about lines of intellectual and spiritual influence—it seems singularly inadequate to the transmission of heritage in general and to these instances in particular. I will not venture an explanation of the public health policies of New York hospitals in the late 1940s or early 1950s, but we can be certain that routine circumcisions were anything but accidental, while the exceptional (if, for Jews, hardly unique) circumstance of a flight from persecution only partly obscures one of the most familiar and least accidental motives for the maintaining of traditional practices, often despite overt skepticism and revulsion: compliance with the wishes of the elders. Those wishes frequently have the power to override not only ideological resistance but also prudence and even self-preservation. In the dangerous historical situation sketched by the anthropologist, it would have been wise, if not for the parents' survival prospects then at least for their child's, to leave the newborn son uncircumcised.

   On the problem of the term as used in ordinary speech, there is a remarkable footnote in J. L. Austin's "A Plea for Excuses": "You have a donkey, so have I, and they graze in the same field. The day comes when I conceive a dislike for mine. I go to shoot it, draw a bead on it, fire: the brute falls in its tracks. I inspect the victim, and find to my horror that it is *your* donkey. I appear on your doorstep with the remains and say—what? 'I say, old sport, I'm awfully sorry, &c., I've shot your donkey *by accident*?' Or '*by mistake*'? Then again, I go to shoot my donkey as before, draw a bead on it, fire—but as I do so, the beasts move, and to my horror yours falls. Again the scene on the doorstep—what do I say? 'By mistake'? Or 'by accident'?" (*Philosophical Papers*, ed. J. O. Urmson and G. J. Warnock, 3d. ed. [Oxford: Oxford University Press, 1979], 185 n. 1). In the light of this analysis, it would not be legitimate to call the circumcision of the anthropologist's sons either an accident or a mistake.

2. Cf. Jacques Derrida, "Signature Event Context," in *Margins of Philosophy*, trans. Alan Bass (Chicago: University of Chicago Press, 1982), 307–30. As will become clear, my interest in Derrida is not in the indeterminacy that Derrida argues to be the condition of iterability but rather in the historical contests over meaning.

3. It is striking that Deuteronomy also explicitly forbids other ritual mutilations: "Ye are the children of the Lord your god: ye shall not cut yourselves, nor make any baldness between your eyes for the dead" (14:1). On the anthropology of Jewish circumcision, see Howard Eiberg-Schwartz, *The Savage in Judaism: An Anthropology of Israelite Religion and Ancient Judaism* (Bloomington: Indiana University Press, 1990), and *God's Phallus and Other Problems for Men and Monotheism* (Boston: Beacon Press, 1994); Bruno Bettelheim, *Symbolic Wounds: Puberty Rites and the Envious Male* (Glencoe, Ill.: Free Press, 1954).

4 This moralization seems based upon the passage in Deuteronomy 10 from which I have quoted: "Only the LORD had a delight in thy fathers to love them, and he chose their seed after them, even you above all people, as it is this day. Circumcise therefore the foreskin of your heart, and be no more stiffnecked. For the LORD your God is God of gods, and Lord of lords, a great God, a mighty, and a terrible, which regardeth not persons, nor taketh reward" (10:15–17). See also Deuteronomy 30:6, and Jeremiah 4:4 and 9:26.

5. Fisher, "A Sermon . . . Preached upon a good Friday, by the same John Fisher, Bishop of Rochester," in *The English Works of John Fisher, Bishop of Rochester*, ed. John E. B. Mayor (London: N. Trübner, 1876), 411. I owe this reference to Lowell Gallagher. Among the many important studies of the significance of the body in medieval spirituality, I owe a particular debt to Peter Brown, *The Body and Society: Men, Women, and Sexual Renunciation in Early Christianity* (New York: Columbia University Press, 1988); Miri Rubin, *Corpus Christi: The Eucharist in Late Medieval Culture* (Cambridge: Cambridge University Press, 1991); and Caroline Bynum, *Fragmentation and Redemption: Essays on Gender and the Human Body in Medieval Religion* (New York: Zone Books, 1991), and *The Resurrection of the Body in Western Christianity* (New York: Columbia University Press, 1995). For the equation of Christ's wounded body with parchment, see Rubin, *Corpus Christi*, 306–8.

6. See Piero Camporesi, *The Incorruptible Flesh: Bodily Mutation and Mortification in Religion and Folklore*, trans. Tania Croft-Murray, Latin texts trans. Helen Elsom (Cambridge: Cambridge University Press, 1988), 3–7.

7. Heinrich Seuse, *Leben*, in *The Exemplar: Life and Writings of Blessed Henry Suso*, trans. M. Ann Edward, 2 vols. (Dubuque, Iowa, 1992), 1:13; quoted in Eric Jager, "The Book of the Heart: Reading and Writing the Medieval Subject," *Speculum* 71 (1996): 16.

8. Jager, "The Book of the Heart," 17.

9. Odoric of Pordenone (1265?–1331), in *Cathay and the Way Thither*, ed. Sir Henry Yule, 2 vols. (London: Hakluyt Society, 1866), 1:142.

10. Moreover, the terms in which Odoric describes the ritual self-annihilation are closely related to the terms of Christian self-mortification. Compare this vision of the anchorites' contempt for the flesh, from *Sermoni di S. Giovanni Climaco, Abbate nel Monte Sinai* (Venice, 1570):

> Their eyes were dull, concave and sunken deeply into their heads, and all their lashes had fallen out; their cheecks were wizened, burned and full of sores from the hot and fervent tears that had coursed down them. Their faces were thin, dry and pale, not unlike the faces of the dead. Their chests likewise had sores and contusions from self-inflicted bleeding and they suffered great pain from the beatings they had given themselves. From their mouths there came forth blood rather than saliva, because of their beaten and broken torsos.... Their clothes were all ragged, full of filth, flea and lice-ridden.... They prayed to the universal Bishop, exhorting him under oath not to let them be worthy of human burial, but that he should cause them to be thrown like beasts into some river or in some field so that they should be devoured by wild animals.

(Quoted, with similar passages, in Camporesi, *The Incorruptible Flesh*, 45.) See also Caroline Bynum, *Holy Feast and Holy Fast: The Religious Significance of Food to Medieval Women* (Berkeley: University of California Press, 1987).

11. The *Oxford English Dictionary* attributes the first printed use of the term *Juggernaut* to W. Bruton (1638) in Hakluyt's *Voyages*.

12. The term Juggernaut—in Sanskrit, "Lord of the World"—refers to the god Krishna, whose enormous image at Puri in Orissa is annually dragged in procession on a huge chariot. Presumably, it was this procession, whose religious fervor and vivid spectacle continue to fill observers with wonder, that was represented, in a distorted form, in Odoric's narrative. But apart from the accidents that inevitably attend vast throngs pulling the immense cart, no deaths beneath the wheels, no acts of self-slaughter, no deliberate mutilations have been reported in modern times, nor do there appear to be Indian accounts of such practices. Either the ultimate expression of faith has changed since Odoric's time or he is reporting (or inventing) a fantasy.

13. Sir John Mandeville, *The Travels of Sir John Mandeville*, trans. C. W. R. D. Moseley (Harmondsworth: Penguin, 1983), 126. For an analysis of the destabilizing power of Mandeville's Travels, see my *Marvelous Possessions: The Wonder of the New World* (Chicago: University of Chicago Press, 1991), 26–51.

14. Fernao Mendes Pinto, *The Travels of Mendes Pinto*, ed. and trans. Rebecca Catz (Chicago: University of Chicago Press, 1989), 339.

15. Pinto, *The Travels of Mendes Pinto*, xliii.

16. Cf. the brief critique of Catz's thesis by Robert Viale in his French translation of Mendes Pinto (*Pérégrination* [Paris: ELA La Différance, 1991], 22). I am grate-

ful to Professor Maria Alzira Seixo of the University of Lisbon for bringing this translation to my attention.

17. See the brilliant account of "the 'trial' of theoretical curiosity," in Hans Blumenberg, *The Legitimacy of the Modern Age*, trans. Robert M. Wallace (Cambridge: MIT Press, 1983), 229–456.

18. Commentary on Romans, in Philipp Melanchton, *Werke*, ed. Hans Engelland and Robert Stupperich (Guterlow: C. Bartelsman, 1951), 5:291–92. I am indebted to Professor Debora Shuger for calling this passage to my attention and translating it, and for many other valuable suggestions and questions.

19. Luther, "Libellus de ritu et moribus Turcorum" (1530). I owe the reference to Debora Shuger.

20. John Bulwer, *Pathomytornia, or A dissection of the significant muscles of the affections of the minde: Being an essay to a new method of observing the most important movings of the muscles of the head, as they are the neerest and immediate organs of the voluntarie and impetuous motions of the mind. With the proposall of a new nomenclature of the muscles* (London, 1649).

21. *The Complete Essays of Montaigne*, trans. Donald M. Frame (Stanford: Stanford University Press, 1958), 392.

22. He provides a sample of this language that English was capable of rendering in utterances like the following: "*obedient alma honasa hul; generati alvah ableuvisse insi locat amorvissem humanet rokoas salah axoret eltah alvah hon ono olephad in se mori melet eri neri meleare; okoriko olo ophaus narratus asa sadoas loboim olet amni Phikepeaa ebellrer elme bosai in re meal olike.*" *TheaurauJohn His Aurora in Trandagorum in Salem Gloria, Or the discussive of the Law & Gospell betwixt the Jew and the Gentile in Salem Resurrectionem* [London, 1655], 54–55; I owe this passage to Thomas Luxon.

23. If we think that the hands are too limited a means of human communication compared with the tongue, Bulwer proposes to show us that their range of expressiveness is actually greater than that of words. In a flight of rhetorical enthusiasm that leads him to forget that he is himself, after all, using words, Bulwer offers his proof by launching into a list of what we do with our hands:

> Sue, entreat, beseech, solicit, call, allure, entice, dismiss, grant, deny, reprove, are suppliant, fear, threaten, abhor, repent, pray, instruct, witness, accuse, declare our silence, condemn, absolve, show our astonishment, proffer, refuse, respect, give honor, adore, worship, despise, prohibit, reject, challenge, bargain, vow, swear, imprecate, humor, allow, give warning, command, reconcile, submit, defy, affront, offer injury, complement, argue, dispute, explode, confute, exhort, admonish, affirm, distinguish, urge, doubt, reproach, mock, approve, dislike, encourage, recommend, flatter, applaud, exhalt, humble, insult, adjure, yield, confess, cherish, demand, crave, covet, bless, number, prove, confirm, congee, salute, congratulate, entertain, give thanks, welcome, bid farewell, chide, brawl, consent, upbraid, envy, reward, offer force, pacify, invite, justify, contemn, disdain, dis-

allow, forgive, offer peace, promise, perform, reply, invoke, request, repell, charge, satisfy, deprecate, lament, condole, bemoan, put in mind, hinder, praise, commend, brag, boast, warrant, assure, inquire, direct, adopt, rejoice, show gladness, complain, despair, grieve, are sad and sorrowful, cry out, bewail, forbid, discomfort, ask, are angry, wonder, admire, pity, assent, order, rebuke, savor, slight, dispraise, disparage, are earnest, importunate, refer, put to compromise, plight our faith, make a league of friendship, strike one good luck, give handsel, take earnest, buy, barter, exchange, show our agreement, express our liberality, show our benevolence, are illiberal, ask mercy, exhibit grace, show our displeasure, fret, chafe, fume, rage, revenge, crave audience, call for silence, prepare for an apology, give liberty of speech, bid one take notice, warn one to forbear, keep off and be gone; take acquaintance, confess ourselves deceived by a mistake, make remonstrance of another's error, weep, give a pledge of aid, comfort, relieve, demonstrate, redargue, persuade, resolve, speak to, appeal, profess a willingness to strike, show ourselves convinced, say we know somewhat which yet we will not tell, present a check for silence, promise secrecy, protect our innocence, manifest our love, enmity, hate, and despite; provoke, hyperbolically extoll, enlarge our mirth with jollity and triumphant acclamations of delight, note and signify another's actions, the manner, place, and time, as how, where, when, etc.

Chirologia: or the Natural Language of the Hand, and Chironomia: or the Art of Manual Rhetoric, ed. James W. Cleary (Carbondale: Southern Illinois University Press, 1974), 20.

This reminder that the Renaissance was the great age of lists is not likely to persuade many readers that "postures of the hand" exceed "the numerical store of words," but it is enough to license Bulwer's lengthy and painstaking analysis of gestures, from scratching the head with one finger (an *"effeminate* gesture betraying a *close inclination to vice"* [130]) to putting forth the middle finger, the rest drawn into a fist ("a natural expression of *scorn* and *contempt*" [132]).

24. After giving an account of circumcision as a widespread practice, Bulwer carefully acknowledges that the Jews were not simply imitating neighboring peoples: "Not that the *Hebrewes* took this fashion from the *Egyptians*, but from the Covenant God made with *Abraham*, Gen. 16. But the Circumcision of Abraham was not new, but at length approved of and sanctified by God" (1650 ed., 210–11). Similarly, he cites the moralization of circumcision in an attempt to explain the departure from nature: "As for Circumcision commanded by God, it was for a moral reason, and had an expresse command; otherwise, as a Grave Divine expresseth it in the case of *Abraham*, as a natural man, it would have seemed the most foolish thing in the world, a matter of great reproach, which would make him, as it made his posterity after him, to seem ridiculous to all the world" (214).

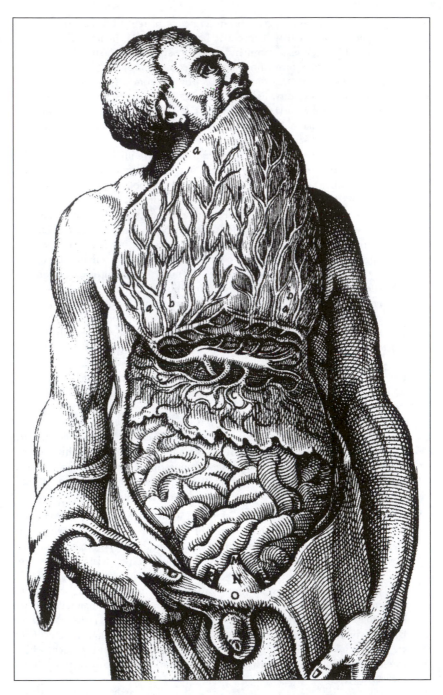

12. Self-demonstrating anatomy from Juan Valverde's *Historia de la composition del cuerpo humano* (Rome, 1556).

12

Fables of the Belly
in Early Modern England

MICHAEL SCHOENFELDT

> We love our food when it is meate, we loathe it when it
> is excrement. When it goes into us we desire it, when it
> passeth through us we despise it.
> —Edward Reynoldes, *Treatise of the Passions*
> *and Faculties of the Soule of Man*

In our current eagerness to establish political readings of early modern texts
—an eagerness whetted by the dearth of such readings in New Criticism—
we have allowed political concerns to consume a range of other discourses
through which individuals in the period attempted to comprehend their
experience of the world and to wring meaning from it. Among these discourses is the historically contingent blend of physiology, psychology, and
ethics that constitutes the period's medical understanding of the complex
relations between corporeal process and dispositional inclination. In early
modern England, the individual consumer was pressured by Galenic physiology, classical ethics, and Protestant theology to conceive all acts of ingestion and excretion as very literal acts of self-fashioning. The stomach, the
organ that accomplishes digestion, provides a particularly intense focus of
inwardness because it is the part of our body that makes its needs felt most

frequently and insistently. It demands to be filled at least a couple of times a day, and to be emptied at least once. When these demands are not met, the entire organism suffers. The exigencies of the stomach require the individual to confront on a daily basis the thin yet necessarily permeable line separating self and other. The purpose of this essay is to explore some of the legends formulated in the period to explain digestion, that magical yet mundane moment when dead animal and vegetable matter is ingested to sustain life, when something alien is brought into the self and something alien is excreted by the self, when, as Edward Reynolds suggests, the object of appetite is rendered the source of repugnance.[1] Far more involuted, conceptually and physiologically, than the voracious orifice of indiscriminate consumption immortalized by Comus, the belly god of Jonson's *Pleasure Reconciled to Virtue* and of Milton's *A Masque*, the stomach occupies a central site of ethical discrimination and devotional interiority in early modern culture.

Because of the predominance of the Galenic regime of the humors, in which all illness was imagined to be the product of a lack or excess of some bodily fluid, the stomach assumed a position of particular importance in early modern regimes of mental and physical health. Whereas our post-Cartesian ontology imagines inwardness and materialism, soul and stomach, as necessarily separate realms of existence, the Galenic regime of the humoral self demanded the invasion of social and psychological realms by biological and environmental processes. At the same time, this regime articulated a variety of strategies for making such invasions a narrative of liberation rather than captivity. Although it imagined that bodies were perpetually in danger of poisoning themselves on their own nutritive material, it also made available a vast array of therapies for purging this harmful excess, and urged frequent and thorough deployment of them. Dedicated to rendering salutary the inevitable permeability of bodies and of selves, this regime located and explained human passion amid a taxonomy of internal organs. As the organ of assimilation and purgation, the stomach assumed a critical role in this taxonomy. The stories that early modern science made available to explain the technology and ethics of digestion, at once so different from and so similar to the narratives of nutritive management to which twentieth-century physiology has subjected us, tell us much about the ways in which early modern individuals inhabited and experienced their bodies.

The process of digestion was imagined to occur in three stages. The first, occurring in the stomach proper, is termed concoction, and converts food into chyle, a fluid that the body can begin to absorb. The next stage of digestion occurs in the liver, and converts the chyle into blood, which can be distributed to the different members of the body through the network of veins. The third and final stage of digestion takes place in the various parts of the body that attract what nourishment they need from the blood. Digestion thus is something that does not happen exclusively in the stomach but occurs throughout the organism. The human body is from this perspective just a giant stomach. Digestion, moreover, is a very literal assimilation of something that is not part of one to the essence of one's being; as Thomas Elyot describes it in his *Castel of Helth* (1541), "Concoction is an alteration in the stomacke of meates and drynkes, accordynge to their qualities, wherby they are made lyke to the substance of the body."[2] Digestion is a continual process of liquefaction and rarefaction, with each stage producing a purer form of nutrition by expelling what is not useful and converting what is. Semen in the male, and milk in the female, are the most rarefied forms of blood. Each stage of digestion, moreover, produces its own excrement: in the stomach, the excrement is feces; in the liver, urine; and in the various parts of the body, sweat, hair, nails, and mucus.

Together with its corollary organs of digestion—the liver and the spleen—the stomach was imagined to complete physiologically a process that begins in the ethical judgment: the discrimination of dross from nutrition, of good from bad. As William Vaughan, author of the popular *Directions for Health* writes, the body is a dynamic and porous edifice continually producing "superfluous excrements" which must be purged:

> Natures providence hath devised and framed sundry passages needfull for the purging, conveiance and evacuation of all such superfluous humours: to wit, the Kidneyes and the Urine-pipes, the empty or fasting Guts, ... the Bladder, Eares, and Pores, appointed for the avoydance expulsion of sweat. And in the most part of these, if obstructions should happen, all the whole filthy masse of noysome humours is thereby kept within the body, and then given violent assault to some of the principall parts.[3]

The stomach is at the center of a system demanding perpetual, anxious osmosis with the outside world. Obstruction rather than flow is cause and evidence of illness. Indeed, the body's emunctory capacities are so important to the health of the organism that curing hemorrhoids can result in sickness and even death. This critical link between health and flow urges revision of the account of the ideal classical body we have inherited from

Bakhtin's compelling work on Rabelais.[4] Under the Galenic regime of the humors, which imagines all illness as an imbalance among the four nutritive fluids produced by digestion—choler, melancholy, phlegm, and blood —soundness of mind and body is achieved not by immuring bodily fluids but rather by carefully manipulating them. This physiology demands not the seamless corporeal enclosure that Bakhtin identifies with the classical body but rather the routine excretory processes that he displaces onto lower-class festivity. Even the notorious diagnostic examination of urine and feces by physicians was simply a technique for investigating just how effectively the patient was accomplishing the critical activities of assimilation and excretion.

An elaborate technology of digestion was invoked to explain the process by which the body separates nutritive material from the pernicious dross that inevitably suffuses it. Nicholas Culpepper's translation of John Veslingus's *Anatomy of the Body of Man* outlines the stomach's ventricular capacities as well as its complex but sometimes cozy relationship to the surrounding organs:

> The inferior Orifice which is on the right side, the Ancients called *Pylorus*, or *Janitor*; for by this the meat digested passeth to the next Guts as by a gate; the heat of the Bowels round about the Stomach, quallify its cold and dry Temperature: the Stomach is in form like the Bag of a pair of Bag-pipes; it is placed by the Wisdome of God in the left *Hypochondrium* under the *Diaphragma*; The right part is committed to the Liver, the left to the Spleen; below, it is cherished by the *Omentum*, and underneath it lies upon the Sweet bread, as it were upon a Pillow.

Indiscriminately mixing anthropomorphic, thermal, musical, domestic, and architectural imagery, Veslingus at once conveys the labyrinthine architecture of the abdomen and infers the intricate processes that the stomach performs in every act of digestion. Thomas Vicary's *A Profitable Treatise of the Anatomie of man's body* offers a similar vision of the stomach's relation to other organs, transforming the stomach's architectonic centrality into a narrative of its physiological priority:

> It hath the lyver on the right side, chafing & heating him with his lobes or figures: & the Splen on the left syde, with his fatnes, and veynes sending to him melancolie, to exercise his appetites: and above him is the Harte, quickening him with his Arteries: Also the brayne, send to him a braunch of Nerves to geve him feeling.[5]

The stomach, according to Vicary, is the recipient of the assiduous attentions of a constellation of internal organs. The liver, Vicary continues, assumes its particular shape and texture because "it should be plycable to the stomacke, like as a hande dothe to an apple, to comforte her digestion; for his heate is to the stomacke as the heate of the fyre is to the Potte or Cauldron that hangeth over it" (69). In both Veslingus's and Vicary's digestive structures, a feeling of snug domesticity alternates with a vocabulary of technical precision.

Vicary's comparison of the stomach to a cauldron heated by the liver's fire involves one of the most frequently used images for the stomach—the comparison of its mechanisms to culinary techniques practiced outside the organism. A very literal kind of cooking occurs within the stomach—"concoction," the technical term for digestion, derives from the Latin *concoctus*, "to boil together"—readying food for delivery to various parts of the body as a cook prepares meals. "Our stomake is our bodies kitchin," remarks William Vaughan in his *Directions for Health.* Joshua Sylvester's translation of *Du Bartas His Divine Weekes and Workes* (1641) calls the stomach "that ready cook concocting every Mess," and explores in some detail the culinary processes involved:

> ... in short time it cunningly converts
> Into pure Liquor fit to feed the parts;
> And then the same doth faithfully deliver
> Into the *Port-vein* passing to the Liver,
> Who turns it soon to blood; and thence again
> Through branching pipes of the great *Hollow-vein*,
> Through all the members doth it duly scatter:
> Much like a Fountain, whose divided Water
> Itself dispersing into hundred Brooks,
> Bathes some fair Garden with her winding crooks ...
> Even so the Blood (bred of good nourishment)
> By divers Pipes to all the body sent,
> Turns here to Bones, there changes into Nerves;
> Here is made Marrow, there for Muscles serves,
> Here skin becoms, there crooking veins, here flesh,
> To make our Limbs more forcefull and more fresh.

Du Bartas imagines the body as a variegated garden nourished by a fountain whose liquid is transformed into the parts it nourishes. Accomplishing the salutary liquefaction of food mass, the stomach is the vital center of a vast system of food preparation and distribution, concocting food solids into nutritive fluid that can then be dispersed through the blood to the different parts of the body as needed.[6]

The stomach, then, is not a passive receptacle but the great feeder of parts. This physiological fact explains in part why in the most famous literary account of the stomach in English Renaissance literature, Menenius Agrippa's fable of the belly in Shakespeare's *Coriolanus*, Agrippa is able to quiet the rebellion of a hungry and angry mob by means of the rather unexpected comparison of aristocrats to the belly. One would not normally think of defending a voracious aristocracy in a subsistence society by likening it to the organ of digestion. In hierarchical readings of bodily organs, moreover, the belly is typically linked to the lower classes, while the upper classes are aligned with the heart or brain. In the marginalia of Fletcher's *Purple Island*, for example, the commentator asserts that

> the whole body may be parted into three regions: the lowest, or belly; the middle, or breast; the highest, or head. In the lowest the liver is soveraigne, whose regiment is the widest, but meanest. In the middle the heart reignes, most necessarie. The brain obtains the highest place, and is as the least in compasse, so the greatest in dignitie.[7]

Against this conventional interpretation of the political order of the body, Agrippa strategically replaces a hierarchy based on the distinction between low and high with a hierarchy based on the distinction between center and periphery, and so underscores the vast importance given to the digestion and distribution of food in the maintenance of the individual body. When the belly is accused of idleness, that "only like a gulf it did remain / I' th' midst a' th' body, idle and unactive, / Still cupboarding the viand, never bearing / Like labor with the rest" (98–101), the belly responds by conceding

> That I receive the general food at first
> Which you do live upon; and fit it is,
> Because I am the store-house and the shop
> Of the whole body . . .
> I send [food] through the rivers of your blood,
> Even to the court, the heart, to th' seat o' th' brain,
> And, through the cranks and offices of man,
> The strongest nerves and small inferior veins
> From me receive that natural competency
> Whereby they live . . .
>   all
> From me do back receive the flour of all,
> And leave me but the bran.

Fantasizing that a society's resources naturally trickle down from its most to its least privileged members, Agrippa uses the physiological centrality of the stomach to mystify a doctrine of social inequality and to obscure the actual labor that is part of the production and distribution of provisions.[8]

Among the most extended accounts of the stomach in early modern English literature is the notorious episode of the Castle of Alma in Spenser's *Faerie Queene*, Book 2. In this book devoted to temperance, the classical virtue by which appetite is made subject to discipline, Arthur and Guyon tour the alimentary tract, entering through the mouth and proceeding down the gullet in order to explore the stomach, the most literal site of human inwardness. Giving the well-worn metaphor of the self as a castle a particular emphasis, and elaborating the cozy domesticity that suffused the portraits of the stomach in Vicary and Culpepper, Spenser likens the stomach to a "stately Hall, / Wherein were many tables faire dispred, / And ready dight with drapets festivall, / Against the viaundes should be ministred" (canto 9, sts. 27–33).[9] The hall is presided over by a steward named "Diet," a figure "rype of age, / And in demeanure sober, and in counsell sage." His marshall is "Appetite," whose job is to "bestow / Both guestes and meate, when ever in they came, / And knew them how to order without blame." These figures of dietary and social order lead Alma, Guyon, and Arthur into the stomach proper, "a vaut ybuilt for great dispence, / With many raunges reard along the wall; / And one great chimney, whose long tonnell thence / The smoke forth threw. And in the midst of all / There placed was a caudron wide and tall, / Upon a mighty furnace, burning whot." The lungs function as "An huge great paire of bellowes, which did styre / Continually, and cooling breath inspyre." A dynamic balance between the heat necessary for cooking and the cooling breath of respiration—a balance central to definitions of temperance as a form of moderation between extremes—is thus attained. The stomach, though, is no placid place but an area of immense bustle: "about the Caudron many Cookes accoyld, / With hookes and ladles, as need did require." These cooks are themselves organized around a carefully divided series of tasks that mirror the different activities for which the stomach was thought to be responsible: "The maister Cooke was cald Concoction, / A carefull man, and full of comely guise." He is accompanied by "Digestion," who "did order all th' Achates in Seemely wise, / And set them forth, as well he could devise." While Digestion dispatches the various fluids that concoction makes available where they are needed, other unnamed cooks assume "severall offices. . . . Some to remove the scum, as it did rise; / Others to beare the same away did mind; / And others it to use according to his kind." The immense complexity of the digestive process is indicated by the number of figures Spenser finds it necessary to include. Apparently for Spenser, too many cooks do not spoil the broth.

A critical issue in the digestion of nutritive material is the elimination of what cannot be assimilated:

> But all the liquour, which was fowle and wast,
> Not good nor serviceable else for ought,
> They in another great round vessell plast,
> Till by a conduit pipe it thence were brought:
> And all the rest, that noyous was, and nought,
> By secret wayes, that none might it espy,
> Was close convaid, and to the back-gate brought,
> That cleped was Port Esquiline, whereby
> It was avoided quite, and throwne out privily.

(canto 9, st. 32)

The process of disposing of the "fowle and wast" material that is in Spenser's phrase "not good nor serviceable" is as important to the health of the organism as is the process of nutrition. "The Guttes," notes Thomas Vicary, "were ordeined in the fyrst creation to convey the drosse of the meate and drinke, & to clense the body of their superfluities." Good digestion demands not just the assimilation of nutritive material but also the expulsion of superfluity. As Thomas Elyot asserts, "[T]hese excrementes be none other, but matter superfluouse and unsavery, which by natural powers may not be converted in to fleshe, but remayning in the body corrupt the members, and therfore desireth to have them expelled."[10]

Indeed, most illness in the period is imagined to derive from the body's inability to rid itself of excess humors. As a result, nearly all medical interventions in the period short of surgery are intended to expel such pernicious excess, through purgation or phlebotomy, or to correct a humoral imbalance through ingestion. "Physicke," notes Robert Burton in *The Anatomy of Melancholy*, "is naught else but *addition and substraction.*" In his larger project of bestowing upon the intrinsically inglorious ethic of temperance the grandeur of heroic action, Spenser bestows upon this system of nutritive addition and excretory subtraction that sustains individual existence the bustling stability of a baroque structure. Like Arthur and Guyon, we are meant to view the continual processing of food, and the perpetual discrimination of noxious from nutritious matter, as a "goodly order" that solicits our admiration for the "great workmans skill" behind it. "Never had they seene so straunge a sight" as the machinery of digestion common to all humans.[11]

The critical role the stomach plays in the life of the organism makes it a central medium for therapies that alter body and mind. The stomach, notes

Thomas Vicary, "is a necessarie member to al the body; for if it fayles in his working, al the members of the body shal corrupte" (66). In *The Touchstone of Complexions*, Levinus Lemnius explicitly links digestive concerns to a humoral physiology and psychology, which connects mental and physical illness to the excess or dearth of one of the four fluids produced by digestion known as humors:

> These [humors] according to the nature of nourishment received, are increased or diminished, ... And albeit these humours being of great force divers wayes, and sundrily affecting the body, yea the minde also with fulsome and unpleasant exhalations and sents is oftentimes greatly annoyed and encumbred, (even as ill & naughty wine bringeth to the braine affects both hurtfull and dangerous). ...
>
> For if the body should not be sustained with nourishment, or if the humours (which moisten every particular member) should lack the preservatives and fomentations wherewith they be maintained, the whole frame of man's body must of necessity decay, and be utterly dissolved.[12]

No firm line could be drawn separating food from medicine. "Physicians hold," notes William Vaughan, "that men be diversly affected, according to the dyet which they use." The point made repeatedly in the vast literature on medical self-help is that all foods do something in one, and to one, physically and mentally. Like the humors they nourish, foods are predominantly either hot or cold, moist or dry, and bestow that disposition on the consumer. To choose one's diet is an act of self-fashioning in the most literal sense. The regulation of what goes into and out of the stomach provides a central site of what Michel Foucault terms "the care of the self," those techniques by which individuals make themselves into subjects by a deliberate exercise of discipline over appetite.[13] Deciding what foods are most appropriate to one's own particular humoral balance, moreover, requires intense self-scrutiny. In *The Castel of Helth*, Elyot describes how the attempt to eat healthily produces a kind of necessary introspection in the consumer: "The quantitie of meate muste be proporcioned after the substaunce and qualitie therof, and according to the complexion of hym that eateth." One must attend not only to one's complexion or particular humoral temperament but also to one's occupation and environment:

> Wherefore of men, which use moch labor or exercise, also of them, which have very cholerike stomackes here in Englande, grosse meates may be eaten in a great quantitie; and in a cholerike stomake biefe is better dygested than a chykens legge, forasmoche as in a hotte stomacke fyne

> meates be shortly aduste and corrupted. Contrarywise in a colde or fleu-
> matyke stomake grosse meate abydeth longe undigested, and maketh
> putrified matter: lyght meates therfore be to suche a stomacke more apt
> and convenyent. The temperate bodye is beste nourysshed with a lyttell
> quantitie of grosse meates: but of temperate meates in substaunce and
> qualytie, they maye safely eate a good quantitie.[14]

Consumption is part of a highly complex network of influences on character and health. The porousness of the stomach is symptomatic of the overall
porousness of the individual. For Robert Burton, the particulars of each
consumer's situation must be weighed so carefully that the dietary recom-
mendations to which he devotes so many pages must be subordinated to
the superior authority of individual experience: "our owne experience is the
best Physitian; that diet which is most propitious to one, is often pernitious
to another; such is the variety of palats, humors, and temperatures, let
every man observe, and be a law unto himselfe." The introspection that
consumption demands precipitates an arena of radical individuation. Even
Paracelsus, whose medical writings in many areas repudiate the Galenic system on which Burton's claims are based, imagines the stomach as an inher-
ently anomalous organ: "If the physician is to understand the correct
meaning of health, he must know that there are more than a hundred,
indeed more than a thousand, kinds of stomach; consequently, if you gather
a thousand persons, each of them will have a different kind of digestion,
each unlike the others."[15] Necessarily situating dietary authority within, the
early modern consumer becomes "a law unto himself," cultivating a self
whose unique experience and temperament mandate axioms superior to
the prescriptions of external authority.

   Diet, then, provided early modern subjects with a repertoire of therapies for avoiding the more deterministic aspects of Galenic humoral psychology. That the individual consumer can alter disposition by diet at once
empowers that individual and pressures all dietary decisions. In *The Anatomy of Melancholy*, Burton describes overeating in a vocabulary that fuses
psychology, medicine, and ethics:

> As a Lampe is choaked with a multitude of oyle, or a little fire with over-
> much wood quite extinguished: so is the natural heat with immoderate
> eating strangled in the body ... an insatiable paunch is a pernitious sinke,
> & the fountaine of all diseases both of body and minde.

Burton, moreover, articulates the processes by which body and soul influence each other:

as the Body workes upon the minde, by his bad humours, troubling the Spirits, sending grosse fumes into the Braine, and so *per consequens* disturbing the Soule, and all the faculties of it ... so on the other side, the minde most effectually workes upon the Body, producing by his passions and perturbations, miraculous alterations; as Melancholy, despaire, cruell diseases, and sometimes death it selfe. Insomuch that it is most true which *Plato* saith [that] ... all the mischiefes of the Body, proceed from the Soule.[16]

Physiology and psychology are merely the same phenomena in different media; the health of both depends upon the efficacy of digestion. In *The Touchstone of Complexions*, Levinus Lemnius explores the strong link between mind and body by attending to the critical role of the spleen in digestion: if the spleen

throughly performe the office, for which it was ordained and doe exactly drinke up the drossie seculency of blood, it maketh a man thereupon wonderfully merry and jocund. For when the blood is sincerely purified, and from all grossnesse and seculency purged, the spirits consequently are made pure, bright, and cleare shining: Whose purity and clearnesse causeth the minde to rejoyce, and among merry companions to laugh and delight in pretty devices. ...

Contrariwise if it be surcharged and overwhelmed with too much confluxe of filthy humour, and be debarred or disappointed of the ordinary helpe and ayde of the Liver, either through imbecility or obstruction, then bringeth it many discommodities and annoyances, no lesse hurtfull and prejudiciall to the minde then to the body, as heavinesse, sorrow, sadnesse, feare and dread of missehap to come.

Diet and digestion were seen to affect not just mood and mental capacity but even the ineffable realms of the soul. "Now for the soules faculties," asks William Vaughan, "how is it possible, but that the smoaky vapours, which breathe from a fat and full paunch, should not interpose a dampish mist of dulnes betwixt the body and the bodies light?"[17] The relationship between gluttony and ungodliness is construed to entail a physiological as well as a moral cause. The Elizabethan "Homilie Against Gluttony and Drunkennesse" even makes good digestion dependent upon divine grace: "except GOD give strengthe to nature to digest, so that we may take profite by [our meats], either shall we filthily vomite them up again, or els shal they lie stinking in our bodies, as in a lothsome sinke or chanell, and so diversely infect the whole body."[18] Every act of eating performs our fragile dependence upon the recalcitrant graces of a predatory world. The processes of assimilation, moreover, demand the continual intervention of divine grace to accomplish the miracle of digestion.

Perhaps this is why the spiritual autobiographies of the period pay such close attention to digestion. As their common etymology would suggest, the regulation of diet and the keeping of diaries are engaged in corollary forms of diurnal inwardness. At the beginning of the *Reliquiae Baxterianae*, Richard Baxter explains why he observes the conditions of his body in a work intended to measure the progress of his soul: "because the Case of my *Body* had a great Operation upon my Soul, . . . I shall here together give you a brief Account of the most of my Afflictions of that kind." A typical passage records that "my chief Troubles were incredible Inflations of Stomach, Bowels, Back, Sides, Head, Thighs, as if I had been daily fill'd with Wind."[19] Baxter, moreover, blames these inward afflictions on his youthful diet—"I am now fully satisfied that all proceeded from Latent Stones in my Reins, occasioned by unsuitable Diet in my Youth"—and imagines their cure in the careful regulation and manipulation of substances that enter and exit his adult body. "My chiefest remedies" for illness are:

> 1. Temperance as to quantity and quality of Food: for every bit of spoonful too much, and all that is not exceeding easie of digestion, and all that is flatulent, do turn all to Wind, and disorder my Head.
> 2. Exercise till I sweat. . . .
> 3. A Constant Extrinsic Heat, by a great Fire, which may keep me still near to a Sweat, if not in it: (for I am seldom well at ease but in a Sweat).
> 4. Beer as hot as my Throat will endure, drunk all at once, to make me Sweat.[20]

For Baxter, health is contingent upon the continual application of therapies of purgation—therapies that themselves offer a physiological version of the spiritual phenomenon of repentance. Tempering what enters the body, and sweating out one's inevitable excess, become essential components of the spiritual life of the subject.

An even more remarkable nexus of spirituality and corporeality is recorded in the diary of Ralph Josselin, another seventeenth-century clergyman. Josselin records that on February 14, 1647/1648, he "tooke above 2 ounces sirrup roses which wrought very kindly with mee, gave me 9 stooles brought away much Choler, I went to bed, with a persuasion after seeking of god, that he would rebuke my distemper." Where Baxter sweats, Josselin defecates, but both imagine corporeal excretion as critical acts of their spiritual life. Josselin here describes a striking link between a tactic of physical purgation that removes a humoral fluid known to produce excessive anger, and the sincere expression of devotional gratitude. The sentence moves without blinking from body to spirit. On another occasion, Josselin remembers: "I was ill in my stomacke, and yett very loth to enter into a course of phisicke[.] [T]his weeke I had a great looseness and griping of my body, avoyding thereby much choller, which I looke upon as a good providence of god towards me." God apparently works in mysterious ways, approaching his creatures even through their digestive tract. As John Harington remarks in his notorious *Metamorphosis of Ajax*, "[A] good stoole might move as great devotion in some man, as a bad sermon."[21] Franciscus Van Helmont's *Paradoxical Discourses* (translated into English in 1685) depicts the stomach as a literal location of divinity, indeed, as the holiest of holies:

> Forasmuch as the Body of Man, according to the testimony of Scripture, is, and should be the Temple of God.... And that in the Temple at Jerusalem, there was an Altar of Burnt-offering, upon which many Beasts, &C. was offered: and seeing that all the meat a man feeds upon enters into the stomach, might not the stomach be compared with the said Altar? And might it not properly be called an Altar in the Temple of God, on which all right and well ordered food for the life of man, is to be offered up?[22]

Indeed, the point of George Herbert's poem "The H. Communion" is that God chooses to enter his creatures "Not in rich furniture, or fine array" but "by the way of nourishment and strength," that is, through the alimentary canal in the eucharistic meal. The stomach is thus the receiving chamber in which God is welcomed into the temple of the self. Herbert's "The Rose," moreover, explores just the linkage between devotional aspiration and therapeutic purgation articulated by Baxter and Josselin. In this poem, Herbert praises the divine wisdom behind the fact that a rose is at once a source of sensual pleasure and a medical purgative: "What is fairer than a rose? / What is sweeter? Yet it purgeth." Explicitly linking the airing of one's inmost sins to the therapeutic removal of humoral excess, Herbert declares that "Repentance is a purge." The poem "Lent" praises fasting by linking "fulnesse" with "sluttish fumes, / Sowre exhalations, and dishonest rheumes," gastrointestinal disorders that "Reveng[e] the delight" one ostensibly took in stuffing oneself (lines 19–24), and contrasting this dyspepsia with "the cleannesse of sweet abstinence," which produces "Quick thoughts and motions at a small expense." Feasting, then, is understood to produce abiding discomfort rather than the gastronomic pleasure it promises. Afflicted with perpetual ill health, Herbert translated Luigi Cornaro's *Treatise of Temperance and Sobrietie*, a work devoted to the pragmatic benefits of the moral virtue of dietary temperance. "He which lives a temperate life," Cornaro promises, "cannot fall into diseases, and very seldom into indispositions; because Temperance takes away the cause of most diseases."[23]

The enormous medical, ethical, and religious significance of what goes in and out of the stomach receives perhaps its most extensive literary statement in *Paradise Lost*, where Milton not only "images forth the cosmos as a vast anthropomorphic digestive system" but also reminds us repeatedly that the originary myth of western culture is a narrative of dietary transgression.[24] After Adam and Eve eat the forbidden fruit and take "their *fill* of love and love's disport" (my italics), they fall asleep, and experience the first terrestrial case of insomnia caused by indigestion:

> Soon as the force of that fallacious fruit,
> That with exhilarating vapor bland
> About their spirits had played, and inmost powers
> Made err, was now exhaled, and grosser sleep
> Bred of unkindly fumes, with conscious dreams
> Encumbered, now had left them, up they rose
> As from unrest.
>
> (9.1042–52)

One of the bitterest jokes suffusing Milton's portrait of the Fall is the indigestion it causes. At the Fall, humanity not only troubles its own house but also inherits the wind. This troubled sleep is in deliberate and stark contrast to Adam's rest before the fall, which "Was aery light, from pure digestion bred, / And temperate vapors bland" (5.4–5). Good digestion occupies a central position in Milton's ethical universe.[25] Indeed, in a poignant letter to Leonard Philaras explaining in detail the symptoms that accompanied the loss of his sight in the hope that Philaras might consult with a French physician about a cure, Milton remembers:

> It is ten years, I think more or less, since I noticed my sight becoming weak and growing dim, and at the same time my spleen and all my viscera burdened and shaken with flatulence.... Certain permanent vapors seem to have settled upon my entire forehead and temples, which press and oppress my eyes.

Milton here records a fascinating link between the onset of gastrointestinal distress—itself an immediate product of the Fall in his account—and the beginnings of his own blindness. Contemporaneous physiology would affirm this causal link between flatulence and the dimming of sight, since internal vapors were known to rise from the smoky furnace of the belly to the head, and cloud the eyes as well as other mental faculties. As Lemnius remarks in *The Touchstone of Complexions*, "[T]he fulsome vapours (which as it were out of a dampishe marshe or stinkinge Camerine) strike upward, do annoye the Brayne with greevous and odious fumes, and distemper the spirits Animall with a strange forreine qualitie."[26]

One of the most chilling passages in *Paradise Lost* is the Bosch-like vision of the manifold diseases—far more devastating than even blindness—that "Intemperance . . . In Meats and Drinks" shall bestow upon humanity:

> Immediately a place
> Before his eyes appeared, sad, noisome, dark,
> A lazar-house it seemed, wherein were laid
> Numbers of all diseas'd, all maladies
> Of ghastly spasm, or racking torture, qualms
> Of heart-sick agony, all feverous kinds,
> Convulsions, epilepsies, fierce catarrhs,
> Intestine stone and ulcer, colic pangs,
> Demoniac frenzy, moping melancholy
> And moon-struck madness, pining atrophy,
> Marasmus, and wide-wasting pestilence,
> Dropsies, and asthmas, and joint-racking rheums.
>
> (11.477–88)

Such variegated corporeal agony, Michael argues, awaits those who "serve ungoverned appetite" and "pervert pure nature's healthful rules / To loathsome sickness." But Michael also promises Adam that "if thou well observe / The rule of not too much, by temperance taught / In what thou eat'st and drink'st, seeking from thence / Due nourishment, not gluttonous delight," he will ameliorate the horrible physical effects of the inevitable corporeal decay that his first act of transgressive consumption has precipitated. If the Fall is a failure to follow a dietary regimen prescribed by God, regulation of what goes into and out of the stomach by reference to the far more challenging "rule of not too much" becomes a central spiritual and physiological therapy.

The stomach, then, can be seen to have played a central role in the development of political individuation and the articulation of devotional inwardness in early modern England. Far more complex than the proverbial paunch of self-indulgence, the early modern stomach was a primal site for the exercise of ethical discrimination and moral virtue. The writers we have explored are not voracious gluttons whose god is their belly but rather judicious consumers whose belly is the way to God. In a commendatory note "To the Readers" prefacing Phineas Fletcher's *Purple Island* (itself an extended imitation of Spenser's Castle of Alma), the Conformist divine Daniel Featley remarks: "he that would learn *Theologie*, must first studie *Autologie*. The way to God is by our selves: It is a blinde and dirty way; it hath many windings, and is easie to be lost: This Poem will make thee understand that way."[27]

Traversing this "blinde and dirty way," through the interior spaces of the consuming subject, is a voyage that a surprising number of early modern writers felt obliged to make. If this alimentary path seems to us a particularly grotesque and unseemly route to knowledge of self and God, the fault perhaps lies not so much in these early modern writers as in our own historically contingent and severely attenuated conceptions of what arenas of knowledge are most pertinent to the comprehension and expression of the inward self.

Notes

1. Edward Reynoldes, *Treatise of the Passions and Faculties of the Soule of Man* (London, 1640), 185–86.

2. Sir Thomas Elyot, *The Castel of Helth (1541)*, ed. Samuel Tannenbaum (New York: Scholars' Facsimiles & Reprints, 1937); 74v. The *Castel* was very popular, going through at least fifteen editions between 1539 and 1610.

3. William Vaughan, *Directions for Health, Naturall and Artificiall* (London, 1626), 168.

4. In "Of a cold and dry Complexion," in *The Touchstone of Complexions*, trans. T. Newton (1565), Levinus Lemnius notes that many have been made ill "by the stayng of their Hemorrhoides, and stopping of their naturall Purgations or Flowers, or by the restraint of some ordinary and accustomed issue" (quoted in *The Frame of Order*, ed. James Winny [London: George Allen, 1957], 51). Mikhail Bakhtin, *Rabelais and his World*, trans. Helene Iswolsky (Cambridge: MIT Press, 1968). Work that has been influenced by Bakhtin includes Peter Stallybrass and Allon White, *The Politics and Poetics and of Transgression* (Ithaca: Cornell University Press, 1986); Peter Stallybrass, "Patriarchal Territories: The Body Enclosed," in *Rewriting the Renaissance: The Discourses of Sexual Difference in Early Modern Europe*, ed. Margaret Ferguson et al. (Chicago: University of Chicago Press, 1986), 123–42; "Reading the Body: The Revenger's Tragedy and the Jacobean Theater of Consumption," *Renaissance Drama* 18 (1987): 121–48; and Gail Kern Paster, *The Body Embarrassed: Drama*

and the Disciplines of Shame in Early Modern Europe (Ithaca: Cornell University Press, 1993). See also Paster's chapter in this volume.

5. John Veslingus, *The Anatomy of the Body of Man*, trans. Nicholas Culpepper (London, 1677), 11–12; Thomas Vicary, *A Profitable Treatise of the Anatomy of Mans Bodie* (London, 1577), 67, 69. Sir Thomas Elyot likewise explains how the liver, a hot organ, "is to the stomake, as fyre under the pot" (*Castel of Helth*, 46v).

6. Vaughan, *Directions for Health*, 168. *Du Bartas His Divine Weekes and Workes*, trans. Joshua Sylvester (London, 1641), Sixth Day, First Week, lines 712–36, in *The Complete Works of Joshuah Sylvester*, ed. A. B. Grosart, 2 vols. (New York: AMS Press, 1967), 1:78. For a further discussion of the blood and veins, see Paster's chapter in this volume.

7. See Kenneth Muir, "Menenius's Fable," *Notes and Queries*, June 1953, 240–42, and Leonard Barkan, *Nature's Work of Art: The Human Body as Image of the World* (New Haven: Yale University Press, 1975), 95–109, on the various deployments of the fable from Plutarch through Shakespeare. Phineas Fletcher, *The Purple Island or the Isle of Man* (Cambridge, 1633), 20, marginalia, note to canto 2, st. 14.

8. The larger patterns of eating in *Coriolanus* have been analyzed well from a psychoanalytic perspective by Janet Adelman, "'Anger's My Meat': Feeding, Dependency, and Aggression in *Coriolanus*," in *Representing Shakespeare: New Psychoanalytic Essays*, ed. Murray Schwartz and Coppelia Kahn (Baltimore: Johns Hopkins University Press, 1980), 129–49. *Coriolanus* 1.1.98–146, from *The Riverside Shakespeare*, ed. G. Blakemore Evans (Boston: Houghton Mifflin, 1974), 1397–98.

9. *Edmund Spenser: The Faerie Queene*, ed. Thomas P. Roche (Harmondsworth: Penguin, 1978). On the literary history of the body as a castle, see Chilton Powell, "The Castle of the Body," *Studies in Philology* 16 (1919): 197–205. Elyot's *Castel of Helth*, of course, gets its title from just this concept.

10. Vicary, *A Profitable Treatise*, 65; Elyot, *Castel of Helth*, 53.

11. Robert Burton, *The Anatomy of Melancholy*, ed. Thomas C. Faulkner, Nicholas Kiessling, and Rhonda Blair, 2 vols. (Oxford: Clarendon Press, 1989), pt 2, sec. 1, mem. 4, subs. 3, 2:18. Jonathan Sawday, "The Uncanny Body," in *The Body Emblazoned: Dissection and the Human Body in Renaissance Culture* (London: Routledge, 1995), 141–82, discusses the blend of familiarity and estrangement in Renaissance accounts of the interior body.

12. Lemnius, "Of a Compound Complexion," in *Touchstone of Complexions*, quoted in *The Frame of Order*, ed. James Winny (London: George Allen, 1957), 29–30 .

13. Michel Foucault, *The Care of the Self*, vol. 3 of *The History of Sexuality*, trans. Robert Hurley (New York: Random House, 1986). Vaughan, *Directions for Health*, 143.

14. Elyot, *Castel of Helth*, 15v–16. William Harrison explains the predilections of English diet by reference to the English climate: "The situation of our region, lying near unto the north, doth cause the heat of our stomachs to be of somewhat greater force; therefore our bodies do crave a little more ample nourishment than the inhabitants of the hotter regions are accustomed withal, whose digestive force is not altogether so vehement, because their internal heat is not so strong as ours, which is kept in by the coldness of the air that from time to time (especially in winter) doth environ our bodies" (*Description of England*, ed. Georges Edelen [Ithaca: Cornell University Press, 1968], 123–24).

15. Burton, *Anatomy of Melancholy*, pt. 2, sec. 2, mem. 1, subs. 2, 2:27. *Paracelsus: Selected Writings*, ed. Jolande Jacobi, trans. Norbert Guterman (Princeton: Bollingen, 1951), 87:

16. *Anatomy of Melancholy*, pt. 1, sec. 2, mem. 2, subs. 2, 1:221; pt. 1, sec. 2, mem. 3, subs. 1, 1:247.

17. Lemnius, "Of a cold and dry Complexion," 50. Vaughan, *Directions for Health*, 62.

18. *Certaine Sermons or Homilies Appointed to be Read in Churches in the Time of Queen Elizabeth (1547–1571): A Facsimile Reproduction of the Edition of 1623*, ed. Mary Ellen Rickey and Thomas B. Stroup, 2 vols. in 1 (Gainesville: Scholars' Facsimiles and Reprints, 1968), 2:98.

19. *Reliquae Baxterianae* (London, 1696), pt. 1, 9; p. 3, 173.

20. *Reliquae*, pt. 1, 10 and 11. This is a less festive regime than it might first appear to modern palates, since beer was at once a far more common drink and a far less alcoholic drink than it is today.

21. *Diary of Ralph Josselin, 1616–1683*, ed. Alan Macfarlane (London: British Academy, 1976), 112, 122. On Josselin, see Lucinda Beier, "In Sickness and in Health: A Seventeenth-Century Family's Experience," and Andrew Wear, "Puritan Perceptions of Illness,"in *Patients and Practitioners: Lay Perceptions of Medicine in Pre-Industrial Society*, ed. Roy Porter (Cambridge: Cambridge University Press, 1985). Sir John Harington, *A New Discourse on a Stale Subject, Called the Metamorphosis of Ajax*, ed. Elizabeth Story Donno (New York: Columbia University Press, 1962), 92.

22. *The Paradoxal Discourses of F. M. Van Helmont, Concerning the Macrocosm and Microcosm of the Greater and Lesser World, and their Union* (London, 1685), 97.

23. I have discussed the relationship between Herbert's dietary practices and his emphasis on devotional inwardness more fully in "George Herbert's Consuming Subject," *George Herbert in the Nineties: Reflections and Reassessments*, ed. Jonathan F. S. Post and Sidney Gottlieb (George Herbert Journal, Special Studies and Monographs, 1995), 105–32. In *The Golden-Grove* (London, 1608), William Vaughan offers a similar defense of the salutary aspects of fasting, noting that "by flesh the body is enflamed, and tormented with hot burning agues, and with innumerable maladies besides. So that the commodities of fasting, do farr exceed and downwaigh the discommodities therof" (bk. 2, chap. 39, "Of Fasting").

24. Barkan, *Nature's Work of Art*, 44–45, commenting on *Paradise Lost* 5.415–26.

25. All citations are to *Paradise Lost*, ed. Scott Elledge (New York: Norton, 1975). In his tract *Of Education*, Milton recommends that students study medicine "that they may know the tempers, the humors, the seasons, and how to manage a crudity," that is, a bout of indigestion; he suggests further that music "would not be unexpedient after meat to assist and cherish nature in her first concoction" (*Complete Prose Works of John Milton* [New Haven: Yale University Press, 1959], 2:392–93, 411).

26. *Complete Prose Works*, 4, pt. II, 869. William Kerrigan discusses this passage with great insight in *The Sacred Complex: On the Psychogenesis of Paradise Lost* (Cambridge: Harvard University Press, 1983), 202–3. In *Health for the Rich and Poor, by Diet, without Physick* (London, 1670), 126, Nicholas Culpepper explains that the dimming of sight in the elderly occurs "because the Optick Nerves are clouded with superfluous Humors and Vapors, whereby the Animal Spirits, which are subservient to the sight, are either darkned or choaked in their progress." This "impediment," Culpepper continues, "is taken away by Sobriety in Diet." Lemnius, "Of a Compound Complexion," 50.

27. Fletcher, *Purple Island*, "To the Readers."

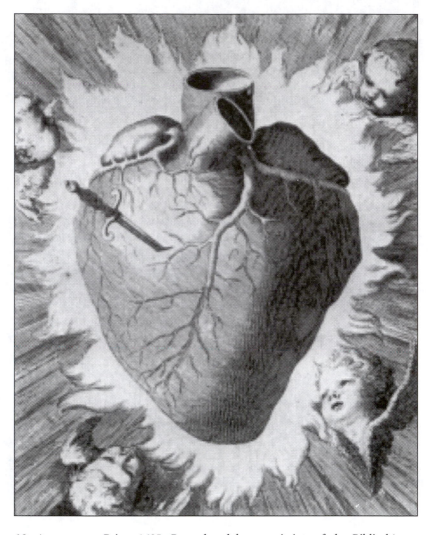

13. Anonymous Print, 1685. Reproduced by permission of the Bibliothèque Nationale de France, Paris.

13

Sacred Heart and Secular Brain

SCOTT MANNING STEVENS

"The Sacred Brain of Jesus"—why should that phrase strike us as shocking or even disturbing when the art of Western Christianity is replete with images of the exposed heart of Christ? Though medical scholars have acknowledged the brain as the center of mental activity (including our emotions and desires) since the late seventeenth century, the brain's representation has remained curiously taboo in Christian iconography. One might find it difficult to visualize an image of Christ's exposed brain and yet his bleeding and disembodied heart is the subject of countless representations in Western art. Explanations of this more traditional iconography focus on the physical heart of Jesus as symbol or metaphor for the incarnation of the divine on earth. Far from being a metaphor for the soul, Christ's heart operates as the reification of his human, fleshly, and mortal body. Ancient and medieval medical authorities alike had long recognized the central importance of both the heart and brain, but the question was one of predominance. Hierarchical systems required an ascending scale of importance in which one organ was seen to "rule"—and so the debate over the brain and heart.

Devotional practices specifically focused on Christ's heart have a long history in the Western church. Bonaventura and Aquinas make frequent references to the Sacred Heart in their scriptural and devotional writings, and a host of medieval mystics record visions that led them to venerate the Sacred Heart. Among these figures are Hildegard of Bingen, Gertrude of Helfta, Julian of Norwich, and Saint Francis of Rome. Significantly, in many of these cases the heart is not the sole object of devotion but, rather, is seen in relationship to the holy wound on Christ's side and the mysteries surrounding the Eucharist. It is not until the latter half of the seventeenth century that the Sacred Heart begins to emerge as a specific object of popular devotion with a liturgy of its own.

The French Jesuit John Eudes and the Visitandine nun Margaret Mary Alacoque are the architects of the specific Counter-Reformation liturgy devoted to the adoration of the Sacred Heart. Whereas earlier attention had focused on the pierced heart as a symbol of suffering and sacrifice, the seventeenth-century liturgy concentrated on the physical heart of Christ as the symbol of his humanity.[1] In Catholic Christological terms the heart of Christ is the symbol of the center of his person. The devotional liturgy of the Sacred Heart gained increasing popularity in Roman Catholic countries throughout the eighteenth and nineteenth centuries. Finally this liturgy was reexamined in the mid-twentieth century by Vatican theologians who believed the church needed to explicitly define its position concerning the nature of the Sacred Heart itself.[2] Pius XII's papal encyclical entitled *Haurietis Aquas* further explicated the devotion, and the Second Vatican Council resolved that Christ "loved with a human heart."[3] It is in regard to the historical belatedness of this formulation of Christ's "person" in the liturgy of the Sacred Heart that I came to my questions concerning what I have referred to as the Sacred Brain of Jesus.

What are the issues involved in a liturgical practice that locates Christ's self in the image of the heart precisely at a juncture in history when medical science is coming to recognize the brain as the center of the human self? What is the impact of anatomy and physiology, which developed with remarkable speed in the period between Vesalius and Harvey, on cultural notions of the body and the discourse of self and subjectivity? With the movement toward a psychophysical parallelism that would come to locate all mental activity—intellect and affect alike—in the brain, what led the church to elevate the heart as a metaphor for person? The paradox of this preference of the heart over the brain as the locus of self (in the face of growing physiological evidence to the contrary) is at the center of my present study. In this context the development of the liturgy of the Sacred Heart may appear to be just one reactionary move among many in the post-Tridentine theology of the Counter-Reformation.[4] Did the church inadvertently remove itself from a "real world" discourse—one in which it had been dominant during the height of Scholasticism's sway over European intellectual life—only to find itself occupying the position of the "merely" metaphorical?[5]

A brief survey of what I shall call the terms of the real debate will help to contextualize these questions. It is easy to fall into a false dichotomy when discussing the respective roles of brain and heart, but such a split would grossly oversimplify the complex and heterodox systems of meaning ascribed to each organ over the centuries. Recently, for example, one scholar has asserted that there was considerably less confusion over brain function in the past than we have been led to believe. Taking as a starting point Shakespeare's well-known lines sung preceding Bassanio's choice of caskets in the *Merchant of Venice*—"Tell me where is fancy bred / Or in the heart, or in the head?"—Ynez Violé O'Neill writes that "this couplet seems to suggest that the bard and other Tudor laymen were confused about the site of the imagination. Contemporary physicians, surgeons, and most artists had no such problem."[6] Such a sweeping generalization about medical authorities in Shakespeare's time ignores the myriad of competing theories of mind in that period, while simultaneously creating the impression that Shakespeare's use of the word *fancy* lacks any poly-valent significance. Both assumptions should be avoided if we are to arrive at an understanding of the debate between brain and heart in the early modern period.

Among the first obstacles we are likely to encounter when investigating historical conceptions of the brain, its function and significance, is a con-fusing array of terminologies concerning the nature of the mind. The words *psyche, pneuma, anima, spiritus,* or *mens* rarely have the satisfactory or con-vincing technical specificity that we have come to demand from scientific language. Hence the desire to generalize among scholars when presenting an overview of the past—even though in the case of the brain we are still faced with similar difficulties in defining spirit and soul or psyche and mind. It is important to keep in mind that although Plato, Theophrastes, Democritus and Diogenes had stressed the brain as the focal point of bodily activity, none of their respective theories agreed with one another and some were in no way biologically based.[7] Aristotle and his followers, on the other hand, laid stress on the heart as the location of the soul as the vital force and source of human agency.

For Plato, the soul was organized along a tripartite model, with the appetitive aspect located in the midriff, passion in the breast, and the rea-soning soul in the brain. One important element of this model—one that would remain potent throughout the Renaissance—was the imposition of hierarchy on this schema. Almost no part of the Platonic model is based on biological observation. Aristotle's notion, by contrast, is greatly complicated by his own ideas of biology and metaphysics. In the end, Aristotle cannot posit a soul independent of the body any more than he could uphold the concept of matter without form. The categories were mutually dependent. While the vital force most like our term *soul* is found throughout the whole body, it emanates from the heart, which is the seat of life and heat. Aristotle worked under the premise that the heart was the first organ formed in the embryonic state and the last organ to cease before death. The life force it contained manifested itself in movement and heat, without which life would not be present. Cognition most likely emanated from the heart in Aristotle's system as well, but repaired to the brain as the organ specifically formed for this purpose.

The development of an organicist model of life in Hippocratic and Aristotelian writings was given further articulation in Rome by the Greek physician Galen. Although Galen had subscribed to inherited Greek notions of the humors and their effect on the human body, he greatly expanded these theories and attempted to provide a more cohesive sense of their relationship to the whole human system.[8] This departed from the Aristotelian model in which the heart controlled the entire body as the source of life and heat. In the Galenic model the three principal members controlled three separate but necessarily interconnected systems within the body. These were the heart, the brain, and the liver. This model put the brain on a higher level than Aristotelian physiology had, but it in turn would be undermined with Avicenna's attempt to reconcile Aristotelianism and Galenic medicine. The heart thus regained its nominal primacy over the other principle members, though they retained an elevated status in the body.

Because Avicenna's work was the primary source for most medieval scholars of the body, the heart's central importance was guaranteed as long as Avicenna's authority held out. But one of the most influential concepts of human physiology in the Middle Ages came from outside the Greco-Arabic medical tradition: the Christian Bible and the patristic writings had a decisive influence on the study of human physiology—especially under the influence of Thomasian Scholasticism.[9] With the achievement of a monumental synthesis of the Aristotelian and Christian traditions, the heart would retain its pride of place in conceptions of its status relative to the other organs of the human body. Brain function continued to be investigated by physicians and anatomists but often with the foregone conclusion that their observations must be made to incorporate an inherited system that had taken on the trappings of dogma. As Nancy Siraisi points out, most medical faculties in Europe required a scholastic liberal arts education as preparation for the study of medicine.[10] This would seem to secure a certain level of stasis in scientific endeavors unless Scholasticism and the authority of Aristotle were challenged.

By briefly surveying the development of these concepts concerning brain and heart function, I wish to point to the heterodox tradition that existed as the Renaissance approached. Most records of medieval physiology show that the contradictions within the various authorities of the past were a primary subject of medical investigation. No one position ever held universal sway, nor did any disappear completely.

Shakespeare's question, then, regarding the location of "fancy" in either heart or head was hardly unproblematic. Nor, for that matter, can one simply assert that the word "fancy" refers to the imagination in an uncomplicated way; in the idiom of Shakespeare's English, "fancy" is just as likely to refer to desire, taste, or (significantly) affect.[11] Where does human desire— or taste, or affect, or imagination—have its source? In the heart or in the brain? The considerable slippage around the term is precisely what motivates Shakespeare's question and points us back to the real terms of the debate. Affect and intellect (which includes imagination) were, according to the majority of authorities, located in the heart and head respectively during this period. The question is, then, which of these has precedence in defining our notions of self? Are we primarily defined by our affective or intellectual qualities? For most of us today, the affective and intellectual are both located in the brain and from this perspective Shakespeare's song might be said to make little sense. But seventeenth-century physiology was only beginning to question the function of the heart as a muscle and not as an organ of thought, or at least not the center of our emotional life. These categories were in no way rigidly defined. Thus Donne can refer to his "naked thinking Heart" in "The Blossom," just as Shakespeare's Prospero describes his "beating mind."[12]

In an intellectual culture given to imposing hierarchies on conceptual models or systems, one would naturally ask which of the organs was in effect the source of the self. According to the principal members theory, one should be in command of the others (though the liver seems never to have been a real contender). The self was surely constituted of both affect and intellect, heart and head, but which should govern?

The heterodox nature of the debate persisted well into (and indeed beyond) the Renaissance. One of the great departures of early modern science and philosophy was from the inherited organicist model toward a mechanistic understanding of the universe and the human body. But always present (if perhaps only in the background) were the semimagical concepts found in the traditions of alchemy, numerology, and astrology. These alternative paradigms for knowing were often upheld by figures who actively pursued what we might now mistakenly term "legitimate" scientific inquiry. Giordano Bruno is the great Continental example of this, and Robert Fludd is the most prominent British figure of the magical-scientific school. Fludd, for example, was able to accept Harvey's notion of the circulation of the blood while busily developing his microcosmic views on the nature of man. Much has been made of Fludd's Rosicrucian beliefs, but I would hold that these views were not so much formative of Fludd's program as indicative of a mind-set that sought to rationalize the supernatural and yet retain its faith.[13] That faith was not only in God but in the equally ancient notion that one could discover the key to the interconnectedness of all meaning (on a macrocosmic level). Such epistemes were naturally the hallmark of a culture confronting the apparent conflict between a nascent positivism and ancient notions of the divine.

Ironically, some of the more discordant aspects found in early mechanists' views of the universe, such as those that Mersenne and Descartes proposed, may make more sense when held in regard to a thinker like Fludd. Whereas Fludd privileged inherited systems over empirical evidence, Descartes put method over all. His program of systematic skepticism should likely have ended in a profound doubt concerning the existence of a divine being and the human soul. Much of his work is of course seen as contributing to a modern rationalist/materialist understanding of the world. Thus, we can draw the conclusion, if we follow Descartes's method, that consciousness is the phenomenon produced by the incomprehensibly complex "machine" we know as the brain. Yet, Descartes never makes this leap; instead he chose to fall back on an inherited notion of the soul. There was naturally a problem inherent in such a conclusion: How did the soul act on the body if it is independent of it? Descartes solved this problem with the curious choice of the pineal gland as the site of interaction between the two worlds of mind (which Descartes used interchangeably with the soul) and body. Aside from the unfortunate choice of the pineal gland as the virtual location of the soul, Descartes is probably best known for the so-called mind-body split. But, in regard to the debate between brain and heart, one might be justified in invoking a "mind-brain split"—we are much more likely to invoke the word "mind" as conceptually separate from the word "brain," whereas "heart" may be used interchangeably as metaphor or physical object.

Descartes did not in fact locate the soul in the pineal gland to the exclusion of the rest of the body. The brain and, specifically, the pineal gland were the physiological sites of interaction (what has been referred to as the *virtual site*) between mind and body, but the soul as mind or consciousness was conceived of as existing throughout the human frame.[14] The conscious or thinking self for Descartes may be seen as having its primary receptors in the brain because it is the terminus of sensory perception—especially given that the organs of sight, hearing, smell, and taste are all located in the head. But the soul in this schema was unitary, unlike the tripartite model inherited from Plato and Aristotle. For Descartes, the unitary soul was the immortal soul of Christian doctrine. The much-discussed Cartesian split between mind and body is not as clearly defined in Descartes's writings as one might presume. In order not to denigrate the physical self or human body, Descartes made the union of body and soul integral to his definition of a human being. In the "Sixth Meditation" he writes, "Nature also teaches me . . . that I am not only lodged in my body as a pilot in a vessel, but that I am very closely united to it, and so to speak so intermingled with it, that I seem to compose with it one whole."[15]

This is significant not only in terms of the debate over the nature of Cartesian dualism but even more so in the larger terms of Descartes's project for the physical sciences and our understanding of empirical evidence. Had dualism been the defining character of Descartes's conception of the self as *res cogitans,* we would merely have been left with another version of idealism. Rather, the seemingly disembodied rational mind is able to interact with and comprehend the material world through abstract and unified conceptual models (based on mathematics) and act as a check on the unreliable senses. The human brain may be physiological or mechanical, but it would ultimately be understood through its own powers of "right reason" and Cartesian method. What I have called the mind-brain split is a radical departure from the conceptions of the composition of self held by most of Descartes's contemporaries.

Among these contemporaries perhaps the most orthodox in his views was Robert Burton; we can thus turn to his work in order to find a more traditional view of mental inwardness and its connection to the body. Burton's physiology is Galenic, though his psychological investigations go beyond the standard medical explanations of his day. Along with the system of the humors, Burton also subscribed to the system of the three principal members:

> Of the noble [parts] there be three principal parts, to which all three belong, and whom they serve, *brain, heart, liver;* according to whose site,

three regions, on a threefold division, is made of the whole body. As first of the *head*, in which the animal organs are contained, and brain itself, which by his nerves give sense and motion to the rest, and is (as it were) a Privy Counsellor, and Chancellor, to the *Heart*. The second region is the chest, or *middle belly*, in which the *Heart* as King keeps his Court, and by his arteries communicates life to the whole body.[16]

Like Bacon and many others, Burton draws on traditional metaphors of the body politic to explain the organization of the principal members.

Burton's employment of a politicized body seems to indicate that the heart, as "king," would have the most effect on our inward state, but it is in fact the brain, his "Privy Counsellor," that turns out to be the power behind the throne. This underscores the issue of precedence in the system of the principal members as well as Burton's own ambivalence as to the respective "rule" of the heart and brain. Jacques Le Goff has recently traced some of these shifts within the political uses of body metaphors from the classical past to the Middle Ages and found considerable flexibility in these paradigms, depending on the rhetorical needs of a given political discourse.[17]

The primary shifts that Le Goff notes in his study occur as the classical period's metaphors are replaced by the political rhetoric of predominantly Christian states in medieval Europe. The heart takes on new prominence because of its central position in the body and, more importantly, because of the authority of biblical metaphors. This reconfiguration of the metaphorical uses of the head and heart correlates with the struggles experienced between the church and state in that period. The church could claim to be the heart of a state while the king was its head—but the question still remained, which had greater authority? Though the heart is the seat of our life force and necessary for the continued existence of the body, it falls short of the brain in defining our selves. The brain, according to Burton, "is the most noble organ under heaven, the dwelling-house and seat of the soul, the habitation of wisdom, memory, and in which man is most like unto God."[18]

The often paradoxical positions held by Burton concerning the nature of the soul and its location in the body should not surprise us, given his love of the arcane and heterodox. His work serves to remind us that there was a myriad of published opinions on the human mind and body circulating in the seventeenth century.[19] Any attempt to reduce these theories to an either-or situation would be facile. As long as the soul was held to exist by the majority of educated people writing in a given period, we can expect to find a wide array of theories that draw on the physical sciences, psychology, metaphysics, and even magic.

Such questions as these concerning the location of the soul, whether it found its seat in the brain or emanated from the heart and was coextensive with the entire body, did not constitute the only issues of the debate between head and heart. This debate was further complicated by the Christian concept of the conscience. "Conscience" and "consciousness," it is worth noting, were used interchangeably in the early modern period; the split in our usage of those terms is, significantly, a post-Cartesian one. For Christians, like the Platonists before them, our moral sensibility was founded on our ability to perceive the good—in the case of Christianity, the Good was defined as the divine or holiness. The source of this goodness was likewise external, but unlike the Platonic system, it was not perceived by the intellect but, rather, by the conscience, which was thought to reside in the heart. In almost all the systems discussed thus far the heart was considered to be the seat of the passions and hence the site of our affective sensibilities, but Christianity brought to it the perceptive abilities of the conscience. Xavier-Léon Dufore has pointed out that the New Testament stresses the heart as "the center of decisive things, of the moral conscience, of unwritten law, [and] of encounters with God."[20] This in effect allowed the heart to "know" things in a way that the brain could not. Confusion is natural in this case because of the considerable slippage within the terminology employed in the discourse of inwardness. Once the Greek *psyche* had become identified with the immortal Christian soul and then later used interchangeably with mind and soul in Descartes's writings, those searching for definitive categories within the early modern period were bound to be frustrated.

Because the heart, enlightened by the Holy Spirit, could *perceive*, it was more than the receptor of the passions. The heart could on some level compete with the brain as a locus of perception through its ability to perceive things unseen. This ability occurred not through the affections but through the moral sensibility of the conscience—as Saint Paul would have it, "the law written in their hearts." Patristic writings expounded on this notion and often opposed conscience to the intellect. (The analogue to the conscience may be the *super ego* of Freudian psychology, but for the Fathers of the church its location was in the heart.)

Sixteenth-century Catholicism produced many manuals of systematic theology to counter the challenges of the Reformation. Again we will choose a typical example—Johannes de Combis's theological work, *Compendium totius theologicae veritatis,* published in Venice in 1554. Here, de Combis locates the soul within the heart and draws on classical and medieval medical authorities to support the church's position. The use of medical texts or those of natural philosophy to support metaphysical claims was not uncommon, given the interconnectedness of these disciplines under the macrosystem of Scholasticism, but it was becoming increasingly complicated to rein in the natural sciences and make them conform to the relative stasis of accepted doctrine.

The church found itself involved in a two-front struggle waged against its authority: on the one hand Protestantism, and on the other, the so-called New Science. Galileo's case is the most infamous illustration of the church's inability to incorporate innovations in scientific method and theory. The debate over head and heart follows a similar trajectory. Roger French has pointed out in his study of Harvey that scholastic science, relying as it did on both classical and biblical texts, was increasingly used to define theological positions. In the case of the soul, French writes, "the purely theological account of the soul from sources like Augustine took on physical attributes and functions."[21] French points to the case of Nicolas de Nancel (1539–1610) as illustrative of the Counter-Reformation response to questions posed by natural philosophy and reform theology alike. In the 1580s, de Nancel wrote his *Problema, An sedes animae in cerebre? an in corde? aut ubi denique?* [22] The debate over the seat of the soul was, of course, an ancient one, but de Nancel's response, which held that the soul is incontrovertibly located in the heart, is typical of the Counter-Reformation's increasingly rigid dogmatic stance in the face of scientific innovation.

It is in fact this dogmatic stance that marks the Counter-Reformation's interaction with the scientific revolution as it progressed throughout the seventeenth century. Figures such as de Nancel would willingly turn to natural philosophy to bolster traditional metaphysical positions but would simultaneously reject much of what we now consider advances in science. Theological dogma's seemingly static epistemological position inevitably pitted it against a progressive scientific model. The scientific triumphalism of the later seventeenth century that led to the Enlightenment was often countered by reactionary policies dictated by the Catholic authorities.

When attempting to understand Descartes's theories of brain function, specifically those concerning the interaction between body and soul, we would do well to recall Robert Merton's thesis, wherein he posits Catholic hostility to the new sciences, without allowing that thesis to supply any foregone conclusions. Descartes, it is known, was careful not to offend Catholic authorities in France and may have suppressed the publication of his own *Treatise on Man* to this end. But fear of reprisal from Catholic authorities does not explain the equation of the soul with consciousness in Descartes's system any more than religious sentimentality would.[23]

Returning to the question of the head and heart, and more specifically the Sacred Brain of Jesus, I wish to examine briefly certain iconographic traditions of the early modern period in relationship to physiology and the self. Vesalian anatomy had done much to demystify the hidden interior of the body. The dramatic advances in anatomy in the subsequent years provide proof of the impact of Vesalius's work, but the physiology of the brain remained obscure. The heart, on the other hand, was more readily comprehensible to anatomists, who like Harvey, began to understand its "mechanical" function.

Harvey, perhaps following Bacon's example, chose not to address metaphysical or theological issues surrounding the heart. By excluding these aspects from his study, he offers a tacit critique of notions concerning the seat of the soul. The debates over Harvey's work in England and on the Continent were concerned with his thesis on the circulation of the blood, not with the soul. Most conservative physicians realized the implications of Harvey's work for the accepted Galenic system and rushed to Galen's defense. Occasionally, this meant drawing on Scholastic authorities and sometimes even theological works, but by the late seventeenth century most leading medical authorities had accepted the Harvean model. This eventually led to a split between medical and theological faculties. The heart was still discussed both as a muscle in material terms and the seat of the soul in what would be seen increasingly as metaphoric terms. Descartes's mechanistic conception of the body still contained mysteries, but it was increasingly obvious from Harvey's work onward that the heart was a muscle best understood as a pump. If the body offered a "real" reification of the self it was to be found in the brain.

Unlike the brain, the heart had enjoyed a long tradition as an unambiguous symbol of love. Since the early Middle Ages Christian iconography had used the heart in poetry and the visual arts to represent one of the most profound of human emotions. With the advent of print technology, the emblem tradition became a popular means of disseminating a devotional literature that combined both text and visual representations. Images of the heart, whether a stylized human heart or the Sacred Heart of Jesus, became favorite subjects of emblem writers in both Catholic and Protestant societies. Barbara Lewalski has pointed out that the Protestant traditions treated the heart as the object of God's transcendent and redeeming will as it was acted upon by the Divine.[24] In keeping with Calvinist belief, the heart was a more passive receptor of God's grace rather than an active participant in the process of redemption. Catholics, on the other hand, traced their emblem tradition back to the Jesuit spiritual exercises whereby the heart is surrendered to God. Later the Counter-Reformation would emphasize this surrender in terms of penance and reparation. Émile Mâle has pointed out the use of the visual arts in seventeenth-century religious controversy as a means of upholding traditional Catholic positions.[25] Central among the Reformation/Counter-Reformation debates was the sacrament of the Eucharist. Though this sacrament had received a tremendous amount of attention throughout the Middle Ages, as Carolyn Walker Bynum has shown us,[26] Mâle points out that representations of the Eucharistic moment in Western art were surprisingly rare before the seventeenth century. It is at that point that the Eucharist and its connection with the Sacred Heart became the subject of countless representations in religious art and literature.

As I noted earlier, the liturgy of the Sacred Heart is a modern invention. Between 1673 and 1675 the French Visitandine nun Margaret Mary Alacoque experienced a series of visions in which she encountered Christ displaying his exposed heart or saw his disembodied heart alone. In each case Alacoque was encouraged by divine instruction to promulgate devotion to Christ's heart. For scholars of religion and church historians alike, Alacoque's visions mark a special moment in the development of a specific liturgy dedicated to the Sacred Heart of Jesus. Accounts of similar visions in the Middle Ages and early Renaissance exist but tend toward a heightened private devotional life for the individual recording such a vision. Alacoque's visions differ in that they specifically call for the creation of a public devotional practice in the form of a liturgy. Counter-Reformation figures such as Francis de Sales and John Eudes had made earlier attempts to establish a similar devotion but were not successful. It was not until Margaret Mary's visions were made known that the new devotion made inroads with the laity and became broadly practiced. The main thrust of earlier Counter-Reformation attempts at establishing this liturgy was to counter what was seen as the Protestant denigration of the Eucharist—or more specifically—the doctrine of transubstantiation. The heart of Christ had traditionally been seen as representing both elements of body and blood and so was the natural focus of such a devotion.

In the visual arts of the Counter-Reformation one of the informing principles behind the choice of subject matter was reparation. The Protestants had attacked various dogmas and sacraments that the Roman church felt obliged to defend. Artists commissioned by ecclesiastical and civic authorities in Catholic Europe turned increasingly toward subjects at the center of these controversies: the assumption of the Virgin, the Real Presence, the sacraments of confession and penitence—all of these were reemphasized and glorified to shore up or repair the church's position. Most scholars agree that Alacoque's visions differ from those of her predecessors primarily in their emphasis on reparation. It is this particular aspect of the devotion that helped pave the way for the new liturgy among the laity and church authorities alike. The indignities suffered by the sacraments at the hands of the Protestants could be righted by a return to the heart. If we keep in mind Burton's assertion that it is in our brains that we most resemble the Almighty, we might say conversely that it is in his heart that Christ most resembles the human. As Orest Ranum has pointed out, by "confusing human passions with Christ's passion, people could identify with his suffering."[27] This is the same devotional sympathy for Christ's *agon* that is at the center of Alacoque's vision.

The new devotion to the Sacred Heart was not without its critics. There was considerable opposition to the cult of the Sacred Heart within the Catholic Church itself in the late seventeenth century. The Jansenists of Port Royal, including Pascal, found such devotions repugnant for their easy voluntaristic piety and formulaic approach to salvation.[28] But the rigorous and masculinist theology of Port Royal, like that of Calvinism, would cease to be a major force in Western Christianity as sentimentalism became the pervasive characteristic of eighteenth- and nineteenth-century popular religion. The problem with the Sacred Heart lay not in its anachronistic relation to the human body and physiology but rather in the popular tendency to devalue it as a symbol of Christ's humanity and treat it as a reification of sentiment.[29]

Unlike the Protestant emblems of the heart, which were stylized to the point of being visual symbols of the heart rather than representations of it, the Sacred Heart of Jesus in Counter-Reformation iconography increasingly took on anatomical precision. Christ's divine humanity was being emphasized in the visual arts so that he could be seen to have loved and suffered with a human heart. The heart's long-standing symbolic centrality allows us to view it as much more than a material fact. The brain, by comparison, presents us with a different problem for the representation of the self altogether. It lacks a stylized visual symbol such as the heart. We know what a heart-shaped object would look like but not a brain-shaped one. Visual representations of the brain from Vesalius onward come to us imbued with what could be called "facticity."[30] Whereas the heart, as a symbol, could absorb the shock of its own realistic representation, the brain seems strangely alien when exposed.

The question remains as to whether the church in some way disabled itself discursively by privileging the heart over the brain as the center of Christ's person. I would argue that within the Christian discourse of the self the church made a logical choice in choosing the heart. The fact that it is difficult to imagine a pictorial representation of Christ's exposed brain is telling. Angus Fletcher long ago reminded us that metaphors should surprise at some level in order to be effective.[31] But one might qualify that notion by adding that a metaphor should not necessarily shock. Obviously tastes change within a culture and are always heterodox to begin with—so what was once distasteful becomes decorous and vice versa. The problem of using the brain as a symbol or metaphor for the self is more complicated still, for though we may assume that the brain is in a certain way the center of our self, it is still difficult to contemplate representations of the brain as a metaphor of the self. Given that I know of no iconographic tradition depicting Christ's exposed brain, we might be better able to imagine the shock of seeing such an image by considering Rembrandt's *The Anatomy Lesson of Dr. Joan Deyman* (1656). Jonathan Sawday has pointed out the uncanny echoes in this work with Mantegna's earlier *Cristo in scurto* (Foreshortened Christ) of c. 1478–1485.[32] In Rembrandt's painting the anatomized corpse lies in roughly the same position as Mantegna's Christ, but here the body is eviscerated and the top of the skull removed exposing the brain. This is appropriate to the anatomy theater but unthinkable, I would argue, for the representation of Christ.

The exposed and flaming heart, no matter how realistically rendered, may still surprise some viewers, but it needs no immediate explanation because of its metaphoric availability. Images of the human brain, on the other hand, have no such corresponding metaphors to shift their signification. For instance, we now know that a heart can be transplanted from one body to another, making the uniqueness of one's heart metaphorical rather than physical, but in the case of the brain its uniqueness as the site of our consciousness (and thus our selves) is inescapably physical. As for representations of the brain, it remains the linguistic partner of the notion of the mind but is itself always the sign of its own materiality.

The heart conversely seems often on the verge of losing its materiality in discourse. This is no doubt due to its semiotic overdetermination; as a physical object and metaphor it signifies on many levels, regardless of medical science's conviction that it is a muscle, a pump. The heart is thus paradoxically freed from a "scientific" discourse of the self—that is, once it is known that the heart is not the locus of mental activity it is no longer available for a purely physiological explanation of consciousness (as is the brain). Instead the heart is allowed to reoccupy a metaphoric space in which it operates as a symbol of the conjunction of body and soul. Beyond connecting the material with the ethereal, the heart remains an enduring link between past and present. We can be moved by such a symbol or metaphor from ages past because of the heart's enduring centrality in the discourse of affect.

Descartes's confusing use of "mind" and "soul" as interchangeable terms demonstrates a profound reluctance on his part to equate the self with the bodily "machine." We may view the brain as the site of the self but Descartes was unable to, as he writes in a letter to one correspondent: "One thing is certain: I know myself as a thought and I positively do not know myself as a brain."[33] I suspect Christians and non-Christians alike would understand this sentiment.

We would do well to remember these changes in discursive modes when applying our own interpretive templates to the past. If we rely too heavily on such models, we will inevitably misconstrue or deny the complexity of systems of meaning that existed in the past or in cultures not our own. Debora Shuger has recently pointed to changes in the discourse of eros that have occurred between the Renaissance and the late modern period. She writes,

> [M]ost recent work on the body tends to presuppose that erotic desire (the longing for union with the beloved) *is* sexual desire (genital arousal). ... In any culture where erotic longing provides the central metaphor for spirituality, desire cannot be the equivalent of sexuality. Erotic desire [in the Renaissance] is physical, but primarily affects the upper body; it is engendered in the eyes and dwells in the heart.[34]

This strikes me as an extremely important point to keep in mind if we are to avoid reductive or homogenizing interpretations of any variety in discourses. Would anyone want to argue that Bernini's *Ecstasy of Saint Theresa* merely depicts the autoerotic experience of a frustrated and cloistered female sexuality? Yet, many psychoanalytic critics insist on enacting a "displacement downwards" when reading the discourse of desire—even when some of their interpretive paradigms require a faith at least as strong as that demanded of a Christian.[35]

We can understand the heart as both sacred and secular or both metaphorical and physical in a way that, I argue, we cannot conceive of the brain. Thus, the church's choice of the Sacred Heart over the "Sacred Brain" may be understood as neither reactionary nor benighted: far from merely dismissing the developments of medical science, early modern theologians acknowledged the complex means of signification available to the human body. A purely positivist or materialist explanation of human life (if that were indeed possible) would be insufficient, given the range of human experience. Reading the symbolism of the body, in parts or whole, allows us to acknowledge that materialist and metaphorical discourses occupy not parallel but exclusive realms—the body is often their most immediate site of interaction. The heart, though its signification is not easily defined, has proven an enduring symbol of both the spiritual and physical worlds—it is, to paraphrase Sir Thomas Browne, that which makes man a "true *Amphibium*," allowing us to exist in both worlds at once.

The brain, on the other hand, seems tied to its own physicality and function, oddly separate from the more evocative term "mind." Perhaps the brain remains taboo because at some level we suspect that its mysteries are knowable. Along with the notion that science may ultimately be able to explain the workings of the human brain may come the fear that if knowledge is indeed power, then understanding the brain would be tantamount to possessing power over the mind. In this age of organ transplants and synthetic parts, the brain may seem to be our last irreplaceable organ—a part uniquely "us." We may be simultaneously protective of the singularity of an individual brain while fearing that a deeper understanding of its functions will reduce mental life to a biological phenomenon (albeit wondrous) and not a spiritual mystery.

Notes

1. For a good general review of the liturgical history of the devotion to the Sacred Heart, see Annice Callahan, Introduction to *Karl Rahner's Spirituality of the Pierced Heart: A Reinterpretation of Devotion to the Sacred Heart* (Lanham, Md.: University Press of America, 1985). See also Joseph Petrovits, *Theology of the Sacred Heart* (Washington, D.C.: Catholic University of America Press, 1917).

2. *The New Dictionary of Catholic Spirituality*, ed. Michael Downey, (Collegeville, Minn.: Liturgical Press, 1993), entry by Annice Callahan, 470–71.

3. Pope Pius XII, "Haurietis Aquas" (encyclical letter of May 15, 1956), *Acta Apostolica Sedis* (Vatican City, 1956), 48:309.

4. The Copernican revolution and Galileo aside, Catholic orthodoxy still has recourse to established dogma in order to respond to contemporary questions such as fertility, contraception, abortion, and euthanasia. Some fifty years ago Robert Merton drew on evidence of Counter-Reformation hostility toward the new sciences in order to formulate the obverse hypothesis: namely, were the

Puritans and other Protestant ascetics better represented among the new scientific communities of the early modern period? Merton's investigation produced the now-classic "Merton thesis" concerning the role of religious values in the sciences. See *Puritanism and the Rise of Modern Science: The Merton Thesis*, ed. I. Bernard Cohen (New Brunswick, N.J.: Rutgers University Press, 1990).

5. Since the period of Bacon and Descartes up through the logical positivism of the Anglo-American philosophical tradition, the world of the physical sciences has claimed pride of place in discussions of the real or actual. This often leaves theology to be interpreted as at best a system of metaphors built over time around a core of ethical beliefs—or at worst a benighted and dangerous superstition. Martin Buber once described this habit of thought, which denies the possible reality of supernatural phenomena, as "the opinion [that] religion has never been anything but an intra-psychic process whose products are 'projected' on a plane in itself fictitious but vested with reality by the soul." Martin Buber, *Eclipse of God*, trans. Norbert Guterman (New York: Harper & Row, 1952), 13.

6. See Ynez Violé O'Neill, "Diagrams of the Medieval Brain: A Study in Cerebral Localization," in *Iconography at the Crossroads*, ed. Brendan Cassidy (Princeton: Princeton University Press, 1993), 91. In the same passage O'Neill goes on to assert, "Few if any of them doubted that fantasy or imagination was located in the front and cognition or reason in the middle, and memories in the back of the head." This is equally misleading, given the possible uses and interpretations of the word "fancy." See note 11 of this essay.

7. See D.H.M. Woollam, "Concepts of the Brain and Its Function in Classical Antiquity," in *The History and Philosophy of Knowledge of the Brain and Its Functions*, ed. F. N. L. Poynter (Oxford: Basil Blackwell, 1958), 5–18.

8. The integration of the concept of the humors with that of the complexions (i.e., temperament or the balance of the elemental qualities of hot, cold, wet, and dry) led Galen to propound a theory of the "principal members" and their associated systems.

9. An excellent overview of medieval medical science is provided by Nancy G. Siraisi, *Medieval and Early Renaissance Medicine* (Chicago: University of Chicago Press, 1990), 97–109.

10. Siraisi, *Medieval and Early Renaissance Medicine*, 91.

11. See Alexander Schmidt, *A Shakespeare Lexicon and Quotation Dictionary*, ed. George Sarrazin (New York: Dover, 1971), 1:399. Schmidt lists six common usages from the period: (1) the power of forming mental images, imagination, (2) image, conception, a thought founded not on reason, but on imagination, (3) fantasticalness, (4) liking, taste, (5) love, (6) a love-song.

12. See Shakespeare, *The Tempest* 4.1.159–63: "Bear with my weakness; my old brain is troubled: / Be not disturbed with my infirmity: / If you be pleased, retire into my cell / And there repose; a turn or two I'll walk, / To still my beating mind." *The Riverside Shakespeare*, ed. G. Blakemore Evans (Boston: Houghton Mifflin, 1973). In examining references to the terms "heart," "mind,"

and "brain" in Shakespeare's works, it is worth noting that although there are numerous uses of the words "heart" and "mind," "brain" occurs much more infrequently and most often in context with the other principal members of the body. This would seem to indicate the use of "brain" instead of "mind" when emphasizing physiology, whereas "heart" and "mind" are not so construed. See Marvin Spivak, *The Harvard Concordance to Shakespeare* (Cambridge: Harvard University Press, Belknap Press, 1973).

13. For a general overview of Fludd's life and works, see Frances Yates, *Theatre of the World* (London: Routledge & Kegan Paul, 1969).

14. René Descartes, *The Passions of the Soul*, trans. Stephen Voss (Indianapolis: Hackett, 1989), 35–37.

15. Descartes, *Meditations on First Philosophy*, in *The Philosophical Works of Descartes*, trans. Elizabeth S. Haldane and G.R.T. Ross (Cambridge: Cambridge University Press, 1931), 192.

16. Robert Burton, *The Anatomy of Melancholy*, ed. Floyd Dell and Paul Jordan Smith (New York: Tudor, 1927), 134.

17. Jacques Le Goff, "Heart or Head? The Political Use of Body Metaphors in the Middle Ages," trans. Patricia Ranum, in *Fragments for a History of the Human Body*, pt. 3, ed. Michel Feher, with Ramona Naddaff and Nadia Tazi (New York: Zone Books, 1989), 12–26.

18. Burton, *The Anatomy of Melancholy*, 131.

19. It is worth noting the variety of authorities (and their conflicting opinions) cited in Burton's work. The variety makes it famously difficult to discern Burton's own position on numerous questions particularly given the undulations of his prose between evidence and counterevidence, authority and counterauthority.

20. Xavier-Léon Dufour, *Dictionnaire du Nouveau Testament* (Paris: Seuil, 1975), 171.

21. Roger French, *William Harvey's Natural Philosophy* (Cambridge: Cambridge University Press, 1994), 221–22.

22. The tract was published as part of Nicolas de Nancel's larger work, *De immortalitate animae*, in 1587. (De Nancel had been trained as a classicist but later turned to medicine. After being forced by religious conflict to retreat to Douai, he returned to Paris and finished his medical studies and eventually became a physician to the royal family.)

23. Both the projects of a systematic skepticism and the reformation of scientific method had raised doubts among the more orthodox in Descartes's own lifetime, and though he retained the notion of the soul, even that hypothesis was open to questioning by his method. The hypothetical model and the method for discerning knowledge are the most enduring features of Descartes's work. Similar to Sir Francis Bacon, who is widely acknowledged to have been a mediocre scientist though a great propagandist for the new sciences, Descartes is now seen as having a method containing the corrective for the faults in his

own scientific enterprise. With the rise of the experimental sciences, positivism and empiricism become most self-assured when arriving at a hypothesis to be tested rather than establishing a dogma. Bacon knew that knowledge would constantly accrue, thus changing the "facts" that science had claimed to know. Rather than viewing this as defeat and falling back into radical skepticism, Bacon saw the need to establish what he calls "stages of certainty." Theology, on the other hand, makes itself vulnerable whenever it steadfastly holds to the stasis of knowledge that it has granted the authority of dogma. Metaphysics may remain safely outside the ken of empiricism, but it runs the risk of becoming obsolete or excluded from what I have called "real world" discourse. The church's position on the physical sciences appears merely benighted or brittle if it is unable to accept innovations.

24. Lewalski emphasizes the differences present in the *Schola Cordis* traditions of both Catholic and Protestant writers of the seventeenth century, comparing for example two works of the same title (*Schola Cordis*) one by the Continental Jesuit Benedict van Haeften the other by the English Protestant Christopher Harvey. See Barbara K. Lewalski, *Protestant Poetics and the Seventeenth-Century Religious Lyric* (Princeton: Princeton University Press, 1985), 179–212.

25. Émile Mâle, *Religious Art from the Twelfth to the Eighteenth Century* (New York: Noonday Press, 1949), 171.

26. Carolyn Walker Bynum, *Holy Feast and Holy Fast: The Religious Significance of Food to Medieval Women* (Berkeley: University of California Press, 1987). Cf. Mâle, *Religious Art from the Twelfth to the Eighteenth Century*, 167.

27. Orest Ranum, "The Refuges of Intimacy," trans. Arthur Goldhammer, in *A History of Private Life: Passions of the Renaissance,* ed. Roger Chartier (Cambridge: Harvard University Press, 1989), 3:235.

28. See Louis Cognet, "Les Jansénistes et Le Sacré-Coeur," in *Le Coeur: Les Études Carmélitaines*, ed. Paul Claudel (Bruges, Belgium: Chez Desclée de Brouwer, 1950), 234–35.

29. On the later developments of sentimental piety and its connection to the devotion to the Sacred Heart, see John B. Knipping, "Heaven on Earth," in *Iconography of the Counter Reformation in the Netherlands* (Nieuwkoop, Netherlands: Bede Graaf, 1974), 1:96–108.

30. It has been suggested that the anatomist's investigations of the human brain were often met with suspicion by ecclesiastical authorities in the early modern period. This atmosphere of suspicion may explain why the great seventeenth-century anatomist Thomas Willis dedicated his work on the anatomy of the brain to the archbishop of Canterbury. See K.B. Roberts and J.D.W. Tomlinson, *The Fabric of the Body: European Traditions of Anatomical Illustrations* (Oxford: Clarendon Press, 1992), 401.

31. Angus Fletcher, *Allegory: The Theory of a Symbolic Mode* (Ithaca: Cornell University Press, 1964).

32. Jonathan Sawday, *The Body Emblazoned: Dissection and the Human Body in Renaissance Culture* (New York: Routledge, 1995), 154–57. Sawday points out

that many copies of Mantegna's famous image of Christ existed as devotional images throughout western Europe.

33. Quoted by Walther Riese, "Descartes' Ideas of Brain Function," *The History and Philosophy of Knowledge of the Brain and Its Functions,* ed. F. N. L. Poynter (Oxford: Basil Blackwell, 1958), 133.

34. Debora Shuger, "Panel Discussion," in *Renaissance Discourses of Desire,* ed. Ted-Larry Pebworth (Columbia, Mo.: University of Missouri Press, 1993), 271–72.

35. The heart as a symbol of human affect, passion, and conscience is thereby translated into a symbol of displaced genital arousal and shame. Recently Michael Carroll has interpreted the liturgy of the Sacred Heart in just such a manner, writing that "the underlying appeal of the devotion to the Sacred Heart: [is] that in making reparation to the physical heart of Jesus, a heart that has been lacerated and punctured, devotees are really gratifying the infantile desire to make reparation for the oral-sadistic attacks launched in fantasy against the father's penis." It is precisely this type of reductiveness that I believe we should avoid. See Michael P. Carroll, *Catholic Cults and Devotions: A Psychological Inquiry* (Montreal: McGill-Queen's University Press, 1989), 153.

14.1 Portrait of Vesalius, *De humani corporis fabrica* (Venice, 1543).

14

"God's handy worke"

Divine Complicity and the Anatomist's Touch

KATHERINE ROWE

> No the soul is as the hand; for the hand is an instrument with
> respect to instruments, the intellect is a form with respect to
> forms, and sense-perception a form with respect to things
> perceived.
> —Aristotle *De anima* 3.8 432ª1

> Reason, is the hand of the Understanding, Speech the hand of
> Reason, and the Hand it selfe, is the hand of Speech. The
> hand executeth those things which are commanded, our com-
> mandments are subiect and obedient to Reason, and Reason
> it selfe is the power, force and efficacie of the understanding.
> —Helkiah Crooke, *Microcosmographia*

For early modern writers, following Aristotle by way of Galen, the location
of agency in relation to the body is the chief intellectual tenor of representations of the hand. The instrumentality of the hand and its capacity to grasp
are the central imaginative vehicles of this figure. As a material sign, the
hand is defined by its functional properties: its ability to gesture, touch,
grip, and demonstrate. Handclasps, for example, stand for consent in the

marriage ceremony of the Church of England, feudal obedience to a lord, formal reconciliation after conflict, and the ratification of a compact or treaty. The raised right hand signifies political suffrage and affirms obedience to civil or royal authority, as in the English National Covenant of 1640.[1] In all of these gestures, the hand represents and effects a point of contact between collective notions of person and the world of interiority, intentions and will.[2] So, for instance, in both political and legal philosophy hands become a familiar topos for relations of office, deputation, and substitution—in which agent and principle exist in some negotiated dependency. John of Salisbury's allegory of the body politic offers a famous and influential example, in his discussion of the natural allegiance of officers to the state:

> And so the hand of the republic is either armed or unarmed. The armed hand is of course that which is occupied with marching and the blood-letting of warfare; the unarmed hand is that which expedites justice and attends to the warfare of legal right, distanced from arms.... And so the armed hand is exercised strictly against enemies, but the unarmed is extended also against the citizen. In addition, discipline is necessary for both because both are notoriously accustomed to being wicked. The use of the hand testifies to the qualities of the head itself because, as Wisdom asserts, the iniquitous king has entirely impious ministers.... For the continence of governors is laudable when they restrain their hands and hold back the hands of others from exactions and injuries. Still, the hand of both sorts of soldiers, namely, armed and unarmed, is the hand of the prince; and unless he constrains both, he is not very continent. And surely the unarmed hand is to be curbed more closely because while the armed hand is commanded to abstain from exactions and rapine, the unarmed hand is also prohibited presents.[3]

The metaphor of the body politic is often read as if it expressed Menenius's strategy of mob control, but while it can be used to justify political hierarchies by analogy to organic structures, John of Salisbury's allegory of the hand proposes a more complex set of problems. Here the concrete possibilities of manual action (hands are grasping, aggressive) undo the organic metaphor just at the moment when the continuity of moral action appears most important to his argument. As John explains the moral import of his figure, its tenor and vehicle mix: the continent prince must use his actual hand to restrain his figurative hand—whose multiplying officers are prone to seizure and graft. The limbs that stand here for deputation and ministry thus emphasize the problematic nature of these substitutions and the moral complications they produce. Far from naturalizing the notion of a single, neatly described person of the state, they signify the mixed and sometimes dangerously contaminated agencies that are the subject of John's ongoing meditation and analysis. In its emphasis on the mobility of hands, their ability to grasp (arms or someone else's property), and its play on their simultaneously figurative and functional nature, the *Policraticus* encapsulates the principal strategies that characterize the use of the hand in early modern representations of agency.

When political fictions make use of the body in this way, they draw on an anatomical history that defines corporeal agency in terms as layered and complex as these meditations on administrative performance and moral culpability. Medical anatomies are particularly interesting because they pursue a *mechanics* of agency relations. They offer insight into the essentialist arguments of early modern culture. What notions of physiology, for example, underlie legal phrases that stand for self-evident guilt, like *hand-habbende* and "red-hand"—or allow the physician John Bulwer to say that "what we put our hand unto we are infallibly understood to will and intend" (50)? Anatomists struggle persistently and intelligently to explain intention and action as bodily functions: by describing the common means of sense perception in touch and by tracing the mechanics of motion and grasp. They explain these functions in mechanical terms that seem familiar to us from the roughly contemporary discourse of Descartes, detailing a process by which internal spiritual motions impel bodily instruments. Yet as late as the early seventeenth century, they also return to medieval analogies of the body as microcosm in ways that seem incompatible with the burgeoning mechanistic forms they describe. This rhetorical strategy recuperates bodiliness as a locus of virtue in a way that is insistently antidualist. By linking analogical and functional analysis to mechanical description, medical anatomies express a persistent sense of the body as a locus of self and agency, not merely the instrument of a noncorporeal essence.

To the extent that early modern anatomies continue to be modeled on the anatomy of the hand—as Galen recommended in his opening book of *De usu partium*—the hand becomes the prominent vehicle for integrating sacred mystery with corporeal mechanism. Its mechanics are paradoxically invested with the external force most important to the form of the body, at once internalizing and illustrating God's agency and design. The dissection of the hand in particular, from Galen to the seventeenth century, persists as one of the central moral *topoi* of anatomy demonstrations: celebrated for its difficulty and beauty, it reveals God's intentions as no other part can. Most important, anatomies construe the *demonstratio* of divine intentions as both a symbolic and a functional property of the hand. To take in hand the rational work of dissection, they imply, is to do what the surgeon John Banister calls "God's handy worke": both to reveal and to perform God's will in the flesh.[4] This argument emerges both in text and image. Manual puns and allusions shape the textual exposition of the hand in medical anatomies and keep the actions of the dissecting hand in close focus. And anatomical illustration, drawing on traditional visual representations of God's hand, returns repeatedly to the image of two clasping hands: suggesting the interlaced and mutual nature of divine and human agency embodied in this part. Readings of the body shaped by a single part produce no more or less true a reading of a body general than others. But they do more clearly remind us of the heterogeneity of the terms with which we invent corporeality and physical experience. By directing our attention to the hand, this essay supports a broader claim about the study of the figurative and corporeal body: "the body" as a site of cultural fiction making brings together various, sometimes contradictory, spheres of reference, fictional strategies, and values. The body imagined in relation to its hand is shaped by those fictions particular to the hand: the principle of rational organization, the capacity for artistry and manufacture, the dependencies of mutual labor and layered agency. These ideas make the body seem less the Foucauldian subject, more nimble and mobile than the horizontal poses of dissected corpses imply, more animate, finally, even when dismembered and anatomized.

The body revealed by sixteenth- and seventeenth-century anatomies can look very different from what I am beginning to describe here. Recent scholarship has emphasized the emergence of the anatomized interior as a separate space, chaotic, confused, and dark; the anatomist navigates this confusion, strategically eliding the violence of his practice and its complicity with forms of state control such as execution.[5] This account depends on a clear split between the body as a locus of passivity and the agencies (here cultural and political) that work on it from the outside. It is precisely this clear split that the dissection of the hand, with its emphasis on function, struggles with and attempts to suspend. By drawing analogies between the internal structures that facilitate grasp (the flexor muscles), the scene of instruments and demonstration immediately surrounding the hand of the anatomist (touching, showing, and cutting), and the spiritual authority that inhabits both (God's hand), this dissection complicates an easy alignment of interiority and intention.

Thus, to take seriously the notion—common to much historical criticism today—that the interior of the body is not separable from the practices that make it visible, we need to retain a sense of the discursive complexity of these practices. By exploring the rhetorical strategies associated with the dissection of the hand, in Helkiah Crooke's *Microcosmographia, A Description of the Body of Man* (1615), I want to direct our attention to a different set of responses to the opened, dissected body. Anatomical investigation moves Crooke to delight, as his frequent use of adjectives like "exquisite" attests. Rational exposition of parts is modulated in a variety of ways: by long clauses that emphasize the contiguity of tissues; by celebratory digression; by reference to ancient and folk authority; by punning allusion to the mucky work of dissection that plays up rather than evades the anatomist's intimate contact with viscera. *Microcosmographia* looks back to medieval visions of the body and forward to Harveian mechanics, and attempts a difficult but compelling synthesis of mechanical analysis and the mystical homologies of the body-as-microcosm.[6] In it, Crooke explores the nature of agency in the body within the same complex, mixed registers—concrete and figurative, corporeal and social—used in political and legal philosophy. How can the relations between parts and wholes be made stable? Where can the boundaries of person and the limits of action be identified? Its underlying physiological puzzle—how do incorporeal motions of the soul move corporeal organs and instruments?—intensifies the contradictions apparent in an attempt to integrate mechanical and analogical modes of analysis. These questions surface throughout Crooke's work, but especially in two related sections: his introduction to anatomy as a discipline and the anatomy of the muscles that move the fingers. Here, the text proposes a kind of corporeal metonymy; focus on the physical contiguity of parts, the property of touch, and the manual activities of dissection anchors this mixed mode of analysis. Crooke's close attention to the habits and functions of the hand in these sections constitutes an early modern theory and practice of touch. And it amply illustrates the mixed complicities exemplified by the hand in early modern literature, exploring in concrete terms an imaginative territory that—as in John of Salisbury's analysis—is both figurative and corporeal, both singular and corporate, partly in and partly of the world of objects. Offering a theory of a specific kind of manual practice, it illuminates a part defined by and constituted in material qualities that are habits, motions, and functions.

❧

Dissections in the sixteenth and seventeenth century began with the parts that decompose soonest: abdomen, torso, and head. In general, the limbs were dissected last.[7] In the case of the arm, the exposition proceeds from the shoulder toward the fingers, and what begins as a necessary response to bodily decay emerges as an implicit argument about the relatedness of parts. These trajectories reinforce one of the central narratives of anatomy: the contiguity of "joynte" and body, part and whole, which maintains continuity of action. Crooke raises two important historical exceptions to this order, both pertaining to the hand proper. He notes that in both Galen and Columbus the location of the hand in the anatomy reflects its preeminence as a part: Galen famously begins *De usu partium* with the hand, Crooke reminds us, because it is the ideal and exemplar of all the other parts; and Columbus treats the hand last for a related reason: "because (sayth he) the wonderfull and miraculous frame therof might remaine infixed in our memories" (785). Crooke seems to imply that the uniquely memorable quality of this dissection constitutes a kind of coherence in itself, reinforcing our sense of the body's perfection as a conceptual unity.[8] As other anatomists suggest, Columbus's strategy also mitigates the vivid disintegration of the body during dissection, since the tissues of the hand "the longest endure uncorrupted."[9]

Whether it is dissected early or late, the analogical character of the hand, following Aristotle's seminal definition, makes it a mediator between the ancient and sacred homologies of the body as microcosm and a rational inquiry into physical mechanics. Crooke follows the order of dissection in his own account of the parts, yet conceptually he follows Galen and Aristotle in emphasizing the ideational primacy of the hand. The hand incorporates an ideal correspondence between parts and wholes, and guides us in understanding their mechanical interactions. The pattern of unity in division it offers is expressed in both its structure and function, as Crooke's meditation on the mechanics of grasp demonstrates:

> The true office of the Hand is to apprehend or to holde, and his proper action is apprehension (for Hand and Hold are Conjugates, as we term them in Schooles)…. The Figure is long and divided into many parts that it might comprehend in one all kinde of Figures, the round or Spherick, the right and the hollow, for all figures are made of three lines, a crooked, a hollow and a straight. Beside, this figure doth equally apprehend both greater bodies and lesse; for small things it holdeth with the ends of two fingers, the great finger or the thumbe and the forefinger…. Now, if the hand had bene made of one continuall peece, it would onelie have apprehended a body of one magnitude. Neyther was it sufficient that the Hande

should be divided into fingers, unlesse the same fingers had beene placed in a divers order and not in the same right line, so as one was to be set or opposed to the other four, which being bowed with a small flection might meete and agree with the action of the other foure opposite unto it. (730)

This description resonates with allusions to the medieval microcosm of the body, whose perfection can square the circle. For Crooke, the divided parts and united action of the hand typify the Baconian ideal of anatomy as an epistemological endeavor: "a diligent and curious Section, undertaken to get knowledge or skil by" (26). Anatomy consists of a fruitful correspondence between cutting, "the action which is done with the hande," and the rational "habite of the minde, that is, the moste perfect action of the intellect" (26).

> The first is called practicall Anatomy, the latter Theorical or contemplative: the first is gained by experience, the second by reason and discourse: the first wee attaine onely by Section and Inspection, the second by the living voice of a Teacher, or by their learned writing: the first we call Historicall Anatomy, the second Scientificall: the first is altogether necessary for the practise of anatomy, the second is only profitable; but yet this profit is oftentimes more beneficiall then the use it self of Anatomy: the first looketh into the structure of the partes, the second into the causes of the structure, and the actions and uses therefrom proceeding. (26)

As he continues his carefully balanced oppositions, Crooke takes pains to distinguish practical anatomy, "Artificiall section," from the accidental investigations of warfare. The first is an orderly history—or telling, as in the French *histoire*—that preserves the integrity of parts as wholes. The second is a Spenserian meander, "rash and at adventure," that obscures the delicate distinctions of the first and threatens violence.

> For oftentimes in great wounds we observe the figure, scituation, magnitude, and structure of the outward and inward parts; but that observation is but confused, for we cannot distinctly perceive the branchings of the Nerves, the Serpentine and writhen Meanders of the Veynes, nor the infinite divarications of the Arteries. Now that a Dissection may be made artificially, it is first requisite that the parts bee so separated one from another, that they may all be preserved whole, not rent and torne asunder. Next, that those which grow not togither, bee gently divided. Thirdly, that those which do grow together, be carefully separated. Fourthly, that we mistake not many parts joyned together for one, nor yet make many parts of one. (26)

In either its order or confusion, the interior of the body can be understood only in relation to the style of investigation. Crooke's phrase, "the action which is done with the hande" is thus not a casual one. It hearkens back to the classical source of anatomical descriptions of the hand: "So the soul is as the hand; for the hand is an instrument with respect to instruments, the intellect is a form with respect to forms." Aristotle's enduring analogies provide anatomy with a marvelous, recursive logic. The hand that actually cuts and orders embodies the rational design it produces: unity in division. Supporting this conceit is the central aesthetic of *Microcosmographia:* a vision of unity and divine providence extrapolated from the marvelous design of the hand. As William Schupbach has shown in his seminal analysis of Rembrandt's *Anatomy of Dr. Nicholas Tulp,* the renowned beauty of the anatomy of the hand developed its own visual and textual tradition. Schupbach summarizes its two central themes: first, the flexor muscles of the hand, which specifically control apprehension, link divine intentions and the work of civilization. In his chapter "Of the excellency of the hands" Crooke extols:

> By the helpe of the hand Lawes are written, Temples built for the service of the Maker, Ships, houses, instruments, and all kind of weapons are formed. I list not to stand upon the nice skill of painting, drawing, carving and such like right noble artes. (729)

Second, the celebrated beauty and sophistication of this anatomy proves the Argument from Design as no other evidence could.[10] In his 1578 *Historie of man,* John Banister expands it this way: "Thus if we wel perpend the construction, and composition of the partes, and bones of the hand, our senses shall soone conceive the maner of the action, with no lesse admiration, in beholdyng the handy worke of the incomprehensible Creator" (fol. 31r).

In emphasizing "the action which is done with the hande," Crooke's definition of practical anatomy adds a specific historical charge to the Argument from Design. In the sixteenth century, when Vesalius began to practice anatomy demonstrations, barbers or surgeons generally wielded the knife, while the higher-ranking physicians lectured from the text. Vesalius condemns the "very capricious division of an art into separate specialties" in his preface to the *Fabrica.* He speaks acidly and at length of the decay in contemporary medical fashions, "miserably distorted," by the avoidance of "treatment made by the hands" and manual "investigation of nature":[11]

[W]e see learned physicians abstain from the use of the hands as from a plague lest the rabbins of medicine decry them before the ignorant mass as barbers and they acquire less wealth and honor than those scarcely half-physicians. . . . Indeed, it is especially this detestable, vulgar opinion that prevents us, even in our age, from taking up the art of treatment as a whole, limiting us to the treatment of only internal diseases, to the great harm of mankind, and—if I may speak frankly—we strive to be physicians only in part. (2v)

Genuine and accurate revelation, he insists, can be gained only through dedicated application of the hand. That "pleasure in the employment of the hands" and zealous use "handed down to posterity" by Galen makes both physician and his practice whole (fol. 2r).

Delicately suggesting this complex of themes, Crooke defines anatomy as a "diligent" and "careful" discipline. He displaces its potential for violence onto an opportunistic, rending, and tearing anatomy of wounds. Treating the interior mechanism of the body through dissection obviously requires touching it, placing the hands inside it, lifting successive layers of tissue to reveal their points of origin and arrival. In other contexts, this activity would produce the pain and physical outrage behind words like "rent and torne asunder." Given these charged associations, it would seem remarkable that Crooke should keep "the action which is done with the hande" in the foreground of his text. Yet he does, in an ongoing series of puns that play on the commonplace of "handlygne" and "touching" a topic. Typically, these passing puns introduce and close the separate chapters of *Microcosmographia*. Sometimes they are gleefully integrated into the exposition. Without the sense of touch, Crooke warns us at one point, physicians "must of necessity grope uncertainlie in darke and palpable ignorance" (649).

In certain respects, "handlynge" puns draw on the same sources that inform the graphic hands that appear in anatomy portraits, as in the portrait of Vesalius facing the first page of the *Fabrica* (figure 14.1). Both invoke a visual tradition of didactic hands to maintain their decorum— even while the pointing fingers of the physician appear entwined in entrails or sinews. In the margins of medieval manuscripts similar pointing indices organize the text and provide moral emphasis. In a related convention, saints are often pictured pointing to the props that symbolize their martyrdom. Read thus, "handlynge" puns continually remind readers and listeners of the indexical, "textual" nature of the hands that dissect. They confirm that the anatomist performs a *demonstratio* when he handles the body. To an audience in a dissection theater, the puns might accordingly evoke a moral context, supporting Crooke's assertion that the hand that sections and inspects is a teacherly hand, the one of "learned writing." To the readers of an anatomy text, the puns evoke the vivid scene of dissection in a way that complicates this moral decorum. From either vantage, the puns test the organic wholeness of hand and body, and the sense of control didactic gestures imply, against the more questionable activities hands can be imagined doing. If Crooke gropes "uncertainlie in darke and palpable ignorance," should it make our guts tighten a little? Wouldn't decorum be more successfully controlled by restraining such play?

To ask this is to raise the corollary question of intention: Whose is expressed in these puns, and to what end? There are two ways to address these questions, both relevant: first, the history of Crooke's relation to the Royal College of Physicians of London, well-traveled but worth summarizing for the complex relation between professional status and anatomical labor it reveals. Discomfort is one of the responses that Crooke knows he is getting from one part of his audience, the fellows of the Royal College. And violating certain kinds of professional decorum is a central part of his project. *Microcosmographia* appeared in English, with a preface addressed to the company of barber surgeons: at the time, barbers and surgeons were still the general practitioners of dissection in England, and few spoke or read Latin. Thus, when Crooke puns in English part of the point—and annoyance—may be that the surgeons will grasp his wit. The college strenuously objected to Crooke's translation, attempting to delay and emend it. They contended that the general circulation of an English-language anatomy was unethical (it would lead to the unscrupulous practice of physic) and improper.[12] During the period when the first three editions of *Microcosmographia* were published, Crooke attempted unsuccessfully to be admitted a fellow of the Royal College. In response, perhaps, he belittles their objections in his prefaces. He implies that their sense of decorum is intellectually obstructive, points out that all of his material had been covered already in public dissection, and stresses its medical necessity. Surgeons must understand anatomical theory; physicians should be versed in anatomical practice.

In this context, it is not surprising that Crooke's first person pronouns reveal an odd betwixt-and-betweenness of address. He uses "we" in his preface to associate himself both with the adept surgeons he formally addresses, and the physicians who are his hoped-for professional peers, his source of authority and his antagonists. In addition, Crooke struggles to define professional boundaries that justify the circulation of medical knowledge while confirming his own ethical, authoritative status. Surgeons and physicians should share manual skills but remain separate in practice, he says: physicians in particular should know how to dissect, but choose not to. Thus, his puns negotiate the charged and mixed allegiances suggested by the definition of anatomy as a "gentle" manual discipline. At the same time they redirect accusations of impropriety by attributing them to weak-minded distaste. He describes with Vesalian acerbity a *physician* whose hands are not practiced in anatomy—the physician whose touch (not the anatomist's) discomfits by groping in palpable ignorance. And if the prospect of such groping discomfits anyone, it is presumably the same physicians—too squeamish to perform dissections—who are left uneasy.

These puns also work at a second, very different register of literary effect, one that suspends the question of intention in order symbolically to integrate the anatomist's gestures with the formal structures they reveal. The puns idealize and internalize the action of the anatomist's hand in the body itself: the body is permeable, Crooke implies repeatedly, in its ideal state and optimum functions. Thus the groping pun that plays on the sense of touch is part of a larger theory of that sense:

> But we in the mean time admiring this majestie & certainty of the senses, will make entrance into so faire and pleasant a field of discourse, and handle every one of them in particular, beginning with the sense of Touching, which as it is more common than the rest, so without doubt deserves the first place: For this is the ground of all the rest ... hence Aristotle, and with him all other Philosophers [call it] The Sense as if they should have said the onely Sense of all Senses. (648)

"O healthfull and Saving Touch, O Searching Sense," he continues, suggesting a moral structure for anatomical inquiry that builds on the physician's healing touch: healthful, saving, searching (649). "But we holde our handes," he finishes, "both Time & the Matter requires that we prosecute the remaining Senses in as few words as we can" (649). Touch is the "innermost" sense, yet its organ—skin—is "nearer to the occursation or confluence of outward objects; because it is the limit and border as it were of all the parts" (84). Its mediating and delimiting role makes the sense of touch so "exquisite," and helps to make the audience comfortable with the movement of the anatomist's hand in and out of the corpse. While touch is the common sense, distributed throughout the body, the hand is its rational and controlling agent: a "Judge and discerner of touch" (730) that directs and analyzes it:

> For albeith this touching vertue or tactive quality be diffused through the
> whole body both within and without, as being the foundation of the
> Animall *Being*, which may be called *Animality*, yet we do more curiouslie
> and exquisitely feele and discerne both the first and second qualities which
> strike the Sense in the Hand than in other parts. (730)

The rational and dignified connotations of "Judge and discerner of touch"
combine in this phrase to help sustain the notion of a "gentle" and "careful"
handling of innermost parts. Yet the term "discerner" implicitly insists on
the primacy of such handling as the means of judgment. To *discern of*, in its
legal contexts, is synonymous with judging: to have cognizance of and to
interpret judiciously; the verb *to discern* also held the sense it retains now,
to perceive distinctions and differences. In the sixteenth and seventeenth
century, however, it also maintained a transitive sense: to separate as distinct, to distinguish and divide. Thus, in the epithets "Judge and discerner
of touch," the perceptual and ethical attributes of touch—the discrimination of moral, logical, and spiritual differences between things—are implicitly located in the manual practices of anatomy.

Most importantly, then, "handlynge" puns alert us that the motion of
the anatomist's hand itself is a symbolically necessary part of anatomical
exposition, as well as a practical requirement. In mechanical terms, the
motion of the hand—and thus its seamless expression of intention and
volition—is a function of its contiguity to the body. In this respect, the
anatomist's hand performs what the sectioned parts display. The dependency of motion on contiguity thus becomes a central theme of the dissection of the arm, as a closer look shows us: first in the textual exposition and
then the illustration of this anatomy.

The practice of "diligent" and "curious" dissection maintains a careful
distinction between parts while preserving their right connections. Even
more, it defines relations and traces continuities *through* rational separation. By way of introducing the parts of the hand proper, Crooke reminds
us that anatomically, the word "hand" denotes the whole limb from shoulder to fingertip.

> There are therefore two kinds of Joyntes, the upper and the lower; the
> upper joyntes are called by the common name of the *Hand*, for the
> Ancients accounted the whole member from the shoulder to the fingers
> ends to bee all the *Hand*. . . . The whole Hand Hippocrates and Galen doe
> devide into three parts in *Brachium*, *Cubitur* and *Summa or extrema
> manum*, that is, the Arme, the Cubit and the Hand as we call it. (728)

Similarly, the illustrations that accompany this section show the whole arm, shoulder muscles fanned out to the clavicle and blade. The exposition of the working parts of the hand emphasizes contiguity and continuity as well. Crooke describes the progress of the flexor muscles across the ulna (ell) and radius (wand) as follows:

> The first Bender ariseth with a round beginning and large, mixed of a fleshy and Nervous substance, from the internall proturberation of the arme under the heads of the Palme-muscle and those two which bend the Wrist, Afterward becomming broader, it passeth thorough the middle and anterior part of the ell and the Wand, and becommeth fleshy and round, yet before it attaine unto the roote of the Wriste his Venter or Belly is angustated or straightned, and divided into four fleshy parts, all which do determine into tendons exquisitely nervous and transparant: and being together involved in one common, thin and mucous membrane; for their more safe progression doe passe along under the annular or round Ligament which is seated overthwart the wrist; and at the second bone of the forefingers nere the middest of the Joynte are divided with a long Section or slit through which the tendons of the next muscle to be described (which lyeth under them) which were to reach unto the third Joynte are transmitted. There they become Broader that they might moove more easily and apprehend or take holde the better, and a little after the division or section they are inserted into the second bones of the foure Fingers. (787)

The long prepositional clauses of this passage seem to emulate the path of the muscles across the two bones of the forearm. Its layered and extended syntax maintains the sense of continuous connection from upper insertion to lower, from muscle to tendon, from single tissue to four-part division.

In Galen's *De usu partium*, as I have noted, the hand serves as the ideal and type of part-whole relationships. When this dissection arrives at its celebrated goal, the finger-insertions of the flexor muscles, its harmony of action facilitated by division moves anatomists to wonder:

> And truly this progresse and insertion of these muscles is an admirable and strange worke of Nature: for they are so severed, that the fingers in their motion might orderly follow one another, and each of them alone bend inward. (787)

Crooke's illustrations, likewise, emphasize continuity in division: they tend to expose or detach the lower rather than the upper insertions of these muscles, as if to imply the continued integrity of the body above the dissection. Later illustrations, with their greater interest in morphology, still

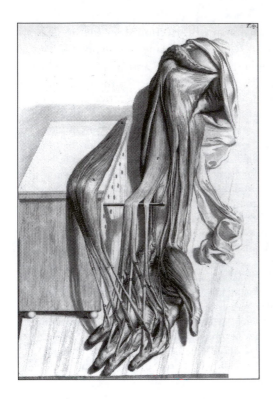

14.2 Muscles of the hand and
forearm from Govard Bidloo,
Anatomia Humani Corporis
(Amsterdam, 1685).

maintain this emphasis. A 1685 engraving for Govaert Bidloo's *Anatomia humani corporis* shows the striking tension and balance between the teleology of this dissection and its interest in contiguity of tissues (figure 14.2). Here the muscles above the flexor-tendons are detached and pulled back at the fingers in order to show their complicated stratification and interpenetration. Still, the dissected tissues are pulled tautly against the heavy arm in a way that emphasizes how well anchored they remain. And even the one detached muscle, the top of the *flexor digitorum superficialis* points stiffly back up to the shoulder, almost blending into the shadow of the upper arm. It points against the pull of gravity as if it still maintained its upper attachment. Thus, this dissection is always implicitly backward looking, emphasizing the contiguity of tissues even at their most exposed. Like its earlier, textual versions, the Bidloo engraving illustrates the dependency of motion and attachment.

The continuities symbolized by the muscles that grasp remain implicit and sustaining characteristics of the hand in early modern political and social rituals, as now. From rhetorical treatises to political theory, the hand symbolizes an apparently seamless continuity between the instrumental part and the person or power that it acts for. Anatomical form seems to confirm this, by explicating the organs of volition:

> Seeing therefore that the proper action of the Hand is Apprehension, and Apprehension a Motion depending upon our will, it was also necessary that the hand should have muscles which are the instruments of voluntary motions whereby it might be mooved altogether and every finger apart. (785)

Yet, to show the physical connections that sustain this logic, they must be severed—a practical necessity that would seem to disrupt the mechanical certainties that make "apprehention a motion depending upon our will." The visual strategies medical anatomies deploy to manage this paradox supply as a corollary the strategy of punning, likewise emphasizing the actions of the dissecting hand. In particular, as William Schupbach has shown, they develop the flexor-muscle dissection as coherent emblem motif, one that shows up especially in early-seventeenth-century title pages and anatomy portraits.[13] Although the muscles displayed are those of a dead and severed part, they remain symbolically inseparable from the process of dissection. The action of the anatomist's hand dissecting the forearm is absorbed into the emblem and the Galenic system of ideas it represents. As scholars since Margaret Tallmadge may have noted, Galen translates Aristotle's definition of the hand in a double sense, and the anatomists of the sixteenth and seventeenth century follow suit: they define the hand as both the supreme example *of* all instruments and tools, and as the tool that uses tools, "the instrument *for* all instruments"[14] (Rowe, 281). Drawing on this tradition, emblems of the flexor-muscle dissection, like the Fabricius title page, make the hand agent, instrument, and patient of the *demonstratio*. In this way, cut tissue and cutting hand become a symbolic unit, signifying effective, voluntary action and the unity of parts.

Anatomy illustrations draw on contemporary visual art in a number of additional ways that emphasize the actions of the hand. Muscle-men and skeletons hold out the specific props of dissection (knives to flay, ropes to suspend) or present the generic ones familiar from emblem books (hourglasses, apples, spades, mirrors, and skulls). These pictures offer the double aesthetics that has become a commonplace of critical scholarship: legible for their symbolic attributes—*vanitas* and *memento mori* motifs—and for their helpful display of the anatomy under examination. Full-figure illustrations gesture toward their anatomized parts or an explanatory table, using

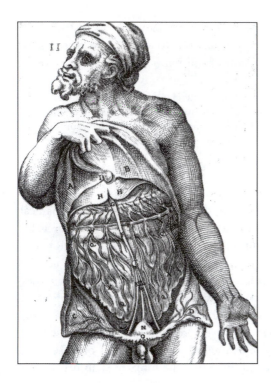

14.3 Self-demonstrating anatomy from Juan Valverde's *Historia de la composision del cuerpo humano* (Rome, 1556).

the body concretely to illustrate the dissection and as a pointer. Increasingly in the seventeenth century, such figures handle themselves: écorchés brandish flayed skins and sharp knives, anatomized torsos pull back their abdominal skin, as in the in famous detail from Valverde's *Historia de la composicion del cuerpo humano* (figure 14.3). Remarkably, these figures rarely make cautionary or protective gestures. Far from warding off investigation, the hands in anatomy illustrations seem to invite and offer it. Unlike the powerful grips of the emblem tradition, their fingers often appear slightly spread, the palm open to view, the arm slanting down—as one might welcome a guest into one's house (see figure 14.3). In later anatomical drawings this open-handed pose is ubiquitous, whether the hand is drawn alone or as part of a body, and it is worth noting that this is not an effect of death. Immediate rigor mortis contracts the fingers more tightly, and the relaxation that follows does not flex them flat again. In his portrait, Vesalius holds the corpse's hand and arm in this classical anatomical position, signaling his formal intervention. Yet contemporary theory of gesture gives this pose a specific valence that shifts its emphasis. In his compendious study, *Chirologia, or the Natural Language of the Hand*, John

14.4 Royal College of
Physicians shield of arms,
1546.

Bulwer interprets this kind of open-handed posture as the habit and sign
of liberality:

> To put forth the right hand spread is the habit of *bounty, liberality* and a
> *free heart*; thus we *reward* and *friendly bestow our gifts*. Hence, TO OPEN THE
> HAND in the Hebrew phrase implies to be *free-hearted, munificent*, and *lib-*
> *eral*. For the Hebrews when they would express a *profuse munificence*, they
> say *jad pethucha*, that is, [an open hand]. (55–56)[15]

Illustrations of the dissected arm show similar postures: palms open
and fingers spread, as though freely offering. These arms tend to emphasize
the mortal weight of gravity, slanting down as if partly relaxed, yet some, as
in figure 14.2, surprise us with the potential force of their invitation.

These mixed modes of representation, naturalistic and emblematic,
have drawn much critical commentary, especially attentive to the apparent
complicity of the corpse in the process of dissection. As Jonathan Sawday
has argued, the helpful postures of anatomy illustrations seem to internalize
the didactic and surgical work of the anatomist's hand in the body dissected. Their liberal gestures suggest a body inviting its own dissection and
actively engaged in the *demonstratio*: signaling the multiple agencies and

shifting authority of the dissection theater.[16] At a formal level, as Glenn Harcourt has shown, illustrations of dissection adopt *demonstratio* as a general aesthetic.[17] Their mixed mode addresses a contemporary problem of representation: the difficulty of painting intention. As Leonardo da Vinci frames it, "The good painter has to paint two principal things, that is to say, man and the intention of his mind. The first is easy and the second difficult, because the latter has to be represented through gestures and movements of the limbs...."[18] The engraving of the flexor muscles for Bidloo's anatomy (figure 14.2), for example, undertakes such a complex representation: although its didactic interests initially seem very far from aesthetic problems, it is striking precisely for the intentional force of its implied invitation. When such figures gesture, the faculty of agency (understood as the animation of the muscles by the motions of the soul) is displayed as an essential feature of the hand, a structural quality like shape and position of the muscles. As Luke Wilson has put it, describing Harvey's dissection of the eye: the process of dissection "restores [the] soul as an intentional structure," implicitly connecting "anatomical procedure and the notion of the body as agent" (81).

For Wilson, this observation leads to deeper recognition of the transactions between anatomist and cadaver, each both agent and patient, produced by mutual agency; the intimate, supportive gesture and entwined fingers of the Vesalius portrait suggest this clearly (68–69, 88). Crooke describes this kind of gesture precisely as a mutual compact, reprising the symbolic tradition of the hand clasp as a sign of reconciliation and truce: "*Numa Pompilius* consecrated the Hands to *Faith*, and therefore all Compacts, Covenants, Truces and enter-courses whatsoever are held inviolably ratified by the very touch of the Hand." (730). Anatomies summon a third agent to this covenant, maintaining that the "action which is done" by the anatomist's hand is Godly handy work. Read in this light, Crooke's insistent return to microcosmic analogies emerges as part of a larger rhetorical strategy. Like his "handlynge" puns, like his theory of touch, these supply a moral framework for dissection that inheres both in the structure of the body and in anatomical procedure. In a defining instance, *Microcosmographia* opens with an analogy frequently found in anatomy texts: the story of Noah's ark, which implicitly compares the practice of dissection with Noah's carpentry. The story of the ark eases the strains of professional decorum that emerge in Crooke's preface by uniting a covenant with the elect and a divine directive to manual labor. Furthermore, the story associates artisanry, measure, and manufacture with dissection, through the etymology of the bones of the arm: brachium, cubit, and ell (the ulna).[19]

> Now the . . . due proportion, composition, or correspondency of the parts
> of mans body, with respect each to other, and of them all to the whole, is
> admirable. This alone for a patterne do all workemen and Arts-maisters
> set before them: to this, as Polycletus rule, do the Surveighers, maister
> Carpenters and Masons, referre all their plottes and projects; they builde
> Temples, Houses, Engines, shipping, forts, yea and the Ark of Noah, as
> it is recorded, was three hundred cubites, the bredth fifty, in heighth thir-
> tie. (6)

The traditional measurement of the ark in human proportions goes back to
Augustine and Origen, to be reprised in early modern treatises on architecture and painting: the trope is a kind of architectural commonplace of the
mystical unities expressed by the proportions of the human body.[20] Names
of the bones and units of measure are mutually derived from the practice of
linear measurement (as the contemporary etymology for cubit and ell has
it). Thus for anatomy, as for architectural practice, the Noah story implies
that ideal qualities of the instrument inhere in procedure and performance
as well as form. Anatomical handy work, like Noah's, emerges as a creative,
constructive, and restorative labor: an undertaking in service to and imitation of God.

If the anatomist's hand does God's work, the hand he dissects is also, by
extension, God's. Medical illustrations of the hand draw on several other
conventions from the emblem and *imprese* tradition in ways that suggest
God's hand as a pattern for anatomical exposition. Illustrations of the arm,
as for example, from Berengario's *Commentaria* (1521), often draw on an
old motif in religious art. God's hand emerges from the clouds, sometimes
surrounded by a nimbus, often swathed in cloth. The clouds or classical
sweep of fabric that circle the shoulder where the limb ends mark the point
past which God's actions must not and cannot be traced. We can see the
evidence of God's work on earth (denoted by the reaching hand), but God's
person and intentions remain inscrutable.

Discussing this tradition in the context of emblem books, Bernard
Scholz points out that secular and religious readings of such "ownerless
arms" sometimes work together, often to suggest human action in accordance with God's will.[21] Contemporary representations of the physician's
hand do just this; typically they integrate the actions of God's hand and the
human hand in the same inscription. A glance at the arms of the Royal
College of Physicians, for example, reminds us of the mixed nature of the
physician's hand (figure 14.4). At first reading, the upper hand looks like
the hand of God: it emerges from a cloudy nimbus at the top of the shield
and grasps a wrist that stretches from the side—the middle space of human

activity. But because it wears an aristocratic ruff and takes a pulse, it is also clearly a physician's hand. The commonplace of the regal and divine healing touch inscribes God's faculties in this human hand. In the context of dissection, as I've argued above, the challenge to anatomists is to assimilate a touch that looks like wounding—the surgeon's touch—into the physician's divine ministry.

To do this, illustrations of the dissected hand must refigure the incision itself, and metonymically, the practice of "section," as a process that makes as well as signifies contiguity of action. In Scholz's compelling analysis of emblem aesthetics, the apparent dismemberment of "ownerless arms" must remain semantically invisible if they are to be read as icons of powerful agency; thus, he argues, the circling clouds and classical swags that serve as "theologically motivated metonymies" in religious emblems function in secular ones "to prevent the semantic interpretation 'cut off' in conjunction with the inscriptions of the other constituent characters ... which cannot have been too far-fetched in an age of man-to-man combat" (258–59, 264).[22] In the conversion of spiritual to secular inscription, he points out, the metonymy is retained as a sign of powerful agency in and of itself; in its secular context, by extension, we cannot read an ownerless arm as forceful if we read it as dismembered. For the anatomist, as Crooke's definition makes clear, the difference between dissection and combat is certainly an important and delicate one. Yet instead of directing our attention away from the boundary between cut and uncut tissue, representations of the dissected arm rework it. In doing so, they seem less concerned with the implicit violence of anatomy than with expanding the possibilities of this visual metonymy—in particular, spiritual and epistemological ones—and with making dismemberment symbolically as well as visually legible.

Illustrations of the dissected arm borrow their circling fabric borders from the earlier visual tradition, reworking them either as cloths and bandages (as in figure 14.2) or incorporating them into the body itself. In Vesalius's portrait, for example (figure 14.1), the skin of the corpse's upper arm curves smoothly around like a sleeve. Unlike their emblem cousins, these border motifs imply scrutability rather than inscrutability. They insist that the boundary of the anatomized limb—either skin or cloth—can be read as a metonymy for coherent connections, epistemological as well as physical. When anatomy illustrations naturalize the cloth boundary, for example, making it part of the corpse, they translate a perceptual and epistemological limit into a mechanical process that can be described fully. Anatomists learn to trace the action of Creation and demonstrate its marvelous ingenuity; and the dissection of the human hand makes visible the trace of God's molding hand in a kind of *imitatio Dei.* As Crooke reminds us: "Because the hand was the most noble and perfect organ or instrument of the body: God the Creator moulded it up of diverse particles, all which for our better understanding we will referre unto foure kindes" (731). A subtle and beautiful revision of the cloth border motif makes this point differently, in the engraving of the forearm dissection for Govaert Bidloo (figure 14.2). Here a loosened bandage trails the arm, visually balancing the stretched flexor muscles. The cloth that would otherwise wrap and border the shoulder curls along the forearm, as if to propose that what used to be an imaginative constraint on the *demonstratio* of God's omnipotence is now gracefully loosened, part of the field of scrutiny. Its symmetrical path beside the flexor muscles suggests that this dissection of the hand somehow surpasses that profound limit of perception and knowledge.

To trace continuous connections across distinct parts is to know the local actions of the hand that manifest the motions of the soul, as I've argued above. As the Galenic panegyric to the hand insists, it is also to know the perfection of the body as a manifestation of God's "handy worke." Again, as John Banister reminds us, "if we wel perpend the construction, and composition of the partes, and bones of the hand, our senses shall soone conceive the maner of the action, with no lesse admiration, in beholdyng the handy worke of the incomprehensible Creator" (fol. 31r). In the dissection of the hand, the mechanics of apprehension stand in for what we could neither apprehend nor experience: God creating. The hand of the anatomist, emulating God's hand as it composes the flexor muscles for display, supplies this missing link.

Notes

Thanks are due to Elizabeth Fowler, Suzanne Keen, Mark Miller, John Norman, and John Rogers for their generous critical readings of this essay, and to Andrew Zurcher for his legwork.

1. On marital handclasps, see Dale Randall's useful essay "The Rank and Earthy Background of Certain Physical Symbols in *The Duchess of Malfi,*" *Renaissance Drama* n.s. 18 (1988): 171–204. On feudal handclasps, see Kathryn Lynch, "'What Hands Are Here?' The Hand as Generative Symbol in Macbeth," *Renaissance English Studies* 39 (1988). For a history of the Renaissance handshake see Herman Roodenburg, "The 'Hand of Friendship': Shaking Hands and Other Gestures in the Dutch Republic," in *A Cultural History of Gesture,* ed. Jan Bremmer and Herman Roodenburg (Cambridge, U.K.: Polity Press, 1991). See

also Joaneath Spicer's "The Renaissance Elbow," in the same volume. On raising the right hand see John Bulwer, *Chirologia: or the Natural Language of the Hand and Chironomia: or the Art of Manual Rhetoric*, ed. James W. Cleary (Carbondale: Southern Illinois University Press: 1974): "Juro," 48 and "Suffragor," 49. Jonathan Goldberg's useful study of the early modern discourse of hand writing, *Writing Matter: From the Hands of the English Renaissance* (Stanford: Stanford University Press, 1990), undertakes the kind of analysis I am aiming for here: to take seriously the idea that actions comprise the iconographic and literary *semes* of the hand, and to give a detailed account of one kind of early modern theory and practice of manual action.

2. Although early modern constructions of agency vary from discourse to discourse, the powerful symbolism of the hand sometimes provides an imaginative link between them; see the discussion of stage dismemberment and representations of agency in Katherine Rowe, "Dismembering and Forgetting in *Titus Andronicus*," *Shakespeare Quarterly* 45, no. 3, (fall 1994). Recent scholarship has been increasingly attentive to the disciplinary and generic cross-pollination in early modern thinking about agency. See Elizabeth Fowler, "Civil Death and the Maiden: Agency and the Conditions of Contract in *Piers Plowman*," *Speculum* 70, no. 4 (October 1995): 760–92. On mixed agency in early modern dissection, see Luke Wilson, "William Harvey's *Prelectiones*: The Performance of the Body in the Renaissance Theater of Anatomy," *Representations* 17 (Winter, 1987): 62–95. On agency in early modern jurisprudence, see A. R. Braunmuller, "'Second Means': Agent and Accessory in Elizabethan Drama," in *The Elizabethan Theater*, vol. 11, ed. A. L. Magnusson and C. E. McGee (Port Credit, Ont.: P. D. Meany, 1990). Michael Neill surveys the wide range of manual symbolism on the Renaissance stage in "Amphitheaters in the Body: Playing with Hands on the Shakespearean Stage," *Shakespeare Survey* 48 (1995): 23–50.

3. John of Salisbury, *Policraticus: Of the Frivolities of Courtiers and the Footprints of Philosophers*, trans. and intro. Cary J. Nederman (Cambridge: Cambridge University Press, 1990), 104–5. As Leonard Barkan has shown, the classical tradition underlying this figure comprises mixed political motives: it can be used to argue for the primacy of the citizen and mutual protection of parts of society, or for their obligation to subordinate to the larger good of the whole. Leonard Barkan, *Nature's Work of Art: The Human Body as Image of the World* (New Haven and London: Yale University Press, 1975), 65–66.

4. John Banister, *The historie of man, sucked from the sappe of the most approved anathomistes* (London, 1578), fol. 60v.

5. Jonathan Sawday's study of the culture of dissection, *The Body Emblazoned: Dissection and the Human Body in Renaissance Culture* (London and New York: Routledge, 1995), advances these arguments in compelling ways; he also traces the history of dualist discourses in the culture of dissection. As I hope to show here, the dissection of the hand is in some senses anomalous—a hybrid or holdout in the shift toward Cartesian and Harveian mechanics.

6. Helkiah Crooke, *Microcosmographia: A Description of the Body of Man. Together with the Controversies thereto Belonging. Collected and Translated out of all the*

Best Authors of Anatomy, Especially out of Gasper Bauhinus and Andreas Laurentius (London: William Jaggard, 1615). Reprinted twice by 1618, the work was published again (corrected, enlarged, and largely outdated) in 1631. As the title page makes clear, it is a compilation and translation of the best of the authorities of the previous century, notably Andreas Laurentius and Caspar Bauhin. It sets out to describe the best of current practice (drawing verbatim from Bauhin) and to survey historical controversies (opining in the more conservative voice of Laurentius); its numerous illustrations derive mostly from Vesalius's *Fabrica* (C. D. O'Malley, "Helkiah Crooke, M.D., F.R.C.P., 1576–1648," *Bulletin of the History of Medicine*, 42, no. 1 [1968]: 5, 8). According to O'Malley, Crooke's work contributed little to the scientific advancement of anatomy but much to its practice in England (12). Because Crooke's sources are not important to my argument, I attribute the quotations below to Crooke; page numbers appear in parentheses.

7. See William Schupbach, *The Paradox of Rembrandt's "Anatomy of Dr. Tulp"* (London: Wellcome Institute for the History of Medicine, 1982), 28, and Sawday, *The Body Emblazoned,* for historical analysis of the order of dissection. For a modern translation of *De usu partium,* see Margaret Tallmadge May, *Galen on the Usefulness of the Parts of the Body* (Ithaca: Cornell University Press, 1968).

8. See Schupbach's discussion of the use of this dissection in anatomy lectures in the Netherlands during the early sixteenth century for a similar argument (*The Paradox of Rembrandt's "Anatomy of Dr. Tulp"*). The deep connection between formal and symbolic properties of the hand and early modern mnemonics can be seen in any chiromancy; these themes are usefully illustrated in William Engel's *Mapping Mortality: The Persistence of Memory and Melancholy in Early Modern England* (Amherst: University of Massachusetts Press, 1995), 12–67.

9. Like Crooke, Banister cites Columbus on this point: "This member is most notable, and worthy longest to be borne in mynde. The muscles whereof (sayth Columbus) will, in dissection, the longest endure uncorrupted" (*The historie of man,* fol. 60v). Crooke and Banister refer to M. Realdus Columbus, *De re anatomica* (Venice, 1559).

10. For the preceding account, see Schupbach, *The Paradox of Rembrandt's "Anatomy of Dr. Tulp,"* 17–19. This chapter is generally indebted to this work; especially his Appendix II, "The Special Significance of the Hand" (56–65), which excerpts the relevant anatomical literature, from Aristotle to *Gray's Anatomy.*

11. Andreas Vesalius, *De humani corporis fabrica libri septem* (Basel, 1543), fol. 2r–v. Translated in C. D. O'Malley, *Andreas Vesalius of Brussels, 1514–1564* (Berkeley: University of California Press, 1964), 317–20.

12. O'Malley (*Bulletin of the History of Medicine*) and Sawday (*The Body Emblazoned*) both give fuller accounts of the publication controversy.

13. See especially the detail of an engraving from Heironymus Fabricius ab Aquapendente, *De visione voci auditu* (Venice, 1600), discussed by Schupbach (*The Paradox of Rembrandt's "Anatomy of Dr. Tulp,"* 19): here Anatomia herself pulls back the superficial flexor muscles of a dissected arm. Other examples of the use of the severed hand as an emblem of anatomical practice can be

found in the title page of Bidloo's *Anatomia humani corporis* (lower right corner, a severed hand on the title page of an anatomy text that two *putti* open curiously) and in the decorated initial letters of Valverde's *Historia de la composicion del cuerpo humano* (Rome, 1556), where *putti* hold up a severed hand (19r).

14. Rowe, "Dismembering and Forgetting," 281.

15. Dilwyn Knox glosses the spread-fingered, open-palmed gesture more specifically as one of invitation. He cites a fifteenth-century Florentine illustration of an inkeeper making this gesture, accompanied by an explanatory caption; see "Ideas on gesture and universal languages c. 1550–1650," in *New Perspectives on Renaissance Thought*, ed. J. Henry and S. Hutton (London: Duckworth, 1990), 104.

16. See Sawday's analysis of écorché gestures, the fullest to date, in chapter 5, "Sacred Anatomy and the Order of Representation," of *The Body Emblazoned*. See also Luke Wilson, "William Harvey's *Prelectiones*," and Glenn Harcourt, "Andreas Vesalius and the Anatomy of Antique Sculpture," *Representations* 17 (winter 1987): 28–61. K. B. Roberts and J. D. W. Tomlinson provide a history of these aesthetics in *The Fabric of the Body: European Traditions of Anatomical Illustration* (Oxford: Clarendon Press, 1992). In *Literature After Dissection in Early Modern England* (forthcoming), John G. Norman discusses emerging representational strategies of the anatomy theater.

17. Harcourt, "Andreas Vesalius," 49.

18. "Posture, Expression and Decorum," in *Leonardo on Painting*, ed. Martin Kemp, selected and translated by Kemp and Margaret Walker (New Haven: Yale University Press, 1989), 144, cited in Spicer, "The Renaissance Elbow," 85. The visual tradition that associates gestures of the hand with expressions of intention is a very old one. Jean-Claude Schmitt summarizes the medieval theories of gestures that Leonardo and his contemporaries drew on and that animate anatomical illustration. See "The Rationale of Gestures in the West: Third to Thirteenth Centuries," in Bremmer and Roodenburg, *A Cultural History of Gesture*, 59–70.

19. Of the manual terms for linear measure in England and Scotland (cubit, ell, hand, span, palm, nail or thumb, and finger), many were still in practical use in the sixteenth century. The cloth measures, ell and thumb, lasted even longer: Elizabeth I's Exchequer standard ell (45 inches) remained the de facto standard until 1824 (R. D. Connor, *The Weights and Measures of England* [London: Her Majesty's Stationery Office, 1987], 95).

20. Leonard Barkan, *Nature's Work of Art: The Human Body as Image of the World* (New Haven and London: Yale University Press, 1975), 142. For the architectural system of human proportions Barkan refers us to Vitruvius's influential *De Architectura* and Giovanni Paolo Lomazzo's *Trattato dell' arte della pittura*, trans. Richard Haydock (London, 1598). According to Lomazzo, "[F]rom the proportions of man's body (the most absolute of all God's creatures) is that measure taken which is called Brachium, wherewith all things are most exactly

measured, being drawne from the similitude of a mans Arme, which is the third part of his length and breadth, and the Arme containeth 3 heads or spans. . ." (108). The essential and practical but still mystical character of these similitudes, preserved in the etymology of *cubit* and *ell*, persisted in seventeenth-century debates about the standardization of measure. See John Greaves's scathing objection to the application of Vitruvius, impractical "unless, as some fancy, that the cubit of the Sanctuary, was taken from the cubit of Adam, he being created in an excellent state of perfection. . . ." (*A Discourse of the Romane Foot.* [M. F. for William Lee], 1647, 9).

21. Bernard F. Scholz, "'Ownerless Legs or Arms Stretching from the Sky': Notes on an Emblematic Motif," in *Andrea Alciato and the Emblem Tradition: Essays in Honor of Virginia Woods Callahan*, ed. Peter M. Daly. (New York: AMS Press, 1989), 62–63. Scholz reminds us of the Mosaic injunction against pictorial representation of God, adopted by the early Christian Fathers, noting that inscriptions of God's hand pun on the Hebrew word *yad*, which means both "hand" and "power" (258–59).

22. Scholz points out that this figure is rarely treated as a key motif in emblem books, as if it lacks its own "symbolic relevance" to their authors and audience (Ibid., 259). I argue that although the emblem books themselves may not index the motif, their audience certainly registered this complicated metonymic occlusion of "cut off" as symbolically relevant. Literary allusions to the motif typically develop dismemberment as a dramatic, narrative and aesthetic problem (see Rowe, "Dismembering and Forgetting").

Part IV

❖

Parting Words

15. From Ottavio Scarlatini, *Homo et ejus partes figuratus et symbolicus* (Bologna, 1684).

15

Footnotes

❖

PETER STALLYBRASS

1. In the nineteenth century, a new foot was invented through the invention of toeshoes. Toeshoes are the material precondition for ballet. The ballerina dances *en pointe*; her foot is transformed into a disappearing act. In ballet, we have the most paradoxical of worlds: a nostalgic world of peasants and dancing swans, of the feudal and the magical; the logical world of the modern individual, an individual who, transcending any material preconditions, no longer touches the earth—or only just touches the earth. Through the ballerina, we can imagine an individual who is not grounded. Like Peter Pan, she flies. But while Peter Pan (in the modern theater) is guided by wires, she is guided by the disappearing act of her own foot.

This transformation of the foot reaches its apotheosis in the circus, a form that, like ballet, speaks profoundly to our nostalgia even as it inscribes modernity. The modern circus is organized around *feet*.[1] The high-wire act takes ballet a step further. The aerial artists, often wearing ballet clothes, ascend into the heavens; their feet no longer touch the ground at all. On the ground, the clowns, part of whose function was originally to clean up the dung of the animal performers, stage their baseness, their groundedness. One juggles, but whereas the aerial jugglist defies gravity, suspending objects in air, the clown's objects collide with one another, break, fall to earth. Another clown wears an enormous pair of shoes, and, while the aerialist walks on air, treads on dung. And then there are the feet of the animals. Elephants with four feet stand on two, their front two transformed into arms. A goat delicately climbs a stepladder. Two-footed animals are transformed into four-footed animals; four-footed animals are transformed into two-footed animals; two-footed animals are transformed into animals without feet. Like ballet, the circus imagines as one of its possibilities a human whose feet have disappeared, transformed into tapering points. These feet that no longer bruise the earth are the logical feet of the bourgeois citizen, the transcendental individual;[2] these feet disown the feet of the clown.

2. In early modern Europe, power is marked not by the absence of feet but by their presence. Marlowe's Tamburlaine makes his enemies his footstool; he puts his feet upon them.[3] One of the most important images in English Protestantism, constantly repeated through reprintings of Foxe's *Actes and Monuments*, is of Emperors kissing the Pope's foot or being trodden upon by him.[4] The 1610 edition of Foxe's *Actes* for instance, depicts "King Iohns supplication to the Pope. Emperours kissing the popes foote. The Image of Antichrist."[5] It is followed by an image of "Pope Coelestinus the fourth crowning the Emperour Henricus the sixt with his feete" (an image that, in fact, depicts the Pope kicking the Emperor's crown off as he kneels).[6] For Foxe, the nadir of history is reached when the head of the Emperor is subordinated to the foot of the Pope. The Pope's power is marked by his ability to put his foot upon his enemies. Equally, to imagine reversing the subordination of Emperor to Pope is to imagine the Emperor with his foot upon the Pope. Immediately following the title page of the second volume of the 1610 edition of Foxe, Henry VIII is shown treading on the neck of the Pope.[7] The image draws, of course, upon a biblical tradition. Psalm 110 begins: "The Lord said vnto my Lord, Sit thou at my right hand, vntil I make thine enemies thy fotestole."[8] In Isaiah, the Lord's power is repeatedly invoked as his ability to tread down his enemy: "vpon my mountaines wil I treade him vnder fote" (14.25). But the biblical emphasis is above all upon the power of those who are already trodden down to stand up and tread upon their enemies. The Lord's chosen will be raised up from being "a nacion … troden vnder fote" (18:7) while the Lord

> wil bring downe them that dwell on hie: the hie citie he will abase: *euen* vnto the grounde wil he cast it downe and bring it vnto dust.
>
> The fote shal treade it downe, *euen* the fete of the poore, *and* the steps of the nedie. (26:5–6)[9]

"The fete of the poore" is in a sense a tautology. The poor, simply in being poor, are already the feet of the social body. They are both what the social body walks with and what the social body bruises. The foot is what is stepped on. But the head of society is never footless; the head's feet are the active instruments of subordination.[10] The Pope puts his feet upon the Holy Roman Emperor; but in the first woodcut of Foxe's *Actes and Monuments*, the capital "C" of Constantine bears within it an image of Elizabeth, the godly ruler.[11] The bottom of the letter "C" is composed of a prostrate Pope with a serpent's tail, his tiara falling from his head. Elizabeth has him quite literally beneath her feet.

3. Feet in the Renaissance may be lowly, but they are also intimately revealing. The foot measures the person:

> Least subject to disguise and change it is,
> Men say, the devill never can change his.[12]

To know a person is to know his or her foot. Hence, Iffida says to Fidus in Lyly's *Euphues and his England*, "[Y]ou shal not know the length of my foote, vntill by your cunning you get commendation," and Henry Smith writes that Satan "marks how every man is inclined, . . . and when he hath the measure of his foote, then he fits him."[13] The foot measures the person. At the same time, the whole body rests upon the feet. They are the body's essential support, emblems of *firmitas* and *soliditas*.[14] Fortune, because she is unstable and unreliable, stands upon a ball. The fortunate person puts "the better foote before"[15] or "the best foot forward"[16] as opposed to the unfortunate or ungodly who "putst the wrong foote before."[17] One gets off on the right or wrong foot. And those who are radically flawed have feet of clay.[18]

The feet, then, although at the base of the body, are crucial to it. If the "Homily against Disobedience and Wilful Rebellion," published in 1570, decries the notion that subjects can judge their princes "as though the foote must judge of the head," Saint Paul legitmated a more complex reading of the foot. In a much cited passage from 1 Corinthians, Paul claimed that "the bodie also is not one member, but many": "If the fote wolde say, Because I am not the hand, I am not of the bodie, is it therefore not of the bodie?" (12:14–15). Here, Paul mocks the foot's pretensions. But the foot's pretensions are immediately juxtaposed to the head's:

> But now *are* there manie membres, yet but one bodie. And the eye can not
> say vnto the hand, I haue no nede of thee: nor the head againe to the fete,
> I haue no nede of you. (12:20–21)

Paul's divisions of the body still correspond to divisions of social function, but the status of the foot is not clear. For God, he claims, has given "the more honour" to precisely those parts "which we thinke moste vnhonest" (12:23–24). It is certainly the equality rather than the subordinations of parts that George Herbert celebrates in the "symmetrie" of the human frame:

> Each part may call the furthest, brother:
> For head with foot hath private amitie.[19]

Similarly, when in *Coriolanus* Menenius derides the Second Citizen[20] as "the great Toe of this Assembly" because "one o'th lowest, basest, poorest" (TLN 163, 165; 1.1.155, 157), Menenius's contempt has to be set both against his own foregrounding of the literal priority of the toe (it "goest formost" [TLN 166; 1.1.158]) and against the Citizen's image of the leg as the "Steed" that carries that head and the heart (TLN 110; 1.1.117). Without the great toe, the body limps, the body politic totters.[21]

4. If the hierarchies of the body are complex for Saint Paul, the hierarchies of gender are not: "I wil that ye knowe, that Christ is the head of euerie man: & the man is the womans head" (1 Cor. 11.3). Undoing Paul's image of the interdependence of foot and hand, Kate in *The Taming of the Shrew* tells her fellow wives to "place your hands below your husbands foote" (TLN 2735; 5.2.177). The hierarchies of gender are intensified by those of age when Prospero turns upon his daughter, Miranda:

> What I say,
> My foote my Tutor? (1.2.469–70)

(One may note in *The Tempest* the discursive violence through which Caliban is subordinated by depicting him not as a foot but as a "footlicker" [TLN 1894; 4.1.219] who says to Stephano, "I will kisse thy foote" [TLN 1194, 1197; 2.2.149, 152].) Yet the complex interplay and transformations of class by gender and gender by class in the Renaissance undo any simple equation of woman to the subordinated foot. At the end of *Loues Labour's Lost*, Don Armado, performing the role of "braue Hector," steps back into his part as "Braggart" only to "adore thy sweet Graces slipper" (TLN 2623; 5.2.667). If he now does homage to the Queen, subordinating the swaggering warrior to the humble servant, he only repeats in more courtly guise his previous subordination to the least courtly of women: Jaquenetta.

I doe affect the very ground (which is base) where her shoe (which is baser) guided by her foote (which is basest) doth tread.

(TLN 470–72; 1.2.167–69)

But the value of the base is never a given.

In *The Shoemakers Holiday*, Simon Eyre mocks Firke for making shoes for "*Sybill* my Lords maid":

fie, defile not thy fine workemanly fingers with the feete of Kitchinstuffe, and basting ladles, Ladies of the Court, fine Ladies, my lads, commit their feete to our apparelling, put grosse worke to *Hans*.[22]

The "gentle" craft of shoemaking may put the male craftsman beneath a woman, but for Eyre, it should be beneath only a woman of rank. The "baser" foot of "Kitchinstuffe" is the domain of a foreign apprentice. But *The Shoemakers Holiday* as a whole works against the habitual notions of female subordination. If the notion of women as clogs or as "a paire of old shooes" (1.1.142) that can be discarded[23] appears in the play, it is set against a craft that transforms a shoe into a fitting offering between lovers, an offering in which the husband can construct a material reminder of himself to put upon his wife's foot. Thus, Rafe gives a shoe to Jane as he parts from her:

Now gentle wife, my louing louely *Iane*,
Rich men at parting, giue their wiues rich gifts,
Iewels and rings, to grace their lillie hands,
Thou know'st our trade makes rings for womens heeles:
Here take this paire of shooes cut out by *Hodge*,
Sticht by my fellow *Firke*, seam'd by my selfe,
Made vp and pinckt, with letters for thy name,
Weare them my deere *Iane*, for thy husbands sake,
And euerie morning when thou pull'st them on,
Remember me, and pray for my returne,
Make much of them, for I haue made them so,
That I can know them from a thousand mo.

(1.224–35)

The shoes that Rafe gives to Jane are a work of corporate homage, since they bear the work of Hodge and Firk, as well as of Rafe himself. But if the shoes are the work of men, and stand in for a man, they are most certainly not Freud's phallic shoes. On the contrary, they are the "rings" into which Jane will put her heels: her feet into his shoes; his body as worn matter, "pinkt" with her name.

5. In the uncorrected copies of Q1 *King Lear*, Goneril says of her husband, Albany: "My foote vsurps my body" (Q1 2025; 4.2.28).[24] The corrected copies emend this to: "A foole vsurps my bed." In 1619, Q2 emended "My foote vsurps my body" to "My foote vsurps my head." Finally, in 1623, the compositors of the First Folio set up a fourth reading: "My Foole vsurpes my body." As Thomas Clayton noted in 1981, Q1's first reading, "My foote vsurps my body," had to that point been "categorically dismissed by editors and textual critics."[25] And yet several puzzles remain. As Clayton observes, the uncorrected line makes perfect sense, and may well accord with the manuscript from which the play was set. Proofreading was sometimes used to get a "better" version without resorting to checking against copy. But the line must at the least have caused some difficulty or otherwise it wouldn't have undergone three emendations in five words: "A" for "My"; "foole" for "foote"; "bed" for "body." And the line again caused difficulty when the play was reset for Q2. But this time, a single emendation sufficed: "head" for "body," to read "My foote vsurps my head."[26] I am concerned here not to defend any of the four readings as "correct" but only to note that all four readings circulated in the early seventeenth century.

In footnotes on feet, my concern is obviously with uncorrected Q1 and Q2. And perhaps the first thing to note about them is how familiarly they chime with the language of head and foot. In *The Batchelars Banquet*, for example, we find the all too predictable view that "The honestest woman and most modest of that sexe, if she weare the breeches" is

> (because a woman) scarce able to gouerne her selfe, much lesse her husband. . . . [W]ere it not so, God would haue made her the head, which sith it is otherwise, what can be more preposterous, then that the head should be gouerned by the foote.[27]

But in Q1 *Lear*, it is the *husband* who is the foot: Goneril is the body. If uncorrected Q1 has given modern editors (and some Renaissance compositors)[28] such trouble, is it partly because of their reluctance to think of Albany, man and duke, as foot? Or because of their inability to imagine a foot that can "usurp"? Just before Q1's "My foote vsurps my body," Goneril gives a chain to Edmund, the Bastard:

> wear this spare speech;
> Decline your head: this kiss, if it durst speake
> Would stretch thy spirits vp into the ayre.

> (Q1 2019–21; 4.2.21–23)

Edmund, the base, stoops his head to be kissed by his mistress; a woman's kiss, a monarch's kiss, that can stretch the spirits of the base, the feet of society, "up." "If thy base will be thy master . . ."[29] Goneril (as woman, foot; as monarch, head) raises Edmund (as bastard, foot; as man, head) by enchaining his head. They are conjoined as equals, both head and feet, even "in the ranks of death" (Q1 2023; 4.2.25).

6. *Usurping Feet/Usurping Heads*: "My foot usurps my head" (*Lear* Q2). But what if the head has usurped the feet? In 1654, the republican John Streater wrote in his anti-Cromwellian newsletter:

> It is a madness for the head to chain the Foot. I pray if it doth, how much liberty hath the head more than the foot? It was the *Basis* of the Government of the State of *Lacedemon*, that all should be free, that all should be able to govern.[30]

And in "A Letter sent by the Maydens of London" in 1567, the maids (that is, servants) assert not only the Pauline image of the body politic and its interdependent parts but also the extent to which "Matrones and Mystresses" are the slothful center, entirely dependent upon their maids:

> For as there are divers and sundry membres in the body, the least whereof the body may not well want or spare: and when any one of them is hurt or greved, the whole body suffreth smart therfore: Even so are we to you (good Mistresses) such as stande you in more steade, than some of the membres stande the body in, yea in as much steade we alone doe stande you in, as divers membres of the body altogether do stande the body in. For one might live although he lacked one of his eyes, one of his hands, one of his legs, and might also see, or handle any thing, and walke abrode. But . . . we are to you very eyes, hands, feete & altogether.[31]

The elite, the "Letter" claims, are "paste paines taking your selves" (37). The taking of pains, the living of pain, has devolved onto the social feet.

In fact, those who materially shaped the social foot—shoemakers—were the leading popular philosophers and radical politicians of early modern Europe, as Eric Hobsbawm and Joan Scott argued in 1980 in an extraordinary essay, "Political Shoemakers."[32] What Hobsbawm and Scott seek to explain is the *persistence* of the radical shoemaker into the era of early industrialism. In the British Chartist movement, shoemakers were the largest single group after weavers (who were a larger part of the working population); in the taking of the Bastille, the twenty-eight shoemakers who were arrested were exceeded by only three other trades, and they were the largest trade among those arrested in the riots of the Champ de Mars in August 1792 and in the opposition to the coup d'état of 1851. In Germany, Weydemeyer wrote to Marx in 1850, the Communist League consisted "only of shoemakers and tailors" (87, 88). And the fear of the popular learning of the shoemaker was testified to by proverbs throughout Europe: "Let the cobbler stick to his last and let the learned men write books"; "preaching cobblers make bad shoes" (90).

But why did the radical shoemaker ever emerge in the first place and why was she or he such a compelling figure in early modern Europe? One of the most compelling aspects of Hobsbawm and Scott's piece is their admission of the inadequacy of available explanations. Their own explanation (and, in my view, an excellent one) is that once shoemaking was recognized as a radical profession, radicals were attracted to it. In other words, stereotypes have a way of coming true, for *better* as well as for worse (98).[33] But what established the connection between shoemaking and radicalism in the first place? It is, I believe, encoded in the very language of the body politic. The shoemaker *is* the social foot (shoemaking was a notoriously poor trade[34]); at the same time, through the fabrication of the shoe, the shoemaker *fabricates* the "basis" of society itself. The shoemaker is thus materially and symbolically the maker of the social (she or he is the foundation of social *movement* in its most literal sense); at the same time, she or he is the person most trodden upon by a hierarchical society that imagines itself in terms of an elite who put their foot upon those whom they subordinate.

The shoe, then, in precapitalist society (that is, within the society of the body politic), figures the social from the ground up. When Thomas Nashe mockingly describes the radical John Leiden ("Botcher") as leader of a world turned upside down, he imagines him as literally putting a shoe on his head:

> That day come, flourishing entred *Iohn Leiden* the Botcher into the field,
> ... and on his head for a helmet a huge high shooe with the bottome
> turnd vpwards, embossed as full of hob-nayles as euer it might sticke.[35]

But Nashe's mockery grasps the material connection. Shoemaking grounds the social through its shoes, and hence through its feet. The people who made the social feet (shoemakers like Jacob Boehme, the German radical, and George Fox, the founder of the Quakers[36]) were more likely than others to be aware of their material role in the founding of the social. The language of the body politic, for better and worse, insisted upon their foundational role (as the "mere" base; as the active fabricators of the possibility of social movement).

So at the beginning of *Julius Caesar* it is a *cobbler* who speaks for the plebeians. He speaks as "a Mender of bad Soules" and tells the patrician Flavius, "if you be out Sir, I can mend you" (TLN 18, 22; 1.1.13, 17). (In *Coriolanus*, Caius Martius imagines the plebeians "feebling such as stand not in their liking, / Below their cobled Shooes" [TLN 207–8; 1.1.195–96]). In 1617, it was said to be a shoemaker named Picard who led the uprising against the Italian statesman Concini, and who "defiled him when dead by roasting and eating his heart."[37] Shoemakers were frequently accused both of religious radicalism and of atheism. In the Cerne Abbas inquiry of 1594, two shoemakers (Robert Hyde and Lodge) were attacked for their material-izations of heaven and hell. Hyde ("of Sherborne shoemaker") is reputed to have said:

> Mr Scarlet you have preachett vnto vs that there is a god, a heauen & a hell, & a resurrecion after this Liffe, and that we shall geiue an accompte of our worckes, and that the soule is immortall; but now sayeth [Hyde] here is a companye aboute this towne that saye, that hell is noe other but pouertie & penurye in this worlde; and heauen is noe other but to be ritch, and enioye pleasueres; and that we dye like beastes, and when we ar gonne there is noe more rememberance of vs &c. and such like.... And alsoe [the deponent] sayeth there is one Lodge a shomaker in Sherborne accompted an Atheiste.[38]

Shoemakers made their own religion from the ground up. As they made the social foot, they cobbled together new visions of the body politic, in which the head would no longer "chain the Foot."

Notes

1. My thoughts on the circus are indebted to Paul Bouissac, *Circus and Culture: A Semiotic Approach* (Bloomington: Indiana University Press. 1976).

2. If the image is a transcendental one, the actual feet of the ballerina or of the aerialist are anything but transcendental, as anyone who has performed in these arts or has looked at the feet of performers will know.

3. Christopher Marlowe, *Tamburlaine, Part 1,* in *The Complete Works of Christopher Marlowe,* ed. Fredson Bowers (Cambridge: Cambridge University Press, 1981) 1:4.2.1, 4.2.14, 5.1. 209.

4. I deliberately preserve the upper case of "Emperor" and "Pope" so as to capture the material hierarchies of print, even though Renaissance print shops were

wonderfully inconsistent, and hence irreverent, in their treatment of the hierarchies of upper and lower case. Joseph Moxon, in his *Mechanicke Exercises* (London, 1683), vol. 2, writes of the "Foot of the Letter" (376) and "the Foot of the Page" (377). On feet and footnotes, Nicholson Baker writes in a footnote to *The Mezzanine* (New York: Vintage Books, 1990): "As Boswell said, 'Upon this tour, when journeying, he [Johnson] wore boots, and a very wide brown cloth great coat, with pockets which might have almost held the two volumes of his folio dictionary; and he carried in his hand a large English oak stick. Let me not be censured for mentioning such minute particulars. Everything relative to so great a man is worth observing. I remember Dr Adam Smith, in his rhetorical lectures at Glasgow, told us he was glad to know that Milton wore latchets in his shoes, instead of buckles.' (Boswell, *Journal of a Tour to the Hebrides* [Penguin, p. 165]. Think of it: *John Milton wore shoelaces!*) Boswell, like Lecky (to get back to the point of this footnote), and Gibbon before him, loved footnotes" (121–22 fn).

5. John Foxe, *Actes and Monuments* (London, 1610), 1:719.

6. Ibid., 1:720. See also Frances Yates, *Astraea: The Imperial Theme in the Sixteenth Century* (London: Routledge, 1975), 42 and Plate 4c; and M. Dorothy George, *English Political Caricature: A Study of Opinion and Propaganda* (Oxford: Clarendon Press, 1959), 1:5.

7. Foxe, *Actes and Monuments*, 2: sig. paragraph.

8. *The Geneva Bible* (Geneva, 1560), Psalms 110:1. See also Matthew 22:44; Mark 12:36; Luke 20:43; Acts 2:35; Hebrews 1:13. In relation to the Pope's putting his head upon the Emperor's neck, see Joshua 10:24: "set you feet vpon the neckes of these Kings."

9. The gloss to these lines in the Geneva Bible reads: "God wil set the poore afflicted ouer ye power of the wicked."

10. But the feet of the proud could also expose their pretensions. It was proverbial that the peacock had fair feathers but foul feet. See Thomas Nashe, *Christs Teares ouer Ierusalem* in *The Works of Thomas Nashe*, ed. Ronald B. McKerrow (Oxford: Basil Blackwell, 1958), 2:112: "Dooth the Peacocke glory in his foule feete? Dooth he not hang downe the tayle when he lookes on them?"

11. Foxe, *Actes and Monuments* (1610), sig. paragraph. See Yates, *Astraea*, 43 and Plate 4a.

12. John Donne, "Loves Progress," 11.77–78 in *John Donne: The Elegies and The Songs and Sonnets,* ed. Helen Gardner (Oxford: Clarendon Press, 1965), 18. Yet Othello, looking down to see Iago's cloven feet, says "that's a Fable" (5.2.351). In Jonson's *The Diuell is an Asse*, Fitzdottrel, as the stage directions tell us, "lookes and suruay's [Pug, a devil's] feet; ouer and ouer" (1.3.8 S.D.), only to be told by Pug "that's a popular error, decieues many" (1.3.30) (in *Ben Jonson*, ed. C. H. Herford, Percy Simpson, and Evelyn Simpson, vol. 6 [Oxford: Clarendon Press, 1954]. A repeated Jacobean and Caroline joke is that you can't see the devil's foot any more because like a courtier he hides his foot under a rose (a

large ornament of ribbons attached to the top of shoes). See Jonson, *The Diuell is an Asse* 1.3.7–9; John Webster, *The White Diuel* in *The Complete Works of John Webster,* ed. F. L. Lucas (Oxford: Oxford University Press, 1937), 5.3.103–5; George Chapman, *The Tragedy of Caesar and Pompey* (in *The Plays and Poems of George Chapman: The Tragedies,* ed. Thomas Marc Parrott (London: Routledge, 1910), 2.1 (p. 358).

13. John Lyly, *Euphues and his England,* in *The Complete Works of John Lyly,* ed. R. Warwick Bond (Oxford: Clarendon Press, 1902), 2:68; Henry Smith, *The Sermons of Mr. Henry Smith* (1657), 491.

14. See Helen Gardner, "Commentary," in Gardner, *John Donne,* 135. Cf. John Donne, "A Valediction: forbidding mourning," ll. 27–28: "Thy soule the fixt foot, makes no show / To move, but doth if th'other doe."

15. William Shakespeare, *Titus Andronicus,* TLN 942, 2.3.192. All further references to Shakespeare's plays, apart from *King Lear,* are incorporated in the text and are from *The First Folio of Shakespeare,* ed. Charlton Hinman (New York: Norton, 1968); through line numbers (TLN) are followed by the act, scene, and line numbers of *The Riverside Shakespeare,* ed. G. Blakemore Evans et al. (Boston: Houghton Mifflin, 1974).

16. Thomas Overbury, *Sir Thomas Ouerbury His Wife* (London, 1638), 164.

17. Arthur Dent, *The Plain Mans Path-way to Heauen* (London, 1601), 141.

18. See Daniel 2:33.

19. "Man" in *The Works of George Herbert,* ed. F. E. Hutchinson (Oxford: Clarendon Press, 1941), 91.

20. In 1.1, most of the speeches of the Folio's Second Citizen are reassigned by modern editors, following Edward Capell's 1768 edition, to the First Citizen— as if the most vocal of the citizens must necessarily be the "first." The emendation is usually justified in terms of "consistency of character" (see Philip Brockbank's comment in his edition of *Coriolanus,* the Arden Shakespeare [London: Methuen, 1976], 98). In terms of the language of the body politic, it makes perfect sense that "the great Toe" of the plebeians should be second rather than first. It's at the very least difficult to see how a compositor could have misread "*2. Cit.*" for "*1. Cit.*" thirteen consecutive times. Moreover, the Second, Third, and Fourth Folios all followed the First Folio in assigning the Citizen's speeches of 1.1.57–167 to the Second Citizen.

21. On the connection between the limping of the body and the limping of the body politic, see *2 Henry IV.* In 1.1, Northumberland enters on a crutch, and in 1.2, Falstaff limps from the pox or the gout in his toe. But if these supposed "rebels" to the body politic limp, the king's legs have given way under him and he has retired to bed.

22. *The Shoemakers Holiday,* in *The Dramatic Works of Thomas Dekker,* ed. Fredson Bowers, vol.1 (Cambridge: Cambridge University Press, 1953), 2.3.79–82. For a fine analysis of the ways in which the play deals with social tension, see David

Scott Kastan, "Workshop and/as Playhouse: Comedy and Commerce in *The Shoemaker's Holiday*," *Studies in Philology* 84 (1987): 324–37.

23. It may be noted that whereas Freud tends to assume in his early work on fetishism that shoes are male, it is more common for shoes in the Renaissance to be gendered female, although their gender tends to be the subject for play rather than for certainties. For Freud, see "Fetishism," in *The Standard Edition of the Complete Psychological Works of Sigmund Freud*, ed. and trans. James Strachey (London: Hogarth Press, 1961), 152–57. For a critique of Freud's assumption, see Jacques Derrida, *The Truth in Painting*, trans. Geoff Bennington and Ian McLeod (Chicago: University of Chicago Press, 1987). For the indeterminate gender of the foot in the Renaissance, see Margreta de Grazia, "The Ideology of Superfluous Things," in *Subject and Object in Renaissance Culture*, ed. Margreta de Grazia, Maureen Quilligan, and Peter Stallybrass (Cambridge: Cambridge University Press, 1996): "'Foot' can refer to either female or male genitalia, through its relation to yard (penis) or to 'foutre' or fault, a woman's genital crack" (39 n. 57).

24. All quotations from *King Lear* are taken from *The Complete King Lear, 1608–1623*, ed. Michael Warren (Berkeley: University of California Press, 1989).

25. Thomas Clayton, "Old Light on the Text of *King Lear*," *Modern Philology* 78 (1981): 347–67, at 348. I am deeply indebted to Clayton's article throughout this note.

26. Clayton, who shows the logic of Q2's emendation and the intelligence of such a reading, nevertheless finds it "grotesque as well as nonsensical" (ibid., 349).

27. F. P. Wilson, ed., *The Batchelars Banquet* (Oxford: Clarendon Press, 1929), 92–93. In addition to the other parallels already cited, one might look at the following: "mean eyes have seen / The foot above the head" (*Timon of Athens*, 1.1.93–94); "many make their head their foote" (Robert Armin, *A Nest of Ninnies* [London, 1608], 56); "goe fetch the head [i.e. the duke] to give the foote a posset" (John Day, *The Ile of Guls* [London, 1606], sig. B2.

28. Only the compositors of Q1 were troubled by the relation of foot to body; the compositors of Q2 went even further in suggesting Goneril's sense of the gap between her potency and her husband's demeaning usurpation of it.

29. John Fletcher, *Women Pleas'd*, in *The Works of Beaumont and Fletcher*, ed. A. R. Waller (Cambridge: Cambridge University Press, 1909), 7:1.1 (p. 242).

30. *Observations Historical, Political, and Philosophical upon Aristotles first Book of Political Government*, no. 1, 4–11 April 1654, 4. (Note the emphasis upon the *Basis* of government, the sense that government itself originates in the base, the foot.) I am deeply indebted to David Norbrook for sending me this reference. I am even further indebted to him for his acute observations on the *limitations* of the language of the body and the body politic. How and why should slaves, to take the most extreme example, think of themselves as participating members of a social body? What would it mean to rethink society (as Marx, for instance, would do) as a body irrevocably fractured by dominance and exploitation, a social body in which the "feet" of an earlier political discourse *produce* the

economy even as their own bodies are literally *consumed* by it? The dream of the body politic is a utopian dream, a dream that, in the hands of the dominant, is already a form of violence.

31. "A Letter sent by the Maydens of London" (1567), ed. R. J. Fehrenbach, in *Women in the Renaissance: Selections from "English Literary Renaissance,"* ed. Kirby Farrell, Elizabeth H. Hageman, and Arthur F. Kinney (Amherst: University of Massachusetts Press, 1990), 28–47, at 37. I am deeply indebted to Ann Rosalind Jones for drawing this passage to my attention and for discussions of the relations between gender and class in the Renaissance.

32. Eric Hobsbawm and Joan Scott, "Political Shoemakers," *Past and Present* 89 (1980): 86–114. This brilliant essay informs all of my thinking on the political activism of the social feet.

33. Hobsbawm and Scott, "Political Shoemakers," 98. At the same time, Hobsbawm and Scott honestly admit that "the shoemaker's proverbial fondness for books and reading is difficult to explain, as there is nothing in the nature of the craft to suggest any occupational connection with the printed word" (94).

34. Hobsbawm and Scott, "Political Shoemakers," 98–105.

35. Thomas Nashe, *The Vnfortunate Traueller* (1594) in *Works*, 2:232.

36. Hobsbawm and Scott, "Political Shoemakers," 91.

37. Hobsbawm and Scott, "Political Shoemakers," 93.

38. Cerne Abbas inquiry, in *Willobie His Auisa,* ed. G. B. Harrison (London: John Lane, 1926), app. 3, 264; quoted in Hobsbawm and Scott, "Political Shoemakers," 92.

Contributors

Marjorie Garber is William R. Kenan, Jr., professor of English and director of the Center for Literary and Cultural Studies at Harvard University. She is the author of *Dream in Shakespeare: From Metaphor to Metamorphosis* (1974), *Coming of Age in Shakespeare* (1981), *Shakespeare's Ghost Writers: Literature as Uncanny Causality* (1987), *Vested Interests: Cross-Dressing and Cultural Study* (1991), *Vice Versa: Bisexuality and the Eroticism of Everyday Life* (1995), and *Dog Love* (1996).

Stephen Greenblatt is Class of 1932 Professor of English at the University of California, Berkeley. His books include *Renaissance Self-Fashioning: From More to Shakespeare* (1980), *Shakespearean Negotiations: The Circulation of Social Energy in Renaissance England* (1988), *Learning to Curse: Essays in Early Modern Culture* (1990), and *Marvelous Possessions: The Wonder of the New World* (1991). He is the general editor of the Norton Shakespeare.

David Hillman is a teaching fellow in the Department of English at Harvard University. He is the editor of *Authority and Representation in Early Modern England*, by Robert Weimann (1996), and coeditor (with William West) of the forthcoming *Shakespeare and the Power of Mimesis*, also by Weimann. He is currently working on a project titled *Shakespeare's Entrails: Solitude, Skepticism, and the Interior of the Body.*

Sergei Lobanov-Rostovsky is Assistant Professor of English at Kenyon College. He is currently working on a project entitled *The Cannibal Banquet: Violence, Enactment, Tragedy*.

Jeffrey Masten is Gardner Cowles Associate Professor in the Humanities at Harvard University, where he teaches in the English department. He is the author of *Textual Intercourse: Collaboration, Authorship, and Sexualities in Renaissance Drama* (1996) and has edited *The Old Law*, which will appear in Oxford's *Collected Works of Middleton*. His current work is on the philology of sex in early modern England.

Carla Mazzio is a teaching fellow in the Department of English at Harvard University. She is coeditor (with Susan Suleiman, Alice Jardine, and Ruth Perry) of *Social Control and the Arts: An International Perspective* (1991). She is currently working on a project entitled *Sins of the Tongue: Rhetoric, Power, and Speech in Early Modern England*.

Katharine Park teaches history and history of medicine at Wellesley College. She is the author of *Doctors and Medicine in Renaissance Florence* (1985) and the coauthor with Lorrain Daston of *Wonders and the Order of Nature, 1150–1750*. She is currently coediting *The Cambridge History of Early Modern Science* and working on a project titled *Knowing the Renaissance Body: Gender, Epistemology, and the Culture of Human Dissection*.

Gail Kern Paster is professor of English at George Washington University. She is the author of *The Idea of the City in the Age of Shakespeare* (1985), *The Body Embarrassed: Drama and the Disciplines of Shame in Early Modern England* (1993), and is currently working on a book on early modern theories of the passions and embodied interiority.

Katherine Rowe is assistant professor of English at Yale University. Her essay is part of a book in progress, titled *The Dead Hand: Agency, Dismemberment and Self-Possession*.

Michael Schoenfeldt is associate professor of English at the University of Michigan. He is the author of *Prayer and Power: George Herbert and Renaissance Courtship* (1991) and is currently working on a project titled *Bodies and Selves in Early Modern England*.

Kathryn Schwarz is assistant professor of English at Vanderbilt University. She is currently completing a project entitled *Mankynde Women: Amazon Encounters in the English Renaissance.*

Peter Stallybrass is professor of English and a member of the Program in comparative literature and literary theory at the University of Pennsylvania. He is coauthor with Allon White of *The Politics and Poetics of Transgression* (1986), coauthor with Ann Rosalind Jones of the forthcoming *Worn Worlds: Clothing and Identity in Early Modern England and Europe*, coeditor with David Scott Kastan of *Staging the Renaissance* (1991), and coeditor with Margreta de Grazia and Maureen Quilligan of *Subject and Object in Renaissance Culture* (1996). He is currently completing a collection of essays on English Renaissance cultural politics.

Scott Manning Stevens is assistant professor of English at Arizona State University. He is currently working on a project titled *The Trials of Modernity: The History of the English Essay in the Seventeenth Century.*

Nancy J. Vickers is professor of French, Italian, and comparative literature at the University of Southern California. She is coeditor with Margaret Ferguson and Maureen Quilligan of *Rewriting the Renaissance: The Discourses of Sexual Difference in Early Modern Europe* (1986) and *Medieval and Renaissance Representation: New Reflections* (1984). She is currently working on a project on the relationship between genre and technology in lyric poetry and music video. In July of this year she will become the seventh president of Bryn Mawr College.

Index